PAIRED-ASSOCIATES LEARNING

PAIRED-ASSOCIATES LEARNING

THE ROLE OF MEANINGFULNESS, SIMILARITY, AND FAMILIARIZATION

by

ALBERT E. GOSS

DEPARTMENT OF PSYCHOLOGY
UNIVERSITY OF MASSACHUSETTS
AMHERST, MASSACHUSETTS

and

CALVIN F. NODINE

DEPARTMENT OF PSYCHOLOGY
CARNEGIE INSTITUTE OF TECHNOLOGY
PITTSBURGH, PENNSYLVANIA

1965

ACADEMIC PRESS   New York and London

LB
1064
.G58
1965

ACADEMIC PRESS INC.
111 Fifth Avenue, New York, New York 10003

United Kingdom Edition published by
ACADEMIC PRESS INC. (LONDON) LTD.
Berkeley Square House, London W.1

LIBRARY OF CONGRESS CATALOG CARD NUMBER: 65-18427

PRINTED IN THE UNITED STATES OF AMERICA.

Preface

Both the rationale for and objectives of this monograph are described in greater detail in the introductory chapter. So, too, are the limitations imposed. Virtually all pertinent information available was examined; thus, the materials selected and described are comprehensive and substantially exhaustive.

In addition to providing a summary and evaluation of information already available, this monograph contains reports of twelve hitherto unpublished experiments. They are described in part in the body of the monograph and more completely in the Appendix. They extend existing information on the role of meaningfulness, similarity, and familiarization of stimuli in paired-associates learning. Moreover, they illustrate, concretely, problems, methods, findings, and theoretical implications of findings.

This monograph was prepared to meet the needs of three different groups. One group, small but growing in size, consists of those individuals currently or prospectively involved in research on the role of meaningfulness, similarity, and familiarization of stimuli in paired-associates learning. For them, the consolidation of information obtained in past research contained in this work should permit greater concentration on future normative and experimental investigations.

Another group, overlapping but larger in size, comprises those who teach courses in verbal behavior and learning, those who are carrying out research in other areas of this field, and those who are attempting to apply findings about paired-associates learning to various extra-laboratory tasks such as second-language learning. A third group, the largest and the one being constantly replenished, consists of students who are or will soon be enrolled in courses and seminars on verbal behavior and learning. Included also are those students who, on their own, desire some exposure to methods, data, and theory in an important area of this field.

Amherst, Massachusetts
June, 1965

A. E. GOSS
C. F. NODINE

v

Acknowledgment

Support for the preparation of this monograph and for the experiments reported in the Appendix came primarily from Contracts 2691(00) and 3357(03) between the Personnel and Training Branch of the Office of Naval Research and the University of Massachusetts. In large measure, therefore, the Office of Naval Research and, specifically, Denzel D. Smith, formerly of the Personnel and Training Branch, and his successor Glenn L. Bryan share the credit for whatever merits this monograph may have. They are in the enviable position of being in no way responsible for any of its faults. By many courtesies, the late Edwin B. Wilson of the Boston Branch Office of the Office of Naval Research facilitated the work carried out under the two contracts.

We are indebted to many others. Fred D. Sheffield's doctoral dissertation and a review of the literature on meaningfulness prepared later by Harvey Lifton were valuable points of departure. Further impetus was provided by the reports and comments of participants in a seminar at the University of Massachusetts in the Fall of 1960 devoted primarily to meaningfulness and similarity in paired-associates learning. The participants were Jean Carl Cohen, Carl Cooper, Barbara S. Musgrave, Barbara F. Nodine, Sally L. Perry, Daniel E. Rosen, and the authors. Subsequently, Merrillee Atkins and Bruce N. Gregory helped to search the literature for pertinent information.

Nancy J. Cobb, Nancy C. Farrick, Bruce N. Gregory, Herbert Levitt, Nancy A. Mello, and Sally L. Perry collaborated as co-authors in the planning, execution, analyses of the resultant data, and preliminary reports of results of one or more of the experiments described in the Appendix. Also assisting in this work were Barbara Jaffarian Dunham, Alice Reilly, and Pauline Gorman Weiss. Joseph Mach constructed the memory drums used for administration of lists to subjects individually.

Helen L. Rowell contributed in diverse ways which include preparation of materials for the experiments, statistical analyses, planning tables and figures, and typing the several drafts of the manuscript. In addition, she caught many of our grammatical lapses and checked source and numerical citations to minimize any inconsistencies and inaccuracies. Finally, with help from Marsha B. Britt, she aided substantially in preparing the author and subject indexes. Nancy C. Farrick also aided in the preparation of materials for the experiments, in statistical analyses, and in preparation of the manuscript.

Suggestions and criticisms of one or more drafts, which have been incorporated in too many places for special acknowledgment, were made by Nancy J. Cobb, Charles N. Cofer, Eleanor J. Gibson, Mary E. W. Goss, Clyde E. Noble, Louis E. Price, and Rudolph W. Schulz.

Information and aid of various kinds were obtained from the University of Massachusetts Press Committee of which Sidney Kaplan was then chairman.

Contents

CHAPTER 1

Introduction

Summarized and evaluated in this monograph are data and theories on the role in paired-associates (PA) learning of meaningfulness, similarity, and familiarization of stimulus and of response members of PA lists. Presented also are the designs, results, and conclusions of twelve new experiments on PA learning in which one or more of the variables have been meaningfulness, similarity, and familiarization of stimulus members, response members, or both. In order to assure continuity of the summary presentation of data and theory, details of the new experiments are reported in the Appendix. When pertinent, however, significant features are also mentioned earlier along with those of other experiments.

The rationale for a summary and evaluation of data and theories on meaningfulness, similarity, and familiarization in PA learning is developed below along with explication of the general objectives and of some important limitations. The over-all plan of the monograph and content of subsequent chapters are then described as are the designs of the experiments reported in the Appendix. Noted last are a number of abbreviations which are to be employed. Some are desirable for brevity and others for continuity with usage elsewhere. For convenience, they are defined both in one place and when first introduced in subsequent chapters.

RATIONALE AND GENERAL OBJECTIVES

Meaningfulness and Verbal Learning was the title and theme of Underwood and Schulz's (1960a) book-length research monograph. A year earlier, Morikawa (1959a) had reviewed available materials on the role of meaningfulness, familiarization, and similarity of stimulus members and of response members in PA learning. More recently, Noble (1963) has summarized his own and his students' theoretical, normative, and experimental work on meaningfulness and

1

familiarization in verbal learning for which Goss (1963) provided a supplementary theoretical analysis. Finally, Umemoto (1963) reviews early contributions to the development and use of "association methods" preliminary to examination of the significance of such methods for investigations of verbal learning and other phenomena of verbal behavior and to discussion of different approaches to specification of meaningfulness, meaning, and semantic similarity.

Further consideration of meaningfulness, similarity, and familiarization in PA learning might, therefore, seem redundant. For several reasons this is not the case. That the redundancy is only apparent is the first reason. The many experiments on the role of meaningfulness and familiarization in PA learning which have appeared since publication of Morikawa's review and since completion of the normative and experimental work reported in *Meaningfulness and Verbal Learning* and by Noble should be classified, reviewed, and evaluated. Indeed, much of the more recent experimentation was an outgrowth of studies described in these previous contributions. Their very influence, therefore, is partly responsible for the need for updating.

The second reason for further consideration of effects of meaningfulness on PA learning is the relative neglect of some important techniques of and data on scalings of meaningfulness and related attributes in one or more of the previous reviews. For example, Morikawa, Underwood and Schulz, and Noble were primarily interested in effects of meaningfulness of discrete stimuli. Consequently, techniques of scaling meaningfulness and related attributes of pairs of stimuli were not considered. Nor were results of such scalings and data on relationships between meaningfulness of discrete stimuli and meaningfulness of pairs of those stimuli examined. A further consequence was omission of information about the influence of meaningfulness and related attributes of pairs of stimuli on PA learning.

The semantic differential format was irrelevant to Underwood and Schulz's objectives; therefore it was not described. Noble's treatment of the semantic differential format was primarily a critique which, while a useful clarification of issues and views, neglected some aspects of the nature and use of semantic differentiation.

In other publications, Underwood and Schulz have contributed substantially to an understanding of the role of similarity in PA learning; but consideration of bases for and data on scalings of similarity of stimulus members was also outside of the scope of *Meaningfulness and Verbal Learning.* As a consequence, findings of effects of similarity of stimulus and response members on PA learning were treated only incidentally. Noble wisely and profitably focused on problems and techniques of the measurement of meaningfulness and on data concerning the influence of meaningfulness of discrete stimuli on PA learning and on serial learning. The scope of Morikawa's review was so great that, in the limited number of pages available to him, bases for and data on scalings of similarity could not be described.

The third reason is to provide a more adequate description of the techniques and problems of construction of lists representing various combinations of meaningfulness, similarity, and other attributes of stimulus and response members and of the assignment of those lists to subjects. While mentioned by others, these techniques and problems have not been examined systematically and in detail.

The fourth reason is to extend the theoretical treatments of the role of meaningfulness in PA learning presented by or summarized in Underwood and Schulz and by Noble to include the role of similarity. While meaningfulness and similarity were both included in Morikawa's analysis, his treatment was necessarily brief. The related and final reason is to bring together a wider range of normative and experimental data bearing on the component propositions of these and other theoretical analyses than, heretofore, have been examined and evaluated.

Some repetition of the content of the Morikawa, Underwood and Schulz, and Noble contributions is unavoidable. But this redundancy has the desirable feature of providing one additional learning trial with the duplicated content and the additional desirable feature of consolidating information on meaningfulness, similarity, and familiarization from four different sources. One of these is long and without an index (Underwood & Schulz), another is not generally accessible (Morikawa), and a third is in Japanese as well as generally inaccessible (Umemoto).

For these reasons, one general objective can be described as the classification, review, and evaluation of techniques and results of scalings of meaningfulness and related attributes of discrete stimuli and of pairs of stimuli and of scalings of similarity among stimuli. The other general objective can be described as classification, review, and evaluation of experimental and theoretical materials on acquisition of correct responses of PA units as functions of meaningfulness and familiarization of stimulus and response members, and of similarity among stimulus and among response members of PA units and between them.

PA tasks may involve one or more units specified by 1:1, n:1, 1:n, or other patterns of pairings of stimulus and response members. Conventionally, for some by definition, PA learning has been with units specified by the 1:1 pattern: each of several different stimulus members is paired with only one of the same number of different response members. For PA learning with units specified by n:1 and 1:n patterns, two or more stimulus members are paired with one response member, or the converse. In general, the data on PA learning considered here were limited to findings obtained with criterion or terminal tasks whose units were specified by the conventional

1:1 pattern. Within such tasks a further restriction was to those involving the production of verbal responses or the selection of stimuli for verbal responses. When directly pertinent to the interpretation of some of the relationships obtained with units specified by the 1:1 pattern, data obtained with units specified by other patterns, for motor responses, or both are, on occasion, examined.

Transfer phenomena other than backward recall of stimulus members and retention are not considered systematically primarily because in only a few experiments are there data on the influence of meaningfulness and familiarization of discrete and paired stimulus members on these phenomena. However, as the occasion arises, available data of pertinence are noted. Relatively little new information on effects of similarity, either intra-task or inter-task, on transfer and retention has appeared since Underwood's (1954, 1961) and Postman's (1961) analytical reviews. Because these reviews are recent and extensive, excluded also was a consideration of the effects of similarity on transfer, other than backward recall, and of similarity on retention.

Some data have been reported on effects of meaningfulness and similarity on acquisition of serial-anticipation and verbal-discrimination tasks (Goss, 1963; Noble, 1963; Umemoto, 1963; Underwood & Schulz, 1960a). Also, theoretical accounts of obtained relationships have been advanced. These data and theories have not been considered in the present monograph primarily because they are not extensive and because they have not been extended substantially beyond the materials covered by Goss and by Noble. Furthermore, because of the confounding of stimulus and response functions in the same unit of serial-anticipation and verbal-discrimination tasks, the better experimental strategy is seemingly first to determine the role of meaningfulness, similarity, and familiarization in the PA task wherein stimulus and response functions can be separated manipulatively.

SUBSEQUENT CHAPTERS

The over-all plan is to describe the techniques of scaling meaningfulness and related attributes and the resultant normative data and then to summarize experimental findings on effects of meaningfulness before discussing theoretical analyses of the role of meaningfulness and similarity in PA learning. The theoretical analyses show the significance of information on the role of similarity of stimulus and of response members in PA learning. Such information is requisite to understanding the aims and significance of the five interrelated approaches to empirical confirmation of various aspects of the theoretical proposals. These approaches have been prior familiarization of stimulus members, response members, or both; acquired-distinctiveness training; induction of meaning and meaningfulness; response-mediated associations; and manipulation of the numbers of and associations among elements of stimulus and of response members. Pertinent findings within each approach are reviewed. Evaluation of the validity of various aspects of the theoretical analyses follows, along with suggestions for further research.

The more specific chapter plan is, in the next chapter, to describe techniques of scaling meaningfulness and related attributes of discrete stimuli and of pairs of stimuli. Results of such scalings are also reported and sug- gestions are made regarding some desirable, additional normative data. Summarized in the third chapter are experimental findings on acquisition and backward recall as functions of meaningfulness and related attributes of stimulus members, response members, and of pairs of stimuli. These findings are presented within a classification of combinations of values of attributes of stimulus and response members and of assignment of those com- binations to lists which is developed at the beginning of the chapter.

The fourth chapter is devoted to the main propositions of the more impor- tant, recent theoretical analyses. Because earlier analyses have been sum- marized adequately elsewhere (Goss, 1963; Noble, 1963), they are largely ignored. For the same reason, certain highly detailed theoretical issues which they consider are ignored here.

Bases for and techniques of scaling similarity among stimuli in addition to those described in connection with the scaling of meaningfulness are described in the fifth chapter. Then summarized in the same chapter are results of a number of scalings of similarity and findings on acquisition and backward recall as functions of similarity of stimulus and response members and of similarity and meaningfulness of stimulus and response members combined.

Prior familiarization is the approach to confirmation of various theoretical propositions which has been investigated most extensively. The entire sixth chapter, therefore, is devoted to description of general and more specific techniques of familiarization and to findings on transfer to PA learning from familiarization of stimulus and response members. Included here, also, are results of investigations of the influence of satiation of stimuli on PA learning.

Considered in the seventh chapter are findings pertinent to evaluation of the effects of acquired-distinctiveness training, experimental induction of meaning and meaningfulness, response-mediated associations, and number of and associations among elements.

In the first part of the eighth chapter is an over-all summary of the second, third, fifth, sixth, and seventh chapters. The theoretical analyses presented in the fourth chapter are then summarized before considering the significance for those analyses of the empirical findings and conclusions. In the last part of this chapter are some general suggestions for further experiments on effects of meaningfulness, similarity, and familiarization on acquisition of PA lists.

DESIGNS OF EXPERIMENTS

Combined in the first of the experiments described in the Appendix (Experiment 1) were the variables of similarity of stimulus members, meaningfulness, and similarity of response members, and percentage of occurrence of response members (%ORM). Following acquisition to a criterion of one perfect trial, retention was tested 24 hours later. Thus, in conjunction with findings of previous experiments (Goss, Nodine, Gregory, Taub & Kennedy, 1962), the results of this experiment provide further information about acquisition and new information on retention.

The lists of Experiment 1 were presented to individual subjects under an anticipation format of presentation. Those of each of the next five experiments were presented to subjects in groups under a recall format of presentation. The five variables of the first of these five experiments (Experiment 2) were meaningfulness of stimulus members, meaningfulness of response members, the similarity of both, and %ORM. The next experiment (Experiment 3) involved the same five variables. In addition, within all 32 combinations of these variables, half of the response members were familiarized and half were not. An additional feature was two presentations rather than one presentation of stimulus members alone after each presentation of stimulus and response members together.

In another experiment (Experiment 4) involving subjects in groups and the recall format, meaningfulness of stimulus members and of response members were combined with similarity of meaning-ease of learning of the pairs constituted of those members.

The lists of the preceding four experiments were what are subsequently labeled unmixed lists. All PA units of an unmixed list represent the same level or combination of levels of meaningfulness and similarity. The lists of the next two experiments were what are subsequently labeled partly mixed. The PA units of each list represented some but not all of the combinations of levels of meaningfulness and similarity. These lists were constructed to provide information about effects on acquisition of meaningfulness and similarity of individual PA units. In one list of the first of the experiments with partly mixed lists (Experiment 5), stimulus members of high meaningfulness, low similarity were paired with response members representing the combinations of high and low meaningfulness and high and low similarity of response members. In the other list, stimulus members of low meaningfulness, high similarity were paired with the same response members. The four PA units of each of the lists of the next experiment (Experiment 6) represented different sets of four of the 16 combinations of high or low meaningfulness and high or low similarity of stimulus and of response members. Prior to acquisition of the PA lists, stimulus members, response members, both, or neither had been familiarized.

In the next five experiments, lists were administered to subjects individually with anticipation or recall formats of presentation the variable of primary interest. The lists of Experiments 7 and 8 were unmixed; those of Experiments 9 and 10 were mixed. Experiment 11 was a replication of Experiment 7. In Experiments 7, 9, and 11, meaningfulness of stimulus and response members were additional variables. In Experiments 8 and 10, similarity of stimulus and of response members were additional variables. Also, the designs of Experiments 9 and 10 permitted assessment of effects of length of list and of whole versus part-whole presentation of lists.

In the last experiment (Experiment 12), the variable of percentage of occurrence of stimulus members (%OSM) was introduced. %ORM was also a variable. Of interest were the effects of both variables separately and in relation to each other on acquisition of four pairs in a mixed list each of which represented one of the combinations of stimulus members and of response members of low or high meaningfulness.

ABBREVIATIONS

The abbreviations used in this monograph are listed in alphabetical order. Both short definitions and sources of more complete definitions and illustrative use are provided. Also noted are equivalences between some of the abbreviations listed here and those used by others (e.g., Noble, 1961, 1963; Underwood & Schulz, 1960a).

a: Noble's (1961) association value, "defined in terms of the relative frequencies of responses exceeding the *None* category" (p. 492). Also, Ellis and Bessemer's (1962) rate constant for curves describing cumulative mean numbers of multiple associations.

a':   Noble's (1961) rated number of associations; means for each stimulus computed by assigning values of 1, 2, 3, 4, 5 to rating categories of none, below average, average, above average, many, respectively.

CVC: trigrams of consonant-vowel-consonant structure; more generally, structures of bigrams, trigrams, dissyllables are described by sequences in which C indicates consonants and V indicates vowels.

D: Osgood, Suci, and Tannenbaum's (1957, pp. 90-97) index of similarity between two semantic differential profiles; also see Flavell (1961a, pp. 308-309) and Jenkins, Russell, and Suci (1958a, 1959).

GV: Underwood and Schulz's (1960a, pp. 250-252) generated values of trigrams obtained by summing proportions of occurrence of a particular letter relative to the most frequent single-letter response to single letters and to bigrams; slightly different procedures are described on pp. 236, 242.

H: entropy of a stimulus defined as equal to $-\Sigma p_i \log_2 p_i$, where
            p_i is the number of occurrences of the ith different response divided
            by the number of respondents (Attneave, 1959; Flavell & Johnson,
            1961; Laffal, 1955).

L-Different Total: "number of distinct and different similarities given by
            . . . subjects to each pair" (Flavell & Johnson, 1961, p. 339).

L-Entropy: same as H above (Flavell & Johnson, 1961, p. 340).

L-Latency: "log centisecond reaction time" (Flavell & Johnson, 1961, pp.
            340-341).

M: not used here, but Underwood and Schulz's (1960a, pp. 9-18)
            generic term for meaningfulness defined by operations of:
            "1. Whether or not a subject 'gets' an association within a limited
                period of time.
              2. The number of associates which an item elicits in a given
                period of time.
              3. The number of associates which the subject thinks a given item
                would elicit" (p. 25).
            Noble (1963) does not use the generic abbreviation, preferring
            a, m, and a' for measures obtained by the preceding three operations,
            respectively.

m: not used here, but common in Noble's (e.g., 1952, 1963) articles;
            the mean of the number of different associates to a stimulus obtained
            by the multiple-association technique.

m':   Noble's (1961, p. 508) scaled meaningfulness obtained by trans-
            formation of rated frequencies into normal deviates by the method
            of successive intervals.

M_a: used here for meaningfulness of stimuli obtained by the single-
            association technique; approximately equivalent to Noble's a.

M_n: used here for meaningfulness of stimuli obtained by the multiple-
            association technique; equivalent to Noble's m.

M_p: meaningfulness based on polarization of ratings obtained by means
            of the semantic-differential formats.

M_r: meaningfulness based on ratings of which M_p is a special case as
            are Noble's a', m', and f (ratings of familiarity, 1961), and Under-
            wood and Schulz's FR (ratings of familiarity, 1960a, p. 186) and
            PR (ratings of pronunciability, pp. 23-25).

n: constant for estimated asymptote of Ellis and Bessemer's (1962) curves for cumulative mean number of multiple associations, hence of the total number of associations.

N-Attributes: "all similarities based upon synonymity, common attributes, or membership in a common class" (Flavell & Johnson, 1961, pp. 340-341).

N-Contiguity(ies): "all interpretable responses other than those scored" under N-Attributes (Flavell & Johnson, 1961, p. 341).

N-Different Attributes: "the reciprocal of the total number of different similarities of the N-Attribute type" (Flavell & Johnson, 1961, p. 341).

N-Different Contiguities: "the reciprocal of the total number of different similarities of the N-Contiguities type" (Flavell & Johnson, 1961, p. 341).

N-Different Total: "the reciprocal of the total number of distinct and different similarities given to a word pair" (Flavell & Johnson, 1961, p. 340).

N-Total: "the reciprocal of the total number of similarities given per word pair in the N condition" (Flavell & Johnson, 1961, p. 340). [N is Flavell and Johnson's label for a condition in which subjects were given "one minute per pair to write down as many similarities or ways alike between pair members as they could" (p. 339).]

ORM: occurrence of response members (Schulz & Runquist, 1960); also written %ORM.

PA: paired associates (units, lists, tasks, situations).

R: relative entropy (Attneave, 1959, p. 9).

RT: (associative) reaction time.

t_0:   constant for estimated time-axis intercept of Ellis and Bessemer's (1962) curves for cumulative mean number of multiple associations.

CHAPTER 2

Scalings of Meaningfulness

Glaze (1928) was apparently the first to scale the association value or meaningfulness of discrete stimuli; the stimuli were discrete consonant-vowel-consonant (CVC) nonsense syllables. Subsequently, meaningfulness and related attributes of discrete stimuli and of pairs of stimuli of different types in various lists have been scaled by different techniques. Among the related attributes of meaningfulness of discrete stimuli are ratings of familiarity including estimated frequency of occurrence and also ratings of estimated ease of learning, pronunciability, emotionality, and wordness. Another attribute is frequency of counted or estimated "actual" occurrence or use. Pairs of stimuli have apparently not been scaled for meaningfulness; however, they have been scaled for ease of learning, estimated strength of the association between members of a pair, estimated co-occurrence of referents of members of a pair, similarity of meaning of members of a pair, and vividness of connotation. Considered first are techniques used to scale meaningfulness and related attributes of discrete stimuli and of pairs of stimuli; results of various studies are then summarized and compared; finally, several areas requiring further research are noted.

TECHNIQUES

Three general techniques of scaling meaningfulness and related attributes can be distinguished; within each there are several more specific techniques. The general techniques are: (a) requiring subjects to produce associations, (b) experimenter-supplied stimuli for responses, and (c) counts of frequency of occurrence or of use. The semantic differential can be considered a special technique within experimenter-supplied stimuli for responses.

Production of Associations

The technique of requiring subjects to produce associations involves presentation of each stimulus for some interval of time during which subjects are instructed to produce an association or associations other than repetition of the stimulus. The number of associations by a single subject to each stimulus may be limited to at most one association, or subjects may be instructed to respond with as many associations as they can within intervals which have extended up to 120 sec. (Ellis & Bessemer, 1962). These two variants are here labeled the single-association technique and the multiple-association technique, respectively. Noble (1952) called the latter the production method. Meaningfulness values obtained by the single-association technique are hereafter designated M_a; those obtained by the multiple-association technique are hereafter designated M_n.

Thus far, associations obtained by both single-association and multiple-association techniques have always been with instructions and other conditions under which subjects have had relative freedom with respect to restrictions on class membership of associations and on their relationships to the stimulus. However, such restrictions could be introduced.

SINGLE-ASSOCIATION TECHNIQUE

Glaze limited the number of associations to each stimulus by a single subject to at most one during the 2–3 sec. each stimulus was presented. During this interval subjects may, as Glaze instructed them, simply indicate whether or not they have an association to each stimulus, or they may, as Hull (1933) and others instructed them, indicate the nature of their association. They may also answer or check "Yes" to any one or "No" to all questions such as: "Is it a word? Does it sound like a word? Does it remind me of a word? Can I use it in a sentence?" (Archer, 1960, p. 2). In all three cases, meaningfulness of each stimulus is expressed as the percentage of subjects who indicated that they had an association, who gave an association, or both, or who answered "Yes." Thus M_a values from 0% to 100% are possible with up to as many steps as there are subjects.

Word-association studies (e.g., Jenkins & Russell, 1960; Schlosberg & Heineman, 1950) suggest the additional measures of frequency of the most frequent response (frequency of the primary, communality), number of different responses (Laffal, 1952, 1955), and number of faults (Laffal, 1955). Laffal (1955, p. 265) has also proposed the use of the entropy measure, H, defined as equal to $-\Sigma p_i \log_2 p_i$, where p_i is the number of occurrences of the ith different response divided by the number of respondents. The ratio of obtained H to maximum H, relative entropy or R (Attneave, 1959, p. 9) has also been used (Battig, 1962). Finally, Vanderplas and Garvin (1959a) have employed content value defined as the "proportion of the total percentage of responses which were words or phrases denoting associations with objects or situations" (p. 153).

Strengths of responses of repeating the stimulus or of first associations other than repeating the stimulus could be specified by response latency [associative reaction time (RT)] or speed and by speed of making the response. J. D. Taylor's (1959) and Glanzer's (1962) scalings excepted, these measures have apparently not been used to scale members of sets of trigrams whose meaningfulness values have been obtained by either single-association or multiple-association techniques. Meaningfulness would presumably be directly related to frequency of the most frequent response and to the speed measures and inversely related to number of different responses, H, and number of faults.

Glanzer (1962) suggests a refinement of classification by grammatical function which may have to be extended to scalings of meaningfulness of words. For English monosyllables of little or no ambiguity with respect to their grammatical function, the rank order of increasing latencies was nouns, adjectives, pronouns, verbs, prepositions, adverbs, and conjunctions. The rank order of increasing numbers of different responses to each stimulus through four trials was nouns, adjectives, verbs, adverbs, pronouns, prepositions, and conjunctions.

The stimuli have usually been sequences of three letters and the expected, if not actual, responses have been complete words or even "ideas." Underwood and Schulz have used single letters of two-letter sequences as stimuli and restricted responses to a single letter. They have combined these more molecular associations, weighted for relative frequencies of single letters, of responses to single letters, and of responses to two-letter sequences to obtain generated values (GV) for three-letter sequences. Such GV might be considered an over-all measure of strengths of chains of the more molecular response components of responses of saying or spelling a word (1960a, pp. 241-244).

For pairs of stimuli, Flavell (1961a, p. 315) noted that similarity of meaning might be scaled by strengthening a response to one member of a pair and determining amount of generalization or positive transfer of the response to the other member of the pair. Generalization or positive transfer from each member to the other might be specified separately or averaged. Also suggested is scaling similarity of meaning by extent of clustering of members of a pair in recall.

MULTIPLE-ASSOCIATION TECHNIQUE

With the multiple-association technique, subjects have been told, "This is a test to see how many words you can think of and write down in a short time. You will be given a *key* word and you are to write down as many *other* words which the key word brings to mind as you can. These other words which you write down may be things, places, ideas, events, or whatever you happen to think of when you see the key word" (Noble, 1952, p. 425). The number of acceptable responses (legible, not perseverative, not failures of set) to each stimulus by each subject were then counted and averaged. The resultant mean value for each stimulus was considered its meaningfulness, which Noble abbreviated m. Medians have also been used.

By counting only first responses within the first 2 or 3 sec., data obtained by the multiple-association technique can be analyzed to obtain values comparable to those obtained by the single-association technique (J. D. Taylor, 1959). Also, frequency of the most frequent first response (Cofer, 1958) and number of different first associations can be obtained, and both first and subsequent responses can be tabulated to obtain frequency of the most frequent response to each stimulus [Mandler's (1955) *associative prepotency*] and number of different responses. Ratings of increasing numbers of responses to each stimulus can be dichotomized into ratings of "none" or all other categories (Noble, 1961; Noble, Stockwell, & Pryer, 1957), and the meaningfulness of that stimulus expressed as the percentage of subjects checking some category other than "none."

Among possible time-based measures are latency or speed of the first association, the time interval between cessation of each response and initiation of the next response, speed of making each response, and time required to make n responses.

Following Laffal (1955), Flavell and Johnson (1961) used single responses by each subject that members of each pair of stimuli were alike or similar to obtain latency of response (L-Latency), number of different similarities suggested (L-Different Total), and entropy (L-Entropy). The latter was defined as equal to $-\Sigma p_1 \log_2 p_1$, where p_1 is the frequency of a particular similarity response divided by the number of subjects.

For pairs of stimuli, Flavell and Johnson (1961) have also used a multiple-association technique in which subjects were given "one minute per pair to write down as many similarities or ways alike between members as they could" (p. 339). The six measures of subjects' responses were reciprocals of: (a) the total number of similarities given per pair of stimuli (N-Total), and (b) the total number of different similarities given per pair of stimuli (N-Different Total); (c) the total number of "similarities based upon synonymity, common attributes, or membership in a common class" (N-Attributes), and (d) the total number of different similarities of this type (N-Different Attributes); (e) all interpretable responses other than attributes (N-Contiguity), and (f) the total number of different responses of this type (N-Different Contiguities).

Experimenter-Supplied Stimuli for Responses

The experimenter may present each stimulus, whose meaningfulness or other attributes are to be scaled, accompanied by one or more discrete stimuli for responses to that stimulus. Alternatively, each stimulus may be accompanied by one or more experimenter-supplied "continuous" stimuli in the form of graphic rating scales. The particular association to or attribute of the stimulus which subjects are to rate is defined by instructions, by single words, bipolar adjectives, or phrases-sentences under or at the ends of the scales, or by both instructions and accompanying further specifications. Meaningfulness based on ratings is designated M_r except for the special case, noted below, of meaningfulness based on polarization with the semantic differential technique which is designated M_p.

Discrete Stimuli for Responses

As has been done for word associations (e.g., Buchwald, 1957; Karwoski & Berthold, 1945; Malamud, 1946; Maller, 1936; Nunnally & Flaugher, 1963; Nunnally, Flaugher, & Hodges, 1963; Riegel, 1959; Terman & Miles, 1936), subjects might be asked to choose associations from lists of possible associations. The meaningfulness of each stimulus would be the mean number of choices. Also, meaningfulness and other attributes of discrete stimuli and of pairs of stimuli might be ranked by traditional paired-comparison techniques (e.g., Haun, 1960) or, particularly for ranking larger numbers of stimuli, by techniques related to or derived from the traditional paired-comparison techniques (e.g., Attneave, 1949). A possible additional measure is the time required for comparisons.

The limiting case of discrete stimuli is merely checking "Yes" or "No" when asked whether each stimulus or pair of stimuli has any one or more or none of the particular attributes specified by a set of questions such as those used by Archer (1960), which were noted previously. This variant of the rating technique is essentially the motor equivalent to the single-association technique in which subjects verbalize whether or not they have an association to the stimulus or pair of stimuli. As with the single-association technique, meaningfulness is scaled as the percentage of subjects who check "Yes." Two slight extensions would be to add a "?" choice, or use of more categories such as "strong," "weak," and "no." Associative RTs of such responses could be obtained and used per se or to weight categorizing responses.

"Continuous" Stimuli for Responses

The general procedure for rating various attributes of stimuli is to present each stimulus for short intervals, usually 4–8 sec. For discrete stimuli, the meaningfulness of each stimulus is defined by instructions to rate in terms of the number of different associations evoked by that stimulus; familiarity is defined by instructions to rate in terms of estimated relative frequency of prior exposure to the stimulus; ease of learning is defined by instructions to estimate the rate at which some stimulus might be learned when, for example, it is the response member of a paired-associates unit; and emotionality is defined by instructions and perhaps by the names of the dimension along which stimuli are rated or by the categories into which the stimuli are placed. Wordness has been specified by checking whether or not a stimulus is a word (Underwood & Postman, 1960, p. 78). For pairs of stimuli, presumably different attributes have been defined by instructions to rate ease of learning, strength of association, co-occurrence, familiarity, similarity of meaning, and vividness.

Ratings of meaningfulness and related attributes have been along 5-point to 15-point graphic scales. Battig's (1960) pairs of stimuli were first rated along a 9-point ordinal scale and 10 weeks later were placed in one of nine categories representing "equal 'intervals' of judged difficulty."

Of little or no concern thus far are possible effects on rated values of the number of points; their designation by numbers, percentages, quantifying adjectives, or combinations of these; and the specific scaling technique. RTs for responses of checking some point may be obtained and used per se or to weight checking responses. Noble (1958a) used relationships to the *GSR* to weight responses to the categories "pleasant," "unpleasant," "mixed," and "neutral."

Each different pair of bipolar adjectives which accompanies each of the n graphic scales of semantic differential assessments (Osgood, Suci, & Tannenbaum, 1957) defines a possible independent association or dimension along which stimuli are rated. Jenkins (1960) has suggested that degree of polarization—the square root of the summed squares of deviations of ratings of a concept from the neutral value—is related to other measures of meaningfulness. Alternatively, semantic profiles (Jenkins, Russell, & Suci, 1958b) might be used to define M_p simply as the number of ratings deviating from the neutral point by some fixed amount.

Differences in semantic differential ratings of stimuli have then been used to specify the similarity of meaning of pairs of stimuli (Jenkins, Russell, & Suci, 1958a, 1959; Osgood, Suci, & Tannenbaum, 1957). Also possible is a set of previously determined associations to each stimulus, with ratings of the relative strength of the associations between a stimulus and some or all of the associations to that stimulus. These, too, might be used to specify the similarity of meaning of pairs of stimuli. Finally, latency of judgments of similarity of or differences between members of a pair might be used (Karwoski & Schachter, 1948).

These several techniques and subtechniques for specifying meaningfulness are classified and summarized in Table 1. Reflected in the table is the initial

TABLE 1

Classification of Techniques of Scaling Meaningfulness in Terms of Origin and Number of Responses and Whether or Not Their Content Is Considered

Content Considered	Production		Experimenter-supplied	
	Single	Multiple	Single	Multiple
Yes	Single word association	Multiple or continuous word association	Multiple-choice word association: choice of one	Multiple-choice word association: choice of more than one
No	M_a	M_n	$M_r{}^a$	$M_p{}^b$

[a] Ratings of other attributes of discrete stimuli and of attributes of pairs of stimuli could also be placed here. Also included are ratings along each of two or more scales which are treated separately.

[b] Based on ratings along two or more scales treated simultaneously.

division into techniques involving subjects' production of responses or their selection or ratings of stimuli for responses supplied by experimenters. Subtechniques are distinguished by the number of responses required and whether or not lexically different responses are noted or "content" of responses is considered. Experimenter-supplied stimuli might be divided further into checking or choice among discrete stimuli and ratings along "continuous" stimuli or graphic scales. Ratings of other attributes of discrete stimuli are generally along a single scale for each stimulus, with the attribute rated defined by instructions. Ratings of attributes of pairs of stimuli are also usually along a single scale with the attribute defined by instructions.

Frequency

Frequency of occurrence of stimuli as counted in samples of words in written texts has also been used to specify familiarity. Assuming a direct relationship between frequency and meaningfulness, frequency can also be considered a basis for inferring meaningfulness of stimuli. With semantic counts, the relationship to meaningfulness is even more direct (Rosenzweig & McNeill, 1962). Specifications of frequency have usually been with words as the unit, for which results of the counts summarized in Thorndike and Lorge (1944) have been used almost exclusively. However, in addition to earlier summaries by Thorndike (e.g., Thorndike, 1921, 1927, 1931) and semantic counts by Lorge (1949) and Lorge and Thorndike (1938), various other counts have been undertaken whose results were reported in part or in full. Among the results of counts of words in various samples of English are those reported by Horn (1926), French, Carter, and Koenig (1930), McLaughlin (1962), and Yule (1944). Results of word counts or lists based on previous word counts of materials in French (Henmon, 1924; Vander-Beke, 1929; Gougenheim, Michea, Rivenc, & Sauvageot, 1956; l'Institut Pédagogique National, 1959a, 1959b), German (Keading, 1898; Morgan, 1928), and Spanish (Buchanan, 1927) are available as is a comparison among frequencies of words for the same concept in English, French, German, and Spanish (Eaton, 1940).

Sequences of two or more words in length might be used and also frequency of single letters or of sequences of two or more letters within words, between one word and the next, or both within and across words. Miller (1951, pp. 86-95) and Herdan (1956, pp. 66-83) summarize some pertinent early data.

E. B. Newman and Gerstman (1952) report frequencies of single letters as first and as first or later letters in a 10,000-word sample largely from Isaiah XXIX-XXXI in the King James Bible. Frequencies of single letters in 5170 words of articles in a San Antonio newspaper and in 5171 words of material from popular magazines have also been counted (Attneave, 1953). Frequencies of occurrence of letters in the two sources correlated .98.

Underwood and Schulz provide estimates of frequencies of occurrence of single letters, two-letter sequences (bigrams), and three-letter sequences (trigrams) within words (1960a, pp. 65-76, 333-369). Also, they have calculated "summed-letter frequency" by assigning values of 1 to 100 to each letter of a trigram, based on absolute frequency of occurrence of the letters, and then added the three values (p. 79). DiMascio (1959) averaged log frequency values of component letters.

The samples used by Bourne and Ford (1961) consisted of 2082 single-word "descriptors" (e.g. magnetic, optical) and 8207 student names with all spaces and special characters removed. There were 16,913 single letters and 16,918 bigrams in the former sample and 141,190 single letters and the same number of bigrams in the latter sample. Frequencies of the single letters in both samples were presented and compared with each other and with frequencies obtained in earlier counts of samples from continuous texts.

Frequency of occurrences of single letters both as first letters of words and as first or later letters, and frequency of occurrences of bigrams and of trigrams have also been counted by Baddelay, Conrad, and Thomson (1960). Their sample of written words was the text of the *London Times* for five consecutive days. Their sample of spoken words was the text of a BBC serial for five consecutive days.

Subsequently, Baddelay (1961b) used frequencies with which one letter was followed by another to specify a measure he labeled predictability. Spaces before and after a word are counted as letters so that any n-letter word can be decomposed into $n-1$ bigrams from left to right and $n-1$ bigrams from right to left, a total of $2(n-1)$ bigrams. For example, a C_1VC_2 trigram is broken into eight bigrams: space-C_1, C_1-V, V-C_2, C_2-space, space-C_2, C_2-V, V-C_1, C_1-space. Each of these bigrams has a rank in terms of the predictability of the second letter from the first letter as such sequences occur in samples of written or spoken words. These ranks are summed and divided by the number of bigrams to yield predictability.

The technique can be used for words with any number of letters. Thus, the Baddelay, Conrad, and Thomson sample from the *London Times* was later used to obtain frequencies of sequences of up through six letters with some information about frequencies of sequences of up through 12 letters (Seibel, 1963).

All words of 3, 4, 5, and 7 letters up to 200 words were recorded in each of 100 samples from different sources to obtain words for Mayzner and Tresselt's (1962) counts of frequencies of single letters and of bigrams. Both frequencies were with respect to word length and letter position.

Frequencies of single English phonemes have been determined for words in the *Oxford English Dictionary* (Trnka, 1935) and for words in lists derived from samples of connected material (Atkins, 1926; Carroll, 1952;

Dewey, 1923; Fowler, 1957). Frequencies of single English phonemes have also been determined for words of samples of telephone conversations (French, Carter, & Koenig, 1930; Tobias, 1959), and more formal oral presentations (Hayden, 1956; Voelker, 1936).

Information about frequencies of consonants and vowels in initial, intermediate, and final positions of words can be found in Trnka who also lists words of various structures such as one vowel and of a vowel and consonant or consonant and vowel. Frequencies of transitions from a vowel to a consonant or the converse are presented.

Carroll (1952, 1958) has counted frequencies of phoneme doublets in a sample of about 20,000 phonemes, as well as frequencies with which given phonemes follow phoneme doublets and frequencies of phoneme triplets. Transitional probabilities such as from the first to the second phoneme of a doublet and the converse were also determined. Tables of frequencies of single phonemes and of sequences of two, three, and four phonemes in Carroll's sample have been prepared by Hultzen, Allen, and Miron (1964).

RESULTS

Table 2 summarizes the subjects, stimuli, procedures, and significant features of the results of a number of scalings of meaningfulness and related attributes of discrete stimuli and pairs of stimuli of different types in various lists. Only studies in which tables of values for individual stimuli or pairs were reported or are seemingly available have been included. Excluded because the values of meaningfulness and related attributes cannot be used with English-speaking subjects are scalings of words and nonsense syllables in other languages (e.g., Umemoto, 1951a; Umemoto, Morikawa, & Ibuki, 1955a). Umemoto's (1963) Table 1 provides a more condensed summary of many of the scalings described in Table 2 and of scalings of Japanese words.

Information about meaningfulness and related attributes of discrete stimuli and about attributes of pairs of stimuli is embodied in or might be derived from the norms obtained in various classical (Jenkins & Russell, 1960; Palermo & Jenkins, 1964a; Woodworth & Schlosberg, 1954) and more recent studies of word associations (e.g., Biase & Marshall, 1964; Bousfield, Cohen, Whitmarsh, & Kincaid, 1961; Castaneda, Fahel, & Odom, 1961; Cohen, Bousfield, & Whitmarsh, 1957; Deese, 1959; Ervin & Landar, 1963; Nunnally, Flaugher, & Hodges, 1963; Palermo & Jenkins, 1963, 1964b; Postman,

TABLE 2

Scalings of Meaningfulness and Related Attributes of Discrete Stimuli and of Pairs of Stimuli Which Report or Make Available Values for Individual Items as Obtained by Production of Associations or by Responses to Experimenter-Supplied Stimuli

Investigator	Attribute	Subjects	Stimuli[a]	Procedure	Results and Remarks
			DISCRETE STIMULI		
			Single Associations		
Glaze (1928)	M_a	15[b]	2019 CVCs[c]	Each stimulus exposed for 2–3 sec. Subjects indicated whether or not had an association but not nature of association	Distribution roughly rectangular with range from 0% to 100%
Hull (1933)	M_a	20	320 CVCs	Stimuli in 20 lists of 16 each presented at 2-sec. rate in serial-anticipation situation under instructions to tell experimenter what any stimulus made subject think of	Distribution markedly skewed positively with range from 0% to 73% and mode at slightly less than 20%

[a]The order is chronological within sets of stimuli which are CVCs; trigrams other than CVCs; words and dissyllables; numbers; and figures.
[b]Unless otherwise noted, indicates number of college student subjects. In some studies, subsets of stimuli were scaled by different subsamples of subjects. Peixotto's (1948) scaling of recognitive values of 300 CVCs was not included here because her table of values was incomplete.
[c]Unless otherwise indicated, CVCs and other syllables are nonwords or nonsense syllables.

(Table continued)

TABLE 2 (*continued*)

Investigator	Attribute	Subjects	Stimuli	Procedure	Results and Remarks
Krueger (1934)	M_a	586	2183 CVCs	Groups of 10 to 47 subjects responded to 300 stimuli in each of four sessions. Experimenter spelled each stimulus twice (about 4 sec.) and subject had 3 sec. to write "idea" it aroused	Distribution markedly skewed negatively with range from 1.45% to 100% and mode at 97%
Trapp & Kausler (1959)	M_a	353	320 CVCs (same as Hull, 1933)	Simulated serial anticipation task for group use. Subjects went through list once, with 1 or 2 sec. to write down anything each stimulus made them think of	Range from 7% to 77% for men and women combined. Rank orders of values obtained for men and women separately about the same. Values of 34 of the stimuli differed from Hull's by more than 20%
Archer[d] (1960)	M_a	216	2480 CVCs including words	Subjects had 4 sec. to pronounce each stimulus and check "Yes," if could so answer any one of four questions about the CVCs; otherwise checked "No." Subjects also given verbal fluency test	Distribution J-shaped with the largest number of stimuli with values of M_a from 91% to 100%. Range of entire distribution from 1% to 100%. Test-retest reliability over 48 hr. of .88. Has been described as scaling for wordness rather than meaningfulness

Witmer (1935)	M_a	25 male adults	4534 CCCs	Each stimulus exposed for 4 sec. Subjects spelled stimulus, then gave its meaning or, if stimulus meant something which subject could not verbalize in the 4 sec., said "Yes"	Distribution slightly skewed positively with range from 0% to 100% and mode at 38%
Taylor (1959)	M_a	100	320 nouns and paralogs of CVCVC structure	Each stimulus presented in associative RT situation	M_a specified by percentages of subjects responding in 2.5 sec. Range from 26% to 95%; distribution skewed negatively. M_a correlated .63 with frequency of responses in dominant category and —.55 with number of different responses
Vanderplas & Garvin (1959a)	M_a	50	180 random shapes: 30 each with 4, 6, 8, 12, 16, or 24 points	Each stimulus exposed for 3 sec. and subjects wrote what shape reminded them of or "Yes" for something not describable in a word or two	Distribution normal with range from 20% to 62% and a mean of 38%. Number of points and M_a correlated negatively; M_a correlated positively with measures of content and of heterogeneity of content
Goldstein (1961)	M_a	140	Same as above except 10 each	Essentially same as above	Results in general agreement with Vanderplas and Garvin's

dArcher's technique could be considered limiting case of rating.

(Table continued)

TABLE 2 (*continued*)

Investigator	Attribute	Subjects	Stimuli	Procedure	Results and Remarks
Battig (1962)	M_a	122	105 random shapes: 7 each representing the combinations of 4, 6, 8, 12, and 16 sides with no, half, or all sides curved	Each stimulus exposed for 8 sec. Subjects wrote down anything stimulus reminded them of and rated strength of association on a 5-point scale	Range of M_a from 13.1% to 89.3% and that of rated strength from 0.26 to 3.26; r of .76 for M_a and rated strength. Both M_a and rated strength correlated negatively with information measures of heterogeneity of content
			Multiple Associations		
Mandler (1955)	M_n	34	100 CVCs with Glaze M_a of 0%, 20%, 40%, 60%, 80%, 100%	Subjects had 30 sec. to respond to each stimulus by writing "all the words that occurred to them, or that they thought of as they looked at, thought of, or pronounced the syllable"	Range from 2.9 to 5.3 with mean of 4.1. Also reports values of associative prepotency for each stimulus and the prepotent response

Shapiro (1963a, 1964)	M_n	600 children: 100 boys and 100 girls in Grades 4, 6, and 8 aged, respectively, 9–10, 11–12, and 13–14	52 word CVCs of Noble m' from 2.64 to 4.78; "is," "are" and 11 function words	Subjects had 18 sec. to write up to five different associations to each word	Ranges of M_n from 0.84 to 3.23, 1.12 to 3.82, and 1.75 to 4.15 for boys in Grades 4, 6, and 8, respectively, and from 0.97 to 3.51, 1.10 to 3.89, and 1.49 to 4.15 for girls in Grades 4, 6, and 8, respectively. No difference between sexes but M_n increased through Grades 4, 6, and 8. Rho's between M_n for each group and Noble m' values from .52 to .66; rho's between M_n for pairs of groups from .88 to .96
Underwood & Schulz (1960a, pp. 264-267)	M_n	54	42 assorted trigrams	Essentially same as Noble's (1952) except that subjects had 40 sec. to write associations to each stimulus	Range of M_n from 5.91 to 10.28. Conclude that interstitials elicit fewer associates than common three-letter nouns and adjectives
Noble (1952)	M_n	119 airmen	96 dissyllables	Subjects wrote as many different words as possible in 60 sec. under instructions to repeat key word covertly as they wrote	Range from 0.99 to 9.61 with mean of 3.65. Mean intergroup reliability coefficient of .98

(Table continued)

TABLE 2 (*continued*)

Investigator	Attribute	Subjects	Stimuli	Procedure	Results and Remarks
Noble & Parker (1960)	M_n	100	Same as Noble (1952)	Same as Noble (1952)	Range for M_n of each stimulus from 2.50 to 11.72 with mean for all stimuli of 5.76. Split-subjects reliability of .99. Mean M_n for all stimuli was 2.11 higher than mean for airmen obtained 10 years earlier; but r between two sets of values of .97
Postman (1961)	M_n, M_r	96, 1000	48 nouns: 24 of high and 24 of low Thorndike-Lorge counted frequencies	Ninety-six subjects responded to stimuli under procedure similar to Noble's (1952) but with 50 sec. to respond. Ratings of familiarity along 5-point scale obtained from 1000 subjects	Words of high Thorndike-Lorge frequencies had higher trigram frequencies, M_n, and M_r than words of low Thorndike-Lorge frequencies
R. C. Johnson (1961)	M_n	30	80 English nouns, adjectives, verbs	Same as Noble (1952)	Range of M_n from 3.23 to 9.20; distribution skewed negatively with median of 7.30

R. C. Johnson, Frincke, & Martin (1961)	M_n	23 (San Jose State College); 79 (U. Calif., Berkeley)	34 English nouns, adjectives, verbs	Same as Noble (1952)	M_n values presented for 16 of 34 stimuli selected on basis of previous ratings of "good" or "bad." M_n for "good" words significantly higher than M_n for "bad" words. Rho of .84 between M_n values for the 16 words for the two groups of subjects
R. C. Johnson, Weiss, & Zelhart (1964)	M_n	122 (including those of Johnson, Frincke, & Martin) 40 institutional psychotic male veterans, mostly schizophrenics	Same as above	Same as Noble (1952)	M_n values presented for all 34 words for students and for psychotics accompanied by ratings along good-bad scale, percentages of non-idiosyncratic responses, and percentages of students and psychotics making the most common association
W. Epstein (1962)	M_n	15	36 words: 12 concrete nouns, 12 abstract nouns, and 12 conjunctions and prepositions	Same as Noble (1952)	For concrete nouns, abstract nouns, and conjunctions and prepositions, respectively, ranges from 7.7 to 10.4, from 6.1 to 9.9, and from 4.3 to 7.2

(Table continued)

TABLE 2 (*continued*)

Investigator	Attribute	Subjects	Stimuli	Procedure	Results and Remarks
Koen (1962)	M_n, M_p	40	60 words of various grammatical functions	On basis of Q sort of 100 words prepared two lists each with 15 neutral and 15 emotional words. One list presented to 20 subjects to obtain M_n by Noble's procedure; other list presented to same subjects for semantic differential ratings along 12 scales, three each representing evaluation, potency, activity, and understandability. Other 20 subjects rated words of former list and produced associations to words of the latter list	M_n and polarization based on M_r (M_p) correlated .61 for neutral words but .02 for emotional words. Correlations between M_n and counted frequency of occurrence of .62 for neutral and .49 for emotional words, and between M_p and frequency of .51 for neutral and −.21 (not significant) for emotional words. Partialling M_n out of correlation between M_p and frequency reduced .51 to .21, whereas partialling frequency out of correlation between M_n and M_p reduced .61 only to .46. No difference between emotional and neutral words in frequency or M_n but emotional words had higher values than neutral words on four-factor polarization and lower ratings on understandability. Significant negative correlations between evaluative ratings (good is "1") and both M_n and frequency for neutral and for emotional words

Ratings Along Single Experimenter-Supplied "Continuous" Stimuli

Noble, Stockwell, & Pryer (1957)	$M_r{}^e$	200	Subjects spelled, pronounced, then rated each stimulus along 5-point scale for number of different things or ideas stimulus made subjects think of	Range of M_r in terms of ratings from 1.28 to 4.44 and in terms of normal deviate transformation of ratings from 0.00 to 3.72. When dichotomized into no association and some association, range from 22% to 100%
		100 CVCs		
Noble (1961)	M_r	200	Essentially same as Noble, Stockwell, and Pryer (1957)	Range of M_r in terms of ratings (a') from 1.06 to 4.78 and in terms of normal deviate transformation of ratings (m') from 0.00 to 4.78. When dichotomized into no association and some association (a), range from 5% to 100%
		2100 CVCs and words		

^{e}Ratings of meaningfulness are first, followed by those of other attributes.

(Table continued)

TABLE 2 (*continued*)

Investigator	Attribute	Subjects	Stimuli	Procedure	Results and Remarks
Cieutat (1963)	M_r	126	148 monosyllables, 150 bisyllables, 148 trisyllables of different numbers and consonant-vowel structures	Subjects rated each stimulus along a 7-point scale "on the number of things or ideas it reminds you of"	The ranges for a, the proportion of subjects checking any point other than "none," were from .31 to 1.00, .34 to 1.00, and .34 to 1.00 for monosyllables, bisyllables, and trisyllables, respectively. All three distributions were J-shaped, negatively skewed. Reliabilities for proportions based on halves of the subjects were from .95 to .97. The ranges for a', the arithmetic mean of the ratings, were from 1.58 to 5.79 for monosyllables, 1.67 to 5.74 for bisyllables, and 1.63 to 5.17 for trisyllables. The distribution for the former stimuli was bimodal, the distributions for the latter two were positively skewed. Reliabilities were .97 upward. Also reported are values for the standard deviations of the ratings of each stimulus and for a linear transformation to obtain distributions with means of 500 and standard deviations of 100 (Z_a')

Battig & Spera (1962)	M_r	95	101 numbers from 0 to 100	"Instructed to rate each number as to 'how many different things or ideas are associated with the number, and how difficult it is to think of these associations,' by circling one of five letters (A–E)"	Range from 0.72 for "31" to 3.56 for "100." r of .30 between values for single digits and of two-digit numbers made up of those digits. Also r of .80 with values obtained in earlier study and r of .85 between values for single digits and mean frequencies of continued associations obtained by Anderson (1961)
Cochran & Wickens (1963a)	M_r	100	Same as Battig and Spera	Each number rated by check mark along 5-in. line with sections labeled none, below average, average, above average, and very many	Range from 0.40 to 3.27, with mean ratings of all but two numbers below those obtained by Battig and Spera. Rank-order correlation of .91 and r of .92 between mean ratings obtained by Cochran and Wickens and by Battig and Spera
Underwood & Schulz (1960a, pp. 23-25)	Pronunciability	181	178 consisting of 100 CVCs, with remainder word CVCs and CCCs	Each stimulus rated along a 9-point scale for ease or difficulty of pronouncing	For 239 different stimuli of this and study below, distribution bimodal; range of pronunciability from 1.50 (easy) to 8.77 (hard). r of .78 between pronunciability and Noble, Stockwell, and Pryer's (1957) M_r values for the 100 CVCs

(Table continued)

TABLE 2 (continued)

Investigator	Attribute	Subjects	Stimuli	Procedure	Results and Remarks
Underwood & Schulz (1960a, pp. 152-153)	Pronunci-ability	70	95 CVCs and CCCs	Thirty-five subjects had instructions of preceding study; 35 subjects had special instructions to avoid rating on basis of frequency and familiarity	rs for mean and median scale values for pronunciability under two sets of instructions were .96 and .95, respectively. Test-retest reliability of mean ratings of 31 syllables common to two studies was .98
Gibson, Pick, Osser, & Hammond (1962)	Pronunci-ability	165	50 (25 pairs of) pseudowords of CVC form but with each consonant or vowel represented by from one to three letters to assure correspondence between these graphemes and the phonemes represented	Essentially the same as Underwood and Schulz	One member of each pair constructed to be easy and the other hard to pronounce. The mean of the ratings for the former was 2.88, for the latter 6.57, with the lower value indicating easier pronunciability. Standard scores of these ratings correlated .85 with number of different pronunciations of the pseudowords

Study	Attribute	Subjects	Stimuli	Method	Results
Underwood & Schulz (1960a, pp. 184-187)	Familiarity	48	80 assorted trigrams	Each stimulus rated along 9-point scale for how often subjects had come in contact with each	Report rank order of values of familiarity of only 36 stimuli along with their rank orders for learning, pronunciability, and counted frequency of occurrence
Haagen (1949)	Familiarity	40	480 two-syllable adjectives	Stimulus rated along 5-point scale	J-shaped distribution with largest number of stimuli highly familiar.
Noble (1953)	Familiarity	200 airmen	Same as Noble (1952)	Twenty-minute session in which subjects rated each stimulus along 5-point scale for the number of times each stimulus had been experienced	Normal deviate transformations of ratings ranged from 0.00 to 5.66
Ledgerwood (1932)	Emotionality	7	20 proper nouns (artificial names) from James Branch Cabell's *The Silver Stallion*	Each word paired twice with every other word so position counterbalanced for paired-comparison scaling. Words also scaled by order-of-merit	r of .96 between values obtained by the two methods

(Table continued)

TABLE 2 (continued)

Investigator	Attribute	Subjects	Stimuli	Procedure	Results and Remarks
Noble (1958a, 1958b)	Emotion-ality	200 airmen	Same as Noble (1952)	Subjects placed each stimulus in one of four categories; neutral, pleasant, unpleasant, or mixed which were weighted 1, 2, 3, 4, respectively	Range of emotionality from 1.85 to 3.00 with corrected intergroup reliability coefficient of .94
Postman (1961)	See above				
Buss (1961)	Emotion-ality (Aggressiveness)	60 males; 78 females	146 words for aggression	Each word rated along scale from 1 (least aggressive) to 9 (most aggressive)	Range of medians of ratings from 1.8 to 8.8 for males and from 2.0 to 8.9 for females
Dixon & Dixon (1964)	Impression value	60 males, 60 females	200 verbs in simple past tense	Verbs presented in 10 different random orders for ratings along an 11-point scale. Ratings were of extent to which an experimenter would have a good to bad impression of a subject who used each verb	Ranges of means of ratings from 4.95 (good) to −4.00 for males and from 4.47 to −4.55 for females. Means of ratings of males and females differed significantly for 40 of the verbs; variability differed significantly for 70

H. Bower (1932)	Distinctiveness of visual image	42 to 183	26 letters; 40 each of various sequences of 2, 3, and 4 letters	Rating on 6-point scale for distinctiveness of "mental picture" or as seen by "your *mind's eye*"	Ranges of values of 2.8 to 3.5 for single letters and of 1.9 to 3.2, 1.9 to 3.5, and 1.6 to 3.2, respectively, for sequences of 2, 3, and 4 letters

Ratings Along Multiple Experimenter-Supplied "Continuous" Stimuli (Semantic Differential)

Jenkins, Russell, & Suci (1958b)	$M_r f$ (Semantic profile)	540	360 words (concepts) from several sources and of various grammatical functions	Eighteen sets of 20 stimuli each administered to different groups of 30 subjects each. Each stimulus rated along 7-point scales specified by bipolar adjectives. Scales selected to sample factors of evaluation, potency, activity, tautness, novelty, and receptivity	Mean ratings of each stimulus along each scale reported. Test-retest reliability of means of stimuli of a sample of 20 was .97; intergroup reliability coefficient based on 400 means was .94

f Treated as ratings along each of 2 separate scales.

(Table continued)

TABLE 2 (continued)

Investigator	Attribute	Subjects	Stimuli	Procedure	Results and Remarks
Jenkins (1960)	M_P	540	As above.	Degree of polarization (M_P) defined as root mean square of deviations of ratings from neutral value of 4	Degree of polarization values for each stimulus reported along with loadings on evaluation, potency, and activity factors
Koen (1962)	See above				

PAIRS OF STIMULI

Ratings Along Single Experimenter-Supplied "Continuous" Stimuli

Richardson & Erlebacher (1958)	Similarity of meaning; ease of learning	110?	73 pairs of adjectives representing four combinations of low or high Thorndike-Lorge frequencies of members; 76 pairs of CVCs and 73 pairs of CCCs representing four combinations of low or high M_a of members	Each pair of stimuli rated for similarity of meaning along a 15-point scale (56 subjects) and for ease of learning with first member of pair as stimulus and second as response (54 subjects)	Values for both similarity of meaning and ease of learning of adjectives almost all higher than values for CVCs which were somewhat higher on the average than those for CCCs. rs between similarity of meaning and ease of learning for adjectives, CVCs, and CCCs of .82, .81, and .59, respectively

Battig (1959)	Ease of learning	82	144 pairs of CVCs of 47%, 53%, Glaze M_a. 105 with stimulus and response in one direction; 39 reversals	Each pair rated along a 9-point ordinal scale	Range from 2.99 to 7.40 with mean of 5.08. Intergroup reliability coefficient of .88
Battig (1960)	Ease of learning	31	210 pairs; same 105 as above with members in both directions	Pairs ranked in terms of nine "equal" intervals of judged difficulty	Range from 1.9 to 7.2 with mean of 4.52. r of .85 between ordinal and interval ratings
Haagen (1949)	Similarity of meaning; strength of association; vividness	240	80 sets of six two-syllable adjectives each; one stimulus of each set paired with each of the others to make 400 pairs	Each stimulus exposed for 8 sec., then 6 sec. and rated along 7-point scale. Eighty subjects rated for similarity of meaning, 80 for strength of association, and 80 for vividness	Distributions for all three attributes skewed toward high end of scale. Intergroup reliability coefficients of .92, .91, and .86 for similarity of meaning, strength of association, and vividness, respectively
Melton & Safier (Hilgard, 1951)	Similarity of meaning	96	300 pairs of adjectives	Details not known	Ratings ranged from 0.01 to 2.85; distribution skewed negatively with median of 1.91

(Table continued)

TABLE 2 (*continued*)

Investigator	Attribute	Subjects	Stimuli	Procedure	Results and Remarks
Haun (1960)	Strength of association	183 for Phase I; 100 for Phase II	30 words from Kent-Rosanoff for Phase I; same 30 words and six most frequent responses to each for Phase II	In Phase I, free association procedure used to obtain six most frequent responses to each Kent-Rosanoff word. In Phase II, paired-comparisons technique used to scale strength of association between each Kent-Rosanoff word and the six responses to that word	Free association frequency of responses to each stimulus reported along with scale values obtained by Thurstone's Case III and Case V solutions. Correlations for free association and paired-comparison ranks for responses to most words small and not significant. Only systematic change in ranks was relatively lower paired-comparison ranks for opposites
Flavell (1961b)	Co-occurrence; similarity of meaning	74	120 consisting of 30 pairs each of concrete nouns, adjectives, concrete nouns-adjectives, and abstract nouns	Each pair rated for similarity of meaning along 7-point scale and each pair, except pairs of abstract nouns, rated for co-occurrence along a 7-point scale. Thirty-seven subjects rated for similarity of meaning and 37 rated for co-occurrence	Ranks of values of similarity of meaning and co-occurrence for pairs of each type of word are presented along with ranks with respect to semantic distance between members of each pair

Ratings Along Multiple Experimenter-Supplied "Continuous" Stimuli (Semantic Differential)

Jenkins, Russell, & Suci (1958a, 1959)	Similarity of meaning (Semantic distances)	540	Same as (1958b)	Similarity of meaning for each of 360 stimuli paired with all other stimuli defined as root mean squares of differences in ratings of members of pairs along the 20 bipolar scales	Similarity of meaning (designated D by the authors) for each pair given in (1958a). Also included are word-association data for each Kent-Rosanoff word used

to be published; Rosenzweig, 1964; Russell & Jenkins, 1954; Schwartz & Rouse, 1961, pp. 124-133; Shapiro, 1963a, 1963b, 1963c, 1964; Tresselt & Mayzner, 1964; Underwood & Richardson, 1956) and of semantic distances and profiles (Jenkins, Russell, & Suci, 1958a, 1958b, 1959). However, only those studies explicitly conceived as pertinent to meaningfulness of discrete stimuli or similarity of meaning of pairs of stimuli have been included in Table 2. Summaries of some of the preceding and of other studies of word association may also be found in Umemoto's Table 1.

Discrete Stimuli

Most scalings of attributes of discrete stimuli have been for meaningful-ness. In early studies, the single-association technique was preferred; in more recent studies, the multiple-association technique and ratings have been preferred. CVC nonsense syllables or, more generally, CVCs were the first stimuli scaled and even now constitute the only long list of the same stimuli scaled more than once. Only Witmer (1935) has scaled meaningful-ness of a substantial number of CCCs. Beginning with Noble (1952), various sets of dissyllables have been scaled.[1] Cieutat (1963) has provided scale values for monosyllables, bisyllables, and trisyllables of various letter lengths and consonant-vowel structures. Numbers from 0 through 100 have been scaled by Battig and Spera (1962). Apparently the only scalings of mean-ingfulness of shapes presented visually, nonsense or otherwise, are those by Vanderplas and Garvin (1959a), Arnoult (1960), Goldstein (1961), and Battig (1962).

Eight of Vanderplas and Garvin's six-point shapes were cut from $\frac{1}{8}$-inch rubber tile and mounted on vinyl tile to serve as the stimuli for Ellis and Bessemer's (1962) assessment of scale values of shapes presented tactually. Subjects made as many associations as possible in two minutes. For each shape, an exponential function was fitted to the cumulative mean numbers of responses in successive 5-sec. intervals. Values for time-axis intercept, rate, and asymptotic constants were determined. Designated t_0, a, and n, respectively, rs of $-.66$, $-.93$ and $.88$ were obtained for the relationships between the values for these constants for each shape and the values obtained by Vanderplas and Garvin.

Using $t_0 + 1/a$ as an estimate of the latency of all responses in the total number of responses, the r for estimated latency and Vanderplas and Garvin's values was .96. The r for the total number of responses and average latency was .91; that for the values of n and a was $-.90$. On the basis of the latter relationship, Ellis and Bessemer suggest that duration of the association period may influence values of M_a and M_n.

Semantic differential ratings from which M_p might be derived have been obtained for various sets of colors and names for colors (e.g. Tanaka,

---

[1] A list of 43,200 dissyllabic words and paralogs is available in Dunlap (1933).

Oyama, & Osgood, 1963; J. E. Williams, 1964; Wright & Rainwater, 1962) and of visual forms (e.g. Elliott & Tannenbaum, 1963; Tanaka, Oyama, & Osgood), including the Rorschach and Holtzman inkblots (e.g. Little, 1959; Otten & Van de Castle, 1963; Rosen, 1960; Sines, 1960; Zax & Benham, 1961). Unfortunately, ratings or factor loadings for individual stimuli along each scale are not usually reported as is the case for semantic differential ratings of complex sounds (Solomon, 1958, 1959b) except for 20 passive sonar recordings (1959a). Without such information, M_p cannot be calculated for individual stimuli.

Garner and Clement (1963) constructed patterns of five dots or of five Xs or 0s arranged in a 3×3 square matrix with at least one dot or one X in each column and each row of the matrix. The resultant 90 patterns were rated for goodness along a 7-point scale. The dot patterns were used again by Clement (1964) along with patterns obtained by filling in cells of a 9×9 square matrix. Both sets of patterns were rated for goodness along a 7-point scale. Also, subjects named each pattern. Latency and content of the names were recorded and response uncertainty (H) was calculated for each pattern.

The common core of the stimuli constructed for semantic differential ratings by Markel and Hamp (1961) were the consonant-consonant sequences gl--, fl--, sm--, sp--, and st--. The former three, particularly, were selected because they occur frequently in English and show "marked properties of connotative meaning." Each was combined with i, pronounced \iy\, and a, pronounced \ah\ and presented aurally for ratings along 15 bipolar scales. Ratings along each scale for each stimulus are presented. When ratings of the same CC-- did not differ significantly, they were interpreted as connotations of the CC--, independently of the terminal phonemes. M_p for the five consonant-consonant sequences could be derived from these ratings.

Relationships between meaningfulness values obtained in different scalings of the same stimuli and also between different measures of meaningfulness obtained in a particular assessment of the same stimuli are examined. Then examined are relationships between meaningfulness and other attributes of the same stimuli and relationships between and among other attributes.

RELATIONSHIPS BETWEEN MEANINGFULNESS VALUES IN DIFFERENT SCALINGS AND BETWEEN DIFFERENT MEASURES OF MEANINGFULNESS

The lists of various scalings of meaningfulness of CVCs have had from 21 to 2100 stimuli in common. Therefore, comparisons can be made of values of meaningfulness obtained for the same stimuli at different times, with different groups of subjects, by different techniques, under different conditions of presentation of stimuli and under different instructions.

Table 3 summarizes the rs between meaningfulness values obtained for the

TABLE 3

Correlations between Values of Meaningfulness Obtained in Different Scalings by
Single-Association and Multiple-Association Techniques of the Same Discrete CVCs[a]

Scale Values Correlated	Number of Syllables	r	Investigator(s)
Glaze vs. Hull	300	.62	Peixotto (1948)
	306	.63	Noble, Stockwell, & Pryer (1957)
Glaze vs. Krueger	300	.65	Peixotto (1948)
	100	.86	Noble, Stockwell, & Pryer (1957)
	1933	.79	Archer (1960)
Glaze vs. Noble, Stockwell, & Pryer	100	.81	Noble, Stockwell, & Pryer (1957)
Glaze vs. Archer	1933	.79	Archer (1960)
Glaze vs. Scheible	27	.79	Scheible (Underwood & Schulz, 1960a, p. 48)
Hull vs. Krueger	300	.70	Peixotto (1948)
	305	.72	Noble, Stockwell, & Pryer (1957)
Hull vs. Noble, Stockwell, & Pryer	21	.55	Noble, Stockwell, & Pryer (1957)
Krueger vs. Mandler	100	.65	Mandler (1955)
Krueger vs. Noble, Stockwell, & Pryer	100	.90	Noble, Stockwell, & Pryer (1957)
Krueger vs. Archer	1933	.85	Archer (1960)
Krueger vs. Noble	100	.88	Noble (1961)

[a] Noble Stockwell, and Pryer's a, Noble's a, and Archer's values, though based on ratings, are included. Peixotto's recognitive values might be considered a measure of learning rather than of meaningfulness; they are here interpreted as meaningfulness.

same CVCs by Glaze (1928), Hull (1933), Krueger (1934), Mandler (1955), Noble, Stockwell, and Pryer (1957), Scheible (Underwood & Schulz, 1960a, p. 48), Archer (1960), and Noble (1961). The Noble values are for the measure he labeled a; this measure is described below. With sets of larger numbers of stimuli there is, perhaps, a slight trend toward higher values of r. The two highest rs, however, were obtained with sets of only 100 syllables. No decrease in r is apparent with increasing amounts of time between studies compared. Finally, the rs are sufficiently high to conclude that relative values, if not absolute values, of meaningfulness of CVCs remain stable under a wide range of conditions.

Noble, Stockwell, and Pryer's (1957) procedure was subsequently used to scale all 2100 CVCs in English with "Y" classified as a consonant (Noble, 1961). The first measure derived from these ratings, which Noble labeled a, was the percentage of 200 subjects responding with ratings in any category above "none"; a corresponds to M_a specified by the single-association technique. The second measure, labeled a', was the mean of values of "1" for ratings of "none" to "5" for ratings of "very many." The a values of a sample of 120 of the trigrams were a negatively accelerated function of a' values. The correlation ratio was .99, the r was .91.

The third measure, labeled m', was first obtained by transforming a and a' values into deviates of the normal distribution function by the method of successive intervals. The relationship between a and m' had initial positive acceleration to m' of 1.5 and subsequent negative acceleration which reached asymptote at m' of 4.0. The a' values increased only a small amount for m' from 0.0 to 1.5, then increased linearly for m' up to 4.5 with slight negative acceleration for the highest m' values.

The relationship between a' and m' was then used to obtain m' values for the remaining 2079 trigrams. Comparison of m' values for the 100 trigrams scaled by Mandler by the multiple-association technique with Mandler's M_n values for those trigrams yielded an r of .72 with essentially linear regression for m' from 0.5 to 3.8. The regression of Archer M_a values for 120 trigrams on Noble m' values for those trigrams was ogival; the correlation ratio for 12 categories of 10 trigrams each was .97; the r was .94. The rs between the a and a' values of these trigrams and their Archer M_a values were .96 and .93, respectively.

Archer (1961) obtained rs from .32 to .68 between his M_a values for syllables in successive 20% intervals and Noble a values for those syllables. Archer notes certain aspects of Noble's procedures of presenting stimuli, recording responses, and scaling which may account for the much lower correlations for the more restricted ranges than for the entire ranges of M_a and a values. However, the restricted ranges per se may have attenuated the correlations.

For apparently the only scaling of meaningfulness of any set of stimuli with children, Shapiro (1963a; 1964) selected 100 boys and 100 girls in each of Grades 4, 6, and 8 of five public elementary schools. M_n values were obtained for 52 CVCs, 26 with Noble m' values from 3.82 to 4.78 ("high") and 26 with Noble m' values from 2.64 to 3.81 ("low"). For each of the six groups, mean M_n values for CVCs of "high" Noble m' were markedly higher than mean M_n values for CVCs of "low" Noble m'. The rho's between M_n and m' values for all 52 CVCs for each grade-sex group separately were from .52 to .66. Thus, for children rather than college students, for production of a maximum of five responses in 18 sec. rather than ratings, and within approximately the upper two fifths of the range of Noble m' values, M_n and m' were related significantly.

At each of the three grades, means, standard deviations, and ranges of M_n values for boys and for girls were essentially the same for CVCs of high or low Noble m' both separately and combined. However, means of M_n values increased from Grade 4 through Grade 8 for both sets of CVCs both separately and combined. Despite the increase in means of M_n values, rho's for all pairwise comparisons between the six groups of children were from .88 to .96.

The mean M_n values of Noble's 96 dissyllables for a sample of college students was 2.11 higher than the mean for airmen tested 10 years earlier (Noble & Parker, 1960). However, the r of .97 indicated that relative positions of the stimuli had not changed. The subjects for Rocklyn, Hessert, and Braun's (1957) calibration of the M_n of 24 of Noble's dissyllables were 16 unemployed males in each of three age intervals of 20–29, 30–49, and 50–66. M_n values based on all 48 subjects correlated .96 with Noble's values for those stimuli. The rs for the three age groups were .96 for 20–29, .94 for 30–49, and .92 for 50–66. Despite a difference in mean M_n values due partly to less stringent scoring criteria, Cieutat (1962) reports an r of .95 between scale values for 24 dissyllables reported by Noble (1952) and values obtained 11 years later with a sample of 54 college undergraduates.

Epstein's (1963) list of five dissyllables of high (mean = 5.40) and five of low (mean = 1.40) Noble M_n values was presented serially at a 2-sec. rate for subjects to reproduce those stimuli perfectly in free recall. Immediately after the list was mastered, meaningfulness of the dissyllables was determined by Noble's (1952) production technique. The means of 8.37 and 3.43 for the sets of high and low Noble values, respectively, were higher than the original means, but the rank-order correlation between the 10 pairs of values was .94.

Johnson, Frincke, and Martin (1961) had 23 subjects from San Jose State College and 79 subjects from the University of California (Berkeley) scale a list of 34 nouns, adjectives, and verbs of essentially equal Thorndike-Lorge

(1944) frequencies by the multiple-association technique. For a subset of 16 words selected on the basis of previous ratings of "good" or "bad," the rho between M_n values for the two groups of subjects was .84.

Percentages of subjects responding within 2.5 sec. to the 320 dissyllables of J. D. Taylor's (1959) list correlated .63 with frequency of responses in the dominant response category and $-.55$ with number of competing responses. The r between the latter two measures was .77. Analyses of covariance designed to control differences in frequency of responses in the dominant category indicated that RTs of dominant responses were not related but that RTs of nondominant responses were related inversely to number of competing responses.

Experimental confirmation of the direct relationship between RT and number of competing responses is reported by Wiggins (1957). Stimuli previously paired with 2, 4, or 8 different responses for 8, 16, or 32 times were presented along with instructions to subjects to respond "with the first other syllable that came to mind." RT of these responses was a direct function of the number of responses which had been paired with the stimuli and an inverse function of frequency of pairing.

Noted previously was Jenkins' (1960) suggestion of a relationship between degree of polarization and meaningfulness. The presumed basis of this proposal was Jenkins and Russell's (1956) finding of a correlation of .71 between M_p and M_n. A rho of .99 was obtained between M_p for 10 words based on ratings by students at the University of Minnesota and those at Arizona State University (Staats & Staats, 1959).

For 17 words common to Jenkins (1960), Noble and Parker (1960), and Thorndike and Lorge (1944), Koen (1962) reports an r of .76 between M_n and M_p. Administering his own sets of 30 emotional and of 30 neutral words to college students, Koen obtained rs between M_n and four-factor polarization (evaluation, potency, activity, understandability) of, respectively, .02 and .61. Partialling Thorndike-Lorge frequency out of the latter zero-order correlation reduced it to .46, which was still significant.

Wimer's (1963) words were 32 nouns with Thorndike-Lorge ratings of AA. M_p for these words was taken from Jenkins, Russell, and Suci (1958a) and M_n was obtained as well as associative variety, "the total number of *different* associations given for a word" by all subjects. M_n correlated .36 with M_p and .72 with associative variety; the r between the latter two was .42.

RELATIONSHIPS BETWEEN MEANINGFULNESS AND OTHER ATTRIBUTES

In general, relationships between meaningfulness and other attributes of bigrams and trigrams are summarized before relationships for dissyllables and words and for shapes. Other attributes comprise counted frequency; ratings of familiarity; emotionality including "goodness," ease of learning, and pronunciability; RT; recognition thresholds; short-term retention by recognition; social values; sound meaning "fit"; memory span, latency of selection; reading rate; and imagery.

Underwood and Schulz found positive relationships between the M_r of the 100 CVCs scaled by Noble, Stockwell, and Pryer and "summed-letter frequency" (pp. 78-79). Glaze M_a and Witmer M_a are directly related to percentages of occurrence of those CVC and CCC trigrams in word counts. Also, percentages of bigrams in the syllables at each level of Witmer M_a are related directly to percentages of those bigrams which appeared in words (Underwood & Schulz, 1960a, pp. 79-82).

With values for trigrams generated from frequencies of responses to single letters and then to bigrams, Underwood and Schulz (p. 236) found only a slight relationship between these GV and M_a values of Witmer's syllables. Similarly, while there was a slight difference between the GV of syllables with Glaze M_a of 0% and 53%, there was no difference between the GV of syllables with Glaze M_a of 53% and 100% (p. 237). Thus, Underwood and Schulz conclude that "the M value of learning materials cannot be generated 'back' with any degree of precision through the use of letter-association data" (p. 239).

For stimuli more complex than trigrams, Cofer and Shevitz (1952) obtained direct relationships between the Thorndike-Lorge frequency of nouns and adjectives and number of different associations during 10 minutes of continuous association. Sines (1962) obtained a correlation coefficient of .90 between the sums of deviations of ratings on 16 semantic differential scales and counted frequency for four words of high and for four words of low Thorndike-Lorge frequencies.

On assumptions that both meaningfulness and familiarity were increasing functions of frequency of prior experiences with stimuli, Noble concluded that familiarity and meaningfulness were directly related. In a plot of familiarity on M_n of 96 dissyllables, familiarity was a direct, negatively accelerated function of M_n (1953). The fitted curve was exponential in form with a correlation for fit to the reduction line of .92.

Lepley (1950) found a direct relationship between familiarity specified by rank-ordering members of sets of five nouns or of five adjectives and M_n as specified by numbers of different synonyms given as associations to those stimuli.

Underwood and Schulz (1960a, pp. 19-20) had 86 of Noble's (1952) dissyllables rated for ease of learning; M_n and ease of learning correlated .90.

For 96 dissyllables previously rated for M_n, Noble (1958a) obtained ratings for affectivity or emotionality. The r between M_n and emotionality was .57. Strassburger and Wertheimer (1959) also found a direct relationship between M_n and emotionality. However, for 27 of Noble's dissyllables presented along with 34 words of "more obvious affective characteristics," Underwood and Schulz (1960a, pp. 151-152) found no relationship between M_n and emotionality. The lack of relationship is considered partial corroboration of their view that Noble's subjects may have rated for familiarity rather than for emotionality and, therefore, that the relationship he obtained was really between M_n and familiarity of the stimuli. Strassburger and Wertheimer's finding would be explained in the same way, as is the case for the positive relationship between Glaze M_a and emotionality of CVCs obtained by Wilson and Becknell (1961).

R. C. Johnson, Thomson, and Frincke (1960) obtained significant differences in semantic-differential ratings of goodness (good-bad as bipolar adjectives) among CVCs of 0%, 47–54%, and 100% Glaze M_a. Subsequently, for words of essentially equal Thorndike-Lorge frequencies, R. C. Johnson, Frincke, and Martin (1961) found that words rated "good" had higher meaningfulness by the multiple-association technique than words rated "bad." However, Underwood and Schulz's suggestion that the ratings of emotionality may actually be ratings of familiarity is an alternative explanation of these relationships between M_n and emotionality. Supporting this alternative is Johnson, Thomson, and Frincke's finding of higher "goodness" ratings following 2, 5, and 10 exposures to words.

R. C. Johnson, Weiss, and Zelhart (1964) report that, for both normal college students and institutionalized psychotic male veterans, words rated "good" relative to those rated "bad" had higher M_n values, evoked fewer idiosyncratic associations, and were responded to more often with the most common association. Ratings by psychotics were generally closer to the "good" extreme than were those by students.

Keppel's (1963) noncollege students used a good-bad scale to rate the CVCs of each of the two samples of 24 on which R. C. Johnson, Thomson, and Frincke (1960) reported ratings of goodness. For the two samples, the values obtained by Keppel and those obtained earlier correlated .82 and .92. Using Noble a rather than Glaze M_a, the correlations between ratings of goodness (low scores "good," and high "bad") and a were −.67 and −.75. The correlations between goodness and pronunciability (low scores, more pronounceable) were .62 and .73; those between pronunciability and a were −.91 and −.82. When effects of pronunciability were partialled out of the correlations between goodness and a, however, they were reduced to nonsignificant values of −.32 and −.34. In contrast, partialling out effects of goodness reduced the rs for pronunciability and a only to −.85 and −.62. Thus, the relationship between meaningfulness and ratings of goodness of CVCs may reflect uncontrolled variations in pronunciability.

For the 17 words noted above, Koen (1962) also reports rs of .80 between M_n and Thorndike-Lorge frequency and .63 between M_p and frequency. The zero-order correlations for his own sets of words were .62 and .49 between M_n and Thorndike-Lorge frequencies of neutral words and emotional words, respectively. The zero-order correlations between M_p and counted frequency were .51 for neutral words and $-.21$ for emotional words. The correlation between M_p and counted frequency for neutral words was reduced from .51 to a nonsignificant .21 by partialling out M_n. Neutral and emotional words did not differ with respect to M_n but the M_p of the latter was significantly larger.

The 16 stimuli used by Terwilliger (1964) were adjectives selected from among the 1000 most frequent words in the Thorndike-Lorge (1944) count. Single associations were obtained from 100 female undergraduates to these and 54 other adjectives. From these single associations Terwilliger calculated H and N (the number of different associations) for each of the 16 adjectives. Each of the 16 adjectives was then paired with every other adjective and the resultant 120 pairs presented to the same subjects for them to choose first the more familiar and, a week later, the more pleasant member of each pair. These choices were expressed as probabilities of choice of an adjective as the more familiar and as the more pleasant member of a pair. With differences in the H and N of members of a pair as additional measures, simple and partial correlations among the four measures were calculated. The coefficients for the partial correlations in which effects of the other two variables were removed indicated that differences in H and in N were related directly as were choices of adjectives as the more familiar and as the more pleasant. Significant negative and positive relationships, respectively, obtained between H and choice of adjectives as the more familiar and between N and such choices. The positive relationship between H and choice of words as the more pleasant and the negative relationship between N and such choices were just beyond and just short of the .05 level, respectively. The values of about .16 and $-.15$, however, are too small to offer reasonable support for Terwilliger's conclusion that pleasant words are better balanced than unpleasant words.

Underwood and Schulz (1960a, pp. 19-20) obtained ratings of ease of learning of 90 of the CVCs of Noble, Stockwell, and Pryer's (1957) calibration; the r was .86. They also obtained ratings of the pronunciability of 239 different trigrams (pp. 23-25, 152-153, 371-372). Ratings of 178, including Noble, Stockwell, and Pryer's 100 CVCs, were obtained in 1957; 95 were rated in 1959. The distribution of values for pronunciability was bimodal, indicating that subjects felt they either could or could not pronounce a particular stimulus. The r between M_r and pronunciability of the 100 CVCs was .78 (p. 25). For 22 trigrams of several consonant and vowel structures, M_n and pronunciability correlated .92 (p. 268). Wilson and Becknell (1961) also found a positive relationship between M_a and pronunciability of CVCs.

Relationships of meaningfulness to visual recognition thresholds have also been investigated. J. A. Taylor (1958) reports no differences among recognition thresholds for CVCs of 0%, 33%, and 60% Glaze M_a within control lists or within experimental lists involving prior frequency or meaning experiences. Although the results are difficult to interpret, Leytham (1957) too apparently found no difference between recognition thresholds for CVCs of different (100% and 20%) Glaze M_a. For words, however, both Kristofferson (1957) and R. C. Johnson, Frincke, and Martin (1961) obtained significant inverse relationships between M_n and recognition thresholds. With female subjects, R. C. Johnson and Zara (1964) obtained inverse relationships between M_n and recognition thresholds for words representing low, intermediate, and high Thorndike-Lorge frequencies. With male subjects, the relationships were inverse for words representing low and intermediate frequencies and direct for words representing high frequencies.

Gibson, Pick, Osser, and Hammond (1962) constructed a set of 25 pseudowords which were regarded as representing a "high spelling-to-sound correlation." For each there was a corresponding pseudoword representing a "low spelling-to-sound correlation." In ratings of the pronunciability of these pseudowords by a modification of the technique used by Underwood and Schulz (1960a), the mean for the former set was 2.88, that for the latter set was 6.57. Over the five-exposure durations of the first experiment, the more pronounceable pseudowords were recognized more often than the less pronounceable pseudowords.

In the second experiment, all 50 pseudowords were presented at a uniform duration of 30 msec. for subjects to choose the pseudoword presented from among four possibilities. About 28% more pronounceable pseudowords were chosen correctly than less pronounceable pseudowords. Among the incidental findings of the control studies of pronunciability were a markedly smaller number of different forms of pronunciation of the more pronounceable than of the less pronounceable pseudowords. The r between standard scores of ratings of pronunciability and of number of different pronunciations was .85.

Gibson, Pick, Osser, and Hammond suggest that the lower recognition thresholds for the more pronounceable pseudowords than, in general, for the less pronounceable corresponding pseudowords, could not "be caused by a difference in the familiarity of the letters taken alone, or even the vowel- and consonant-clusters taken alone, for the same clusters were used in the two lists" (p. 564). Anisfeld (1964), however, used Underwood and Schulz's (1960a) count to sum frequencies of the successive $n-1$ bigrams of each of the 50 pseudowords. For 22 of the 25 pairs of a more and a less pronounceable pseudoword, summed bigram frequencies of the former were higher. Thus, summed bigram frequencies and pronunciability were related inversely. Also, summed bigram frequencies and recognition thresholds were related directly to suggest that Gibson, Pick, Osser, and Hammond did not entirely eliminate differences in frequency attributes of the more and less pronounceable pseudowords. In a further analysis (Gibson, 1964), a pronounceability proved more potent than frequency. In another experiment, Gibson, Osser, and Pick (1963) seemingly modify their interpretation of the role of frequency when they propose "a frequency count of initial 'G' would be pointless. But a count of initial 'G' before a given vowel or vowel cluster and representing a given sound would be relevant" (p. 143). Bigram frequencies can approximate such counts.

The more immediate concern of the Gibson, Osser, and Pick experiment, however, was recognition thresholds for a set of words of several trigram structures, for a set of nonword CVCs each of which was constituted of the same letters as one of the words (pronounceable), and for a set of nonword CCVs each of which was also constituted of the same letters as the words (unpronounceable). Presented in addition were the 25 complementary pairs of pseudowords of larger numbers of letters used by Gibson, Pick, Osser, and Hammond. The subjects were 12 boys and 12 girls who participated just after completion of first grade and the same numbers of boys and girls who had just completed third grade. All stimuli were exposed at a uniform duration of 40 msec., and spelling the stimulus was the criterion form of response. Except for third-grade girls, percentages of correct recognitions increased in the order unpronounceable CCVs, pronounceable CVCs, and pronounceable words. First-grade subjects recognized fewer stimuli than third-grade subjects.

Recognition thresholds for the pseudowords of larger numbers of letters did not differ between the more and less pronounceable words for first-grade subjects who recognized only about 5% of both sets of words correctly. For third-grade subjects, percentages of correct recognitions increased to 35% for pronounceable and to 19% for unpronounceable pseudowords. The difference by a two-tailed sign test was significant at less than .01.

Both trigram and summed bigram frequencies (Underwood & Schulz, 1960a) were higher for the words than for the CVCs and CCVs. Trigram frequencies of CVCs and CCVs were both low with a slightly greater total for the latter. But summed bigram frequencies for CVCs were considerably higher than those for CCVs. Thus, summed bigram frequencies and pronunciability were again confounded.

The 12 triads of trigrams prepared by Gibson, Bishop, Schiff, and Smith (1964) each contained a trigram of low meaningfulness, low pronunciability (control), one of low meaningfulness and high pronunciability (pronounceable), and a third of high meaningfulness, low pronunciability (meaningful). Mean thresholds of recognition were successively higher for pronounceable, meaningful, and control trigrams. Percentages of correct recognitions of the trigrams, however, were in the order control $<$ pronounceable $<$ meaningful and percentages of the trigrams recalled were in the same order. Equation of bigram and trigram frequencies is again a problem. For example, the means of trigram frequencies for control, meaningful, and pronounceable trigrams were 5.9, 2.8, and 11.9, respectively.

As a subsidiary aspect of an experiment on perception of the 128 patterns produced by a 7-line matrix, Klemmer (1961) had 10 subjects write down as many names as possible for each pattern. Number of responses to each pattern by all subjects correlated .47 with ease of reproduction of the patterns when presented tachistoscopically.

Associative RTs were measured for each of Hull's 320 CVCs (Beck, Phillips, & Bloodsworth, 1962). Median RTs to those stimuli for 18 subjects correlated $-.19$ with Archer M_a of the stimuli and $-.23$ with their Trapp and Kausler M_a. Although low, both rs were significant. Distributions of means and medians for RT of free associations to CVCs of 100% Glaze M_a were, in one case, completely and, in the other case, almost completely below the distributions of RTs for CVCs of 20% Glaze M_a (Leytham, 1957).

Short-term retention by recognition of 20 critical words differing in M_p among 78 test words (Jenkins, 1960) was investigated by Kjeldergaard and Higa (1962). M_p and percentages of subjects recognizing the words correctly correlated .59. Karen (1956) had earlier presented a list of 15 CVCs of 20–30% Hull values and of 15 words with Thorndike-Lorge frequencies of at least 1/1,000,000 to subjects under intentional and incidental instructions. Under both instructions more words than CVCs were picked from among the stimuli seen previously and 30 decoys.

Noble's (1952) technique was used with 125 undergraduates in psychology to obtain M_n values for 10 words representing each of Spranger's aesthetic, economic, political, religious, theoretical, and social values (Bousfield & Samborski, 1955). Resultant M_n values and scores obtained by Allport, Vernon, and Lindzey (1951) for religious and theoretical words correlated .39 and .37, respectively. The rs for words representing each of the other four values were not significant.

In addition to M_n, M_p, and associative variety, Wimer (1963) used values along 10 different semantic differential scales taken from Jenkins, Russell, and Suci (1958b). Of 30 correlations, 11 were significantly positive at .05 and one was significantly negative. The largest absolute value was .76.

J. H. Weiss (1963) obtained judgments of the sound-meaning "fit" of 127 monosyllabic words of high Thorndike-Lorge frequency from one group of subjects and of the emotionality of those words from another group of subjects. On the basis of these judgments he prepared a list of 20 words of which five represented each of the combinations of low and high "fit" and low and high emotionality. Each of these words was then rated along one or more semantic differential scales for evaluation, potency, activity, novelty, and tautness. For means of the sums of absolute deviations, significantly larger deviations were obtained for words of high than of low emotionality on scales for evaluation and potency. Significantly larger deviations were obtained for words of high fit than of low fit on scales for potency and activity and for words of low fit than of high fit on scales for evaluation and novelty.

Words could be scaled in terms of extent of retention in immediate memory. Brener (1940) obtained better retention of presumably more meaningful concrete words than of presumably less meaningful nonsense syllables. In a more elaborate investigation by Bousfield and Cowan (1964), memory span for CVCs which were pronounced in ordered recall was related linearly to Archer M_a values and to Noble a, a', and m' values. Memory span for CVCs which were spelled in ordered recall was related to each of those measures of meaningfulness in positively accelerated fashion. Regardless of measures and values of meaningfulness, longer memory spans were obtained when CVCs were pronounced than when they were spelled. At least for Archer M_a values, essentially the same direct relationships were obtained with free recall as with ordered recall.

Schulz and Lovelace (1964) divided the aperture of a memory drum into a one-inch slot on subjects' left and an eight-inch slot on their right. Each member of sets of CVCs of high and of low Archer M_a was presented alone on the left and simultaneously, along with the nine other members of a set, on the right. The CVC presented alone on the left was to be selected as rapidly as possible from among those on the right by pressing a button under that CVC. Through 10 trials, latencies of selection of the CVC presented on the left were lower for CVCs of high M_a than for those of low M_a. Moreover, no convergence of the curves was evident. Thus, CVCs of high M_a were consistently and persistently selected faster than those of low M_a. Among the suggested explanations was longer reading time for CVCs of low than of high M_a and consequently longer latencies of selection. Cited in partial support of this explanation was Conrad's (1962) findings of a direct relationship between meaningfulness and rate of reading CVCs.

Sixteen "concrete" nouns and 16 "abstract" nouns, all with Thorndike-Lorge frequencies of 50 or more per 1,000,000, were Paivio's (1964) stimuli. M_n values were obtained for these words as were "ratings of the capacity of the words to arouse sensory 'images'" and of auditory familiarity. The rs among these measures were .90 for M_n and imagery, .75 for M_n and auditory familiarity, and .76 for imagery and auditory familiarity.

Vanderplas and Garvin (1959a) report correlations between M_a for nonsense shapes and their H and their content of .48 and .35, respectively. The M_a values for Battig's (1962) nonsense shapes correlated $-.50$ with H,

$-.76$ with relative entropy, and .76 with rated strength of associations. Battig was unable to entirely reconcile his negative correlation between M_a and H with the positive correlation reported by Vanderplas and Garvin. The results of both scalings suggested that M_a was not related strongly to various physical characteristics of the shapes. Arnoult (1960) obtained generally stronger relationships between M_a and physical characteristics of shapes and between familiarity and physical characteristics. Goldstein (1961) also found a significant inverse relationship between M_a and complexity.

For dot patterns, Clement (1964) obtained rs of .71, .87, and .84 for ratings of goodness and H, for ratings and latency of naming responses, and for H and latency, respectively. The corresponding rs for square patterns were .66, .77, and .78.

RELATIONSHIPS BETWEEN OTHER ATTRIBUTES

The other attributes of stimuli considered here are those for which strong relationships to meaningfulness have been demonstrated and for which values of the attributes have been obtained under conditions which resemble those for the scalings of meaningfulness, particularly with experimenter-supplied continuous stimuli or scales. Specifically, the attributes are frequency, familiarity, ease of learning, pronunciability, and GV. Subsumed under GV is probability of single-letter responses to single letters and to bigrams which are part of or complete words. Excluded from detailed summary, because so treated elsewhere (W. P. Brown, 1961, pp. 12-15), are investigations involving relationships of various attributes of words to their recognition thresholds. In general, such thresholds are related inversely to experienced frequency in an experimental context, to Thorndike-Lorge frequency, to ratings of familiarity and, perhaps, to ratings along a good-bad scale (W. P. Brown, 1961; Doehring, 1962; Newbigging, 1961a, 1961b; Newbigging & Hay, 1962; Riegel & Riegel, 1961; J. T. Spence, 1963a).

Under some conditions, however, such as subjects' knowledge of members of a set of words (Pierce, 1963) and experimental isolation of the variable of strength of competing responses (Havens & Foote, 1963), the relationship between word frequency and recognition thresholds of words may be attenuated or disappear. Whether frequency of nonword trigrams is (Anisfeld, 1964) or is not (Postman & Conger, 1954) related to recognition thresholds is conjectural.

Attneave (1953) reports corrected correlations between counted frequency of occurrence of letters and judged or guessed frequencies under different instructions of, respectively, .81 and from .45 to .86.

In Mayzner and Tresselt's (1962) experimental condition, the stimuli were 100 "skeleton" words; each consisted of a single letter in one position, dashes for from two to six additional letters, and a double dash for three accompanying letters. Subjects ranked the letters with respect to frequency with which those letters would follow the letter of the stimulus. Resultant bigrams were then ranked for frequency. In one control condition, the letter of each stimulus was blacked out; in the other, the letter was absent. More of the entire 100 stimuli and, eventually, of 19 "critical" stimuli were ranked correctly for single-letter and bigram frequencies by subjects of the experimental than of the control conditions with the latter conditions essentially equal. On the basis of these findings, ratings of frequencies of single letters and bigrams are regarded not only as related directly to differences in counted frequencies but also as reflecting effects of word length and letter position.

With 100 pairs of bigrams or 150 pairs of trigrams as stimuli, Underwood and Schulz (1960a, pp. 52-55) had subjects designate the more frequent member of each pair. Percentage of correct choices of both bigrams and trigrams increased in approximately linear fashion for successively greater differences in counted frequencies of members of the pairs. Correct choices of the more frequent member of each of 44 pairs with one member with a frequency of less than 25 and the other member with a frequency of more than 25 correlated .76 with differences in frequencies.

Underwood and Schulz (1960a, pp. 184-187) also had both University of California (Berkeley) and Northwestern students rate trigrams of several vowel-consonant structures for relative frequency of contact. For one subset of 36 trigrams, familiarity and frequency correlated .46; for another subset of 36, the correlation was .51. These correlations indicate a direct relationship between familiarity and frequency. That familiarity of dissyllables reflects amount of prior experience with those stimuli is indicated by Noble's (1954) report of a negatively accelerated increase in familiarity as a function of number of experimentally controlled exposures to dissyllables of low M_n. Arnoult (1956) reports a similar relationship between familiarity and frequency of prior exposure to nonsense forms.

For one sample of 36 trigrams, Underwood and Schulz found no relationship between pronunciability and counted frequency (p. 171). For another sample of 36 trigrams, the rho was .30 (p. 187). For these same trigrams and for another sample of trigrams, the rs for pronunciability and rated familiarity were .73 and .79 (p. 186), respectively. For six different lists of eight stimuli each, rs for pronunciability and GV ranged from .52 to .84 with an over-all r of .72 (p. 247). For still another set of 86 trigrams, pronunciability and ease of learning correlated .92 (p. 25).

All three-letter words of CVC structure in the Thorndike-Lorge list were classified in terms of Lorge magazine count frequencies of 0–50, 51–100, 100–200, 201–600, and more than 600 (Underwood & Schulz, 1960a, pp. 238-239). For larger counted frequencies, increasing numbers of subjects responded with second letters which were part of and third letters which completed words. They conclude that vowels produced by subjects in response to single-letter stimuli are more likely to be the middle letter of words of high than of low counted frequency.

Counted frequency of words and judgments of their frequency are also related directly. In rank orderings of frequencies of words, Howes (1954) obtained corrected correlations between counted frequencies (Thorndike-Lorge magazine count) and ranks assigned by college students of .78 in Experiment I, of .88 in Experiment II, and of .85, .84, and .60 for the three samples of words of Experiment III. Reliabilities of student rankings were .94 or higher.

For subjects in each of three different age groups, Riegel and Riegel (1964) found significant negative values for the relationships between counted frequencies of words and both relative entropy of associations to the words and the proportions of associations which were single responses. Significant positive correlations were found between readability scores and both relative entropy and proportions of single responses.

As noted previously, Wimer (1963) also used ratings along 10 semantic differential scales including *usual-unusual* which was considered to define familiarity. Fifteen of 33 positive coefficients were significant at .05; two of 12 negative coefficients were significant. The values ranged from $-.51$ to .87.

Summary

For CVCs particularly, the same and different measures of meaningfulness obtained under different conditions of presentation and instructions and with subjects ranging from grade-school-aged children to college students have intercorrelated positively. For the entire range, or a substantial part of the range, of values of M_a, M_n, and M_r, coefficients have ranged from .52 upward to values as high as .99. In addition, one or more of the several measures of meaningfulness have proved consistently related to "summed letter frequency," probability of occurrence of CVCs and CCCs in words, and associative RT. Significant relationships have also been obtained with ratings of familiarity, emotionality, ease of learning, and pronunciability. However, meaningfulness of trigrams is only slightly and not usefully related to GV and, perhaps, to recognition thresholds.

Ratings of familiarity correlate with counted frequency which constitutes validation of ratings of familiarity and of frequency. Pronunciability is only weakly related to counted frequency but is related to GV and to ratings of familiarity and ease of learning.

Meaningfulness values of dissyllables and words expressed as M_a, M_n, M_r, or M_p have correlated with each other from .71 to .99. Demonstrations of relationships have been obtained between one or more of these measures of meaningfulness and a number of attributes: counted frequency; ratings of familiarity, ease of learning, emotionality including "goodness"; recognition thresholds; short-term retention by recognition; social values; sound meaning "fit"; memory span, latency of selection; reading rate; and imagery.

Whether emotionality including goodness of CVCs and of dissyllables and words constitutes an independent attribute or attributes is questionable. Ratings on which these values are based may have actually been with respect to other attributes such as familiarity, pronunciability, or both.

Substantial reliability of measures of meaningfulness and of other attributes is indicated by the generally high intercorrelations. Also, Noble and Parker (1960) and Archer (1960) report high conventional measures of reliability.

Pairs of Stimuli

Haagen's (1949) 400 word pairs were rated along 7-point scales for strength of associations, what he termed closeness of associative connection, for similarity of meaning, and for vividness. The reliability of ratings of all three attributes was high. The correlation between strength of association and similarity of meaning was .90, but because the full range of strength was not sampled, Haagen rejected the conclusion that strength of association and similarity of meaning are identical. The rs of .17 for strength of association and vividness and of .09 for similarity of meaning and vividness indicate that vividness is an essentially independent attribute. Cofer (1957) has shown that Haagen's similarity of meaning values are directly related to an index of the overlap of responses elicited by members of the pairs presented separately.

Twenty of Haagen's pairs of adjectives were scaled for synonymity by adults from 30 to 70 years of age (Rocklyn, Hessert, & Braun, 1957). For subjects at high and low educational levels separately, the rs between values of synonymity and Haagen's values were .79 and .77, respectively. The r between values for subjects at the two levels was .79.

Haagen's procedure was the basis of a more extensive study by Umemoto, Morikawa, and Ibuki (1955b). The stimuli of the pairs were 120 adjectives for each of which from 15 to 20 other adjectives were responses. Meaningfulness, similarity of meaning, and familiarity of responses are reported.

Richardson and Erlebacher (1958) found high correlations between ratings of ease of learning and similarity of meaning of lists of pairs of adjectives, pairs of CVCs, and pairs of CCCs. The adjective pairs represented the four combinations of stimuli and responses of high or low Thorndike-Lorge frequencies; the CVC-CCC pairs represented the four combinations of stimuli and responses of high or low values of Glaze M_a or of Witmer M_a.

Examination of Richardson and Erlebacher's Table 2 suggests that the highest values of ease of learning and similarity of meaning were for pairs whose members both had high Thorndike-Lorge frequencies or high M_a, and that the lowest values of ease of learning and similarity of meaning were for pairs whose members both had low Thorndike-Lorge frequencies or low M_a. Intermediate values of ease of learning and similarity of meaning were obtained with pairs with one member of high Thorndike-Lorge frequency or high M_a and the other member of low Thorndike-Lorge frequency or low M_a. Thus, these results suggest at least slight direct relationships between ease of learning and similarity of meaning of pairs on the one hand, and, on the other hand, Thorndike-Lorge frequency or M_a of their members.

The CVCs of Battig's pairs were all of 47% or 53% Glaze M_a. Despite this homogeneity of M_a, ratings of ease of learning along a 9-point ordinal scale ranged from 2.99 to 7.40 (Battig, 1959), and ratings with respect to nine categories at equal-appearing intervals ranged from 1.9 to 7.2 (Battig, 1960). The r for values of pairs by the two techniques was .85; for individual subjects the rs ranged from .02 to .60 about a median of .37. The ranges of values obtained by Battig were considerably greater than those obtained along a 15-point scale by Richardson and Erlebacher for any one of the four combinations of high or low Glaze M_a of the stimuli and responses of their pairs of CVCs. Thus, Battig's data suggest that the ease of learning of pairs of CVCs and perhaps their similarity of meaning may not be at all related or only weakly related to M_a of their members. However, using values of M_a from Archer's recalibration of Glaze's CVCs, Battig obtained an r of .69 between ratings of ease of learning of pairs of stimuli and averages of the M_a of members of each pair.

Flavell (1961b) reports scale values for similarity of meaning and co-occurrence for each of three sets of 30 pairs of stimuli. The members of the pairs of these sets were both concrete nouns, both adjectives, or a concrete noun and an adjective. Co-occurrence, along with the distance between the semantic differential ratings of members of these pairs (D) obtained by Jenkins, Russell, and Suci (1958a, 1959), were used as separate and joint predictors of similarity of meaning. For concrete noun-concrete noun, adjective-adjective, and adjective-concrete noun pairs, the zero-order correlations of similarity of meaning and co-occurrence were .84, .95, and .94, respectively, and those of similarity of meaning and D were .79, .86, and .40. Contrary to Flavell's expectations, combining co-occurrence and D produced essentially no better predictions of similarity of meaning than were obtained with co-occurrence alone. For another set of 30 pairs whose members were two abstract nouns, the r for similarity of meaning and D was .76, which is consistent with Rowan's (Osgood, Suci, & Tannenbaum,

1957, pp. 143-146) earlier finding for pairs of somewhat similar types of nouns of high correlations between factors derived from judgments of similarity and factors derived from semantic differential ratings.

Subsequently, Flavell and Johnson (1961) had different groups of subjects respond to each of 30 concrete noun-concrete noun pairs by the single-association and multiple-association techniques described earlier. L-Latency, L-Different Total, and L-Entropy were determined from responses obtained by the single-association technique; and the N-Total, N-Different Total, N-Attributes, N-Different Attributes, N-Contiguity, and N-Different Contiguities were determined from responses obtained by the multiple-association technique. Values for these nine measures for the 30 concrete noun-concrete noun pairs and the values of similarity of meaning, co-occurrence, and D measures for these same pairs obtained by Flavell (1961b) were then intercorrelated. Of Flavell and Johnson's nine measures, similarity of meaning correlated significantly with but three, L-Entropy, N-Total, and N-Attributes for which the rs were .70, .57, and .40, respectively. The correlation between similarity of meaning and N-Total was less than the correlation of .91 for somewhat different words reported by Attneave (1951); Flavell and Johnson offer reasons for the disagreement. Combining co-occurrence, D, L-Entropy, and N-Total as predictors of similarity of meaning produced a multiple correlation of .92.

Various of the zero-order correlations among Flavell and Johnson's nine measures were also significant. For example, L-Different Total and L-Entropy correlated .93, which is the value of r (.925) obtained by Laffal (1955) for the same two measures of responses to a set of 100 single words which were nouns, verbs, adjectives, or of mixed grammatical function.

For pairs of black-on-white geometrical forms, values of similarity obtained by the method of graded dichotomies (Attneave, 1949) correlated .85 with numbers of verbalized similarities (Attneave, 1951).

In an experiment growing out of previous studies by Flavell (1956) and Benedetti (1958), Flavell and Flavell (1959) investigated judged strengths of relationships between members of pairs as functions of the "logico-grammatical" categories of members and of instructions. The instructions to college students were to select the pair of each of 275 pairs of pairs whose members were "closer in meaning," "more closely related in meaning," or more closely associated. Under all three instructions, there were differences among categories with respect to judged strengths of relationships. The rho between the rank orders of the categories under the first two, very similar instructions was .99; these rank orders of categories correlated .49 and .57 with the rank order of the categories under association instructions. Thus, judged strengths of relationships is seemingly influenced by logico-grammatical category of members of pairs and by instructions.

In a later developmental study, Flavell and Stedman (1961) obtained judgments of strengths of relationships between members of pairs in the same 11 categories under "closer in meaning" instructions. Rank orders of scores for the categories for subjects in each of Grades 2 through 9 were each correlated with the rank order for college students obtained by Flavell and Flavell. The correlations increased from about .30 for second-grade children to about .90 for fifth-grade and older children. For second-grade children administered the test in groups of two rather than in their regular classroom, the rank order of scores for the categories correlated about .85 with the rank order for college students. Logico-grammatical category of members of pairs influenced judgments of strengths of associations in children as young as second graders, and the rank orders of scores for the categories were reasonably stable across a wide range of ages.

Pairs of stimuli can be formed on the basis of a stimulus and its associative primary. For 52 of such pairs obtained from Russell and Jenkins' (1954) norms, Pollio (1964a) found correlations of .52, .25, and .36 for ratings on evaluative, potency, and activity dimensions obtained by Jenkins, Russell, and Suci (1958a). For 38 of such pairs obtained from Woodrow and Lowell's (1916) norms for children, the corresponding correlations were .64, .69, and .44. In a further analysis, Pollio found the correlations to hold for the stimulus word and low-probability primaries but not for the stimulus word and high-probability primaries. Thus, similar semantic differential profiles can be expected only for stimulus words for which the primaries are relatively weak.

Pollio also computed the mean semantic distance between the 68 Kent-Rosanoff words of Jenkins, Russell, and Suci's atlas and the available associations to those words. As ratings along the evaluative dimension became less positive and more negative, mean semantic distances increased. This relationship did not obtain for ratings along activity and potency dimensions. Only for the evaluative dimension, therefore, were the ratings for a discrete stimulus predictive of the semantic distance between that stimulus and other stimuli.

Visual recognition of members of pairs of CVCs has been investigated (L'Abate, 1960). For pairs representing combinations of Glaze M_a of 100–100%, 0–100%, 47–47%, 100–0%, and 0–0%, the respective mean numbers of correct recognitions of left members and of right members combined were 4.01, 3.50, 3.34, 3.53, and 3.17. Left members were recognized more often than right members. Also reported were significant positive correlations between learning scores for pairs and number of recognitions of their members.

FURTHER AREAS FOR RESEARCH

Preliminary to almost all further normative studies are extensive estimates of contemporary actual frequencies of occurrence of words and derivative data regarding frequencies of letters and of phonemes singly and in sequences of two (bigrams) and three (trigrams). The most recent of the Thorndike counts (Thorndike & Lorge, 1944), useful as it has been, is obsolete for several reasons. The first is its limitation to printed text. Required are samples not only of printed materials from newspapers, magazines, books, and letters, but also of aurally presented materials such as radio and TV scripts and commentary, conversations, songs, and sermons. Furthermore, these samples should be selected to reflect any differences in the printed and spoken words to which individuals differing in sex, age, social and economic status, education, and other characteristics are exposed.

Letter counts have been of some value. Of greater value, however, would be updated and more extensive counts of phonemes within both printed and spoken material. Frequencies of occurrence of single letters or phonemes should be in terms of position in words of different length. Sequences of two and three letters or phonemes within and between words should be distinguished. These, too, might be in terms of position of the first letter or phoneme of the bigram or trigram and of word length. Carroll's (1952) counts are of value here. However, they were for a sample of phonemes in the words of plays for "young people" which is too limited in scope.

Of related concern is semantic counts (Lorge, 1949; Lorge & Thorndike, 1938; West, 1953) within the samples for frequency counts. Information about frequencies of occurrence of different meanings of words might clarify experiential bases of differences in the meaningfulness of words and decreasingly similar nonwords as well as indicate likely associations to particular words (Rosenzweig & McNeill, 1962). The derivative significance of semantic counts for lexicographers is obvious.

Already noted are needs for information about frequency and time measures like those developed in investigations of word associations and about relationships between these attributes and meaningfulness. Some of the problems and techniques of word-association studies are also germane to several of the other areas in which further research on meaningfulness of discrete stimuli and of pairs of stimuli is desirable.

One area is, interestingly, further scaling of all bigrams, all CVCs, and possibly an extensive sample of trigrams of other consonant-vowel structures by multiple associations. Checking "Yes" or "No" and ratings are no substitutes for specification of the actual associations necessary, as noted below, for specifying common meaning or response-mediated similarity between members of pairs or among members of larger sets of stimuli. Despite the apparent congruence between single and multiple associations (Cofer, 1958; Laffal & Feldman, 1962, 1963), multiple associations are preferred as likely to provide more precise information about the nature and extent of hierarchies of individual subjects. Accompanying multiple associations should be ratings of pronunciability by the same subjects so that intra-subject correlations between meaningfulness and pronunciability can be determined.

A second area is an even more extensive scaling of words than J. D. Taylor's (1959). In this connection, sizable samples of frequent, important words of French, German, Spanish, and one or two other widely studied languages and of the most common English meanings of those words might be scaled by multiple associations and for pronunciability. These words, particularly those of the second languages, should be presented visually and aurally. Not only would the pool of stimuli available for experimentation be extended but also such scalings are preliminary to much experimentation on second-language learning. Indeed, the lack of values for the meaningfulness and pronunciability of words in second languages precludes satisfactory analytical experimentation on a variety of problems involving characteristics of the materials.

A third area is scalings of at least CVCs for meaningfulness by multiple associations, for pronunciability, and perhaps for familiarity by groups of children representing the range from 3 or 4 through 16 or 17. At present, except for the 52 CVCs of Shapiro's (1963a, 1964) study, it must be assumed that values of meaningfulness and other attributes of stimuli as scaled primarily by college students correlate positively with potential values of scalings by younger subjects. Extensions to noncollege subjects of the same age (Keppel, 1963) and to older groups (Rocklyn, Hessert, & Braun, 1957) might also prove useful. A related consideration is scalings, particularly by children, of meaningfulness of nonverbal stimuli such as pictures and models of objects, colors, and nonsense forms.

A fourth area is the same scalings carried out with aural presentation of the stimuli. Carroll, Horowitz, and Burke (personal communication, 1964) have obtained ratings of the meaningfulness of 320 phonemic syllables of CVC structure presented aurally. These syllables had been part of a list of approximately 800 previously scaled for meaningfulness by a response latency technique by Horowitz in connection with his Ph.D. dissertation (Horowitz, 1955). The rating procedure used by these investigators was Cieutat's (1963).

Pertinent to the planning of scalings of sequences of phonemes presented aurally are considerations with respect to the correspondence between the phonemes of English and their graphic representation. Because of the larger number of phonemes than of letters, more different sequences of two, three or more phonemes of particular consonant and vowel structure can be constructed than are possible for sequences of letters. Were the limitation of the same number of letters as phonemes removed, the correspondence between phonemes and graphemes could be increased and many more grapheme sequences would be possible. Illustrative of such grapheme sequences are those constructed and presented by Gibson, Pick, Osser, and Hammond (1962, p. 561).

Another area is obtaining more extensive information about the adequacy of assumptions that norms based on groups are reasonably congruent with the manner in which individual subjects react to stimuli. In the case of word-association data, for example, a common assumption is that individual subjects respond to a particular stimulus with responses that are essentially the same as those which occur in the group and that the relative strengths of responses by individual subjects parallel frequencies of those responses in the group data. Rosen and Russell (1957) found the relative frequency and nature of the second of two successive associations to be consistent with the "assumption that the cultural frequency of an association may be taken as an index of the strength of the response" (p. 122).

In the case of four of five single-letter stimuli, Duncan (1960) obtained significant agreement between rankings of letter responses and frequency of occurrence of those letters as free associations to the single-letter stimuli. However, both of these studies provide only indirect evidence of the existence of response hierarchies for individual subjects. Also, Rosen and Russell's instructions and Duncan's instructions and procedures may be special conditions highly favorable to obtaining apparent hierarchic responses by individual subjects. Therefore, the bounds within which the assumption of congruence between group and individual hierarchies is justified should be determined more directly.

Brody (1964) has provided such more direct evidence of a correspondence between hierarchies for groups of subjects and for individual subjects. His words were 15 of low H and 15 of high H from Laffal's (1955) list. Each subject made 15 responses to each of these words. Values of H based on the first association to each word were determined for the 30 subjects as a group. Also, values of H based on all 15 associations to each word were determined for each subject. The Kendall tau for the relationship between values of H for the subjects as a group and means of values of H for subjects individually was .68. A tau of .65 was obtained for the relationship between number of different associations for the group and for individual subjects. Both taus were significant at $<.01$.

A value of .82 was obtained for the correlation between initial frequency of associations for the group and the mean number of subsequent repetitions of those associations. Finally, a value of .72 was obtained for the correlation between initial frequency of associations for the group and the probability of the occurrence of those associations for subjects who did not make them as the first response. Although only for three associations, Shapiro (1963a) also reports evidence of the latter relationship.

Estes (1960) has even questioned the existence of hierarchies of responses, except under the special case of compound stimuli to each of whose elements different responses had been conditioned previously. Whatever the requisite conditions, further development of procedures for establishing hierarchies experimentally is desirable so that the meaningfulness of stimuli can be varied by training rather than by selection (Goss & Cobb, in press).

A further area is determining the extent to which meaningfulness, familiarity, pronunciability, and ease of learning of trigrams, particularly CVCs, can be used to generate the meaningfulness, familiarity, pronunciability and ease of learning of dissyllables constructed of two trigrams.

Meaningfulness measures disregard the particular responses to each stimulus. Knowledge of particular responses, however, is important for specifying possible response-mediated similarity between or among stimuli (Bousfield, 1961; Bousfield, Whitmarsh, & Danick, 1958; Cofer, 1957; Deese, 1962; Marshall & Cofer, 1963; Umemoto, 1963) and also for predicting possible stimulus-response pairs whose association might be facilitated or retarded by mediating responses. At present, the only source of much information is word-association norms with hierarchies based on frequencies of responses in a group rather than by individuals, and the most extensive lists of words are only 444 with frequencies based on responses of but 50 subjects (Deese, 1959) and 400 with frequencies based on responses by 150 subjects (Bousfield, Cohen, Whitmarsh, & Kincaid, 1961). The norms for semantic distances provided by Jenkins, Russell, and Suci (1958a, 1959) provide some basis for inferring response-mediated similarity. But the meaning of stimuli in the ordinary sense of the particular responses evoked in one or several contexts and the relative strengths of those responses is, at best, only approximated by ratings along a common set of dimensions specified by bipolar adjectives. Interpretation of these ratings may be complicated by use of some pairs of bipolar adjectives whose profiles or meanings are similar or the same rather than, as is assumed, different or opposed (Mordkoff, 1963). Finally, very little is known of the comparability of responses to stimuli in the scaling situations and of responses to those same stimuli in various actual learning and performance situations. For example, meaningfulness conceived as the number of responses to a stimulus may be merely a correlate of response integration, the factor of apparent actual importance at least with respect to effects on PA learning of variations in response members. And Reed (1918a, p. 154) reports that the types and relative frequencies of associations obtained in a PA situation did not parallel those obtained by free association (Woodrow & Lowell, 1916).

With respect to pairs of stimuli, Cofer's (1957) results as well as the relationships suggested by Richardson and Erlebacher's table and Battig's r for ease of learning of pairs of stimuli and average Archer M_a of members of each pair indicate that values of attributes of pairs of stimuli can be generated from knowledge of values of attributes of discrete stimuli. The modification of values of attributes of discrete stimuli by pairing them with quantifying adverbs (Cliff, 1959; Howe, 1963) is an interesting, special problem. However, refinement and extension of these and other procedures (e.g., Bousfield, Whitmarsh, & Danick, 1958; Marshall & Cofer, 1963) entails further scalings of attributes of pairs of stimuli. Also desirable for pairs of stimuli are scalings of their meaningfulness, association norms, developmental norms for their various attributes, information about the soundness of inferences to individual reactions from group norms, more adequate specification of particular responses to each pair, and observations of responses to pairs in actual learning and performance situations.

CHAPTER 3

Meaningfulness in Paired-Associates Learning

Meaningfulness and other attributes of stimulus members and response members of PA units and also attributes of pairs of stimuli can vary independently. Experiments concerned with effects on PA learning of variations in attributes of stimulus members and response members have differed markedly with respect to particular combinations of variations employed and in manner of assignment of such combinations to lists and to subjects. In order to classify, compare, and interpret actual designs and resultant findings, therefore, more general aspects of construction and use of lists in which attributes of stimulus members and response members and of pairs of stimuli are varied must be considered. Experimental findings are then summarized and evaluated. With occasional exceptions, suggestions for further research based on these findings are deferred until the final chapter as are suggestions for new experiments arising from findings on effects of similarity, familiarization, and other variables.

CONSTRUCTION AND USE OF LISTS

The design of experiments concerned with effects on PA learning of meaningfulness and other attributes of stimulus members and response members and of attributes of pairs of stimuli involves five interrelated problems of construction and use of lists. The first is the particular combinations of values of meaningfulness or of other attributes of stimulus members and of response members which are used. The second and third are assignment of these combinations to lists and of subjects to lists or combinations. Further, these problems must be generalized to designs involving an attribute of pairs of stimuli, and to designs involving combinations of values of each of two or more different attributes of stimulus members and response members. The fifth problem is the manner of allowance for generalization to other lists whose pairs exemplify the same combinations of values of attributes.

Combinations of Values of Attributes

The center square of Fig. 1 is an over-all scheme of possible combinations

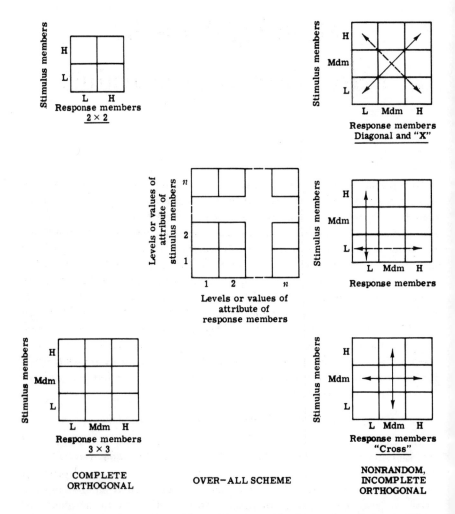

FIG. 1. Over-all scheme of possible combinations of levels or values of meaningfulness or any other attribute of stimulus members and response members along with illustrative complete orthogonal and nonrandom, incomplete orthogonal variants usually involving high (H) and low (L) or high, intermediate (Mdm) and low relative levels or values of the variables.

of values of meaningfulness or of any other attribute of stimulus members and response members. In practice, these possible combinations have been realized either in complete orthogonal designs, two variants of which are shown to the left of the center square, or in nonrandom, incomplete orthogonal designs, three variants of which are shown to the right of the center square. The simplest orthogonal design is one in which two different values of meaningfulness or some attribute of stimulus members are combined with the same values of that attribute of response members. Permitted are conclusions regarding effects of comparable variations in the particular attribute of stimulus members and response members. A 3×3 design is the minimum necessary to determine linearity or nonlinearity of curves relating learning measures to an attribute of stimulus members and response members, and, if the curves are nonlinear, to determine comparability of form and other characteristics.

Complete orthogonal designs may not always be necessary or practical. For example, it may be known or seem likely that learning is influenced by meaningfulness of stimulus members but not by the meaningfulness of response members, or the converse. Or, within the number of subjects available or amount of time per subject possible or practical, complete orthogonality of order 3×3 or higher may entail too many groups of subjects, lists which are too long for acquisition in an hour or less, or both. For these and other reasons, many experimenters have selected one of the nonrandom, incomplete orthogonal designs shown to the right of the center square. In the square at the upper right, the solid two-tipped arrow from bottom left to upper right shows combinations of values of meaningfulness of stimulus members and response members of a number of experiments. In this design, both stimulus members and response members of a pair have the same value of meaningfulness or of any other attributes; thus values of the attribute of stimulus members are completely confounded with values of that attribute of response members. The broken two-tipped arrow from bottom right to top left shows combinations in which meaningfulness or any other attribute of stimulus members and response members are also completely confounded. In the former set of combinations, values of meaningfulness or other attributes of stimulus members and response members are positively "correlated"; in the latter set of combinations, they are negatively "correlated." Neither permits assessment of relative effects of an attribute of stimulus members and response members.

When three or more positively correlated and negatively correlated values are combined to form an "X," however, the combination at the center can be removed to yield one or more 2×2 complete orthogonal designs. For example, with low, medium, and high values along both diagonals, elimination of the center combination collapses the design to a 2×2 combination of low or high values of the attribute of stimulus members with low or high values of the attribute of response members. For "X" designs in $n \times n$ matrices, removal of the center combination results in $n - 2$ of the 2×2 complete orthogonal designs.

The square at the center right shows two other related designs. The double-tipped solid arrow represents variations in just the meaningfulness or some other attribute of stimulus members, each with the same value of that attribute of response members. The specific design involves low, medium, and high values of an attribute of stimulus members with the attribute of response members at low. But the attribute of response members might have been at medium or high. The double-tipped broken arrow represents variations in an attribute of response members each with the same value of that attribute of stimulus members. The value of that attribute of stimulus members might be low as shown, or medium or high. Neither design provides information about relative effects of an attribute of stimulus members and response members.

Shown in the square at bottom right is a "cross" design in which two or more values of an attribute of stimulus members are each combined with an intermediate value of that attribute of response members, and in which the pairings are reversed so that the same two or more values of the attribute characterize response members, and stimulus members have the intermediate value. Relative effects of stimulus members and response members can be assessed with respect to intermediate values of response members and of stimulus members, respectively, but effects of variations in stimulus members at two or more levels of response members, and the converse, cannot be determined directly.

Other nonrandom, incomplete orthogonal designs are possible. For example, with five values of stimulus members and of response members only for extremes of values for response member and stimulus member, the design might be a "hollow square" involving only the 16 combinations of conditions around the sides, rather than the 25 combinations of a 5×5 complete orthogonal design. Relative effects of stimulus members and response members could be determined for the two extreme levels but not for the three intermediate levels of response members and stimulus members, respectively.

Assignment of Combinations to Lists

Combinations of values of meaningfulness and other attributes of stimulus members and response members of a design can be realized in lists in three different ways. The most common way is a separate list of n PA units for each different combination. The units of such lists are unmixed or homogeneous with respect to the particular combinations of values of an attribute of stimulus members, of response members, or both which they represent.

Lists may also be constructed so that there is at least one unit representing each of the combinations of values. Such lists are mixed or heterogeneous. Finally, some but not all combinations of values can be represented in one list, with the remaining combinations represented in one or more additional lists. Such lists are partly mixed or heterogeneous. Examples of all three manners of assignment are: (a) four lists each representing one of the four combinations of low or high values of meaningfulness of stimulus members and of response members (unmixed); (b) a single list of four units, each of which represents one of those combinations (mixed); and (c) two lists, one representing the combination of low meaningfulness of stimulus members with low and high values of response members, and another representing the combination of high meaningfulness of stimulus members with low and high values of response members.

Assignment of Subjects to Combinations

With mixed lists, all subjects learn the one or more pairs representing all combinations of meaningfulness or some other attribute of stimulus members and of response members. With unmixed lists, each list or each combination may be learned by a different group of subjects. A different group may learn some but not all of the lists, or the same group may learn all lists of combinations. Similarly, with partly mixed lists, each list or set of some but not all combinations might be learned by a different group of subjects. Each different group might learn two or more lists which represent two sets of different combinations, but not all combinations, or the same group might learn the two or more lists representing all combinations. Lindquist (1953), Federer (1955), Winer (1962), and other texts on experimental design provide a wide range of models which can be adapted to represent assignment of subjects to combinations of conditions.

Combinations Involving an Attribute of Pairs of Stimuli, and Involving Two or More Attributes of Stimulus Members and of Response Members

Thus far, only attributes of discrete stimulus members and response members have been considered. Should an attribute of pairs of stimuli be added, possible designs can be represented within cubes. The minimum complete orthogonal design is $2 \times 2 \times 2$; a $3 \times 3 \times 3$ design is the minimum necessary to determine linearity or nonlinearity and, if nonlinear, comparability of the form and other characteristics of curves relating learning measures to attributes of stimulus members and of response members and to attributes of pairs of stimuli.

Various nonrandom, incomplete orthogonal designs are possible. For example, pairs of stimuli might be selected, each unit of which has stimulus members and response members of the same value of an attribute, and which, as a pair, represent some additional attribute which is positively or negatively correlated with the positively correlated attribute of stimulus members and of response members. Illustratively, each member of one pair of stimuli might be of low meaningfulness and the pair might be of low similarity of meaning, and each member of another pair of stimuli might be of high meaningfulness and the pair might be of high similarity of meaning.

Should two or more attributes of stimulus members and response members be varied simultaneously, the squares in Fig. 1 used to depict possible combinations of values of those attributes of stimulus members and of response members must be extended into four dimensions. One consequence is greater difficulty in representing designs. More importantly, choices of combinations of values of the attributes of stimulus members and of response members and of mode of assignment of combinations to lists and subjects become more difficult. The greater difficulty is in terms both of complexity and of relative lack of knowledge of direction and extent of possible differential consequences of assignment of combinations to unmixed, partly mixed, and mixed lists. Fortunately, present evidence suggests that differences between mixed and unmixed lists in rank orders of effects of particular combinations of conditions may be negligible (Battig, Brown, & Nelson, 1962; Experiments 9 & 10 in the Appendix). They may sometimes consist only of uniform over-all elevations of acquisition measures (Underwood & Schulz, 1960a, p. 181). But a difference between mixed and unmixed lists in backward recall of stimulus members has been observed (E. Weiss, 1963) to suggest that parallel outcomes may not always occur.

The simplest complete orthogonal design involving values of two attributes of stimulus members and of response members is of order $2 \times 2 \times 2 \times 2$. A mixed list with at least 16 units is required (Cooper, 1964; Nodine, 1963), one for each combination of conditions or, at the other extreme, there must be 16 unmixed lists of n units each. Therefore, nonrandom, incomplete orthogonal designs, partly mixed or mixed lists, or both devices for reducing number of combinations and of lists are more likely to be used. Such solutions become almost unavoidable when two attributes of stimulus members and response members have three or more values, when more than two attributes of stimulus members and response members are varied, and when two attributes of stimulus members and response members are combined with additional variables such as distribution of trials. The possible outcomes under such circumstances are too numerous and complex for development here, as is the case when an attribute of pairs of stimuli is added to increase the number of variables to five.

Generalization to Other Lists

The one or more pairs of stimuli which exemplify each particular combination of values of attributes constitute a sample, random or otherwise, from among all possible pairs of stimuli which exemplify those combinations. In most experiments, each particular combination of values has been exemplified by but one sample of one or more pairs of stimuli. Hence, only by assumption can the results obtained with each set of pairs of stimuli be treated as holding for other samples of pairs of stimuli which exemplify the same particular combination of values of attributes.

Greater assurance of generalizability can be obtained by using two or more parallel lists in which each particular combination of values of attributes is exemplified by two or more different samples of pairs of stimuli. One technique for generating parallel lists is reversal. Stimulus members become response members and the converse. Entirely new stimuli may be selected for each parallel list. Or, stimuli selected for a list may be returned for possible inclusion in other parallel lists. Differences due to lists can then be assessed in subsequent statistical analyses.

The problem of generalization from results obtained with one or more sets of stimuli which exemplify each particular combination of values of attributes is discussed in greater detail by Coleman (1964). It warrants additional attention, particularly with respect to appropriate analysis of variance designs.

RESULTS

Effects on PA learning of meaningfulness and related attributes of discrete stimuli have been investigated more extensively than have effects of similarity of meaning and other attributes of pairs of stimuli.[2] For this rea-

[2] Sheffield (1946), Gannon and Noble (1961), and Hakes (1961b) summarize methods and results of three earlier studies (Cason, 1933; Waters, 1939; Winzen, 1921) which, for this reason, and because of relatively inconclusive findings, are not reviewed here.

A related problem of infrequent but persistent interest over four decades has been the relationship between emotionally or affectivity of words and acquisition and retention of PA lists in which those words serve as stimulus members, response members, or both. Emotionality is usually varied by means of words representing two or all three of the categories pleasant, neutral, unpleasant. In turn, these categories or attributes have most often been specified by means of ratings of the words by the same or comparable subjects. Occasionally, aggressive meanings (e.g., Holzberg, Bursten, & Santiccioli, 1955), sexual references (e.g., Kott, 1955), association disturbances (Laffal, 1952), and arousal in terms of the GSR (e.g., Walker & Tarte, 1963) have been used instead of or as equivalent to "unpleasant." Investigations primarily concerned with effects of emotionality of words on acquisition and other phenomena of PA learning are not considered here because, while counted frequency of the words has sometimes been controlled, meaningfulness of the words has not usually been controlled either by selection or by partial correlation. Thus, interpretations of relationships between emotionality and acquisition rate are ambiguous, particularly when a U-shaped relationship obtains, with pairs which contain pleasant or unpleasant words acquired faster than pairs which contain neutral words.

son, and also because it seems desirable to proceed from attributes of members of pairs singly to attributes of members jointly, findings for discrete stimuli are considered before those for pairs of stimuli. Effects of meaningfulness and related attributes of discrete stimuli and of pairs of stimuli on other transfer phenomena and on retention are relatively uninvestigated. Although not treated separately, pertinent findings on transfer and retention are noted.

More information about effects of combinations of meaningfulness or other attributes of discrete stimuli and pairs of stimuli can be obtained from complete orthogonal designs than from the nonrandom, incomplete orthogonal designs used thus far. Findings of experiments employing complete orthogonal designs are considered first in order to establish tentative generalizations against which findings of experiments employing nonrandom, incomplete designs can be compared. Unmixed lists do not involve the possible complication of interaction among sets of pairs of different values or combinations of values of meaningfulness over and above possible interactions among units representing the same combination of values. Within each design, therefore, findings with unmixed lists are considered before those with partly mixed or mixed lists. In general, findings with CVCs and other trigram and bigram

---

Prominent among the exceptions to the stricture of failure to control for meaningfulness are 14 experiments carried out by Anisfeld and Lambert (1964). The pleasant and unpleasant words of their List 1 and the pleasant and unpleasant adjectives of their List 2 were equated both for Thorndike-Lorge frequency and for M_n. In seven of nine experiments with CVCs as stimulus members, pleasant words as response members were acquired significantly faster than unpleasant words. The relationship held under a modified recall format and under an anticipation format with both selection and production of response members. However, in none of the four experiments with words or numbers as stimulus members were differences in rates of acquisition of pleasant and unpleasant words as response members significant. Also, with CVCs as response members, pairs with pleasant words as stimulus members were acquired no faster than pairs with unpleasant words as stimulus members. Anisfeld and Lambert review various earlier investigations of the relationships of emotionality of words to acquisition and retention not only with PA but also with list ("recall") tasks.

Bummer and Rosenthal (1963) also controlled for meaningfulness of the 10 "common" and the 10 "trauma" words which served as response members of different lists. The same CVCs of 20% Hull values served as the stimulus members of these lists. The response members were selected from among those of longer lists of common and trauma words which 12 graduates had rated as of average meaningfulness. Regardless of level of manifest anxiety as specified by scores on the Taylor scale and of level of intelligence as measured by scores on the Shipley-Hartford test, common words were recalled better after three pairings than were trauma words. These results with CVCs as stimulus members are consistent with those obtained by Anisfeld and Lambert when the stimulus members were CVCs. Assumed is an equivalence of common and pleasant.

forms are described, then those with longer words and dissyllables and with forms. Noted, finally, are findings for backward recall of stimulus members.

Meaningfulness of Discrete Stimuli: Complete Orthogonal Designs

In the experiments summarized here and in various of the experiments with other designs summarized subsequently, meaningfulness of stimulus members and of response members, or of one of these variables may have been combined with other variables. Results are first described for meaningfulness of stimulus members and of response members, disregarding any other variables. When pertinent, effects across or as modified by other variables are mentioned with the exception of similarity as well as of familiarization and other pretraining variables. Experiments involving meaningfulness variables combined with the latter variables are described when those variables are considered.

Unmixed Lists

Cieutat, Stockwell, and Noble's (1958) Experiment II is apparently the only study using a 3×3 orthogonal design with unmixed lists of paired CVCs; the CVCs were from Noble, Stockwell, and Pryer's (1957) list. Across and at each of the three levels of M_r of stimulus members, M_r of response members was related directly to correct responses during the 20 learning trials. With response members of low and medium M_r, number of correct responses increased with greater M_r of stimulus members. With response members of high M_r and stimulus members of low, medium, and high M_r, however, means of correct responses were 30.5, 77.5, and 54.8, respectively, suggesting an inverted-V function. Across the three levels of M_r of response members, means for low, medium, and high M_r of stimulus members were 17.7, 42.1, and 41.0. Thus, the data suggest a positively accelerated relationship between correct responses and M_r of response members, and a negatively accelerated relationship between correct responses and M_r of stimulus members. But the number of points is small and the relationhsip between correct responses and M_r of stimulus members questionable. Also, the significant interaction of M_r of stimulus members and M_r of response members suggests that relationships between acquisition rate and M_r of stimulus members or response members are, in part, contingent on the particular level of the other variable. Therefore, to draw conclusions regarding forms of functions either across all values or for particular values of the other variable is premature. Across all levels of the other variable, the mean square for M_r of response members was twice that for M_r of stimulus members. At low and medium but not high levels of M_r of stimulus members and M_r of response members, the latter variable had a greater effect than the former.

CVCs have been the stimulus members and response members of most

2×2 designs with unmixed lists (Experiment 7 in the Appendix; Cieutat, 1959, 1961; Harleston, 1963; Harleston & Cunningham, 1961; L'Abate, 1959, 1962; R. L. Weiss, 1958). For continuity with the description of an antecedent study with lists in which meaningfulness of stimulus and response members were positively correlated, another experiment (Battig, 1964, pp. 19-21) with a 2×2 design realized in unmixed lists of pairs of CVCs is discussed below. In other experiments with 2×2 designs, stimulus members and response members have been dissyllables from Noble's (1952) list (Cieutat, Stockwell, & Noble, 1958, Exp. I; W. Epstein, 1963; Hunt, 1959). Also, 2×2 designs have been realized with dissyllables as stimulus members and/or response members of high meaningfulness and nonsense syllables as responses and/or stimulus members of low meaningfulness (Haraguchi, 1957; Morikawa, 1959b). The subjects of these experiments, with the exception of Cieutat's (1959) mostly schizophrenic male patients, were college students usually of both sexes. (Unless otherwise noted, the subjects of the experiments described were largely or exclusively college undergraduates.) Memory-drum presentation to subjects individually has been the most common technique of administration; but group techniques have been used by Cieutat (1961) and also for several of the experiments described in greater detail in the Appendix. Haraguchi used both naive and experienced subjects, and both he and Morikawa administered four lists representing the different combinations of values of meaningfulness of stimulus members and response members to the same subjects in counterbalanced order.

In general, whether the lists were administered to subjects singly or by a group technique, in constant or varied order, and under anticipation or recall formats, successively faster acquisition rates have been obtained with stimulus members and response members both of low meaningfulness (low-low), with stimulus members of high meaningfulness and response members of low meaningfulness (high-low), with stimulus members of low meaningfulness and response members of high meaningfulness (low-high), and with stimulus members and response members both of high meaningfulness (high-high). Reflected in this order is greater potency of meaningfulness of response members than of meaningfulness of stimulus members; but the interaction of the two variables may or may not be significant. The generalization of increasingly faster acquisition in the order low-low, high-low, low-high and high-high also holds whether subjects were college students or hospitalized mental patients (Cieutat, 1959) and also whether they were high-anxious or low-anxious males or females (Harleston, 1963; Harleston & Cunningham, 1961; L'Abate, 1959, 1962).

Within each of the four combinations of constant and varied orders of occurrence of pairs under both recall and anticipation formats of presentation, Battig, Brown, and Nelson (Exp. IV, 1962) apparently found successively better acquisition with low-low, high-low, low-high, and high-high lists. Paralleling these findings for varied orders of occurrence are the results of Experiment 7 in the Appendix. Under both recall and anticipation formats of presentation, trials through criterion decreased in the order low-low, high-low, low-high, and high-high.

One exception to the generalization of faster acquisition with low-low, high-low, low-high, and high-high combinations is Cieutat's (1961) rank order of increasing numbers of correct responses of low-low, low-high, high-low, and high-high; M_r of stimulus members had a greater effect than M_r of response members. Each of his four unmixed lists of CVCs (Noble, Stockwell, & Pryer values, 1957) was administered to a different group of 17 high school sophomores. The group technique of administration required circling the correct one of three responses accompanying each stimulus member with guidance or correction from correct pairings at the top of the page. To explain the more pronounced effect of M_r of stimulus members than of M_r of response members, Cieutat suggested that guidance or correction by means of correct pairs at the top of the page may have required a discrimination in which M_r of stimulus members was a more important factor than M_r of response members.

As noted below, under W. Epstein and Streib's (1962) condition of easy recognition of the correct one of three choices, meaningfulness of response members had no differential effect. Because meaningfulness of stimulus members was not varied, no semi-replicatory information is available concerning effects of meaningfulness of stimulus members when responses are selected rather than produced.

A possible second exception is Morikawa's (1959b) finding of a low-low, low-high, high-low, and high-high order of correct responses in forward recall of response members to stimulus members presented alone on test trials after subjects had reached criteria of six of nine correct anticipations, and of one and three perfect trials. However, the superiority of high-low to low-high was slight.

Means of correct responses for the high-anxious females of Harleston and Cunningham's (1961) experiment increased in the order low-low, high-low, low-high, high-high; but some slight deviations from this order were observed for the other three combinations of low-anxious females and both low- and high-anxious males. With only six subjects in each combination for each list, the deviations from expected order probably reflect sampling error. Across all four combinations, the order was low-low < high-low < low-high < high-high.

Adding the variable of ability level of subjects specified by rate of acquisition of a practice list, Harleston (1963) investigated effects of M_a of stimulus and M_a of response members with high- and low-anxious males and females who were slow, moderate, and fast learners. In four of six comparisons, correct responses in 30 trials increased in the order low-low, high-low, low-high, high-high. The exceptions were high-low $<$ low-low for slow-learning, high-anxious subjects and low-high $<$ high-low for high-anxious subjects learning at a moderate rate. Again, with only six subjects in each cell, these inversions for expected order probably reflect sampling factors. Disregarding anxiety and ability, both M_a of stimulus members and M_a of response members were related directly to correct responses with the mean square for the latter three times the mean square for the former. However, the two variables did not interact significantly nor, although ability had a significant main effect, did these variables, singly or together, interact with ability. No information is reported on effects of sex; presumably this variable made no significant contribution. Analysis of each of the four lists separately with ability, anxiety, and trials as variables indicated that ability but not anxiety was related directly to acquisition rate for all four combinations of M_a of stimulus members and M_a of response members.

A clear exception to the expected order, however, is L'Abate's (1962) finding of more correct responses in 10 trials with high-low (100%–0% Glaze M_a) than with low-high lists of 10 pairs within all four combinations of high-anxious and low-anxious men and women. The high-high and low-low combinations yield, as expected, the largest and smallest means of correct responses. Examination of the pattern of differences among means for the four combinations indicated that M_a of stimulus members was more potent than M_a of response members; but a significant interaction between the two variables seemed unlikely. While women learned the high-high list sufficiently faster than men to produce a significant effect of sex, the difference was confined to the high-high list. Anxiety was not a significant factor.[3]

Turning to experiments with words and dissyllables, the lists of Kothurkar's (1963) experiment consisted of 10 pairs of dissyllables representing combinations of high and low Noble M_n of stimulus and of response members. For low-low, high-low, low-high, and high-high lists, respectively, trials to an errorless trial were 33.70, 14.13, 12.55, and 10.85. Both M_n of stimulus

---

[3] Data on transfer within A-B and C-B, A-B and A-C, and A-B and C-D paradigms are reported. Adjustments of scores on the transfer task precluded assessing the main effects of M_a of stimulus members and M_a of response members. However, interactive consequences of these variables for transfer could be determined within the 12 combinations of paradigms, sex, and anxiety. In the analysis of variance, the four combinations of M_a of stimulus members and of response members interacted significantly with sex and anxiety. While M_a of stimulus and M_a of response members were not separated, examination of tabled values suggested that both variables had significant effects on transfer with both direction and extent contingent on the particular combination of paradigm, sex, and anxiety. The particular patterns of relationships among means, however, are too complex for description here.

members and M_n of response members were related directly to acquisition rate. The latter variable was slightly more potent and the two variables interacted significantly in the form of a greater difference due to M_n of stimulus members or of response members for low than for high M_n of the other variable.

For retention after 24 hr., 48 hr., 96 hr., and 1 wk., more responses were correct on the first retention trial with the low-high than with the high-high list. The same results were obtained with percent savings in relearning. More responses were correct with the low-high and high-high lists than with high-low and low-low lists. With the latter two lists, the order was better retention of high-low than of low-low after 24 hr. and 96 hr., and better retention of low-low than of high-low after 48 hr. and 1 wk.

The unmixed lists of 10 pairs of dissyllables prepared by W. Epstein (1963) represented the four combinations of high or low Noble M_n of stimulus and response members. Without familiarization of response members by learning to recall them, trials to criterion increased in the order low-low, high-low, high-high, and low-high; with prior familiarization the order was low-low, high-low, low-high, and high-high. The direct effects of M_n of response members but not of M_n of stimulus members were significant but the two variables did not interact significantly with each other or with familiarization. Both with and without familiarization, trials until response members were available decreased in the order low-low, high-low, low-high, and high-high.

In Postman's (1962) Experiment I, unmixed lists of words representing combinations of stimulus members and of response members of high, medium, and low Thorndike-Lorge frequencies were learned to a criterion of one perfect trial. Number of trials to criterion was a direct function of counted frequency of response members, disregarding frequency of stimulus members, and a V-shaped function of frequency of stimulus members, disregarding frequency of response members. The interaction of the two variables was not significant. Frequency of response members had no effect on retention after 30 sec. or 7 days. While frequency of stimulus members had no effect on relearning after 30 sec., it was related by a V-shaped function to trials to relearn after 7 days.

Randomly selected letters of the alphabet were the familiar stimulus members or response members of Cook and Brown's (1963) 8-pair lists; the unfamiliar stimulus members or response members were forms constituted of single dots randomly placed in an 8×8 matrix. For number of correct items, number of different legitimate responses, the ratio between the former and the latter, and number of legitimate responses, both number of responses and size of the ratio increased in the order unfamiliar-unfamiliar, familiar-unfamiliar, unfamiliar-familiar, and familiar-familiar.

Without exception in 2×2 designs with unmixed lists, though differences between levels of meaningfulness have not always been significant, acquisition rate has been a direct function of meaningfulness of stimulus members and of meaningfulness of response members. Also, with L'Abate's (1962) and possibly Cieutat's (1961) findings as the only exceptions of reasonable reliability, meaningfulness of response members has produced a greater difference than meaningfulness of stimulus members. Haraguchi (1957) found more pronounced effects of both meaningfulness of stimulus members and meaningfulness of response members with naive than with experienced subjects.

PARTLY MIXED LISTS

Sheffield (1946) used four partly mixed lists; in Experiment 6 of the Appendix there were eight basic forms of partly mixed lists. In both experiments, summing across various lists for particular combinations of M_a of stimulus members and response members, faster learning occurred in the order low-low, high-low, low-high, high-high, with M_a of response members more potent than M_a of stimulus members. Differences between particular combinations within the various lists were consistent with these over-all trends.

Mandler and Campbell (1957) first used three partly mixed lists of six pairs of CVCs each; two pairs of each list represented one of the nine combinations of stimulus members and response members of low, medium, and high Mandler M_n (1955). They then used a mixed list of 18 pairs of CVCs, two pairs for each of the nine combinations. The results of the two experiments were reasonably consistent only with respect to direct relationships between acquisition rate and M_n of response members, disregarding levels of M_n of stimulus members. With partly mixed lists, across the three levels of M_n of response members, the relationship between acquisition rate and M_n of stimulus members was an inverted-V, while, with the mixed list, acquisition rate was directly related to M_n of stimulus members. With the partly mixed lists, relationships between acquisition rate and M_n of stimulus members and M_n of response members were different for the same levels of the other variable. With the mixed list, relationships between acquisition rate and M_n for stimulus members with response members of low or high M_n were reasonably direct as were those for response members with stimulus members of low or high M_n. But, for stimulus members of medium M_n, fastest learning occurred with response members of medium M_n; for response members of medium M_n, fastest learning also occurred with stimulus members of medium M_n.

Use of trials to criterion with the partly mixed list and number of correct responses in 30 trials with the mixed list may have been one source of differences in results. Underwood and Schulz (1960a, p. 41) give several other reasons for the discrepancies between the results of two Mandler and Campbell experiments and also between the results of their first experiment with partly mixed lists and findings of other experiments.

MIXED LISTS

Described in greater detail in the Appendix (Experiment 9) are findings with mixed lists of four or 12 pairs within which one or three pairs, respectively, represented combinations of Noble M_r of low-low, high-low, low-high, and high-high. These lists were learned under both anticipation and recall formats. Within both 4-pair and 12-pair lists under both formats, acquisition rate increased in the order low-low, high-low, low-high, and high-high.

One of the 4-pair lists of Experiment 9 was selected for use in the experiment reported in the Appendix as Experiment 12. This list was acquired under schedules of 100% occurrence of both stimulus and response members (100% OSRM), of 100% occurrence of stimulus members and 25% occurrence of response members (25% ORM), and of 25% occurrence of stimulus members and 100% occurrence of response members (25% OSM). The orders of trials on which the first correct responses occurred were high-high $<$ low-high $<$ low-low $<$ high-low under 100% OSRM and 25% ORM, and high-low $<$ high-high $<$ low-low $<$ low-high under 25% OSM. Disregarding schedules, the order was high-high $<$ high-low $<$ low-high $<$ low-low with a significant F for M_a of stimulus members but not for M_a of response members.

Paivio (1964) prepared mixed lists of 16 pairs of which four pairs each were concrete nouns-concrete nouns (CC), concrete nouns-abstract nouns (CA), abstract nouns-concrete nouns (AC), and abstract nouns-abstract nouns (AA). On the basis of scalings by other groups of subjects, he established that the concrete nouns had higher values for M_n, imagery, and aural familiarity than did the abstract nouns. The rs among values for these attributes were .75 or higher. Thus, the CC, CA, AC, and AA pairs, respectively, might be regarded as representing combinations of high-high, high-low, low-high, and low-low values with respect to any one or all three attributes. Both across and during each of four trials, more responses were recalled correctly in the order of AA $<$ AC $<$ CA $<$ CC. The mean square for abstractness of stimulus members was eight times the mean square for abstractness of response members to indicate greater potency of the former variable. Both Fs based on these mean squares were significant; the F for the interaction of the two variables was not significant. Higher point biserial coefficients of correlation were obtained between recall scores and values of stimulus members for M_n, imagery, and familiarity than between recall scores and values of response members for those attributes. The values of the coefficients for concreteness were the same as those for imagery. Thus, variation in M_n, imagery, familiarity, and concreteness of stimulus members all entered into stronger relationships than did variations in these attributes of response members.

The results of Experiment 9 in the Appendix but not those for Experiment 12 or Paivio's experiment were consistent with the typical findings with unmixed lists of faster acquisition in the order low-low $<$ high-low $<$ low-high $<$ high-high. In Experiment 12, under 100% OSRM and 25% ORM the only inversion from the expected order was the faster acquisition of the low-low pair than of the high-low pair. Since only single pairs were involved, sampling of CVCs could easily account for this discrepancy. Under 25% OSM, potency of meaningfulness of stimulus members might be expected to increase relative to potency of meaningfulness of response members. A marked change in relative potency could have occasioned the inversion of the high-low and low-high combinations. Again, however, the inversion of the high-low and high-high combinations and, particularly, that of the low-low and low-high combinations are best attributed, tentatively, to sampling of the CVCs.

Paivio's finding of a greater potency of concreteness of stimulus members, and inferentially of their M_n, imagery, and familiarity, than of those attributes of response members might be due to selection of the nouns in terms of rather imprecise specification of concreteness; to failure to control for differences in M_n, imagery, or familiarity a priori; or both. The same stricture applies to two other experiments of Paivio's (1963) which are described subsequently.

BACKWARD RECALL OF STIMULUS MEMBERS

For backward recall of stimulus members as responses to response members, Hunt (1959) reported decreasing numbers of errors with low-low, low-high, high-low, and high-high lists. The effect of M_a of stimulus members on backward recall was significant and that of M_a of response members approached significance; but the interaction of the two variables was not significant.

For recall of stimulus members after subjects had reached criteria of six of nine correct and of one and three perfect trials, Morikawa (1959b) also found increasing recall for low-low, low-high, high-low, and high-high lists. However, R. L. Weiss (1958) reports increasing recall in the order low-low, low-high, high-high, and high-low; the high-high and high-low difference was not significant.

As described in Experiment 7 in the Appendix, whether acquired under recall or anticipation formats of presentation, number of CVC stimulus members of low similarity recalled correctly increased in the order low-low, low-high, high-low, and high-high. Meaningfulness of stimulus members and of response members were related directly to number of stimulus members recalled. However, in both an analysis of variance and an analysis of covariance involving adjustment of numbers of stimulus members recalled for differences in trials to criterion, Fs for meaningfulness of stimulus members were significant but not those for meaningfulness of response members.

Meaningfulness of Discrete Stimuli: Incomplete Orthogonal Designs

The "X" and "cross" designs of Fig. 1 provide more information than do the diagonal designs or designs in which variations in meaningfulness of stimulus members or response members are paired with, respectively, a fixed value of meaningfulness of response members or stimulus members. L'Abate (1959), whose results were noted above, added another combination—pairs with stimulus members and response members of intermediate meaningfulness —which enlarged the design to an "X." Levitt and Goss (1961) paired stimulus members of high or low M_a with response members of intermediate M_a and the reverse; thus their design was a "cross" with the center cell eliminated. Results of both experiments were consistent with or reconcilable with those obtained with complete orthogonal designs, as were Umemoto's (1951b) earlier findings.

In Paivio's (1963) lists, abstract and concrete nouns served as stimulus members or as response members with adjectives as response members or stimulus members, respectively. Thus, the design was that employed by Levitt and Goss. The lists of Experiment I were partly mixed; those of Experiment II were unmixed. The same subjects, however, learned both a list of nouns-adjectives and a list of adjectives-nouns.

In both experiments, more responses were recalled correctly with nouns as stimulus members than with nouns as response members. Recall was better with concrete nouns as stimulus members or as response members than with abstract nouns as stimulus members or as response members. In Experiment I, but not in Experiment II, the difference between recall with abstract and concrete nouns was sufficiently greater when they were stimulus members than when they were response members to yield a significant interaction of abstractness and order. The nouns of these experiments were different than those of the experiment described above (Paivio, 1964) for which Paivio had obtained values for M_n, imagery, and aural familiarity. On the assumption of the same condition of lower values of M_n, imagery, and aural familiarity for the abstract than for the concrete nouns of the experiments considered here, the results can be interpreted as suggesting direct relationships between acquisition rate and the correlated attributes of M_n, imagery, and aural familiarity of stimulus and of response members. Presumably the relationships are somewhat stronger with the nouns as stimulus members than as response members.

The first phase of Cochran and Wickens' (1963b) study involved two separate ratings of 50 numbers between 1 and 100 by students in an elementary psychology course. Twenty-nine subjects were then selected whose ratings of the numbers were such that three numbers each could be found which fell in the categories of high for the group and high for the individual, high for the group and low for the individual, low for the group and high for the individual, and low for the group and low for the individual. Fourteen of the 29 learned a list in which the 12 numbers selected to fit the categories served as stimulus members. Twelve words among the 1000 most frequent words in the Thorndike-Lorge count served as response members. The remaining 15 subjects learned a list in which the words served as stimulus members and the numbers as response members. Thus, meaningfulness of stimulus members was varied with meaningfulness of response members constant, or the converse.

With numbers as stimulus members, means of numbers of trials to a criterion of one perfect trial increased in the order high group-high individual < high group-low individual < low group-high indivdiual < low group-low individual. With numbers as response members, the same order obtained with, however, only a slight difference between means for the latter two combinations. Across both lists, the direct relationship between acquisition rate and group values for M_r was significant at <.01; the less pronounced direct relationship between acquisition rate and individual values for M_r was short of significance at .05. Somewhat more trials were necessary to learn with numbers as stimulus members than with numbers as response members. However, the difference was not significant nor was there any indication of a greater effect of M_r of response members than of M_r of stimulus members.

In addition, meaningfulness and other attributes have been varied in positively correlated and negatively correlated relationships. Attributes of stimulus members or response members have also been varied with attributes of response members or stimulus members held constant.

POSITIVELY CORRELATED VALUES OF ATTRIBUTES

The three lists used for Merikle and Battig's (1963) first task were 12 pairs of CVCs whose members were of 97–100% Archer M_a, nine pairs whose members were of 47% M_a, and six pairs whose members were CCCs with weak associative connections between letters (low meaningfulness). Despite the decreasing lengths of lists, means of trials to criterion were, respectively, 5.25, 12.00, and 15.17. In the second task, the response members of one third of the pairs were changed to realize an A-B, A-C paradigm; the response members of another third were reversed to realize an A-B, A-B$_r$ paradigm; and both stimulus and response members of the remaining third of the pairs were replaced by new stimuli of the same meaningfulness to realize an A-B, C-D paradigm.

Means of errors with these new lists for the A-B, A-C, the A-B, A-B$_r$, and the A-B, C-D paradigms were, respectively, 6.50, 4.08, and 6.42 for the low-meaningfulness list, 7.50, 6.64, and 7.03 for the medium-meaningfulness list, and 2.88, 3.50, and 2.29 for the high-meaningfulness list. Disregarding transfer paradigms, the smallest number of second-task errors was with the high-meaningfulness list. However, more errors occurred with the medium-meaningfulness list than with the low-meaningfulness list. The interaction of meaningfulness and paradigms was significant. When stimulus and response members were of low meaningfulness, positive transfer occurred with the A-B, A-B$_r$ paradigm. There was little or no transfer with this paradigm when stimulus and response members were of medium meaningfulness, and negative transfer when they were of high meaningfulness. With the A-B, A-C paradigm, as meaningfulness increased, amount of negative transfer increased slightly.

For a second experiment on effects of meaningfulness on transfer, Battig (1964, pp. 19-21) prepared unmixed lists of eight pairs representing combinations of high or low Archer M_a of stimulus and response members. The first task involved acquisition of different lists to a criterion of two successive correct responses with each pair. The second task involved acquisition of a common list to the same criterion. As in the previous experiment, the second task involved A-B$_r$, A-C, and C-D changes to which a C-B change was added. The latter change involved the same response members and different but similar stimulus members.

Means of total errors during acquisition of the lists of the first task were in the order low-low < high-low < low-high < high-high. The same order obtained for acquisition of the lists of the second task for all but the A-B, C-B paradigm. For that paradigm there was one inversion in the form of slight superiority of the high-low to the low-high list. Acquisition within the A-B, C-D paradigm served as the baseline for percentage transfer scores. Analysis of covariance but not of variance indicated significant negative transfer for the A-B, A-B$_r$ paradigm with the high-high list and significant positive transfer with the high-low and low-low lists. By analysis of variance, negative transfer occurred with the high-high list for the A-B, A-C paradigm, and positive transfer occurred with the high-low list for the A-B, B-C paradigm.

Stimulus and response members of the six-pair unmixed lists of Newman and Gray's (1963) second and third experiments were both CVCs of high or of low pronunciability. Across 21 acquisition trials, means of correct anticipations for the list of high pronunciability CVCs were about 60; means for CVCs of low pronunciability were about 10. Backward recall of stimulus members and recall of stimulus members and of response members were also related directly to pronunciability.

Mandler and Huttenlocher (1956) constructed two lists of eight pairs of CVCs with members of the pairs sampled from eight equal intervals of Mandler's (1955) M_n values. For one of their lists, the relationship of *logs* of trials through the second trial of successive correct responses to M_n had a markedly larger linear than nonlinear component; for the other list, the linear component was larger than the nonlinear component at $p = .10$.

These relationships between acquisition rates and positively correlated values of meaningfulness of stimulus and of response members could be generated by various combinations of relationships to acquisition rate of meaningfulness of response members, disregarding meaningfulness of stimulus members, and of meaningfulness of stimulus members, disregarding meaningfulness of response members. Precluded for positively correlated and for negatively correlated designs, therefore, are precise inferences from functions along the diagonal to relative potency of meaningfulness of stimulus members and of response members or to functions relating acquisition rate to meaningfulness of stimulus members, of response members, or of both on either side of the diagonal.

Two pairs of CVCs at each of five levels of M_r as determined by Noble, Stockwell, and Pryer (1957) made up their two PA lists. For Trials 2–4, the relationship between errors and M_r obtained by Noble, Stockwell, and Pryer was negative and positively accelerated; this relationship was more pronounced for Trials 2–11. But for Trials 9–11, errors and M_r were related linearly. Thus, for CVCs in mixed lists the relationship between acquisition rate and M_r along the positively correlated diagonal seemingly is or becomes linear.

Across all levels and at each level of similarity of stimulus members to response members, Young (1961) obtained fewer correct responses with pairs made up of stimulus members and response members of low M_a than with those made up of stimulus members and response members of high M_a.

In his first experiment, Baddelay (1961b) prepared two lists of eight pairs of CVCs each whose stimulus members and response members were both of high predictability or were both of low predictability; the M_a of the CVCs was around 50% and the two lists were of equal mean M_a. For all but the first of 10 trials, more correct responses were made with pairs of high predictability than with those of low predictability.

In a second experiment, lists were prepared with pairs whose stimulus members and response members were also both of high M_a or both of low M_a. Transitional probabilities between last letters of the stimulus members and first letters of the responses (compatibility) were high for two lists whose pairs were of high or of low M_a. Compatibility was low for the other two lists whose pairs were of high or of low M_a. These four lists were matched for predictability. Both for the two lists of low compatibility and for the two lists of high compatibility, differences between acquisition of the list with pairs of low M_a and the list with pairs of high M_a were not significant.

Also in this experiment, lists were prepared whose stimulus members and response members were both of low predictability or of high predictability. There was low compatibility between the stimulus members and response members of two lists whose pairs were of low or high predictability, and high compatibility between the stimulus members and response members of the other two lists. M_a of stimulus members and response members of these lists was held constant. Regardless of compatibility, faster learning occurred with pairs of high predictability than with those of low predictability. In both of the preceding experiments, compatibility was directly related to acquisition rate.

Baddelay subsequently pooled the 40 pairs of these eight lists and, for pairs of high compatibility and those of low compatibility separately, computed rank-order coefficients between learning scores for pairs and their values for Archer M_a, Noble M_r, pronunciability, trigram frequency, and predictability. For high compatibility pairs, the coefficients were from .12 to .25; for low compatibility pairs they were from .23 to .49. In both sets, predictability yielded the highest value.

In Battig, Brown, and Nelson's (1962) Experiment IV there was a fifth list, comprised of five high-high and five low-low pairs of CVCs, which was also learned with constant or varied orders of presentation under both recall and anticipation formats. For each combination of order and format, fewer errors occurred with high-high than with low-low pairs. Performance with the high-high and low-low pairs in the mixed list was somewhat but not significantly better than performance with those pairs within the unmixed high-high and low-low lists.

Kimble and Dufort (1955) and Noble and McNeely (1957) both used 10 pairs of Noble's (1952) dissyllables in a positively correlated design with each pair representing roughly equal increments in equal values of M_n of its members. With criteria of number of trials to reach the first correct association for each pair and of errors in 20 trials, relationships between acquisition rate and M_n were direct and approximately linear.

Epstein, Rock, and Zuckerman (1960) prepared two sets of lists; each set consisted of a list of six pairs of nouns (considered familiar, and meaningful), a list of six pairs of prepositions and conjunctions (considered as familiar as nouns, but less meaningful), and a list of six pairs of CVCs (considered least familiar and less meaningful). Half of the subjects had one learning and one recall trial with each of the lists of one set; order of lists was counterbalanced. Between the one learning trial and recall there was 1 min. of interpolated activity. Recall was by saying the response to each stimulus member (Exp. II) or selecting the correct response (Exp. III).

For both sets of lists, by both methods of eliciting responses, there were decreasing numbers of correct responses with nouns, prepositions and conjunctions, and CVCs. When one considers that the stimulus members and response members of the former two types of pairs were regarded as of higher meaningfulness than the meaningfulness of pairs of CVCs, their results also suggest that pairs with stimulus members and response members both of high meaningfulness are learned faster than pairs with stimulus members and response members both of low meaningfulness.

Epstein, Rock, and Zuckerman (1960, Exp. VI) also prepared two series of pairs of pictures of objects, of concrete nouns, of abstract nouns, and of verbs. If it is assumed that average meaningfulness of these types of pairs decreases approximately in the stated order, the four sets of pairs realize a positively correlated diagonal design. The obtained order of mastery of pictures > concrete nouns > abstract nouns = verbs is reasonably consistent with expectations within such a design. Earlier, with lists of eight pairs administered to school children by a group method, Busemann (1911) obtained decreasing numbers of correct responses with pairs of concrete nouns, abstract nouns, adjectives, verbs, and meaningless words.

Lists of eight pairs of concrete nouns, abstract nouns, and prepositions and conjunctions were prepared by W. Epstein (1962) who obtained M_n values for the three classes of words of 7.7–10.4, 6.1–9.9, and 4.3–7.2, respectively. Thus, the three lists could be regarded as high-high, medium-medium, and low-low. When the correct response for a pair occurred during the test phase of a recall format, that response member was presented on the next trial for recall of its stimulus member; the pair was then discarded. Trials to criterion decreased, and number of pairs learned during the first trial increased in the order low-low, medium-medium, and high-high. Various measures of recall of stimulus members increased in the same order. Since the prepositions and conjunctions had higher Thorndike-Lorge frequencies than did the concrete nouns or abstract nouns, Epstein concluded that effects of meaningfulness do not reduce entirely to effects of frequency. Suggested as possible bases for these results were differences in transitional probabilities and, more strongly, one or more of several related consequences of presumed mediating responses.

The list constituted of prepositions and conjunctions, as Glanzer (1962) suggests, might also have been acquired least rapidly because of presentation of such function words out of their usual context. Thus, in Glanzer's third experiment, function words and content words were presented sandwiched between CVCs in compound response members. In contrast to findings for the words alone as response members, triplets containing function words were learned better than those containing content words. Indeed, negative correlations were obtained between responses correct for words representing

different grammatical categories presented in triplet form and responses correct for those words presented alone as stimulus members or as response
members. The differences between nouns and function words of Epstein,
Rock, and Zuckerman's Experiments II and III might also be, in part, attributable to the relatively more unusual context or task requirement for the
function words than for the content words. But differences related to grammatical category may be due to differences in ease of pronunciation (Cofer,
1964).

Investigating the adequacy of a group PA technique, Cieutat (1960b) used
one list made up of pairs of Noble's dissyllables whose stimulus members
and response members were of low M_n and another list whose stimulus
members and response members were of high M_n. Both for total responses
and total responses correct, high-high pairs were learned faster than low-
low pairs.

Cieutat and Cieutat (1961) used adult males of high or low verbal ability
and good (hospital staff) or poor (patients) adjustment to whom they administered a mixed list with three pairs of Noble's dissyllables at each of three
levels of stimulus members and response members of equal M_n. The curve
showing a direct relationship between correct responses and M_n for subjects
of low verbal ability was below and steeper than the curve for subjects of
high verbal ability. Cieutat and Cieutat describe additional interactions
among their variables. Over-all, their results with a mixed list of low-low,
medium-medium, and high-high pairs agree with those with unmixed lists.

Weitz (1964) prepared unmixed lists of eight pairs whose stimulus and
response members were both of low Noble M_n (hard) or both of high M_n
(easy). They were administered to subjects by a procedure similar to Cieutat's (1961). In the first pair of experiments, half of the subjects had 15
one-minute trials with the easy list and then 15 one-minute trials with the
hard list, and half learned the hard list and then the easy list. In both experiments, regardless of order, the easy list was acquired faster than the hard
list. The same relationship held in a further experiment in which subjects
learned either two hard lists or two easy lists.

Both stimulus and response members of the three lists prepared by Williams and Derks (1963) were CVCs of low pronunciability (Underwood &
Schulz, 1960a), CVCs of high pronunciability, or familiar words of CVC
structure. Means of Archer M_a values for these three lists were 32%, 82%,
and 100%, respectively. All three lists were presented visually, aurally, and
in both modalities combined. With all three manners of presentation, a direct
relationship obtained between pronunciability or M_a and medians of the
number of responses recalled correctly through three trials. Each of the
three lists was acquired faster when presented in the two modalities combined than when presented in the modalities separately. When presented in

the visual or aural modality, the lists of CVCs of low pronunciability and of familiar words were acquired to about equal levels. But the list of CVCs of high pronunciability was learned better when presented in the visual than in the aural modality. Despite the significant interaction of attributes and manner of presentation, whether or not the form of the relationship differs among the modalities separately and combined must be regarded as still conjectural.

Alternate sets of lists of 4, 8, 12, or 20 pairs whose stimulus and response members were both of low, medium, or high meaningfulness were prepared by Carroll and Burke (in press). The stimuli of these lists were CVCs of 0% to 35% Archer M_a values, five-letter words with Thorndike-Lorge frequencies of .5 to 2 per million, and words of varying length with Thorndike-Lorge frequencies of A or AA, respectively. Boys and girls in tenth grade learned these lists; they were divided into those above and below the median of raw scores on the *Modern Language Aptitude Test* (Carroll & Sapon, 1958). Across and at each length of list and level of ability, acquisition rate expressed as the logarithm to the base e of time to learn a specified number of pairs was related directly to meaningfulness of the pairs.

NEGATIVELY CORRELATED VALUES OF ATTRIBUTES

Relative potency of meaningfulness of stimulus members and response members has also been investigated by means of two lists, one with stimulus members of high meaningfulness and response members of low meaningfulness (high-low), the other with stimulus members of low meaningfulness and response members of high meaningfulness (low-high). Faster learning with the latter list has been interpreted as indicating greater weight of meaningfulness of response members than of meaningfulness of stimulus members. Such designs are, of course, negatively correlated diagonal designs which, considering observed values in just the two cells, do not permit precise inferences about the relative potency of meaningfulness of stimulus members or of response members. However, with unmixed lists in a 2×2 design, within the exceptions noted, the rank order of increasing acquisition rates has been low-low, high-low, low-high, and high-high. Therefore, any finding with negatively correlated designs in which the acquisition rate for high-low is less than that for low-high can be considered some corroboration of the high-low, low-high order of increasing rate with unmixed lists in a 2×2 design. The same holds for findings with mixed lists.

Across and at each of 25%, 50%, and 100% percentages of occurrence of response members (ORM), Wilcoxon, Wilson, and Wise (1961) obtained faster learning of pairs with CVCs as stimulus members and adjectives as response members (low-high) than of pairs with adjectives as stimulus members and CVCs as response members (high-low). With a mixed list of pairs with 12 nonsense syllables as stimulus members (low) and six loaded or six neutral words as response members (high), or the reverse, Feldman, Lang, and Levine (1959) report faster learning and relearning of nonsense syllable-word pairs (low-high) than of word-syllable pairs (high-low).

The pairs of Glanzer's (1962) lists had English words as stimulus members and CVCs as response members, or the converse. One each of the words represented nouns, adjectives, verbs, adverbs, pronouns, prepositions, and conjunctions. More correct anticipations occurred with the CVC-word or low-high lists than with the word-CVC or high-low lists. For word-CVC lists, the rank order for grammatical categories was more correct responses in the order conjunctions, pronouns, prepositions, verbs, adverbs, adjectives, nouns. For CVC-word lists the order was conjunctions, prepositions, adverbs, pronouns, verbs, adjectives, and nouns. The rho between these orders was .82.

As noted previously, Glanzer also found differences in word-association latencies and number of associations to words placed in the seven categories. These differences among categories in latencies and number of associations, and differences among categories in the H of associations were correlated with number of correct responses for each of the categories within both word-CVC and CVC-word lists. Significant rhos were obtained between correct responses with CVC-word lists and both latencies and number of associations, and between number correct with word-CVC lists and number of associations.

The paralogs of W. Epstein and Streib's (1962) lists of 10 high-low or low-high pairs were from Noble's list. Both lists were acquired to one perfect trial under an anticipation format with presentation at a 2:2-sec. rate. Alternatively, they were acquired under a selection or recognition format in which the correct response member was to be selected from among three choices during the first 2 sec. with the correct pair exposed during the next 2 sec. Easy recognition involved wrong choices which were not correct responses to other stimulus members of the list; difficult recognition involved wrong choices which were correct responses to other stimulus members of the list. Elimination of response learning under the recognition format, it was proposed, would equalize effects of meaningfulness of stimulus and of response members and hence rates of acquisition of low-high and high-low lists.

Under the anticipation format, trials to mastery of the high-low and low-high lists were 23.56 and 14.00, respectively. While 3.31 trials were required to master both lists when recognition was easy, when recognition was difficult mastery of the high-low list required 7.40 trials and of the low-high list 15.18 trials. The latter difference, significant at less than .05, was not only contrary to the expectation of no difference but also in a direction inconsistent with the generalization of relatively greater potency of meaningfulness of response members than of stimulus members. The proffered explanation was facilitation of associations in the associative stage by meaningfulness of stimulus members which, under the anticipation format, is obscured by differences in response learning. Presumably learning with easy recognition was too fast to reveal differential effects of meaningfulness of stimulus members.

E. Weiss (1963) obtained faster learning to criterion of 10 pairs of nonsense syllables-words than of words-nonsense syllables. In transfer to backward recall of five stimulus members paired with their original response members and of five stimulus members repaired with different response members, there was no evidence of better backward recall of words than of nonsense syllables. The difference between this finding with a heterogeneous or mixed transfer list and Weiss's (1962) earlier finding of better backward recall of words than of nonsense syllables with homogeneous or unmixed transfer lists was attributed to absence of class-descriptive cues in the unmixed lists.

Also fitting the high-low and low-high design are lists with stimulus members in the learner's first language and response members in a second language, and the converse. One of Stoddard's (1929) two groups of children learned from French words to English words; the children of the other group learned from English words to French words. The test administered to both groups consisted of 25 French words for which the English equivalent was to be written, and 25 English words for which the French equivalent was to be written. For recall in the same direction as learning, 15.1 of 25 English words and 8.0 of 25 French words were recalled. Thus the low-high combination produced better learning than the high-low combination.

Kuraishi (1937) found better acquisition of German-Japanese than of Japanese-German pairs. In additional experiments with other types of stimuli which could be considered high-low and low-high pairs, the latter were easier to learn.

ATTRIBUTES OF STIMULUS MEMBERS

Data on acquisition rate as functions of meaningfulness and related attributes of stimulus members and response members, with a fixed value of the particular attribute(s) of response members or stimulus members, respectively, are reported in a number of experiments. Eight of Noble's (1952) dissyllables of high M_n were the stimulus members of one of Lifton and Goss's (1962) two lists of pairs of dissyllables. Eight dissyllables of low M_n were stimulus members of the other list; both lists had the same dissyllable response members of intermediate M_n. These lists were presented first aurally, then visually or first visually, then aurally. For aural or visual original learning and for visual or aural relearning, stimulus members of high M_n led to faster learning than stimulus members of low M_n. Williams and Derks's (1963) and these may be the only data on effects of M_n on original learning with aural presentation of unmixed lists.

Nouns of two syllables which occurred in the Thorndike-Lorge count with frequencies of 1000–3000, 1–33, and 1–3 times out of 4,500,000 served as stimulus members of high, medium, and low frequency of usage in Postman's (1964) lists. Instead of acquiring responses supplied by the experimenter, subjects acquired self-supplied responses under a requirement of a different response to each stimulus member. Acquisition was to a criterion of three consistent repetitions. Recall of the responses and their relearning were tested 30 seconds or 48 hours later.

Since means of trials to criterion for groups tested for retention after 30 seconds and 48 hours did not differ, the scores were pooled. Means of trials to criterion for the lists with stimulus members of high, medium, and low frequency of usage were 8.38, 6.10, and 7.00, respectively, for which the F was significant at .01. The V-shaped relationship was interpreted as due to direct relationships between frequency of usage and both strength of pre-experimentally established associations to each stimulus member and degree of competition among responses. Facilitative effects on acquisition of the former were presumed to increase less rapidly than inhibitory effects of the latter to produce the fall-off in rate of acquisition with stimulus members of high frequency of usage. For recall and relearning after 30 seconds or 48 hours, differences among lists with stimulus members of high, medium and low frequency of usage were small. Nonetheless, across retention intervals the inverse relationship between frequency of usage and both amount recalled and rate of relearning were significant at $<.05$ and $<.01$.

R. E. Johnson (1964) administered only single pairs which were constituted of one of two dissyllable stimulus members of low meaningfulness and of one of two of high meaningfulness. Each was paired with a CVC response member of intermediate Glaze and Krueger M_a. Each pair was administered to a different group of subjects with recall to the stimulus member alone after 25 seconds, 3 minutes, 24 hours, or 2 weeks. At each of these intervals, more responses were made to the stimulus members of high M_a than to those of low M_a, but these differences were not significant.

The stimulus members of the lists used by Pimsleur, Sundland, Bankowski, and Mosberg (1964) were of low or high pronunciability as specified by large or small discrepancies between spelling of the words and their pronunciation, respectively. Scores for original learning of the lists with presentation of the stimuli in visual or aural modalities were not given. In general, for relearning with presentation of the stimuli in aural or visual modalities, respectively, fewer errors and larger savings scores were obtained with stimulus members of high than with those of low pronunciability.

Two of Cohen and Musgrave's (1964a) lists of CVC-letter pairs had stimuli of high or low Archer M_a which required, respectively, 16.38 and 20.75 trials to one perfect trial. Four additional lists had compound stimulus members which were pairs of CVCs representing each of the four combinations of high or low M_a of the first member and of the second member of each pair or compound. The list with high-high compounds was learned to criterion in 17.25 trials; the lists with high-low, low-high, and low-low compounds were mastered in 18.22, 23.88, and 24.71 trials, respectively, to suggest that the difference in M_a of CVCs in the first position was more potent than the difference in M_a of CVCs in the second position.

When CVCs of high M_a and low M_a were then presented separately, more correct responses were made to stimulus members of high than of low M_a. The larger number of correct responses to CVCs of high than of low M_a held whether the CVC of high M_a had been the first or second member.

The stimulus members of one of Sundland and Wickens' (1962) five lists were six-letter words from among the 1000 most frequent of the Thorndike-Lorge words. The stimulus members of another list were pairs of CVCs of 7% Glaze M_a. Responses of three-letter words from among the 100 most frequent in the Thorndike-Lorge list were acquired more rapidly to word stimuli of presumed high meaningfulness than to the CVCs of low M_a.

The stimulus members of Underwood, Ham, and Ekstrand's (1962) seven pairs were compounds of colors and CVC words of high Thorndike-Lorge frequencies or compounds of colors and CCCs of low associative connections between letters. Serving as response members were digits 2 through 8. Acquisition was faster with color-word than with color-CCC stimulus members. During 10 transfer trials involving continued compounds, words or CCCs separately, and colors separately, the list with words separately as stimulus members was acquired faster than the list with CCCs separately as stimulus members. In an experiment which differed only in requiring half of the subjects to spell the trigrams and in substitution of names of colors for colors, Jenkins and Bailey (1964) obtained similar results.

During the 10 trials of a follow-up experiment, 38.8 correct responses were obtained with CCCs as stimulus members in contrast to 51.2 correct responses with words as stimulus members. Thus, with or without color as an additional element or context, meaningfulness of stimulus members was apparently related directly to acquisition rate. Complicating this conclusion, however, is the greater formal similarity among the CCCs than among the words: the differences in acquisition rate in the main and follow-up experiments may have been due to inverse effects of similarity among words and among CCCs.

Jantz and Underwood (1958) prepared a mixed list with two trigram stimulus members at each of four levels of M_a (0%, 33%, 67%, 100%) paired with adjectives. Correct anticipations of response members during 4, 12, or 24 trials and M_a of stimulus members were related directly. When the list was reversed for backward recall, both M_a of stimulus members and number of learning trials were related directly to correct anticipations of the former stimulus members on the first trial of strengthening the "backward" associations and to amount of positive transfer to such strengthening over 10 trials. Lists with the same words were administered to seminarians by Cassen and Kausler (1962) for six acquisition trials at two exposure durations; these were followed by backward recall also at two exposure durations. Although results for acquisition are not reported, they presumably confirmed Jantz and Underwood's finding of a direct relationship between correct anticipations and M_a of stimulus members. Regardless of exposure duration, M_a of stimulus members was related directly to the number of letters of stimulus members which were recalled correctly.

Underwood and Schulz (1960a) also used lists with six different sets of eight trigrams as stimulus members and single digits as response members (Exp. 15) or pronounceable dissyllables of lowest possible Noble M_n as response members (Exp. 16). The trigrams represented a wide range of pronunciability and GV. For the lists with numbers as response members, the rs between mean number of correct anticipations in 20 trials and pronunciability for each list separately ranged from .62 to .99 with an over-all r of .73; the rs between number correct and GV for the lists separately ranged from .39 to .82 with an over-all r of .55. For the two lists with dissyllables as response members, rs between number correct and pronunciability and between number correct and GV were not reported. However, inspection of a plot of correct responses against pronunciability and against GV for both digits and dissyllables (p. 263) indicates that rs for lists with dissyllables as response members would be about the same as those for lists with digits as response members. With digits and with dissyllables as response members, pronunciability was a better predictor of acquisition rate than was GV.

Underwood and Schulz (1960a, pp. 264-269) later obtained the M_n of 22 of the 48 trigrams of Experiment 15. With trigrams as stimulus members and digits as response members, the rs between number correct and M_n and between number correct and pronunciability were .79 and .86, respectively. With digits as stimulus members and trigrams as response members (XYZ removed), the corresponding rs were .84 and .91. Thus, pronunciability was a better predictor of acquisition rate than M_n. Further, removal of pronunciability from the rs for number correct and M_n by partial correlation eliminated the relationship between number correct and M_n.

The stimulus members of each of the two mixed lists of Martin and Schulz's (1963) experiment consisted of two trigrams at each of four levels of pronunciability. Digits served as response members. The lists were presented aurally under a recall format with 2 or 6 sec. between onset of stimulus and of response members and 2-sec. presentations of stimulus members alone. Indicating a direct relationship between pronunciability and number of correct responses in 15 trials were a significant F and correlations between pronunciability and correct responses of .78 and .75 with 2-sec. and 6-sec. inter-onset intervals, respectively.

During the last of three learning trials with a list consisting of words or CVCs as stimulus members and numbers as response members, Asch and Lindner (1963) obtained more correct responses to words than to CVCs. Also, in both forward and backward orders, words were recalled better than CVCs.

The nouns for which Wimer (1963) had obtained values for M_n, M_p, associative variety, and familiarity were the stimulus members of six-pair lists for which the response members were CVCs of low meaningfulness. None of the values for the four correlations between acquisition rate and the measures of meaningfulness or the measure of familiarity approached significance.

Chapman and Gilbert (1937) prepared lists in which half of the pairs had familiar 7-letter English words as stimulus members and half had unfamiliar English words as stimulus members; the response members were 7-letter Hindustani words. The familiar words were almost certainly of higher meaningfulness than the unfamiliar words. Pairs with familiar words as stimulus members were learned more rapidly and retained better after 14 days than pairs with unfamiliar stimulus members.

ATTRIBUTES OF RESPONSE MEMBERS

The four unmixed lists prepared by Palermo, Flamer, and Jenkins (1964) had the same set of adjectives of 4 or 5 letters as stimulus members and different sets of CVCs of about 20%, 50% or 80% Archer M_a values or numbers from 1 to 6 as response members. In Experiment I, these lists were administered to children in Grade 5 with criteria of three successive errorless trials or a maximum of 18 trials; in Experiment II, they were administered to college students with criteria of 18 consecutive correct responses or a maximum of 18 trials.

In Experiment I, the means of errors were 62.5, 53.5, 47.5, and 33.9, respectively, for the lists of 20%, 50%, and 80% Archer M_a or with numbers from 1 to 6 as response members. In Experiment II, the respective means of errors for these lists were 26.6, 18.5, 7.3, and 18.4. Thus, for both younger and older subjects, direct relationships held between acquisition rate and M_a of CVC response members. While the younger subjects learned the list with numbers as response members faster than any of the lists with CVCs as response members, the older children learned the latter list only at the rate they learned the list with response members of 50% M_a. Even allowing for a slightly easier criterion for the older subjects, they acquired each list much more rapidly than did the younger children.

The results of the Palermo, Flamer, and Jenkins experiment for the three lists with CVCs of different M_a are seemingly the only data available on effects of meaningfulness of response members of CVC or other consonant and vowel structures in unmixed lists. However, Underwood and Schulz (1960a, Exp. 5) did construct four lists with the same single-digit stimulus members for which response members were CCCs of 0–21% or of 67–79% Witmer M_a, CVCs of 47–53% Glaze M_a, or common word CVCs. Thus the lists were unmixed but of two different consonant and vowel structures. Fastest and slowest learning was obtained with the first and fourth sets of response members. More correct responses occurred with the 47–53% CVCs than with the 67–79% CCCs to suggest that structure (pronunciability?) as well as meaningfulness may influence acquisition rate.

Morikawa (1958) used 2-letter syllables (high nonassociation values, conversely low meaningfulness) and words (low nonassociation values, conversely high meaningfulness) to form five pairs with syllables as stimulus members and response members (low-low) and six pairs with syllables as stimulus members and words as response members (low-high). After six trials, subjects were tested for forward or backward recall by right-association and recognition techniques. With the right-associate technique, better forward and better backward recall scores were obtained with low-high than with low-low. With the recognition technique, low-high and low-low did not differ in either forward or backward recall.

Reanalysis of learning scores for 22 of the 48 trigrams of Underwood and Schulz's Experiment 15 (p. 268) yielded an r of .80 between those scores and M_a. Learning scores and pronunciability correlated .81.

The stimulus members of Jung's (1963) unmixed lists were two-syllable adjectives; the response members were trigrams with summed-letter counts (Underwood & Schulz, 1960a) of from 9 to 14 for low values and from 46 to 79 for high values. More than twice as many trials were required to reach criterion with trigram response members of low than of high summed-letter counts. In the transfer sessions, with each of the three transfer paradigms of A-B and C-B, A-B and C-D, and A-B and A-C, more correct responses were obtained with response members of high than of low summed-letter counts during the first two and all 10 trials. Positive transfer with the A-B and C-B paradigm was greater with response members of low than of high summed-letter counts; the converse held for negative transfer with the A-B and A-C paradigm.

With CVCs as stimulus members and words of varying Thorndike-Lorge frequencies as response members, Jacobs (1955) obtained an r of .74 between numbers of correct responses and log frequency.

For Underwood and Schulz's Experiment 6, single digits were the stimulus members of four different sets of CVCs representing a wide range of values of pronunciability and of frequency. Number of correct responses in 20 trials was related directly to pronunciability and to frequency, with higher rs for pronunciability than for frequency. The same 12 two-digit numbers were stimulus members for two sets of single letters (Exp. 9), two sets of bigrams (Exp. 10), and three sets of trigrams (Exp. 11) of varying counted frequency. The rs between number of correct responses in 15 trials and frequency decreased from values of .68 (r) and .50 (rho) with single letters as response members to a lower and nonsignificant r and also rho with bigrams as response members and to even lower values of the coefficients with trigrams as response members (p. 172). In all cases, while acquisition rate and frequency were related directly, for response members made up of an increasing number of letters, strength of the relationship between acquisition rate and frequency decreased. For the relationship between acquisition rate and pronunciability of the 36 trigrams of Experiment 11, the r was .57 and the rho .68. Thus, pronunciability was much more strongly related to acquisition rate than was frequency.

In Experiment 12, numbers from 1 to 12 served as stimulus members for response members which were the three sets of trigrams of Experiment 11. The over-all rho and r between correct responses and pronunciability of .82 and .76, respectively, were somewhat larger than the corresponding coefficients for acquisition with two-digit numbers as stimulus members (Exp. 11). Correct anticipations per item, overt errors, and error-rate scores indicated that the largely single-digit stimulus members were less similar than two-digit stimulus members. As a consequence, Underwood and Schulz suggested that similarity of stimulus members might be inversely related to strength of the relationship between acquisition rate and pronunciability.

The three unmixed lists of Underwood and Schulz's Experiment 13 had numbers from 1 to 12 as stimulus members paired with trigrams of low, medium, or high frequency. Within each list, pronunciation ratings of response members ranged from low to high. One third of the response members of each of the three mixed lists were of low, medium, and high frequency. The mean of correct responses for the list of medium frequency was larger than the means for the other two lists; thus acquisition rate and frequency were not related directly. However, for mixed and unmixed lists, respectively, the rs for correct responses and pronunciability of response members for all pairs were .82 and .80 (adjusted). As in earlier experiments, therefore, acquisition rate was a function of pronunciability rather than of frequency. And relationships between acquisition rate and pronunciability in both unmixed and mixed lists were essentially equal.

The mixed lists of Experiment 13 were also learned under a recall format in which 15 learning trials with stimulus members and response members together alternated with 15 test trials with stimulus members alone (Exp. 14). The rs between number correct and pronunciability of response members for the three lists separately were .71, .73, and .81 and those between number correct and counted frequency were −.06, .08, and .35. Thus, for acquisition under both anticipation and recall formats, acquisition rate was related to pronunciability rather than to frequency.

When ratings of frequency (familiarity) became available, Underwood and Schulz carried out further analyses of the data of Experiments 12 and 13 (pp. 184-191). Whereas acquisition rate and counted frequency for all 36 pairs correlated .16 in Experiment 12 and .08 in Experiment 13, acquisition rate and rated familiarity correlated .69 in Experiment 12 and .68 in Experiment 13. The latter values, however, were still somewhat less than the respective rs of .76 and .82 for acquisition rate and pronunciability.

The 72 trigrams of Experiments 12 and 13 were subdivided by consonant and vowel sequences. For CVC, VCC, and CCV sequences, rs between correct responses and pronunciability were .86, .81, and .70, respectively, and those between correct responses and counted frequency were .51, .03, and −.08. The rs for correct responses and pronunciability and for correct responses and counted frequency for CCCs were not significant: Underwood and Schulz suggest that the nonsignificant r for pronunciability may have been due to truncated ranges of values of correct responses and of pronunciability.

Statistical manipulations of the data of Experiments 6, 12, and 13 in which pronunciability was held constant and counted frequency varied, or pronunciability was varied and frequency held constant, also indicated that acquisition rate was related to pronunciability but not to frequency. Providing indirect support for this conclusion is the finding that, with words and three-letter sequences of equal frequency, words were learned faster, perhaps because they were easier to pronounce (Exp. 7).

Arguing that "the frequency with which trigrams appear as units of English speech is a better measure of frequency, in terms of predictive power, than is frequency of contiguity of three-letter sequences" (p. 235), R. C. Johnson (1962) essentially replicated Underwood and Schulz's Experiments 6 and 11. Response members were classified as words, syllables, and nonsyllables; the order presumably represented decreasing occurrences of the trigrams as units. Correct responses increased in the order nonsyllables, syllables, and words. But no differences in correct responses were obtained between trigrams within each of these classes which were above or below median pronunciability values. Johnson concluded, therefore, that frequency of occurrences of trigrams as discrete units is a potent factor while pronunciability simply indicates whether a trigram is a word, syllable, or nonsyllable.

In a second experiment, Johnson added the syllables of Underwood and Schulz's Experiment 15. Subjects were required to write down as many different words as possible in which each syllable occurred. The rhos between the number of words listed for each syllable and number of correct associations in PA learning were .48, .64, and .75 for the syllables of Experiments 6, 11, and 15, respectively. Thus this measure, which can be regarded as related to M_n, also predicts acquisition rate.

Terwilliger (1962) had 50 female undergraduates rate the familiarity of 36 trigrams of Underwood and Schulz's Experiment 13. The rs between these familiarity values and rate at which the trigrams were learned were .77 for mixed lists and .76 for unmixed lists. Multiple Rs between pronunciability and familiarity as predictors and acquisition rate were .85 for mixed lists and .83 for unmixed lists. Adding counted frequency as a predictor did not increase the multiple Rs. With pronunciability held constant, the coefficients between rated familiarity and acquisition rate were .35 for mixed and .31 for unmixed lists. With familiarity held constant, coefficients of correlation between pronunciability and acquisition rate of .57 and .51 were obtained for mixed and unmixed lists, respectively. Thus, both familiarity and pronunciability predicted acquisition rate, with the latter the better predictor.

When dichotomized into trigrams easy to pronounce and hard to pronounce, the rs for number correct and pronunciability, only for syllables easy to pronounce, were .59, .71, and .69, respectively, for data from Underwood and Schulz's Experiments 6, 12, and 13 (p. 190). The corresponding rs, only for syllables hard to pronounce, were .57, .38, and .08. The rs for syllables easy and hard to pronounce for the eight-pair lists of Experiment 15 resembled those for the eight-pair lists of Experiment 6. And the comparable rs for the 12-pair lists of Experiment 14 resembled those for the 12-pair lists of Experiments 12 and 13. Accordingly, Underwood and Schulz hypothesized that, with hard-to-pronounce syllables, acquisition rate and pronunciability are directly related with eight-pair lists but, at most, weakly related with 12-pair lists.

The second condition of Experiment 15 involved two lists with single digits as stimulus members paired with CVCs of varying pronunciability and GV; the second condition of Experiment 16 involved two lists with pronounceable dissyllables of lowest possible M_n as stimulus members and the CVCs of Experiment 15. For the lists with digits as stimulus members, rs between number correct and pronunciability ranged from .61 to .97 with an over-all r of .87 (p. 247). The rs between number correct and GV ranged from .67 to .89 with an over-all r of .76. For the lists with dissyllables as stimulus members, corresponding rs for number correct and GV were not reported. The curves for these relationships (Underwood and Schulz, 1960a, Fig. 33, p. 263), however, suggest that the rs for number correct and pronunciability would be slightly higher than those for number correct and GV.

In Underwood and Schulz's Fig. 33, the pair of curves relating number correct to pronunciability and to GV for trigrams-numbers were above the pairs of curves for digits-trigrams, dissyllables-trigrams and trigrams-dissyllables. The pairs of curves for trigrams-numbers and trigrams-dissyllables, while the most widely separated, were essentially parallel, and had only slight positive slopes. The digits-trigrams curves were above those for dissyllables-trigrams with essentially equal slopes which were steeper than those for the other two pairs of curves. Comparing curves for the four combinations of types of stimulus members and response members, on the assumption that meaningfulness of the digits was greater than that (M_n) of the dissyllables, Underwood and Schulz concluded that meaningfulness of stimulus members did not interact with meaningfulness of response members.

Martin and Schulz (1963) reversed their pairs so that stimulus members were numbers, and response members were trigrams at four levels of pronunciability. Pronunciability of response members and number of correct responses correlated .91 and .90 for, respectively, 2 sec. and 6 sec. between onsets of stimulus and response members. Both the higher correlations and steeper slopes of regressions of number correct on pronunciability indicated that pronunciability of response members had a greater effect than pronunciability of stimulus members.

Asch and Lindner (1963) also reversed their pairs with CVCs and words as stimulus members and numbers as response members. About four times as many words were correct during the last of three learning trials which was a greater difference than was obtained with variations in meaningfulness of stimulus members. Words were recalled better than CVCs in both forward and backward orders.

In Keppel's (1963) first experiment, one list had numbers from 1 through 6 as stimulus members. Three subsets of two CVCs each of high, medium, and low Noble a served as response members, with one CVC of each subset rated relatively "good" and the other rated relatively "bad" on a good-bad scale. Across the three levels of Noble a, response members rated "good" were learned significantly faster than those rated "bad." The second list of this experiment also had numbers as stimulus members and three subsets of two CVCs each as response members. Ratings of these stimuli along the good-bad scale were about equal; one CVC of each subset was of high a and the other of low a. Response members of high a were learned faster than those of low a.

In Keppel's second experiment, numbers from 1 through 14 served as stimulus members for response members comprising seven words rated "good" and seven words rated "bad" which were of equal counted frequency and meaningfulness. Number of correct anticipations of "good" words during 10 trials was not significantly different than number of correct anticipations of "bad" words. The results of this experiment and, compensating for easier pronunciability of the "good" than of the "bad" words, of the first experiment were interpreted as contrary to an interpretation of goodness of response members as a significant variable.

Each of R. C. Johnson and Fehmi's (1963) three 15-pair lists had five response members representing each of three types of words. One type was words of low counted frequency in written material (e.g., feint) which have high frequency homophones (e.g., faint). Another type was words whose written frequencies were the same as those for the homophones of low frequency. The remaining type was words whose frequencies were the same as the sum of the frequencies of both members of homophone pairs. Three-digit numbers served as stimulus members. The mean of 4.3 correct anticipations of homophones in 21 trials did not differ from the mean of 4.5 anticipations of low frequency words; both means were significantly lower than the mean of 8.3 for words of frequencies equal to the summed frequencies of both members of homophone pairs. Johnson and Fehmi entertain "the assumption that low frequency homophones occur more frequently as heard-spoken sounds than do low-frequency words that are not homophones." On this assumption they interpret the results to "suggest that there is no discernible transfer of effect from aural-oral to written word frequency with regard to the rate at which Ss learn written stimulus materials" (p. 128).

In what may be the only study with nonverbal stimulus members (Vanderplas & Garvin, 1959b), nonsense-syllable responses were conditioned to forms with 6, 12, or 24 points which were of low, medium, or high M_a. For groups which had 16 trials, at least for the 6- and 12-point forms, there was slight evidence of more correct responses to forms of high and medium M_a than to those of low M_a; but the significance of these differences was not assessed.

Conclusions Regarding Meaningfulness and Related Attributes of Discrete Stimulus Members

On the whole, relationships between acquisition rate and meaningfulness of stimulus members and of response members obtained in nonrandom, incomplete orthogonal designs are consistent with those obtained in complete orthogonal designs. In terms of the 2×2 design, the rank order of increasing acquisition rates is typically low-low, high-low, low-high, and high-high, and, contingent on particular combinations of conditions, meaningfulness of response members is from slightly to several times more potent than meaningfulness of stimulus members. When meaningfulness of stimulus members and meaningfulness of response members interact, the pattern is typically a greater difference in effects of one variable with decreasing meaningfulness of the other. But available data are still too scanty either to account for exceptions to this generalization on rational grounds or to lead to more precise, reliable generalizations about patterns of families of functions.

Underwood and Schulz's (1960a) analyses of relative strengths of relationships between acquisition rate and meaningfulness, counted frequency, GV, familiarity, and pronunciability suggest that, in general, GV and pronunciability may be the best predictors, with pronunciability the better of the two. These relationships among predictors led them to two further conclusions. The first, based on the superiorities of GV to meaningfulness and, particularly, of pronunciability to meaningfulness, was that "M (defined as number of associates elicited, or number of subjects getting an association within a limited period of time) was not a relevant attribute for the response-learning phase of verbal units" (p. 284). The second conclusion, which is an attempt to retain a frequency hypothesis despite the superiority of GV and pronunciability as predictors to counted frequency and familiarity, is that "the most critical frequency for the development of associative connections is emitted frequency" (p. 290). Emitted frequency is apparently conceived as involving both vocal and writing responses.

Pairs of Stimulus Members

PA learning, like classical conditioning, has traditionally been conceived as involving the strengthening of associations between stimulus members and responses to response members from an initial zero or near-zero level of strength. Indeed, particular stimuli are usually paired to minimize direct or indirect associations between a stimulus member and the response of its paired response member. In part for this reason, perhaps, there has been little experimental interest in more precise determination of effects on PA learning of similarity of meaning and other attributes of pairs of stimulus members.

Considered here are those few experiments in which attributes of pairs of stimulus members were specified independently of subjects' performance or accounts of their performance in the criterion PA task. Excluded thereby are experiments in which subjects provided information about associative aids and mediating responses (e.g., Reed, 1918a, 1918b; Underwood & Schulz, 1960a, pp. 298-300). In the first set of experiments, initial strength of associations between pairs has been specified by values of ratings of associative strength, common meaning or ease of learning. Included also are experiments in which the specification of strength has been by experimenters' conjectures or by reinterpretation. In the second set of experiments, initial strength of associations has been specified by probabilities or orders of occurrence of responses as associations in word-association tests.

SPECIFICATION BY RATINGS, CONJECTURE, REINTERPRETATION

The eight lists used in Experiment 4 in the Appendix were constructed to represent combinations of high or low M_a of stimulus members, high or low M_a of response members, and high or low similarity of meaning-ease of learning of pairs of stimulus and response members. In part to minimize intra-list similarity, and also because of the correlation between similarity of meaning-ease of learning of pairs of stimulus members and M_a values of members of the pairs discretely, high or low values of similarity of meaning-ease of learning of the pairs were not perfectly orthogonal to M_a of stimulus members and M_a of response members.

The direct relationship between number correct in 12 trials and similarity of meaning-ease of learning of pairs of stimulus members was greater than the contribution of M_a of response members; M_a of stimulus members did not have a significant effect. For high similarity of meaning-ease of learning the expected low-low $<$ high-low $<$ low-high $<$ high-high order obtained; but for low similarity of meaning-ease of learning the order was low-low $<$ high-high $<$ high-low $<$ low-high.

The rhos between ease of learning and number correct and between number correct and similarity of meaning, disregarding M_a of stimulus members and response members, were .46 and .64 ($p < .05$), respectively. Since values for similarity of meaning were slightly more homogeneous than those for ease of learning, the larger rho for similarity of meaning suggests that ratings of this attribute may be a better predictor of actual learning than ratings of ease of learning.

Spence and co-workers (e.g., Besch, 1959; Sherman, 1957; Spence, Farber, & McFann, 1956; Spence, Taylor, & Ketchel, 1956) have used Haagen's norms for the strengths of association of paired adjectives to construct noncompetitive and competitive lists. The stimulus members and response members of noncompetitive lists were selected so that the stimulus members and response members of a particular pair had ratings of high associative strength but neither was associated strongly with any other stimulus member or response member. Intra-list associations on the basis of meaning were minimized as was formal similarity. Each of several sets of pairs of competitive lists consisted of a pair with high strength of association between its stimulus member and response member; stimulus members of other pairs of the set were strongly associated to the response member of the first pair and weakly associated to the response members with which they were paired. Also, stimulus members of strongly associated and weakly associated pairs were synonyms so that each might be an associate of the others.

Noncompetitive lists were learned more rapidly than competitive lists. Within competitive lists, pairs with stimulus members and response members of high associative strength were learned faster than pairs with stimulus members and response members of low associative strength.

Lovaas (1960a) used five pairs from Haagen's list with high strengths of association between stimulus members and response members and five pairs with low strengths of association. Subsequently (1960b) he used Spence, Taylor, and Ketchel's competitive list. In both experiments, pairs with high associative strength were learned faster than those with low associative strength. Therefore, disregarding the arrangement of associations of the competitive lists, the results of these five experiments suggest that strength of association of pairs of stimulus members, like its correlates, similarity of meaning, and presumably ease of learning, is directly related to acquisition rate.

In J. T. Spence's (1963b) Experiment I, initial association strength was also specified by ratings. Because of the continuity between this experiment and three further experiments in which initial strength was specified by word-association norms, consideration of this experiment is deferred.

The 15 pairs of Adams and Vidulich's (1962) lists consisted of nouns for which the adjective response members were "congruent" or "incongruent." "Congruent" can be interpreted as high strength and "incongruent" as low strength of associations between stimulus members and response members. The former lists were learned faster than the latter lists both by subjects scoring high and by those scoring low on the Rokeach dogmatism scale.

For their Experiment V, Epstein, Rock, and Zuckerman (1960) prepared two series of three parallel sets of pairs of stimulus members. One type of set consisted of pairs made up of verbs, articles, adverbs, prepositions, and conjunctions which were considered to have high transitional probabilities from stimulus members to response members. The second type consisted of conjunction-preposition pairs of low transitional probability. The noun pairs of their second experiment were the third type of set. The superiority of the first type to the second type was attributed to higher transitional probability, but the better learning with the third type than with the first type was considered evidence against reduction of the influence of meaning to differences in transitional probability.

One list for Epstein, Rock, and Zuckerman's Experiment VIIa consisted of pairs of nouns between which there was an "intelligible connective" (e.g., *cake* near *road*). The pairs of another list consisted of the same nouns and an "unintelligible connective"; those of a third list had no connective. The pairs of a fourth list had grammatically correct but presumably less intelligible connectives which, however, presumably provided for the same transitional probabilities as the connectives of the first list. The better performance with the first list than with the other three lists was regarded as support for Köhler's "organizational explanation" (pp. 1-2). However, until the transitional probabilities from one word to another in the units of their lists are determined and equated by some more satisfactory procedure than experimenters' judgments, a transitional probability explanation of observed differences cannot be rejected. Nor, for the same reason, can a transitional probability interpretation of the findings of Experiment VII be rejected. Since experimenters also judged the transitional probabilities of the pairs in Experiment V, this criticism is partly applicable to the results of that experiment. Therefore, these experiments add little to an understanding of relationships between acquisition rate and attributes of pairs of stimulus members.

Semler and Iscoe (1963; Iscoe & Semler, 1964) describe the stimulus and response members of each of the six paired associates of their "similar" list as possessing "high associative value in terms of categorical or functional similarity." Banana-orange and toothbrush-comb are two such pairs. For their "dissimilar" list, the stimulus and response members of these pairs were repaired "to maximize differences in conceptual similarity." The members of the pairs of the "similar" condition were selected on the basis of results of a sorting pretest. The members of these pairs might also be considered "similar" in terms of semantic similarity. The interpretation of "similar" here, however, is of strong initial associations between members of these pairs. The stimulus members of each pair of the "dissimilar" list presumably had a weak initial association with the response member of that pair but a strong initial association with the response member of another pair. Members of the pairs were presented as actual objects (concrete) or as color pictures of the objects (abstract).

In the first experiment (Semler & Iscoe, 1963), one or the other list was learned by white and Negro children of ages 5, 6, 7, 8, and 9. Through 12 trials, both across and essentially for each combination of race, age, and form of presentation, the "similar" or strong initial association list was acquired more rapidly than the "dissimilar" or weak initial association list. Most of the interactions among the variables were nonsignificant.

In the second experiment (Iscoe & Semler, 1964), the subjects were 6-year-old normal children and 12-year-old mentally retarded children; the two groups were matched for MA. Again through 12 trials, both across and for each combination of type of subject and form of presentation, the "similar" list was acquired more rapidly than the "dissimilar" list.

The four pairs of two of Kothurkar's (1964) four lists represented high or low initial strength of association between stimulus members and response members as specified by word-association norms (Kent & Rosanoff, 1910). The four pairs of the other two lists represented the presence or absence of "the relation of logical entailment between the members." Presence or absence of logical entailment is here presumed to reflect differences in initial strengths of association between the members of a pair. Through four acquisition trials, the means of correct responses were 24.6 and 14.0 for sets of pairs, representing high or low initial strengths, respectively, and 24.8 and 12.5 for sets of pairs for which logical entailment was present or absent, respectively. For retention, the corresponding means were 3.2 and 2.0; and 3.1 and 1.6.

Specification by Probabilities or Orders of Word Associations

A common assumption is the greater the frequency of a response to a particular stimulus member, as obtained by the word-association technique, the greater the strength of that stimulus-response association. Peterson (1956), in what might be considered a selective-learning PA situation, found acquisition rate to be directly related to frequency of responses in the Minnesota word-association norms (Russell & Jenkins, 1954).

The word-association norms obtained by Castaneda, Fahel, and Odom (1961) were used to specify strong and weak initial strengths of associations between stimulus and response members. The direct relationship between acquisition rate and initial associative strength which they found has been confirmed and extended by McCullers (1961, 1963). In addition, in the second of these experiments, McCullers employed three patterns of initial associations designed to provide differences in intra-list interference. The first was the pattern which guided construction of competitive lists employed by Spence and co-workers: a strong association between the stimulus member and response member of one pair; strong associations between the stimulus members of other pairs and the response member of the first pair and weak associations with their own response members; and strong associations among stimulus members. Changed from this pattern in the second pattern were associations between stimulus members of other pairs and the response member of the first pair. They were of zero or low strength. Changed from the first pattern in the third pattern were associations among stimulus members; they were presumably of zero or low strength. With strong initial associations, patterns of associations had no differential effects; with weak associations, learning was progressively slower with the second, third, and first of the patterns.

Shapiro (1963b) constructed one list (noncompetitive) of four pairs with high and of four pairs with low initial associative strengths between stimulus members and responses to response members. In another list (competitive), stimulus and response members were paired so that each stimulus member of the pairs with high initial associative strength between stimulus and response member was paired not with that response member but with the response member of one of the other pairs of high initial associative strength. These lists were learned under 50% and 100% ORM by 80 fifth-grade boys and girls from among those children used to obtain word associations when they were in Grade 4. Half of the children had high and half had low commonality scores for their word associations.

Fewer trials to criterion were required for pairs of high than of low initial associative strength, for noncompetitive than competitive pairings, for high than for low commonality scores, and under 100% than under 50% ORM. Of two significant interactions only one was of importance, the interaction of initial associative strength and pairings. With noncompetitive pairings, the means of trials to criterion for high and low initial associative strengths were 4.95 and 12.33, respectively, while for competitive pairings the means were identical at 24.13. Although the latter pair of means were equal rather than showing faster acquisition with low than with high initial associative strength, the competitive pairings clearly reduced the difference in relative acquisition rate and slowed the rates relative to those for noncompetitive pairings.

Wicklund, Palermo, and Jenkins (1964) based their lists on norms for fourth-grade children obtained by Palermo and Jenkins (1964b). The response members of one list were primary associations to the stimulus members; the response members of the other two lists were associations of intermediate and low strength. Within the first list, half of the primaries had been given by 49% or more of the subjects and half had been given by less than 19% of the subjects. Half of the response members of the other two lists were for words which had strong primaries; half were for words which had weak primaries. In each of two experiments these lists were learned by fourth-grade children to criteria of three consecutive errorless trials or a maximum of 15 trials. In the second experiment, however, the children had one familiarization trial with the stimulus and response pairs prior to the first anticipation trial.

In both experiments, rate of acquisition was related directly to initial strength of associations between stimulus members and response members. With the list with primaries as response members, those of high strength were acquired more rapidly than those of low strength in the first but not in the second experiment. With the other two lists, differences between acquisition of responses to words which had high strength primaries and of responses to words which had low strength primaries were negligible. For comparable lists and pairs, fewer errors occurred in the second than in the first experiment.

Beginning with Castaneda, Fahel, and Odom, the subjects of the preceding experiments have been children. With adults as subjects, even with lists as long as 35 pairs, Jenkins (in press) was unable to demonstrate faster acquisition of response members of high than of low initial association strengths as specified by "free" association norms. Again with adults as subjects, even under relatively difficult conditions of presentation Haun (1960) failed to obtain differences in rate of acquisition between response members of high and low initial strengths of association with stimulus members.

One of the two lists of Postman's (1962) second experiment had stimulus members of high counted frequency; the other list had stimulus members of low frequency. Half of the stimulus members of each list were paired with response members which, by free association norms, were the primary response to each stimulus member. The other half of the stimulus members of each list had response members which, by free association norms, were weakly associated with the stimulus members. For the list with stimulus members of high frequency, there was a slight inverse relationship between acquisition rate and strength of associations between stimulus members and response members. For the list with stimulus members of low frequency, acquisition rate was a direct function of associative strength. Disregarding strength of associations between stimulus members and response members, learning was markedly faster with stimulus members of high than with those of low frequency.

The lists of J. T. Spence's (1963b) Experiment I consisted of four sets of three pairs of adjectives from Haagen's (1949) list. The presumed strengths of initial stimulus-response relationships within each set were as follows:

Type of pair	Stimulus member		Response member
HC	S		R
LC-E	S		R
LC-C	S		R

The solid lines indicate strong and the broken lines weak initial associations; direction of the arrowhead indicates direction of the association. Within each set strong initial associations exist between the stimulus members of HC and LC-E pairs and between those members and the response member of the HC pair. The initial association between the stimulus member and response member of the LC-E pair is weak. Weak initial associations exist between the stimulus member of the LC-C pair and all other stimulus and response members. Weak initial associations also exist between the stimulus members of the HC and LC-E pairs and the response member of the LC-C pair and among the response members of the three pairs. The particular initial association strengths and derivative patterns of relationships were expected to produce interference with acquisition of LC-E pairs. HC pairs would presumably benefit from the strong initial association between stimulus and response members and LC-C pairs would presumably be subject to minimum intra-list interference.

For parallel lists, means of correct responses were 39.8 and 42.4 for HC pairs, 22.7 and 23.6 for LC-E pairs, and 29.2 and 29.8 for LC-C pairs. Thus, as expected, the strong initial association strength between the stimulus member and response member of the HC pairs led to relatively rapid learning but the strong initial association between the stimulus member of the LC-E pairs and the response members of the HC pairs occasioned interference with the occurrence of response members of the LC-E pairs and thus retarded their acquisition relative to the LC-C pairs.

In Spence's Experiment II, strength of initial associations was specified by probabilities of occurrence of response members as word associations (Russell & Jenkins, 1954) rather than by ratings of associative strengths between members of pairs of stimuli. Added to the types of pairs of the paradigm above were pairs designated HC-C, for which a strong forward association existed between the stimulus member and response member of the pair but not between those members and the stimulus and response members of any other pair. In this experiment, initial backward associations between response members and stimulus members of all pairs were all presumably weak. The HC pairs of Experiment I were redesignated HC-E. There were five pairs of each type to yield a 20-pair list.

The means of trials to one perfect recitation were 2.50 for HC-E pairs, 2.91 for HC-C pairs, 6.27 for LC-E pairs, and 6.23 for LC-C pairs. While the more rapid acquisition of the former two types of pairs was expected and consistent with the results of Experiment I, the failure to obtain faster acquisition of LC-C than of LC-E pairs was not. Suggested as an explanation of the latter finding was early development of a discrimination between HC-E and HC-C pairs, on the one hand, and LC-E and LC-C pairs on the other hand with, consequently, little or no interference of response members of HC-E pairs with acquisition of response members of LC-E pairs. Experiment II was designed to investigate the proffered explanation.

For the experimental list of Experiment III, each stimulus member was paired with a response member with which, by word-association norms, the initial association strength was weak. But each stimulus member had a strong initial association with the response member of another pair within the list. For the control list, the response members were the same but there were weak initial associations between the stimulus members and both paired and other response members.

More correct responses were made during the 15 trials with the control list than with the experimental list. While only 6 of 20 subjects who were administered the latter list exhibited overt cross-association intrusions, these subjects acquired the list less rapidly than those subjects who did not exhibit such intrusions.

The experimental and control lists employed by J. T. Spence and Lair (1964) paralleled the lists of Spence's Experiment III: the only important difference was the use of eight rather than of 12 pairs as previously. During 15 trials with the control list, schizophrenics made 87.8 and normals 83.4 correct responses; with the experimental list, schizophrenics made 106.7 and normals 110.9 correct responses. As in the preceding experiment, for both schizophrenics and normals strong initial associations between stimulus members of each pair and response members of some other pair slowed acquisition.

Association hierarchies for individual subjects were the basis for Coleman's (1963) selection of 10 to 13 pairs of noun-adjective paired associates. The response members of each pair had the same latencies as responses to the stimulus members but differed in the number of associations which had preceded them. The paired associates with response members whose occurrence had been preceded by many associations were considered high interference; the paired associates with response members whose occurrence had been preceded by few associations were considered low interference.

These paired associates, along with enough filler paired associates to bring the list to 27, were presented with *is* between members. Recall trials continued until subjects recalled 20 or more of the response members correctly. A one-minute interval filled with adding two-digit numbers was interpolated between joint presentation of stimulus and response members and presentation of stimulus members alone. A retention test was administered from 7 to 14 days later.

The mean of 15.0 errors with low-interference paired associates during acquisition was significantly lower than the mean of 18.5 errors with high-interference paired associates. Fewer errors occurred with low-interference paired associates than with high-interference paired associates in 122 of the matched pairs, and the converse in 73 pairs. In the retention test, the means of errors were 6.38 for the low-interference and 7.77 for the high-interference paired associates. Seventy-four of the former were retained better than the latter; retention was poorer for 38.

Instead of words, Underwood and Keppel's (1963) lists consisted of nine letter pairs of high (HA) or low (LA) initial forward strengths of associations between the stimulus member and response member of each pair. Other response members and other stimulus members within a list along with letters from outside of a list were identified as possible sources of interference with strengthening of the association between a particular stimulus member and the response to its response member. All three sources were stronger within the LA list than within the HA list. These lists were administered to different groups of subjects for 2, 4, 6, 10, 15, or 25 trials; retention was tested 1 day or 7 days later by a recall trial and four additional relearning trials.

For each number of trials, acquisition was consistently better with the HA list than with the LA list. When degree of learning of individual pairs was equated in terms of expected recall after 3 seconds, whether tested after 1 day or 7 days, retention of HA and LA pairs was equal. For pairs which had been experienced through different numbers of trials but which were equal in expected recall after 3 seconds, again HA and LA pairs were retained equally 1 day or 7 days later. In general, therefore, amount retained was a function of degree of acquisition but not of rate of acquisition per se.

For pairs whose strengths of stimulus-response associations were based on Underwood and Richardson's (1956) norms, Underwood and Schulz (1960b) report a similar direct relationship. S. Epstein and Levitt (1962) also found faster learning of pairs with high initial associative strengths between stimulus members and response members than of pairs with low initial associative strengths.

Providing indirect support for a conclusion of a direct relationship between acquisition rate and initial associative strength as inferred from word associations are studies in which rate of concept formation is a function of parameters of associations between stimuli and responses such as their absolute strength, rank, and variability (e.g., Freedman & Mednick, 1958; Mednick & Halpern, 1962; Schulz, Miller, & Radtke, 1963; Underwood & Richardson, 1956).

Instead of words, Wallace (1964) employed stimuli which were combinations of three values along each of four physical dimensions of color, form, number, and number of borderlines. When limited to responses of naming values along two of these dimensions, subjects responded in terms of color-form more often than in terms of number-color. Thus, initial strengths of associations were presumably stronger for the former than for the latter responses.

These stimuli were then used in an experiment on concept formation. Across six combinations of auditory or visual feedback of mild, moderate or strong intensity and for all but the verbal-high combination, fewer total instances were required for subjects to acquire color-form concepts than to acquire number-color concepts.

In addition to the preceding results, indirect support for a conclusion of a direct relationship between acquisition rate and initial associative strength comes from results of studies in which word-association norms have been used to construct chains of mediating responses and to specify response-mediated similarity among stimulus members (Jenkins, 1963a).

SUMMARY

Initial strengths of associations between members of pairs have been specified by ratings or by probabilities or orders of occurrence of responses in word-association tests. By either basis of specification, although the experimental evidence is not extensive and some is indirect, available findings for words and for letters suggest a direct relationship between acquisition rate and initial strength of associations between the stimulus and response members of a pair. The relationship is seemingly less pronounced with adult subjects for whom strength is specified by probabilities of responses obtained as free associations. Moreover, the particular patterns of initial strengths of associations between and among stimulus and response members can be expected to have differential effects on acquisition rate.

CHAPTER 4

Theoretical Analyses

D escribed thus far were findings of relationships among meaningfulness and other attributes of discrete stimuli and of pairs of stimuli and findings of relationships between some of these attributes and rate of acquisition of correct responses of PA tasks. This network of empirical generalizations—which might be called a low-order theory—is a useful summary of demonstrated relationships. Also, this network is a convenient way of preceding from one of the inter-related concepts to others; such derivations are aided by the relatively precise equations for some of the component relationships which Noble (1963) has formulated.

The theoretical analyses of interest here, however, are not such networks of empirical generalizations involving meaningfulness per se but rather attempts to account for some of the component relationships, particularly those of meaningfulness of stimulus members and of response members to acquisition rate, by means of more general stimulus-response concepts and principles such as contiguity, similarity, and frequency. The various theoretical analyses of the role of meaningfulness of discrete and paired stimuli considered here have usually been in terms of these attributes as properties of or as bases for inferring more general properties of stimulus members, of response members, and of relationships between stimulus and response members. Following an overview of attributes of stimuli are summaries of various specific analyses of the roles in PA learning of attributes of stimulus members, of response members, and of relationships between them. Then described are approaches to the confirmation of these analyses.

OVERVIEW AND SPECIFIC ANALYSES

Overview

Assessment of attributes of stimuli is or should be preliminary to use of those stimuli in learning tasks in general and in PA lists in particular. To refer to attributes of stimuli, however, is misleading. Actually, the attributes are of relationships between stimuli and responses to them. By convention and for convenience, often with consequent confusion, attributes of relationships between stimuli and responses are referred to as attributes of the stimuli.

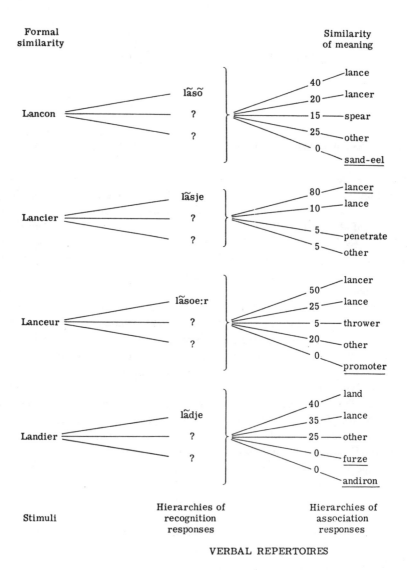

Fig. 2. Hypothesized stimulus-response elements and relationships of illustrative repertoires for each of four verbal stimuli for English-speaking subjects naive with respect to French. The underlined association responses are among the English equivalents of the French words. Indicated also are the bases for formal and semantic similarity among these stimuli.

The relationships between stimuli and responses, among those stimuli, and among the responses to them necessary for understanding various theoretical proposals, are schematized in Fig. 2. Four French words are the stimuli. The hypothesized responses to those stimuli are for groups of or by individual English-speaking subjects naive with respect to French. These responses comprise recognition responses to the stimuli and responses of an association hierarchy. Together they are the verbal repertoire of each stimulus. A more exhaustive analysis of antecedents to and properties of verbal repertoires than is presented here can be found in Goss (1963).

Verbal repertoires can be limited to single words. Formal and semantic similarity are defined by relationships between or among stimuli and also between or among stimuli and resultant responses. When two or more stimuli are paired and presented as units of a PA list, attributes both of their verbal repertoires and their similarity are potentially significant variables. The particular values of these variables constitute part of the initial states of an experimental arrangement.

RECOGNITION AND ASSOCIATION RESPONSES

For word and letter sequences, recognition responses is a convenient name for responses of spelling or pronouncing all or part of the word or sequence, whether or not in an approved or correct manner. For stimuli which are not words, nonverbal stimuli, recognition responses is a convenient name for the one or more conventional labels for the nonverbal stimuli, or for attempts to provide such labels.

Each stimulus of Fig. 2 is shown as eliciting one or more recognition responses. Words and letter sequences can be presented aurally or visually, and responses may be oral or graphic to generate four combinations of stimulus and response modalities and hence four possible repertoires of recognition responses. Extent of congruence among repertoires of recognition responses obtained under the four combinations is of practical and theoretical significance.

In addition to and partly contingent on the form (different pronunciations, spellings) of recognition responses, each French word is shown as eliciting several words which, collectively, are designated responses of an association hierarchy for that word. The numbers in parentheses are hypothetical percentages of subjects making the particular responses as their first responses to a word other than recognition of the word or hypothetical percentages of occurrence of those responses by an individual subject. Alternatively, for individual subjects, numbers might be inserted in the parentheses to indicate order of occurrence of each word in multiple associations. The underlined associations are among the English equivalents of the French words; all but one is presumed to have zero initial strength.

Recognition responses have been assessed by means of recognition thresholds (W. P. Brown, 1961). The complete data of such assessments constitute estimates of probabilities of occurrence of both correct and incorrect

recognition responses under each of several combinations of values of duration, intensity or amplitude, contrast between stimulus and surround or
signal-to-noise ratio, and other parameters of the presentation of stimuli.

Latency, form, and duration of each recognition response to a stimulus may
be assessed whether stimuli are presented below, at, or above the threshold
of correct recognition. Ratings of pronunciability of a word and, conceivably,
of its familiarity, emotionality, and other attributes are known or are presumed to be correlates of latency, form, and duration of recognition
responses (Goss, 1963). Such ratings can also be viewed as indicants of
those attributes. Analyses of the relationships between rating as reference or
criterion responses and attributes of recognition responses in terms of more
general stimulus-response concepts and principles are both recent and incomplete (Bousfield, 1961; Goss, 1963).

Responses of the association hierarchy of each word can be obtained under
variations in parameters of presentation which are the same as those employed for assessments of recognition responses. The critical difference is one
of instructions: for assessments of associations, overt occurrence of recognition responses is usually forbidden. The number of different forms of association responses, and the latency and duration of each response, are attributes
of association hierarchies for groups or an individual subject. Meaningfulness as specified by M_a, M_n, and M_r is either defined by or is presumably
related to latency, form, and, perhaps, duration of association responses.

Frequencies of occurrence of associations produced by subjects are one
way of estimating initial strengths of relationships between stimulus members
and response members. Selection of associations and ratings of attributes
of pairs provide estimates of initial strengths of relationships between stimulus members and responses which have been supplied by the experimenter.

SIMILARITY

Words and their response repertoires cannot be considered in isolation.
Both in terms of overlap of letters or phonemes, particularly letters or phonemes in the same order, and in terms of forms of recognition responses, each
stimulus of a set can be conceived as at different distances from or of varying
similarity to other stimuli within and outside of the particular set. Distance
or similarity thus specified is often labeled formal similarity or similarity
in terms of common elements. The four words of Fig. 2 are of high formal
similarity.

The two responses highest in the association hierarchies of the top three
words are the same. They differ only in the hypothesized relative percentages
of occurrence. Words vary in congruence between percentages of occurrence
of the same associations or, conversely, in degree to which they elicit different responses. Similarity thus specified is often called similarity of meaning

or semantic similarity. (More analytically, overlap of associations can also be conceived as similarity in terms of common elements.) Both formal and semantic similarity can be quantified; techniques for doing so are described subsequently in Chapter 5 on similarity in PA learning.

Specific Analyses

The overview of attributes of verbal and nonverbal stimuli has been for those stimuli in general rather than as paired to constitute PA lists. Theoretical analyses of PA learning have often started not with attributes of stimuli but with already constituted pairs. Attributes of stimulus members, of response members, and of relationships between them are then hypothesized which might predict or might account for the anticipated or the observed course of acquisition. Some analyses, particularly those of Noble (1963) and Underwood and Schulz (1960a), because they are recent and readily available, are treated less extensively than would otherwise be warranted. Ignored are various relatively casual suggestions or suggestions specific to the data which have been advanced in the discussion section of reports of experiments.

STIMULUS MEMBERS

During the past 25 years the starting point of virtually all attempts to relate meaningfulness to properties of stimulus members has been Gibson's (1940) definition of *meaning* as "a characteristic of a verbal or visual item which serves to differentiate it from other items" (p. 205). Gibson did not distinguish between *meaning* and *meaningfulness*. In fact, she apparently treats the two concepts as interchangeable. Presumably, then, the greater the meaning or meaningfulness of a stimulus the greater its differentiation from other items. From this definition of meaning and postulates 9 and 10 (p. 207) in particular, she derives four predictions, two of which are pertinent here:

XV If differentiation has been set up within a list, less generalization will occur in learning a new list which includes the same stimulus items paired with different responses; and the trials required to learn the new list will tend to be reduced by reduction of the internal generalization (p. 222).

XVI More trials will be required to learn a list in which the stimulus items are nonsense syllables, than one in which they are meaningful words. . . . An exception to this prediction should be a case in which the stimulus items are *mutually synonymous* meaningful words. This situation has actually been shown, in the Smith College Laboratory, to increase learning difficulty as compared with unrelated stimulus words (p. 223).

The vague, perhaps circular, definition of meaning is one shortcoming of Gibson's analysis. Also, meaning and meaningfulness were not distinguished explicitly. Stimulus items may differ in physical characteristics; but these were probably not the differences which Gibson considered the basis of different meanings. The particular characteristics of stimulus items or of subjects' responses to those items which did differentiate among them, however, were, at most, specified by example rather than by general criteria. Consequently, differences in meaning could not be specified or quantified adequately as was the case for procedures to establish meaning or meaningfulness experimentally.

Morikawa's (1959a) notion of *stimulus discrimination*, which he equated with Gibson's stimulus differentiation, is subject to the same strictures. Nor are these shortcomings satisfactorily overcome by Saltz's (1960) two statements: "differentiation of the term can be defined as increasing as a function of the frequency with which the term has been presented and responded to (e.g., 'familiarization' training, Noble, 1955)," and "increased differentiation of the stimulus term is assumed to increase the probability that the stimulus term will elicit its appropriate response" (pp. 3-4).

Miller and Dollard (1941) did not consider meaning or meaningfulness as so labeled. But they did suggest a basis for differentiating among stimulus items in addition to physical characteristics. That basis was responses which produce cues: "The stimuli which are produced by the subject's own responses have exactly the same properties as any other stimuli . . . to the extent that these stimuli are distinctive, they have cue value" (pp. 54-55).

Gibson's and Miller and Dollard's analyses—respectively, meaning with no basis, and a basis with no meaning—Sheffield integrated. He defined the meaning of a stimulus as "the complex of responses that is aroused by the stimulus pattern because of past learning" (1946, p. 11). This definition was further refined into intrinsic meaning—"the part of the meaning that is based on stimulations provided by the stimulus-object which is the source of the stimulus pattern"—and extrinsic meaning—"that part of the meaning that is not part of the intrinsic meaning" (p. 12). Differences in intrinsic meaning and in extrinsic meaning are differences in perceptual responses to stimulus items. Differences in the stimuli produced by these responses were viewed as not only supplementing differences in physical characteristics but also as possibly more potent bases of differentiation than physical characteristics. Orientation to more discriminable features of stimulus items is a third source of differentiation based on subjects' responses to stimulus items. Sheffield recognized that a conception of meaningfulness in part in terms of the number of responses which constituted the extrinsic meaning of a stimulus might imply greater trial-to-trial variability in response-produced stimuli. In turn, such variability might retard acquisition of correct responses to stimulus members, an implication contrary to the apparent direct relationship between meaningfulness of stimulus members and acquisition rate.

However, through steps which are not fully developed, Sheffield generated the more satisfactory implication of a direct relationship between acquisition rate and specificity-constancy of the meaning of a word.

Mandler's (1954) symbolic responses are essentially equivalent to Sheffield's perceptual responses as are R. L. Weiss's (1958) identifying responses. Neither Mandler nor Weiss distinguished between intrinsic meaning and extrinsic meaning. For Mandler, both degree of differentiation of symbolic responses and strength of attachment of inhibitory responses to symbolic responses influence acquisition of new responses to old stimuli.

In Cook and Kendler's (1956) analysis of paired-associates learning "the mediating chain of S-R connections is presumed to be the *sine qua non* for learning to occur." The first link in such a chain is implicit responses to stimulus members. For McGuire (1961) "the first postulated link in this habit chain [for a paired-associates item] involves associating with each S a mediating stimulus-producing response, r. This r is a partial representation of the S to which it becomes connected, encoding some aspect of the S which discriminates that S from the others in the list" (p. 335).

Sheffield's analysis of the bases of effects of meaningfulness of stimulus members was also the starting point of Goss's (1963) analysis. Goss substituted verbal mediating responses for Sheffield's perceptual responses, and repetition or naming (recognition) responses and responses of association hierarchies for, respectively, Sheffield's intrinsic meaning and extrinsic meaning. One advantage of the latter changes is a somewhat more satisfactory specification of extrinsic meaning than "that part of the meaning that is not part of the intrinsic meaning." Goss proposed that meaningfulness of stimulus members was, in general, a direct indicant of speed of occurrence and completion and of stability of form of repetition and naming or recognition responses. Also, meaningfulness of stimulus members was considered a direct indicant of dissimilarity among responses of association hierarchies, synonymous or near-synonymous stimulus members excepted. Dissimilar repetition and naming or recognition responses, it was proposed, led to response-mediated dissimilarity among stimulus members based on more stable and dissimilar response-produced stimuli, and on orienting responses to more distinctive features of the stimulus members. The latter consequence might facilitate acquisition of new discriminative responses to the stimulus members not only by reducing similarity among but also by occasioning a further reduction in their similarity through distinctive verbal responses to those more discriminable features.

Faster and more stable recognition responses were also conceived as allowing more time for the rehearsal of those responses and for occurrence and rehearsal of association responses to stimulus members, of anticipations of recognition responses to response members, and of association responses to response members. Finally, fast, stable, and dissimilar recognition responses presumably facilitated division of the stimuli of a list into intra-list and extra-list stimuli and into stimulus members or response members. Meaningfulness of stimulus members, therefore, was not considered important as such but as a direct indicant or positive correlate of properties and consequences of, particularly, recognition responses to stimulus members.

Noble (1955) had earlier suggested that integration of recognition responses to stimuli of serial lists, with consequent lowered stimulus variability, might be the basis for the direct relationship between meaningfulness and rate of serial learning. That integration of stimulus members influences PA learning has been suggested by Baddelay (1961b).

Underwood and Schulz (1960a, pp. 293-295) rejected stimulus integration as a basis for facilitative effects of meaningfulness of stimulus members. More recently, however, S. E. Newman (1960) attributed Underwood and Schulz's findings of a direct relationship between rate of acquisition of stimulus members and their pronunciability to the greater integration of mediating responses to stimulus members of high than to those of low pronunciability. Newman (1961) later distinguished three types of repetition responses to letter sequences: pronouncing, spelling and "a response to some smaller-than-presented number of elements comprising the term." Hard-to-pronounce stimulus members are conceived as slowing acquisition by reducing discrimination among stimulus members, and by allowing less time for other events. In a later analysis, Newman (1963a) has elaborated the responses comprising the hierarchy and has suggested factors which determine which response is strengthened relative to the others.

RESPONSE MEMBERS

Gibson (1940) was simply not concerned with meaningfulness of response members. For Sheffield (1946), meaningfulness of response members was a direct indicant of response patterning defined as "the coordination of successive response elements into a sequence that behaves as a single unit of response" (p. 15). Response patterning was conceived as reducing the number of connections to be learned as well as increasing the distinctiveness of response-produced stimuli at successive points in a sequence and reducing interference due to response similarity and stimulus similarity.

Morikawa's *R item-acquisition* is probably the same as Sheffield's notion of a reduction in the number of connections to be learned. Mentioned as pertinent was Mandler's (1954) treatment of response integration. Response integration has also been emphasized by Cook and Kendler (1956), R. L. Weiss (1958), Underwood and Schulz (1960a, pp. 284-290), Newman (1960, 1963a), McGuire (1961), and Baddelay (1961b). For Newman, response integration may involve strengthening of mediating pronouncing responses to the response member, strengthening of overt spelling responses to stimuli produced by pronouncing responses, and strengthening of connections among components of the overt spelling responses. Implicit in all of the preceding suggestions about response integration is the related notion that more integrated responses will be available sooner and more consistently than less integrated responses.

Goss (1963) viewed meaningfulness of response members as a correlate or indicant of essentially the same properties and consequences of recognition responses to response members or to stimulus members. However, greater weight was given to the notion that faster and more stable recognition responses would increase the likelihood of their occurrence in short anticipation or recall intervals, provide more opportunity for rehearsal of those responses as well as of association responses to both stimulus members and response members, and facilitate identification of response members as belonging to a particular list and as response members rather than stimulus members.

The number of different responses to response members indicated by meaningfulness was considered of little or no importance except perhaps as a basis for indirect associations between stimulus members or stimuli produced by responses to stimulus members and recognition responses to response members. In contrast, Noble (1963) argues that meaningfulness in the form of the number of responses associated with the response member is the critical factor. The general principles underlying this expectation, however, have not been stated.

RELATIONSHIPS BETWEEN STIMULUS AND RESPONSE MEMBERS

Gibson did not consider relationships between stimulus members and response members of pairs of lists. *Direct mediation* and *mediation with associated perceptions* were the "mechanisms" hypothesized by Sheffield. The former was sequences of verbal stimulus, perceptual response and stimulus, verbal response and the latter was sequences of verbal stimulus, two or more perceptual responses and stimuli, verbal response. Subsequently, Sheffield suggested that "the subject may have no prior practice at the direct stimulus-response connections between the words, but two words, in combination, frequently suggest a perceptual response, or a series of perceptual responses that links the two words through past experience" (p. 29). The greater the meaningfulness of stimulus and of response members, the greater the likelihood of such mediated connections between members of a pair.

Sheffield's suggestion had been partially anticipated in notions of mediate associations (e.g., Peters, .935) and associative aids (e.g., Reed, 1918a, 1918b). Underwood and Schulz's recent version was advanced to account for the associative stage of PA learning. Their associative probability hypothesis was "the greater the number of associates elicited by a stimulus, the greater is the probability that one of them will link up with another item" (p. 296). As Goss (1963) has noted, however, a possible dilemma of these formulations is more mediated associations between a stimulus member and responses to response members of other pairs than to the response to the response member paired with that stimulus. The implication is greater retardation rather than facilitation of learning.

Goss distinguished between direct and indirect relationships. One form of direct relationship is a pre-established association between the last letter or syllable of stimulus members and the response of saying the first letter or syllable of the response members. Baddelay (1961a) has labeled this relationship S-R compatibility. Also, associations might have been established between stimulus members as a complete unit and the complete responses to response members. Another form of direct association is based on similarity of members of a pair to two previously associated syllables or units. For example, the word PILSEN provides a basis for generalization of a strong association between PIL and SAN, SUN, SIN, or SON, as well as PIL and ZEN, ZAN, ZUN, ZIN, or ZON.

One form of indirect relationship is mediation by association responses to the stimulus member, to the response member, or to both members of a pair. An example of the first is NAV-SUR mediated by the association "navy" to NAV. An example of the second is the same pairing mediated by "officer" as a response to SUR, and an example of the latter is the same pairing mediated by the sequence "navy, officer," which was based on the former as a response to NAV and the latter as a response to SUR. Like Sheffield's and Underwood and Schulz's proposals, the unresolved dilemma is why the presumed increasing numbers of associations to stimulus members and response members would not bring about greater amounts of response-mediated interference and thus retard acquisition.

Goss describes another form of indirect relationship by means of principles. The manner of construction of most PA lists, however, is such that this form of indirect relationship is probably a rare occurrence.

APPROACHES

The general and more specific approaches to confirmation of features of the preceding theoretical analyses are previewed here briefly. The procedures and pertinent findings are elaborated in the next three chapters. Also described briefly here are the stimulus-response elements and relationships both initially and as changed during acquisition which are emphasized in each specific approach.

Description

One general approach to confirmation of proposed bases of effects of meaningfulness of stimulus and of response members has been transfer to acquisition of PA lists from prior experiences in an experimental context of familiarization and satiation, of stimulus predifferentiation or acquired distinctiveness training, and of experimental induction of meaning and meaningfulness. Verbal reports of the use of pre-experimentally acquired associative aids provide some support for notions of effects of meaningfulness of stimulus and response members based on indirect or response-mediated associations between stimulus members and recognition responses to them on one hand and recognition responses to response members on the other. Therefore, findings of investigations in which mediate or response-mediated associations have been established in an experimental context are of some pertinence. These investigations, too, have involved transfer from one or more lists to a final list.

A general approach which has not involved transfer has been manipulation of the numbers of and associations among elements of stimulus members and response members. Closely related to such investigations are experiments on transfer from stimulus compounds to elements thereof or the converse.

The procedures for familiarization, acquired-distinctiveness training, and induction of meaning-meaningfulness have often been used as somewhat, if not completely, interchangeable. In the present context, familiarization refers to training in which the stimuli have been verbal and the specific procedures have been designed to strengthen pre-experimentally established recognition responses. Predifferentiation, acquired-distinctiveness training, or training to establish response-mediated dissimilarity refers to conditioning or associating different, new verbal or motor responses to each different nonverbal or verbal stimulus. Experimental induction of meaning and meaningfulness refers to conditioning or associating one or more new responses to each different stimulus. The same or different new responses may be conditioned to each stimulus. Conditioning one different, new response to each stimulus is the same as acquired-distinctiveness training. Contingent on the relationships to previously established recognition responses, these new responses might function as new recognition responses or as additional association responses.

The paradigm for verbal satiation has typically consisted of three sessions and two different tasks (Lambert & Jakobovits, 1960; Yelen & Schulz, 1963). In the first and third sessions, stimuli are rated by semantic differentiation. In the second session, recognition responses to the stimuli are repeated rapidly during a fixed time interval. The stimuli have usually been familiar words but, except for this nonessential difference, satiation is essentially the same as familiarization by repetition of recognition responses. The before and after sessions of semantic differentiation are also not essential to defining satiation.

These specifications of familiarization and satiation, acquired-distinctiveness training, and induction of meaning-meaningfulness are in terms of training procedures. Contingent on similarity among initiating stimuli, among mediating responses and stimuli, and among terminating stimuli, and on the particular patterns of relationships among these elements, any of these three training procedures may lead to the conditions or mechanisms of response-mediated dissimilarity and discrimination or of response-mediated similarity and generalization (Dollard & Miller, 1950; Goss, 1955).

Implicitly or explicitly, most of the theoretical analyses assume some type of relationship between meaningfulness and similarity of stimulus and of response members. Accordingly, as a background to such considerations, scalings of similarity of stimuli and data on the role of similarity of stimulus and of response members in PA learning are reviewed before summarizing and evaluating data on effects of familiarization and satiation, acquired-distinctiveness training, and induction of meaning and meaningfulness. Examined finally are selected data on manipulation of numbers of and associations among elements of stimulus and response members, on response-mediated associations between stimulus members and recognition responses to response members, and on stimulus compounds.

Emphases

Figure 3 summarizes the more important of the stimulus-response elements and relationships and changes therein presumed in one or more of the theoretical analyses and in the consequent general and more specific approaches to confirmation of those analyses. The stimuli are those of Fig. 2 now paired as the stimulus members and response members of two paired-associates units. Both formal and semantic similarity between stimulus members, between response members, and between stimulus members and response members are high.

When overt occurrence of recognition responses to stimulus members is required, reduction in latency and duration of those responses and fixation of their form might require a number of trials. Should the stimuli produced by fast, stable recognition responses of repeating entire stimulus members be less similar than the stimulus members per se, those recognition responses and stimuli are the presumed basis of acquired distinctiveness of cues or response-mediated dissimilarity.

Occurrence of association responses is partly contingent on length of the association interval; often the interval is too short for the occurrence of any or more than one association response. Were the anticipation interval sufficiently long for the occurrence of dissimilar association responses and stimuli, these would also provide response-mediated dissimilarity. But occurrence of the same association response to each stimulus, as might be the case were "Lancier" and "Lanceur" the stimuli, would occasion acquired equivalence of cues or response-mediated similarity.

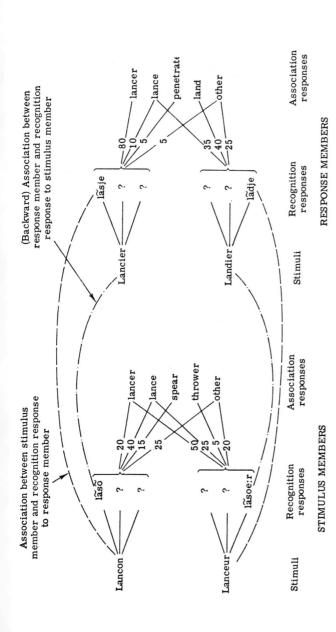

Fig. 3. Some of the more important of the stimulus-response elements and relationships and changes therein presumed in one or more of the theoretical analyses of PA tasks. Both formal and semantic similarity between stimulus members, between response members, and between stimulus and response members are high. Formation of associations between stimulus members and recognition responses to response members is the criterion achievement. But formation of (backward) associations between response members and recognition responses to stimulus members is sometimes tested. Not shown are possible relationships of association responses to stimulus members to each other or to association responses to response members and possible relationships of association responses to response members to each other and to association responses to stimulus members.

When overt occurrence of recognition responses is not required, subjects might learn to fixate first at the center of each stimulus to minimize the time necessary for maximally effective reception of the only differential cues, "c" in "Lancier" and "d" in "Landier." Fixation of such more distinctive aspects of the stimulus members along with the truncated recognition responses and consequent stimuli also constitute response-mediated dissimilarity.

Subjects are usually required to anticipate or recall the complete recognition response to response members. Accordingly, acquisition should proceed faster when those responses are elicited and completed rapidly in stable form. Only the initial part of the response need be conditioned to all or part of paired stimulus members, or to stimuli produced by recognition and association responses to stimulus members. Chaining of the elements comprising the recognition response is at least a semi-independent set of changes which may have taken place previously or may occur simultaneously.

Familiarization and satiation can be viewed as occasioning prior changes primarily in recognition responses to stimulus members and to response members. Contingent on the specific task, acquired-distinctiveness training may influence recognition responses to stimulus members, association responses to stimulus members, or both. Induction of meaning and meaningfulness focusses on association responses; recognition responses may also be changed.

Prior associations may exist or may be established between association responses to stimulus members and recognition responses to response members, the converse, and also between association responses. Such relationships introduce the possibility of mediate associations or response-mediated associations. Finally, in general, the greater the number of components of stimulus members and of response members, the longer the time required to integrate recognition responses to stimulus members, to response members, or to both as well as to select maximally dissimilar components, primarily of stimulus members. Manipulation of number and strength of associations between elements of stimulus and of response members is pertinent as is transfer from compounds to elements and the converse.

CHAPTER 5

Similarity

Considered first are bases of and more specific techniques for scaling similarity between and among stimuli along with some results of such scalings. Findings of experiments on relationships between similarity of stimulus and of response members and acquisition rate as well as backward recall of stimulus members are then summarized and evaluated. Finally, available data on effects of similarity in combination with meaningfulness on acquisition and backward recall are examined.

SCALINGS

Bases and Techniques

The bases for scalings of similarity between and among stimuli have been relative distance(s) along physical dimensions, common letters or phonemes, common meaning, and subjects' reactions in the form of judgments or interstimulus generalization errors. The same or different grammatical function is a possible additional basis which is ignored here.

DISTANCE(S) ALONG PHYSICAL DIMENSIONS

When two or more stimuli lie at different distances from each other along a single physical dimension such as intensity or wave length, the similarity of one stimulus to another is the distance between them along the dimension. Similarity among all members of a set of stimuli can be expressed as the mean of distances between the $n(n-1)/2$ pairs of stimuli. Conceivably, means may be supplemented by or expressed in relation to variances and higher moments of the distributions of distances between pairs.

When two or more stimuli lie at different distances from each other along two or more physical dimensions such as intensity and wave length, the manner of specification of distances is unsettled. Indeed, few, if any, investi-

125

gators have ventured such specification. A possible technique, subject to the stricture of combining "apples" and "pears," is to treat the different dimensions as homogeneous. Distances between members of each pair of stimuli can be calculated by the Euclidean rule. Such distances among all members of a set can be expressed in the same ways as distances among members along a single dimension.

An alternative and preferred technique is to regard each dimension of variation as a separate variable. The minimum requirement for assessment of effects of different degrees of similarity along two dimensions is a complete 2×2 orthogonal design. For differences along n dimensions, the design would entail a minimum of two values along each of the n dimensions combined orthogonally.

Beginning with a pair of complex forms with the same number of points, LaBerge and Lawrence (1957) describe two related techniques for generating matrices of forms with physical specification of equal distances between successive adjacent pairs in columns and in rows in terms of minimum sums of squared distances. Column and row distances need not be the same.

COMMON LETTERS OR PHONEMES

Scalings by common letters yield only relatively gross differences. Typically, lists of high similarity are made up of stimulus members, response members, or both which contain the smallest possible number (provide the greatest overlap or duplication) of different consonants and vowels. The stimulus members, response members, or both of lists of low similarity are constituted of the largest possible number of different consonants and vowels. Illustrative lists representing combinations of CVCs of high or low similarity among stimulus members and among response members with low similarity between stimulus and response members in terms of common elements which are also of high or low M_a may be found in Table A2 in the Appendix.

The ordinal position in which duplication of letters occurs is a possible further determinant of similarity. For example, generalization between JEX and JEZ might be different than generalization between JEX and ZEJ. In allowing for ordinal position, two words of different lengths can be placed side by side at their first letters or at their last letters. Also, their first and last letters might both be placed side by side with the remaining letters occurring sequentially to the right or forward from the first letters, backward from the last letters, and in other arrangements.

Shown in Table 4 are illustrative ratios and resultant percentages for similarity between pairs in terms of common letters in the same ordinal position. First letters were placed side by side and the counting was forward with no skipped letter positions through the last letter of the shorter word. Values for common letters in the same ordinal position are the numerators

TABLE 4

Matrices of Values for Similarity between Pairs of Words in Terms of Common Elements as Specified by Ratios and Resultant Percentages (in Parentheses) of the Same Letters in the Same Ordinal Position from the First Letter of Both Words

	Lancon	Lancier	Lanceur	Landier	Lance	Land	Spear	Despair
Lancon		4/7 (57)	4/7 (57)	3/7 (43)	4/5 (80)	3/4 (75)	0/5 (0)	0/7 (0)
Lancier	4/6 (67)		6/7 (86)	6/7 (86)	4/5 (80)	3/4 (75)	0/5 (0)	1/7 (14)
Lanceur	4/6 (67)	6/7 (86)		5/7 (72)	4/5 (80)	3/4 (75)	0/5 (0)	1/7 (14)
Landier	4/6 (67)	6/7 (86)	5/7 (72)		3/5 (60)	4/4 (100)	0/5 (0)	1/7 (14)
Lance	4/6 (67)	4/7 (57)	4/7 (57)	3/7 (43)		3/4 (75)	0/5 (0)	0/7 (0)
Land	3/6 (50)	3/7 (43)	3/7 (43)	4/7 (57)	3/5 (60)		0/5 (0)	0/7 (0)
Spear	0/6 (0)	0/7 (0)	0/7 (0)	0/7 (0)	0/5 (0)	0/4 (0)		0/7 (0)
Despair	0/6 (0)	1/7 (14)	1/7 (14)	1/7 (14)	0/5 (0)	0/4 (0)	0/5 (0)	

of the ratio; numbers of letters in the words are the denominators. For comparison, these ratios are expressed as percentages. Not reflected in this index is length of runs of common letters, which is a possible future extension of the index. Also, percentages for pairs could be averaged.

Overlap of phonemes has not usually been employed as such. However, such overlap is involved in variations in pronunciation and is often a consequence of overlap of letters. Overlap of phonemes could be scaled explicitly in essentially the same ways as overlap of letters.

COMMON MEANING

Scalings of the common meaning of pairs of stimuli by subjects' judgments in the form of ratings, as described in Chapter 2, are best considered among the techniques of scalings by subjects' reactions others of which are described below. The basis for scalings of similarity by common meaning considered here is associations either produced by or selected by subjects.

Production

Marshall and Cofer (1963) describe and compare 10 indices of what they term word relatedness. These indices were developed in terms of but are not limited to associations which are produced. Of the 10 indices they examined, four are considered here. Described in addition to these four are Rothkopf's (1960) index of overlap, Garskof and Houston's (1963) relatedness coefficient, and Pollio's (1963) degree of cohesiveness.

Computation of all but the Garskof and Houston coefficient can be illustrated by use of the hypothetical repertoires of a recognition response and hierarchies of associations for each of four stimulus words of Table 5. Strengths of presumed recognition responses and of each association are

TABLE 5

Repertoires of Recognition and Association Responses Unique to Each Initiating Stimulus and, for Computation of Indices of Similarity, Rearranged in a Matrix to Show Responses to Any Stimulus as Actual or Possible Responses to Any Other Stimulus; Strength is in Terms of Both Frequencies and Proportions of Response Occurrences

Response	CAT	f	p	LION	f	p	DOG	f	p	WOLF	f	p
Recognition	Cat	100	1.00	Lion	100	1.00	Dog	100	1.00	Wolf	100	1.00
Association												
Primary	Dog	50	.50	Cat	60	.60	Cat	45	.45	Dog	60	.60
Secondary	Mouse	25	.25	Tiger	20	.20	Man	20	.20	Howl	20	.20
Tertiary	Bird	15	.15	Mouse	10	.10	Bite	20	.20	Prowl	10	.10
Quaternary	Lion	10	.10	Bite	10	.10	Wolf	15	.15	Bite	10	.10
Recognition or association												
Cat		100	1.00		60	.60		45	.45			
Lion		10	.10		100	1.00						
Dog		50	.50					100	1.00		60	.60
Wolf								15	.15		100	1.00
association												
Bird		15	.15									
Bite					10	.10		20	.20		10	.10
Howl											20	.20
Man								20	.20			
Mouse		25	.25		10	.10						
Prowl											10	.10
Tiger					20	.20						

expressed in terms of frequency of proportion of their occurrences among 100 subjects. For ease of computation, the repertoires in the upper half have been placed in the matrix of the lower half of the table. In the upper part of the matrix, each initiating stimulus appears as a recognition response or as an association response to the other stimuli. In the lower part of the matrix are all other responses which occurred to any stimulus in alphabetical order.

Similarity of hierarchies and repertoires can be specified between members of possible pairs of n stimuli or among all n stimuli. For extent to which members of a pair have common responses, P. M. Jenkins and Cofer (1957) and Bousfield, Whitmarsh, and Berkowitz (1958) proposed an index of mutual frequency or relatedness. Mutual frequency is defined as the sum of the smaller of the two frequencies of each response common to both stimuli divided by the sum of the total possible responses to each stimulus. For Cat and Lion, the common responses are the recognition or association responses of "Cat" and "Lion" and the association "Mouse." The smaller frequencies of occurrence for these reponses of 60, 10, and 10, respectively, sum to 80. Dividing 80 by 200, the sum of the 100 association responses to Cat and the 100 association responses to Lion, yields an index of .40.

An alternative index, proposed by Rothkopf (1960) and labeled associative overlap (AO), is defined as:

$$AO_{AB} = \sum_{i}^{2n} P_{Ai} P_{Bi}$$

The n most common associations to stimulus A and the n most common associations to stimulus B are determined; thus there are $2n$ associations. For the ith of the $2n$ associations, P_{Ai} is the proportion of occurrences of that response to stimulus A, and P_{Bi} is the proportion of occurrences of that response to stimulus B. These products are computed for the $2n$ responses and then summed. Recognition responses apparently were not but could be included.

For the n of five responses to Cat, including recognition responses, and the n of five responses to Lion, three products are greater than zero ($1.00 \times .60 = .60$; $.10 \times 1.00 = .10$, and $.25 \times .10 = .025$). Because either P_{Ai} or P_{Bi} is zero, seven products are zero. The nonzero products sum to an AO of .725. Excluding recognition responses, AO is .025, the one nonzero product of $.25 \times .10$. No satisfactory data exist as to which of these three indices for hierarchies and repertoires of pairs of stimuli yields, in general, the best predictions of response measures for those stimuli in other assessment situations and in investigations of change.

Similarity among hierarchies and repertoires for all n stimuli of a set can be defined by several different measures including interitem associative strength and indices of total association and of concept cohesiveness. Interitem associative strength (Deese, 1959) is based on those association responses to each stimulus of a set which are recognition responses to the other stimuli of the set. Thus, only the association responses of the middle part (recognition or association) of the matrix of Table 5 are pertinent. Proportions of these association responses to each initiating stimulus are summed and these totals summed and divided by number of initiating stimuli. For the values in Table 5, the index is .60 obtained from $[(.10+.50)+.60+(.45+.15)+.60]/4$.

Both parts of the matrix of Table 5 enter computation of the index of total association which is based on the proportions of all association responses to each stimulus which were also responses to at least one other stimulus. Proportions of such responses to each initiating stimulus are summed; these totals are then summed and divided by the number of initiating stimuli. The sums of proportions for Cat, Lion, Dog, and Wolf are, respectively,

.85(.10+.50+.25), .80(.60+.10+.10), .65(.45+.20), and .70(.60+.10); their sum of 3.00 is divided by 4 to yield a value of .75.

The index of concept cohesiveness is obtained by summing the frequencies or proportions of association responses common to all initiating stimuli and dividing this sum by the sum of the frequencies or proportions of association responses common to any two or more stimuli. In the matrix of Table 5, no association response was common to all initiating stimuli. Therefore, the index of concept cohesiveness is .00.

The relatedness coefficient (RC) developed by Garskof and Houston (1963) permits specification of extent of overlap between multiple associations to each of two words by individual subjects. The definition is

$$RC = \frac{\overline{A} \cdot \overline{B}}{(A \cdot B) - [n^p - (n-1)^p]^2}$$

where A is the m associations to one word, B is the associations to another word n in number, $\overline{A}$ and $\overline{B}$ are the ranks in A and B of the common associations, and p is a fixed number ≥ 0. The following hypothetical orders of associations to the word Cat and to the word Lion by a single subject provide the values necessary to compute RC.

Cat		Lion	
Association	Rank	Association	Rank
Cat	5	Lion	5
Dog	4	Cat	4
Mouse	3	Tiger	3
Bird	2	Mouse	2
Lion	1	Bite	1

Assumed are recognition responses to each stimulus followed by associations. Taking p as 1, the ranks are assigned by $(n-j+1)^p$ where n is the number of associations to the word with the largest number of associations and j is the ordinal position of the a_j association of the series of associations. Recognition responses presumably occur first. The values for A and B are, respectively, (5,4,3,2,1) and (5,4,3,2,1). The values for $\overline{A}$ are (5,3,1). These are the ranks of associations to "cat" which were also associations to "lion." The values for $\overline{B}$ are (4,2,5), the ranks of those same associations to "lion." Substituting these values in the formula gives

$$RC = \frac{(5,3,1) \cdot (4,2,5)}{(5,4,3,2,1) \cdot (5,4,3,2,1) - 1} = .57$$

The RC values obtained by Garskof and Houston (pp. 282-284) for 24 word pairs using both $p=1$ and $p=2$ were correlated with subjects' judgments of the relatedness of members of the pairs by ratings along a 5-in. line. For $p=1$, the rhos ranged from .63 to .90; for $p=2$, the rhos ranged from .65 to .94. When RCs and judgments were averaged for all 20 subjects, the rho between the two measures was .94.

Other measures of similarity among hierarchies of n initiating stimuli are possible. For example, indices of generalization or of mutual frequency might be computed for all possible pairs among n stimuli and then averaged. As with measures for pairs of stimuli, available data do not permit specification of the generally best measure.

Pollio's (1963) degree of cohesiveness (C) characterizes what he labels a W matrix; the matrix is derived from associations to some particular word, S_i, here designated S_1. S_1 might evoke n first associations, R_2, . . . , R_{n+1}. In turn, the n first associations might be regarded as n stimuli, S_2, . . . , S_{n+1}, to each of which the recognition response to S_1 (R_1), and any one of the $n-1$ other associations to S_1, might occur. These relationships can be represented in a matrix in which S_1 and the n associations to it specify $n+1$ rows and R_1 and the associations to S_1 specify $n+1$ columns. A value of 1 is entered in any cell when the association specifying the column is an association to the stimulus word specifying a row. Diagonals are assigned a value of 0. Cell entires of 1 are summed and divided by the number of pairs $[n(n-1)]$ to yield C which varies from 0 to 1 and reflects directly the number of associations among the words as stimuli and responses. A numerical example is provided. Elsewhere, Pollio (1964b) defines a measure of relative cohesiveness which allows for differences in size of W matrices.

Selection

The indices described for associations could also be used with associations which are selected among discrete stimuli or, in some cases, which are indicated by ratings along continuous scales. In addition, as described in Chapter 2, similarity between pairs can be based on differences in profiles of semantic differential ratings (Jenkins, Russell, & Suci, 1958a, 1959; Osgood, Suci, & Tannenbaum, 1957).

Subjects' Reactions

As mentioned with respect to common meaning, subjects' reactions to pairs of stimuli in the form of ratings of common meaning and other attributes have been used to scale similarity between members of pairs. However, such ratings are probably best interpreted as estimates of strengths of associations between one or both stimuli as stimuli and the stimulus as a response. They were so regarded in Chapter 3.

Judgments for pairs of stimuli can be elaborated into judgments for sets of stimuli either as a whole or divided into subsets such as all possible pairs. Various scaling techniques (e.g., Coombs, 1958; Shepard, 1958; Torgerson, 1958; K. V. Wilson, 1963) can be applied to place members of a set along a single dimension of distance from or similarity to each other. These techniques are both too numerous and the space necessary for their exposition too great to warrant description here.

Results

Scalings of similarity are both less common and less extensive than scalings of meaningfulness. The few intercorrelations among various measures suggest that there is reasonable agreement among values obtained by judgments, interstimulus generalization or substitution errors, and even common meaning.

Among the sets of stimuli scaled for similarity by means of subjects' judgments or by their interstimulus generalization errors are Gibson's (1941) 12 sets of nonsense figures. Each set consisted of a standard and three variations, and similarity was specified by "the extent to which the subjects responded to the variation *as if it were the standard.*" Yum (1931) had earlier prepared sets of stimuli consisting of an original stimulus and four variations; 15 judges then arranged the variations in order of similarity to the original.

Plotkin (1943) obtained ratings of similarity between pairs of signals of the International Morse Code. Subsequently, Rothkopf (1957) scaled similarity among those signals by judgments that members of pairs of the same or different signals were the "same" or "different." Percentages of same judgments to pairs made up of the same members correlated −.69 and −.70 with substitution error responses to those stimuli observed previously by Plotkin (1943) and by Keller and Taubman (1943), respectively.

The matrix of correct and incorrect responses in PA learning was the basis for Shepard's (1958) scaling of nine colored circles. The nine responses of a motor PA task were scaled by the same procedure. These values are presented and could be used for specifying similarity of those stimuli and of those motor choices.

Shown in LaBerge and Lawrence (1957) are the individual forms of a 6×6 matrix generated by one of the techniques they describe and of a 6×21 matrix generated by the other technique. With the former matrix, three groups of 20 subjects each judged the similarity between the six stimuli of a given row or column (identifier stimuli) and the stimuli of the same row or column and of remaining rows or columns. Values calculated for average placements of stimuli with respect to the identifier stimuli increased with greater physical distance. A second experiment showed that average placements were not influenced by systematic or random ordering of identifier forms.

The 6×21 matrix was divided into three 6×6 matrices with which judgments of similarity were obtained in the manner of the first two experiments. Average placements for each of the three 6×6 matrices separately are shown for row forms and for column forms as identifiers. While monotonic, the relationships between objective distances and placements by judgments were not necessarily linear. Nor were the relationships the same for comparisons across columns and across rows even with equal physical distances between particular columns or particular rows.

Similarity among the six English stopped consonants and among those consonants plus 10 others has been assessed by Miller and Nicely (1955). Identification of the consonants was under different signal-to-noise ratios and different degrees of acoustic filtering. Degree to which each consonant was identified correctly or confused with each of the other consonants is shown in resultant confusion matrices. Subsequently, K. V. Wilson (1963) calculated distances between consonants in one of the matrices for the six stopped consonants and in one for the 16 consonants by Shepard's (1958) formula and by his own formula. These distances were then subjected to factor analysis by the Principal Axes method without rotation. For the stopped consonants, loadings on each of three factors are reported; for the 16, loadings on each of four factors are reported.

Bloomer (1959) had college students rate phonetic elements in terms of discriminability. Subsequently, those elements entered into construction of a list of words to provide what Haspiel and Bloomer (1961) labeled maximum auditory perception among sounds. Accompanying each word is an index based on discriminability among the component elements. Very possibly this list could be used to develop lists of words of varying similarity with respect to phonetic elements or sounds.

Judgments of whether members of a pair were the same or different were the basis of Rothkopf's (1960) scaling of similarity among six components of an hydraulic pressure regulator. Similarity among the six components was also scaled by means of associative overlap for each four classes of associations. The greater the similarity as scaled by judgments or by associative overlap, the greater the number of substitution errors in PA learning. When the former measure was partialled out, associative overlap and substitution errors were not related significantly.

In the most extensive investigation of relationships among measures of similarity reported thus far, Wimer (1963) obtained or used values for similarity between all pairs of 32 words as indicated by six different scaling techniques. The techniques were ratings along a seven-point scale (judged similarity), "semantic distance between words" (connotative similarity),

"number of associations common to both words in a pair" (associative overlap within individuals), "all instances of associations in common . . . both
within and between Ss" (total associative overlap), "number of *different*
associations that each word had in common for the group as a whole" (variety of associative overlap), and "number of times that either member of the pair
was given as an association for the other member" (associative reciprocity).

The correlations between judged similarity and the values for similarity
specified by the other five techniques ranged from .55 for connotative similarity to .69 for associative overlap within individuals. The only other significant correlation involving connotative similarity was with associative reciprocity for which the value was .40. The correlations between values obtained
by the remaining four techniques were from .67 to .98. These latter values
were not entirely independent in origin which partly accounts for their size.

Correlations were also obtained between values for similarity specified
by each of these techniques and values for 13 other measures. The correlations involving measures of similarity and three measures of meaningfulness
ranged from −.07 to .71; 12 of the 18 were significant at .05. Ratings of
familiarity in terms of the bipolar adjectives *usual-unusual* correlated significantly with only one of the measures of similarity, connotative similarity.

The remaining nine measures were those obtained previously by Jenkins,
Russell, and Suci (1958b) for various semantic differential scales. Many of
the 54 correlations between values for measures of similarity and those along
these scales were significant. But whether or not significant, these correlations
seem of little importance, theoretical or otherwise.

Garskof, Houston, and Ehrlich (1963) later distinguish associations between one member of a pair of stimuli and the recognition response to the
other (association strength, intra-hierarchical relatedness) from associations
between both members of a pair and one or more other common responses
(inter-hierarchical relatedness). Inter-hierarchical relatedness is specified by
RC values for 12 pairs of words and also for another 20 pairs, some from
the preceding 12 and some from the 24 pairs scaled by Garskof and Houston
(1963). Intra-hierarchical relatedness for each pair is specified by the average
of the percentages with which each member of a pair evoked the other as a
word association. Correlation of RC values and association strengths for the
pairs of the former list and of the latter list yielded rank-order coefficients of
.92 and .66, respectively.

Houston and Garskof (1963) selected 128 word pairs and obtained associations to the members of each pair. The frequencies with which each member of a pair evoked the other were summed and correlated with values for
the overlap of associations to members of the pairs. The *r* of .59 was interpreted as indicating that words which evoke each other evoke common
responses.

The stimuli to which P. E. Johnson (1964) obtained associations were 18 concepts in physics such as volume, density, and weight. From the resultant associations, a value for the index of mutual frequency or relatedness (Marshall & Cofer, 1963), or what Johnson termed an intersection coefficient, was calculated for each pair of concepts.

Pollio (1946b) obtained continuous associations to four words each of which represented one of the combinations of abstract or concrete and high or low semantic differential ratings along the evaluative dimension. Fast, medium, or slow associations to the words were determined and then employed as stimuli to which subjects responded with eight associations and with ratings along semantic differential scales. The resultant associations to and ratings of the latter stimuli were used to specify associative cohesiveness and semantic distances among those stimuli. The greater the speed with which those stimuli have been evoked as associations, the greater their associative cohesiveness and the smaller the semantic distance among them.

Clearly desirable are further scalings of, particularly, more extensive samples of various types of forms and of words, both from English and from other languages, which cannot be readily scaled by common letters or common phonemes. A wide range of simpler physical dimensions alone and combined orthogonally might also be used to obtain stimuli of varying similarity.

EFFECTS OF SIMILARITY ON ACQUISITION AND BACKWARD RECALL

Lists have been constructed with verbal stimuli and also with nonverbal stimuli. With verbal stimuli, similarity of stimulus members and of response members have been varied in both complete and incomplete orthogonal designs. Similarity between stimulus and response members has been varied but not orthogonally with the former two variables. In addition, similarity of stimulus and response members has been combined with their meaningfulness and, as described in the next chapter, with familiarization. With nonverbal stimuli, similarity of stimulus members or similarity of response members has been varied. In no experiments, apparently, have similarity of nonverbal stimulus members and of nonverbal response members been combined orthogonally.

Verbal Stimuli

Considered first are findings for complete orthogonal combinations of similarity of stimulus and of response members. Then examined are findings for positively correlated values; for variations in similarity of stimulus members, similarity of response members constant; for variations in similarity of response members, similarity of stimulus members constant; for similarity between stimulus and response members; for other incomplete orthogonal designs in which similarity of stimulus and of response members have been varied; and for similarity and meaningfulness of stimulus and of response members in complete and incomplete orthogonal combinations. Noted finally are effects of similarity on backward recall of stimulus members.

COMPLETE ORTHOGONAL

In apparently the first experiment with a complete orthogonal design, Feldman and Underwood (1957) combined nonsense-syllable stimulus members of high or low formal similarity with adjective response members of high or low similarity in terms of common meaning. Both similarity of stimulus members and similarity of response members were inversely related to acquisition rate; the former was the more potent.

The five lists of Underwood and Schulz's (1961) Experiment III represented the four combinations of low or high similarity of stimulus members and of response members in terms of common meaning. There were two high-high lists which differed with respect to pairings of stimulus and response members. In one list, stimulus members all from the same category were paired with response members also all from the same category but one different from that of the stimulus members. In the other list, stimulus members from a particular category were each paired with a response member from different categories. Under massed practice, increasing numbers of correct responses were obtained in the order high-high, high-low, low-high, and low-low with no difference between the two high-high lists. Under distributed practice, the pattern was the same except for an inversion in the form of low-high inferior to high-low.

In Experiments 8 and 10 reported in the Appendix, the same CVCs were used to construct unmixed lists of six pairs representing the four combinations of high or low formal similarity of stimulus and of response members (Experiment 8) and mixed lists of four and 12 pairs with one and three pairs, respectively, representing each of those combinations of similarity (Experiment 10). These lists were acquired both under anticipation and under recall formats of presentation.

With unmixed lists under the anticipation format, trials to criterion decreased successively for high-high, high-low, low-high, and low-low combinations; under recall there was an inversion in the form of low-high slower than high-low. With mixed lists, whether the lists were of four or 12 pairs and whether they were learned under anticipation or recall, acquisition was faster with the high-high than with the low-low combination. However, the low-high combination was inferior to high-low in two of four comparisons and inferior to high-high in two of four comparisons. Thus, the expected order of decreasing trials to criterion of high-high, high-low, low-high, and

EFFECTS OF SIMILARITY ON ACQUISITION AND BACKWARD RECALL   137

low-low was not obtained consistently. Whether with unmixed or mixed lists, acquisition did not occur consistently faster under recall than under anticipation, or the converse.

The unmixed lists of CVCs of low-low, low-high, high-low, and high-high formal similarity used by Newman and Buckhout (1962) each consisted of seven pairs. Over 39 trials, the largest number of syllables correct was with the low-low list followed by the high-low, low-high, and high-high lists. While both similarity of stimulus members and similarity of response members were related inversely to number of syllables correct, similarity of responses was the more potent as was the case for effects of similarity of stimulus and of response members on number of letters correct and number of different responses.

Two of Kanarick's (1963) lists had presumably similar code lines as stimulus members and dissimilar letters as response members (high-low), or the converse (low-high). Another list had two-digit numbers as stimulus members and letters as response members. Code lines were both stimulus members and response members of the fourth list. These lists were considered low-low and high-high, respectively, to complete the four combinations. Numbers of correct responses per trial were approximately .15, .75, 1.27, and 2.03 for the high-high, low-high, high-low, and low-low combinations, respectively. Thus, both similarity of stimulus members and of response members were related inversely to correct responses per trial with the latter variable the more potent. Precluding general significance for these findings, however, are the nonhomogeneous sets of stimulus members and of response members and the largely presumptive bases of the different degrees of similarity among members of those sets.

The response members of Hawker's (1964) experiment were selected from among nonsense figures which had been constructed by connecting three of the nine dots of a 3×3 matrix with two straight lines. Similarity among these nonsense forms was scaled by judgments of the "physical resemblance between items." Sets of figures of high and of low similarity were selected to serve as stimulus members or response members of pairs whose response members or stimulus members were sets of adjectives of low or of high semantic similarity. The resultant eight lists represented combinations of similarity of stimulus members, similarity of response members, and form-word or word-form sequence of stimulus and response members. All eight combinations were presented under prompting and confirmation formats with two joint presentations followed by one presentation of the stimulus members alone. Responding was by subjects' pushing a switch under the response member considered correct. Under the confirmation format, selections continued until selection of the correct response member. Five minutes after the acquisition trials, subjects recalled the response members by reproducing them on a sheet of paper.

Means of numbers of correct responses through seven test trials were related inversely to similarity of stimulus members and to similarity of response members. The interaction of these two variables was not significant but a significant interaction obtained for similarity of response members and form-word or word-form sequence. The inverse relationship held for figures as response members but not for words. For the subsequent reproduction of response members, significant Fs were obtained for similarity of response members and for the interaction of this variable and sequence but not for similarity of stimulus members. Again, effects of similarity of response members held only for the figures. At present, Hawker's use of nonhomogeneous sets of stimulus and response members with selection of responses strain comparisons between the results of this experiment and those of experiments involving homogeneous stimuli and production of responses. Also, the prompting and confirmation formats of presentation differ somewhat from conventional anticipation and recall formats.

POSITIVELY CORRELATED VALUES

Stimulus members and response members of Battig and Brackett's (1963) 12-pair lists of CVCs were both of high, medium, or low formal similarity. Following verbal-discrimination training, pairs were formed of discriminated, familiarized, or control members. They were presented with 50% and 100% ORM under recall and anticipation formats to a criterion of two successive perfect trials, or for 24 trials.

Acquisition rate and similarity were related inversely for all four combinations of %ORM and format. The only deviation from monotonic relationships was a slight decrease in responses correct from the list of high to that of medium similarity with 50% ORM under recall. Similarity did not interact significantly with %ORM, format of or type of prior training. The significant interaction of similarity, %ORM, and format was largely due to the above-noted unexpectedly slow learning of the medium similarity list with 50% ORM under recall, which probably reflects sampling error. In agreement with the findings of Experiments 8 and 10 reported here, acquisition under the recall format was not consistently faster than acquisition under the anticipation format.

One of Schoer's (1963) lists consisted of synonymous stimulus members and of synonymous response members of high familiarity. Semantic similarity among the stimulus members and among the response members of the other list were both low; familiarity was high. Thus the lists represented combinations of low-low and high-high semantic similarity. Subjects at both high and low levels of ability, as specified by a vocabulary test, acquired the low-low list faster than the high-high list.

SIMILARITY OF STIMULUS MEMBERS

Beecroft's (1956) four eight-pair lists contained no synonymous stimulus members, four sets of two synonymous stimulus members, two sets of four synonymous stimulus members, or one set of eight synonymous stimulus members. Up through the fifth trial, number of correct responses decreased with increasing common-meaning similarity of stimulus members; subsequently, correct responses were unrelated to similarity.

The 16 adjectives which served as stimulus members of Richardson's (1958) lists were of high or of low semantic similarity. They were paired with 2, 4, and 8 CVCs of 47% or 53% M_a and low formal similarity. Thus the pairings were n (8, 4, or 2) stimulus members to one response member. The 2, 4, or 8 response members were assigned to stimulus members to achieve maximum similarity between stimulus members paired with the same or paired with different response members.

In general, responses correct on Trial 25 were higher for the lists with stimulus members of high similarity and assignment of responses to achieve maximum similarity between stimulus members than for the lists with stimulus members of low similarity. The smallest numbers of correct responses were for the high-similarity lists with response members assigned to achieve maximum similarity between stimulus members paired with different responses. The interaction of similarity and number of responses was significant but not sufficient to indicate differences in rank orders for different numbers of responses not reasonably attributable to chance fluctuations. Because the two modes of assignment of response members to stimulus members are not realizable with one-to-one pairings of stimulus and response members, the differences between these two conditions of similarity cannot be generalized to conventional PA pairings. However, for n:1 pairings, Richardson's findings suggest that effects of similarity of stimulus members are in part contingent on manner of assignment of response members.

Sutton's (1958) two lists had 12 adjective stimulus members of low or of high similarity in terms of meaning. The response members were also adjectives. By various criteria, with or without warm up, the list with stimulus members of high similarity was learned faster than the list with stimulus members of low similarity. But the differences were not significant.

The eight CVC stimulus members of high or low formal similarity of Marshall and Runquist's (1963) lists were paired with numbers from 1 to 8 or with eight numbers from 1 to 16. Acquisition was for 16 trials with 4-sec. or 1-min. intertrial intervals. For each of the four combinations of numbers available as responses and intertrial intervals, acquisition was slower with stimulus members of high than with those of low similarity.

In Newman and Taylor's (1963) seven-pair lists, stimulus members made up of four consonants and two vowels or of 10 consonants and the same two vowels were paired with single digits. Nearly four times as many trials were required to reach criterion with stimulus members of high than with those of low similarity.

In two experiments which are the most elaborate of those available on effects of similarity of stimulus members, Cohen and Musgrave (1964b) varied similarity of CVCs in compounds of two CVCs. The CVCs of the compounds were both of high similarity (high-high), both of low similarity (low-low), or one was of high similarity and the other of low similarity with the former in the first position (high-low) or in the second position (low-high). In two other combinations, the CVCs of the compounds were both of high similarity or one was of high and the other was of low similarity but each occurred with equal frequency in the first and second positions. The stimulus members of two additional lists of the first experiment were single CVCs of high or of low similarity. Single letters served as response members.

The results for the compounds in both experiments were in close agreement. Rate of acquisition of responses to compounds with members in a fixed position was in the order high-high $<$ high-low $<$ low-high $<$ low-low. Responses to high-high compounds with members not in a fixed position were acquired faster than responses to high-high compounds with members in a fixed position; responses to single CVCs of high similarity were acquired faster than responses to the latter compounds. Rate of acquisition of responses to compounds of CVCs of high and low similarity with members not in a fixed position was intermediate between the rates for responses to low-high and high-low compounds with members in a fixed position. Responses were acquired slightly faster to the single CVCs of low similarity than to low-low compounds. Finally, responses were acquired faster to single CVCs of low than of high similarity.

Thornton's (1958) lists of eight pairs had four stimulus members which had no similarity in terms of meaning either to each other or to the other four stimulus members. The latter consisted of two pairs whose members were of high similarity to each other but not to the members of the other pair. For normal, schizophrenic, and organic subjects, more correct anticipations occurred to stimulus members of low similarity than to those of high similarity.

Kazusa's (1961) stimulus members were pair of adjectives in Japanese of high or of low semantic similarity. Members of these pairs were each accompanied by a different nonsense-syllable response member or by the same nonsense-syllable response member. In each of two experiments, with one-to-one pairings, there were essentially no differences in trials to one and to five perfect trials due to similarity between stimulus members. With two-to-one pairings, acquisition was faster for pairs with similar than for pairs with dissimilar stimulus members.

For the first of two experiments with CVCs as stimulus members, Restle and Trabasso (Restle, 1962) prepared two lists. In one list there was no duplication among the consonants of the eight stimulus members. In the other, four of the stimulus members had no consonants in common with each other or with the consonants of the other four stimulus members which were two pairs, each of whose members differed only in the vowel. Each stimulus member was paired with a different digit from 1 to 8. Correct pairings of stimulus and response members were learned faster with the stimulus members of low similarity than with those of high similarity.

The same stimulus members were used in the lists of the second experiment but two stimulus members were paired with each response member. The response members were digits from 1 to 4. For the control list, pairs of stimulus members of low similarity were each paired with a different response member. Members of each pair of similar stimulus members were paired with the same response member to produce facilitation pairings. For confusion pairings, members of each pair of similar stimulus members were assigned different response members, either the response member for the other pair of similar stimulus members or one of the two response members for the four dissimilar stimulus members. Acquisition was fastest with facilitation pairings and slowest with confusion pairings. Thus, wth 2:1 pairings of stimulus and response members or, more generally, with the n:1 pairings of concept-formation tasks, whether similarity of stimulus members is facilitative or inhibitory may be partly dependent on the manner of pairing stimulus members of high or low similarity with response members.

From the 32 nouns scaled for various attributes, Wimer (1963) prepared 32 lists with each word appearing as a stimulus member in six different lists. The same six CVCs of low meaningfulness served as response members of all 32 lists. Trials to a criterion of one perfect trial correlated .428 with judged similarity, .202 with connotative similarity, .334 with associative overlap within individuals, .405 with total associative overlap, .305 with variety of associative overlap, and .434 with associative reciprocity. The three values which exceed .349 are significant at .05.

Each of the three different sets of three stimulus members of Rotberg and Woolman's (1963) lists consisted of four-letter nonsense sequences with high formal similarity among members of a particular set and low formal similarity among the different sets. The response members were four-letter words. Members of these sets were either presented one after the other or with other pairs interspersed. These arrangements were labeled "similar and dissimilar learning groupings," respectively. In three different experiments, more correct responses occurred with similar than with dissimilar learning groupings.

With reduction in the separation among sets of similar stimulus members, the difference in rate of acquisition with the two groupings disappeared (Rotberg, 1964). "Similar and dissimilar learning groupings," it should be noted, represent new and different referents for "similar" and "dissimilar" which are not entirely in accord with current convention. A better term would be high or low temporal contiguity or proximity for which there is precedent. The same stricture with respect to use or interpretation of "similar" and "dissimilar" is applicable to Rotberg's (1963) findings.

SIMILARITY OF RESPONSE MEMBERS

In the verbal pretraining phase of Gerjuoy's (1953) investigation of acquired distinctiveness of cues, second-, third-, and fourth-grade boys and girls learned different similar or dissimilar nonsense-syllable names to lights in different positions. The dissimilar names were learned faster than similar names. In the verbal pretraining phase of Foster's (1953) experiments on acquired distinctiveness, airmen learned to respond to forms with sets of formally similar or dissimilar trigrams. Even at the end of many trials, fewer errors were made with dissimilar than with similar trigrams. Gerjuoy controlled for meaningfulness but Foster did not. Consequently, Foster's findings may reflect differences between responses of low meaningfulness, high similarity and of high meaningfulness, low similarity.

In two experiments using lists of 10 nonsense syllables paired with adjectives of low or high similarity in terms of common meaning, Underwood, Runquist, and Schulz (1959) obtained better learning with response members of low similarity than with those of high similarity. Prior familiarization with response members facilitated acquisition of response members of low similarity and also of high similarity. However, the interaction of similarity and familiarization was not significant. Saltz (1961) reports comparable findings.

The members of each of the six pairs of stimulus members of Higa's (1963) six experimental lists were of high similarity to each other as specified by six different techniques: antonyms, coordinates in given taxonomic categories, stimuli and their high frequency primaries excluding antonyms and coordinates (free association), partial-response-identity (Bousfield, Whitmarsh, & Danick, 1958), synonyms in terms of dictionary meaning from among pairs of words low in distances with respect to the semantic differential, and nonsynonymous words with small semantic differential differences (connotation). The 12 stimulus members of the control list were not associated with each other and were very different in terms of semantic differentiation. The response members for all seven sets of stimulus members were alternative sets of 12 CVCs which were pronounceable, dissimilar, with a median M_a of 64%.

Each of 72 subjects learned one of the experimental lists and the control list in counterbalanced order. The lists with high similarity between pairs specified by synonymity and by free association primaries were learned significantly less rapidly than the control list and, although the difference was only significant at .10, similarity specified by the antonym relationship also slowed acquisition relative to the control list. Rates of acquisition of the lists with similarity between pairs specified by the other three techniques did not differ significantly or markedly from rate of acquisition of the control list. Thus, the relationship between similarity and acquisition rate was in part contingent on the manner of specification of similarity. Indeed, in the case of synonyms, antonyms, and free association, semantic similarity need not be introduced as an explanatory variable since intralist interference of stimulus members with response members due to direct interstimulus associations could easily account for the slower learning of these lists.

Rotberg and Woolman (1963) and Rotberg (1964) inverted the lists in which similar stimulus members had been presented one after the other or with other stimulus members interspersed to realize similar and dissimilar groupings of response members. No differences obtained. But, as noted previously, high or low temporal contiguity are less ambiguous labels than similar or dissimilar.

OTHER INCOMPLETE ORTHOGONAL DESIGNS

In the first of Underwood's (1951) experiments on similarity of stimulus and response members in PA learning, similarity of stimulus members, of response members, and between stimulus and response members were confounded. Arbitrarily, this experiment is described here rather than under similarity between stimulus and response members. Adjectives were paired to obtain unmixed lists of high and of low similarity in terms of common meaning. Across three intertrial intervals of 4, 30, and 120 sec., 50% more trials were required to reach criterion with the lists of high similarity than with the lists of low similarity.

Two subsequent experiments by Underwood involved more but still incomplete orthogonal combinations of similarity of stimulus and response members. Again, they are most conveniently treated as other incomplete orthogonal designs. The lists of pairs of CVCs of the first experiment (Underwood, 1953a) represented five combinations of formal similarity of stimulus and response members: low-low, medium-low, high-low, low-medium, and low-high. These were combined with intertrial intervals of 4, 30, and 60 sec. Trials to criterion were inversely related to stimulus similarity but were not related to response similarity. While overt errors per trial were directly related to response similarity they were not related to stimulus similarity.

The stimulus and response members of the paired adjectives of the second experiment (Underwood, 1953b) represented six combinations of high or low similarity in terms of meaning: low-zero, medium-zero, high-zero, zero-low, zero-medium, and zero-high. Faster learning occurred with stimulus members of low or high similarity than with those of medium similarity; errors were not related to similarity of stimulus members. While trials to criterion were not related to similarity of response members, overt errors increased with greater similarity of response members. The incomplete orthogonal designs of these experiments preclude conclusions regarding the interaction of similarity of stimulus and response members or over-all assessment of relative potency of the two variables.

For lists in which adjectives of low common meaning (semantic similarity) were paired with adjective response members of low or high semantic similarity, Morikawa (1959a) obtained better learning with response members of low similarity. With stimulus members of low and high similarity and response members of low similarity, acquisition was faster with stimulus members of low similarity. Comparable results were obtained with lists of nonsense syllables representing pairs of low common-element or phonetic similarity of stimulus and response members, low similarity of stimulus members and high similarity of response members, and high similarity of stimulus members and low similarity of response members. In terms of common meaning and in terms of common elements, similarity of stimulus members had a more pronounced effect than similarity of response members. Similarity of response members, in terms of common elements, did not have a significant effect.

Using a matching test which minimized response learning and maximized associative learning, Horowitz (1962) found faster learning with CCCs of low similarity paired with English words than with CCCs of high similarity paired with the same words. This was also the case with CCCs as response members and words as stimulus members; but similarity of stimulus members did not have a greater effect than similarity of response members.

SIMILARITY BETWEEN STIMULUS AND RESPONSE MEMBERS

Umemoto (1958) constructed lists representing several degrees of similarity between stimulus and response members. In one list, the same items appeared as stimulus and response members; this is the condition of maximum similarity between stimulus and response members. In another list, half of the stimulus and response members were the same to specify an intermediate degree of similarity. In a third list, the stimulus members were all different than the response members. In two other lists, stimulus and response members were different, but in one stimulus members were similar to response members while in the other stimulus and response members were dissimilar. In general, the greater the similarity between stimulus and response members, the poorer the recall.

In Umemoto and Hilgard's (1961) first experiment, the three degrees of formal similarity of stimulus members to response members were related to increasing errors in the order high, low, and medium similarity during the stage from 0% to 50% learning and in the order low, medium, high similarity during the 50% to 100% stage and over the entire course of learning. Thus, the early advantage with stimulus and response members of high similarity, which was due to fewer different syllables to learn, became a disadvantage in the later association-discrimination stage.

Japanese adjectives were the stimulus members and response members of the eight pairs of three unmixed lists of Umemoto's (1962) first experiment. Members of pairs were of high, medium, or low similarity of meaning. Similarity and familiarity of stimulus members of the lists were high as were similarity and familiarity of response members. Trials to criterion and overt errors were both inversely related to similarity of meaning of stimulus members and response members and hence presumably to strength of associations between stimulus members and response members. In a second experiment with pairs of English adjectives, however, lists of high, medium, or low similarity of meaning of stimulus and response members of associative strength required, respectively, 14.9, 24.5, and 18.8 trials to criterion. Thus the relationship was an inverted-V rather than inverse.

The first of Newman's (1964) three lists consisted of six pairs of CVCs with the stimulus member of one pair the response member of another pair. Stimulus members and response members of the second list were constituted of the same nine consonants; those of the third list were constituted of different sets of nine consonants. Thus, stimulus and response members of the three lists were identical, similar, and dissimilar. During 21 learning trials, the respective means of correct responses for these three lists were 15.6, 27.0, and 56.0, and the means for correct backward recall of stimulus members were .67, 1.00, and 2.08. Both rate of acquisition and amount of backward recall were related inversely to similarity between stimulus and response members.

SIMILARITY AND MEANINGFULNESS IN COMBINATION

The unmixed lists of four pairs of CVCs of Goss, Nodine, Gregory, Taub, and Kennedy's (1962) Experiments IA and IB represented the 16 combinations of high or low similarity and high or low M_a of stimulus and response members. Disregarding similarity, M_a of stimulus members had less influence on acquisition rate than M_a of response members. Disregarding M_a, the inverse relationship between acquisition rate and similarity of stimulus members was slightly stronger than that for similarity of response members.

For five of the eight combinations of %ORM and stimulus and response members of high or low M_a, decreasing trials to criterion were obtained for the four combinations of similarity of stimulus and response members in the order high-high, high-low, low-high, and low-low. For two other combinations of %ORM and M_a, the order was high-high, low-high, high-low, and low-low. The remaining order was low-high, high-high, high-low, low-low; low-high was displaced two steps to the left.

While similarity of stimulus members and of response members were more potent than M_a of stimulus members and of response members, respectively, only two of the interactions involving these factors were significant. One was the interaction of similarity of stimulus members, M_a of stimulus members, and M_a of response members which includes the significant interaction of similarity and M_a of stimulus members. With stimulus members of low similarity, the direct relationship between acquisition rate and M_a of stimulus members was stronger with response members of low M_a than with response members of high M_a. With stimulus members of high similarity, faster learning occurred with stimulus members of high M_a than with stimulus members of low M_a when combined with response members of high M_a. But, when combined with response members of low M_a, acquisition with stimulus members of high M_a was slower than acquisition with stimulus members of low M_a. The latter finding is inconsistent with most other results; it is probably due to chance factors. These relationships of similarity and M_a of stimulus and response members to acquisition rate were essentially the same for acquisition with 25% and with 100% ORM.

In a subsequent experiment, stimulus members which were of low similarity, high M_a or of high similarity, low M_a were combined with response members representing the four combinations of high or low similarity and M_a. For the same combinations of similarity and M_a of stimulus and response members, similarity and M_a apparently did not interact. Unfortunately, the combinations used did not permit a further test of the significant interactions of Experiments IA and IB.

These experiments were for acquisition under the anticipation format under individual administration. They were later extended by experiments with the same unmixed lists but with acquisition by recall under group administration (Experiments 2 and 3 in Appendix). Again, the evidence regarding interactions of M_a and similarity of stimulus and response members was largely negative. As previously, the most common rank order of acquisition rates for similarity of stimulus and response members for each combination of %ORM and M_a of stimulus and response members was high-high < high-low < low-high < low-low.

Levitt and Goss (1961) constructed four unmixed lists of pairs of CVCs representing combinations of stimulus members of low or high M_a and high or low similarity with response members of intermediate M_a and similarity.

These lists were then reversed. Similarity of stimulus members and of response members were both inversely related to number of correct responses; but similarity did not interact with M_a.

Levitt (1959) used partly mixed lists in which stimulus members of low similarity and high M_a (easy) or of high similarity and low M_a (hard) were paired with response members representing the four combinations of low or high similarity and high or low M_a. For both hard and easy stimulus members, disregarding similarity of response members, number correct was directly related to M_a of response members. Also described in the Appendix are two experiments (Experiments 5 and 6) with partly mixed lists with acquisition by recall under group administration. The lists of Experiment 5 were those which Levitt had employed. The results were consistent with findings for unmixed lists and, in general, with Levitt's findings.

Each of the 16 pairs of Nodine's (1963) mixed list represented one of the 16 combinations of high or low similarity and high or low M_a of stimulus and response members. Acquisition of this mixed list was for 21 trials with anticipation and four trials with recall under each of the 16 combinations of $\frac{1}{2}$-, 1-, 2-, and 4-sec. durations of stimulus members alone and $\frac{1}{2}$-, 1-, 2-, and 4-sec. durations of the stimulus and response members together. A coefficient of concordance of .83 was obtained among rank orders of responses recalled correctly for each of the 16 combinations of similarity and M_a of stimulus and response members across the combinations of durations. Thus, effects of similarity and M_a of stimulus and response members were essentially invariant with respect to duration of stimulus members alone and of stimulus and response members together. The effects of similarity and M_a of stimulus and response members were generally consistent with those described in Experiments 1, 2, 3, 5, and 6 in the Appendix and by Goss, Nodine, Gregory, Taub, and Kennedy (1962). However, similarity of response members was more potent than similarity of stimulus members and a number of interactions among similarity and M_a of stimulus and response members, including the interaction of all four variables, were significant. The rank order of the correct responses for the 16 combinations of similarity and M_a of stimulus and response members, disregarding durations, correlated .68 with the rank order of trials to criterion for the same 16 combinations of attributes obtained by Goss, Nodine, Gregory, Taub, and Kennedy.

Cooper (1964) administered Nodine's list by recall under group administration. The rank orders of acquisition rates for the 16 combinations of similarity and M_a of stimulus and response members obtained in the Cooper and in the Nodine experiments correlated .90.

Described by Saltz (1960) was an experiment in which response members of high or low similarity were paired with stimulus members of low or high M_a. The difference between response members of low or high similarity was greater with stimulus members of low M_a than with stimulus members of high M_a. The difference between these differences was significant at .05. However, nonorthogonality of similarity of M_a of stimulus and response members precludes conclusions regarding interactions of similarity and M_a.

Young (1961) constructed lists representing three degrees of similarity between stimulus and response members with CVCs of 20% or 90% Glaze M_a. For both trials and overt errors per trial to criterion, similarity between stimulus and response members was inversely related to acquisition rate, while M_a was directly related to rate. With pairs of 90% M_a, the relationship of similarity to trials to learn had linear or slight positive acceleration as was the case for overt errors; with pairs of 20% M_a, the relationship was negatively accelerated for trials and essentially flat for overt errors. Thus, there was an apparent interaction of similarity between stimulus and response members with M_a of stimulus and response members. But this suggested interaction is of limited significance since similarity was between stimulus and response members rather than of stimulus members, of response members, or of both, and M_a of stimulus and of response members were confounded.

At present, for the particular procedures for specifying meaningfulness, formal similarity of stimulus and response members, and the levels of meaningfulness and similarity employed, there is no convincing evidence of interactions of similarity and meaningfulness of stimulus members, of response members, or of both. This holds for both unmixed and partly mixed lists. Since meaningfulness of stimulus and of response members were confounded in Young's lists, his findings are, at best, suggestive of a possible interaction.

Evidence provided by these and by subsequent studies must, of course, be evaluated within the constraint that any interactions or lack of interactions may be special cases of effects of several factors. One such factor is the particular scalings of meaningfulness used to specify levels of meaningfulness. Noble's m' values, and possibly his a' values, seemingly differentiate among trigrams at both extremes of meaningfulness to a greater degree than do Archer's values (Noble, 1961).[4] The apparent wider range of the former values may lead to interactions not demonstrable with extremes of Archer values. The number and values of levels of meaningfulness, whatever the scaling used to specify those values, may also influence the mode of combination of meaningfulness with similarity as might the particular manner of defining similarity and the number of values of levels of similarity. Whether meaningfulness and similarity are combined in unmixed, partly mixed, or mixed lists may be a further factor.

---

[4] Both Archer (1961) and Saltz and Ager (1962) advance criticisms of various aspects of Noble's scaling which, if valid, might vitiate this apparent advantage of Noble's values. Noble (1962) regards these criticisms as largely invalid or irrelevant.

Backward Recall of Stimulus Members

In post-acquisition presentation on the memory drum, Feldman and Underwood (1957) found backward recall of stimulus members to be an inverse function of similarity of stimulus members. But backward recall was not related to similarity of response members.

Subsequent to the thirty-ninth acquisition trial of Newman and Buckhout's (1962) experiment, stimulus members were recalled to response members presented on the memory drum for 2.5 sec. with 2.5 sec. to write the stimulus members. Stimulus members were also recalled to response members presented on cards with unlimited time for recall. For the measures of number of correct syllables, letters, and different responses from the list without reference to position, stimulus recall was related inversely to similarity of stimulus and of response members. Order of increasing numbers of stimulus members recalled was not consistently high-high, high-low, low-high, and low-low although best recall was always with the latter combination.

Morikawa (1959a) describes backward recall with unmixed lists representing high-low, low-high, and low-low combinations of phonetic or common-elements similarity and of semantic similarity. With the lists in which phonetic similarity was varied, following attainment of a criterion of one perfect trial, increasing numbers of stimulus members were recalled for low-low, low-high, and high-low combinations. A direct relationship obtained between stimulus members recalled and similarity of stimulus members for response members of low similarity; an inverse relationship obtained between stimulus recall and similarity of response members for stimulus members of low similarity. Following achievement of criteria of 3/6 correct responses and three successive perfect trials, recall was better for the high-low combination than for the other two which were about equal.

With the lists in which semantic similarity was varied, following attainment of criteria of one and three successive perfect trials, differences in stimulus recall among the three combinations were neither marked nor consistent. Following attainment of a criterion of 5/9 correct responses, recall of stimulus members increased in the order low-high, high-low, and low-low. Thus, only for this criterion was there any suggestion of significant effects of semantic similarity on recall of stimulus members.

In Experiment 8 of the Appendix, backward recall of stimulus members is reported for the four combinations of high and low common-element similarity of stimulus and response members. Neither in an analysis of variance nor in an analysis of covariance involving adjustment for trials to criterion did either variable have significant effects on backward recall. In the analysis of covariance the interaction of the two variables with format of presentation was significant at .05. The principal basis of this effect was greater superiority of backward recall for the high-low combination relative to the other three combinations following acquisition under recall than under anticipation. The pattern of relationships among the four means under the former format, however, was not readily interpretable.

Nonverbal Stimuli

Gibson's (1942) experiment was apparently the first on acquisition of correct nonsense-syllable responses of a PA task as a function of (intra-list) similarity of nonverbal (nonsense forms) stimuli. The list with stimulus members of low similarity was learned to a criterion of one perfect trial in about half the number of trials required for lists with stimulus members of high similarity. Moreover, responses to the same form were uniformly acquired more rapidly with the list with stimulus members of low similarity than with the lists with stimulus members of high similarity.

Murdock (1958, Exp. II) specified similarity among the four members of sets of light patterns in terms of identical elements and redundancy. Patterns of high, medium, and low similarity were associated with increasingly better learning of four CVCs of high M_a, low similarity.

The 12 pairs of Rothkopf's (1958) lists consisted of single aural, Morse signals as stimuli and their letter or number equivalents as responses. In Experiments II and III, the stimuli of one list were similar; those of another list were relatively dissimilar. When presented so that similar or relatively dissimilar stimuli were grouped, there was no difference in the rate of acquisition of the two lists in Experiment II and a slight, but not significant superiority of the latter list during the first two days in Experiment III.

Sets of three nonsense forms each were the stimuli to which the preschool children of Dietze's (1955) experiment responded with three similar or three dissimilar names. Subsequently (Dietze, 1959), both sequence and similarity of responses were varied. In both experiments more discrimination errors and more generalization errors occurred with similar than with dissimilar responses.

With line drawings of Indian children's faces as stimuli, the kindergarten children of Norcross's (1958) experiment had verbal pretraining with similar or with dissimilar CVCs as responses. During both learning and relearning, more correct responses were made with dissimilar than with similar CVCs.

Reese (1960) used two pairs of similar trigrams and two pairs of dissimilar trigrams as responses to lights of different hues. One of the pairs of similar trigrams led to slower learning than either of the pairs of dissimilar trigrams; but the other pair of similar trigrams was learned at the same rate as the latter pairs.

In Murdock's (1960) fifth experiment, the four adjective responses to different patterns of lights were of high or of low similarity in terms of association with each other. The responses of low similarity were learned faster, but not significantly faster, than those of high similarity.

The nine solid black circles which served as stimulus members for Mc-Guire's (1961) lists differed in .07-cm. and .14-cm. steps. Across other conditions, more correct anticipations occurred with the circles separated by .14-cm. steps than with those separated by .07-cm. steps.

Restle (1962) describes the results of an experiment by Bower and Levine with an apparently mixed list whose stimulus members were sets of three Korean characters each with 0, 1, 2, or 3 elements in common. Total number of errors in anticipating English nouns to these stimuli varied inversely with number of common elements.

Two sets of eight color caps, one step or five steps apart in hue, served as the sets of similar and dissimilar stimulus members of an experiment by Smith, Jones, and Thomas (1963). The CVC response members of low similarity and M_a less than 50% were always available. In addition to similarity, the variables were number of stimuli per responses (1, 2, or 4) and whether the members of pairs or tetrads of stimulus members assigned to a response were adjacent to each other or separated. The response measure was $R - W/n - 1$ with R = right, W = wrong, and n = the number of response categories, specifically 2, 4, or 8.

With one-to-one pairings of stimulus members and response members, the mean of scores for performance with dissimilar stimulus members was more than twice that for performance with similar stimulus members. For two and four stimuli per response both for assignment to adjacent and to non-adjacent stimuli, performance was better with dissimilar than with similar stimulus members.

Members of the sets of similar nonsense forms which served as stimulus members of Gagné's (1950) paired associates were presented one after the other or separated. Learning was better under the former sequence of presentation than under the latter. Were presentation of units with similar stimulus members one after the other considered a condition producing greater similarity among stimulus members than presentation of those members separately, the relationship between acquisition rate and similarity was direct. As mentioned previously, specification of similarity in terms of temporal proximity is a new criterion not in accord with current convention.

Von Restorff (1933) constructed eight-pair lists. Within each list, four pairs consisted of all syllables, figures, numbers, letters, or colors. The stimuli of each of the other four pairs represented a different one of the remaining four types. Also constructed were lists made up of six pairs which consisted of all syllables, figures, or numbers, and two other pairs each of which was comprised of stimuli from a different one of the remaining two types. These lists might be viewed as made up of both verbal and nonverbal stimuli with the four to six pairs made up of one type of stimulus as of high similarity and the other four to two pairs as of low similarity. The percentages of correct responses with pairs made up of different types of stimuli were considerably higher than percentages with pairs made up of the same type of stimuli.

Summary

With verbal stimuli in general, but with less consistency than for meaningfulness, both similarity of stimuli and similarity of responses, whether specified by common elements or by common meaning, are inversely related to acquisition rate. Furthermore, although data are limited and exceptions have occurred, similarity of stimuli is apparently more potent than similarity of responses. These relationships seemingly hold for unmixed, partly mixed, and mixed lists presented under both anticipation and recall formats and across variations in several other variables such as %ORM.

Effects of similarity of stimulus members and of response members on backward recall have been investigated in a few experiments. But the findings are too inconsistent to warrant even tentative generalizations regarding effects of similarity.

With nonverbal stimuli of varying similarity, the relationship to acquisition rate is also inverse. Apparently similarity of nonverbal stimuli and of verbal responses have not been varied orthogonally.

CHAPTER 6

Familiarization

Familiarization is a convenient and now conventional label for several different experiences with stimuli usually but not necessarily before their pairing as stimulus members or response members of the criterion PA list. Preliminary specifications of familiarization, satiation, acquired-distinctiveness training, and induction of meaning and meaningfulness were outlined in Chapter 4. These are elaborated for familiarization and satiation in this chapter and for acquired-distinctiveness training and induction of meaning and meaningfulness in the next.

Considered first are the general techniques for producing familiarization and satiation experiences and variations within those techniques. Familiarization and satiation experiences can be placed in the broader framework of paradigms for experiments on transfer. Such placement is discussed briefly. Data on effects of familiarization on PA learning are then described and summarized.

TECHNIQUES

Techniques of familiarization can be viewed as experiences which serve primarily to increase the integration of recognition responses to stimuli. Familiarization of stimuli has been carried out prior to pairing those stimuli with other stimuli to serve as stimulus members or response members of PA lists. However, familiarization and satiation of stimuli could alternate with their presentation as members of PA units.

Strengthening of recognition responses can be approached directly by eliciting such responses to stimuli. Elicitation of recognition responses, of course, may not always strengthen the association between them and the eliciting stimuli. Regardless of effects on strength, such elicitation is one general technique. Stimuli have been presented in prior learning tasks other than PA tasks. Also, responses other than recognition responses to stimuli have been strengthened. These two techniques of familiarization presumably involve incidental strengthening of recognition responses.

With some exceptions (e.g., Sheffield, 1946, pp. 57-72), development and use of all three general techniques and variants thereof appears to have been more a matter of hunch and convenience than of explicit theoretical rationale. And, at present, no information is apparently available on relative effects on subsequent learning phenomena of various of these general techniques and variations thereof.

Recognition Responses

Strengthening of recognition responses to verbal stimuli has involved presentation of each stimulus one or more times for subjects to write the recognition response to the stimulus one or more times (e.g., Experiments 3 and 6 in the Appendix) or for subjects to say the stimulus to themselves or out loud (e.g., Gannon & Noble, 1961; Goss, Nodine, Gregory, Taub, & Kennedy, 1962). The latter variant, as noted in Chapter 4, is the same as the satiation procedure employed by Lambert and collaborators (Kanungo & Lambert, 1963; Kanungo, Lambert, & Mauer, 1962; Lambert & Jakobovits, 1960) and others (Yelen & Schulz, 1963). Another, possibly simpler procedure is for subjects to look at stimuli for a certain period of time (Cieutat, 1960a); this procedure has also been regarded as satiation (Smith & Raygor, 1956). Schulz and Martin's (1964) subjects spelled the stimuli with no overt articulation; the stimuli were recalled after every 10 trials.

DeBold's (1964) "frequency plus differentiation training" involved subjects' pronouncing aloud each member of pairs of stimuli and then rating them for pronunciability.

Comparable variations for nonverbal stimuli would be one or more presentations of each stimulus or presentation of each stimulus for a certain period of time. Degree of familiarization might also be varied along steps such as subjects' simply looking at the stimulus, subjects' looking at the stimulus and making recognition responses, and subjects' looking at, making recognition responses to, and attempting to search out and name discriminable features of each stimulus (Goss & Greenfeld, 1958).

Underwood and Schulz (1960a, p. 103) presented successive syllables at a 2-sec. rate for subjects to spell out loud. Blocks of such trials alternated with test trials in which subjects filled in the letter omitted from each syllable. On test trials with nonverbal stimuli, subjects would presumably draw in or describe the missing part(s) of each figure. Similar but slightly different procedures have been employed by R. L. Weiss (1958), Underwood, Runquist, and Schulz (1959), Underwood and Schulz (1960a, pp. 114-115), and Saltz (1961).

Morikawa (1959b) familiarized stimuli by using first letters of two-letter words as stimuli and second letters as responses of a PA task. The variation used by Besch (1961) was presentation of the first two letters of some of Haagen's (1949) adjectives as stimuli for anticipations of entire words.

Prior Learning Tasks

Epstein, Rock, and Zuckerman (1960, p. 6) had subjects learn 12 short lists, each of which consisted of a nonsense syllable and four numbers. The syllables were later paired to form lists of pairs of familiarized stimuli.

The procedure used by Battig, Williams, and Williams (1962) involved discriminating the correct from the incorrect member of each pair of nonsense syllables of a verbal discrimination task. Both members of some pairs became the stimulus or response members of pairs for PA learning. Members of other pairs were separated and paired with syllables which subjects had not seen previously.

Battig (1964, p. 10) has also familiarized stimuli by presenting them in lists and requiring recall of the letters of those stimuli either in any order or in the exact order in which they had appeared.

Responses Other than Recognition Responses

The procedure which Sheffield (1946) considered familiarization involved "seeing a printed word or syllable in exactly the same form as it was to be shown later in paired-associates learning, vocalizing the word as soon as it was shown, and then finding the word as quickly as possible in a list of three-letter words and syllables. When the word was found it was marked and vocalized again" (p. 59). Each subject marked all words of a list in the same one of 10 different ways. Sheffield's symbolic training was essentially the same except that each word was marked in a different way. These procedures, as noted subsequently, are, perhaps, better regarded as acquired-equivalence and acquired-distinctiveness training. However, recognition responses were made and may have been strengthened.

Battig's (1964) technique of selection of a stimulus from among several arranged in a matrix is more elaborate than the verbal discrimination technique. One variation of the former technique (p. 6) involved presenting each stimulus to be familiarized in a 3×3 matrix in which four of the other stimuli differed from the stimulus to be familiarized by only one letter, two other stimuli differed by two letters, and the remaining two differed by positions of two of the correct letters. Each of the stimuli to be familiarized was placed in four different cells to generate four matrices. Subjects' choices of the stimulus to be familiarized was by saying a number which designated the location of that stimulus in the matrix. Acquisition of correct choices was by a noncorrection procedure to a criterion of one perfect trial or for a maximum of 10 trials. Various aspects of the technique can be and have been varied. Presumably saying the number is preceded by covert vocalization of the recognition response to the stimulus selected.

FAMILIARIZATION AND TRANSFER

The simplest paradigms of transfer of training with PA tasks comprise but two tasks, each acquired in a different session. The first task can be represented as

$$\begin{pmatrix} S_{11} & S_{12} \\ S_{21} & S_{22} \end{pmatrix}$$

with the stimuli in the first column as stimulus members and those in the second column as response members. The first subscript indicates the pair; the second subscript whether the stimulus is a stimulus member (1) or response member (2). The second task may be the same but is usually one in which one of four changes has occurred: (a) stimulus members are different

$$\begin{pmatrix} S'_{11} & S_{12} \\ S'_{21} & S_{22} \end{pmatrix}$$

as indicated by accents; (b) response members are different

$$\begin{pmatrix} S_{11} & S'_{12} \\ S_{21} & S'_{22} \end{pmatrix}$$

(c) both stimulus and response members are different

$$\begin{pmatrix} S'_{11} & S'_{12} \\ S'_{21} & S'_{22} \end{pmatrix}$$

and (d) response members are reversed

$$\begin{pmatrix} S_{11} & S_{22} \\ S_{21} & S_{12} \end{pmatrix}$$

In both the first task and the second task, stimuli are presented as pairs under instructions to learn to anticipate or recall the response member paired with each stimulus member. Recognition responses to stimulus members, response members, or both may change. But such changes are not usually observed and recorded. While responses learned in the first task might occur as mediating responses in the second task, particularly when response members or both stimulus and response members are changed, the relatively short time intervals for anticipation or recall usually employed make such chaining difficult.

In contrast to these paradigms, the first and most common of the general techniques of familiarization described earlier focused on stimuli alone rather than paired. Furthermore, the emphasis has been the strengthening of recognition responses, not formation and strengthening of associations between stimulus members and recognition responses to response members. Successive occurrences of the same recognition response, however, might occasion strengthening of a closed chain of such responses to a stimulus (Kanungo & Lambert, 1963; Kanungo, Lambert, & Mauer, 1962). Also, associations may develop among familiarized stimuli. But, in terms of experimenters' intentions, the occurrence of either type of association is artifactual.

The other two general techniques of familiarization, with that of Battig and collaborators (Battig, Williams, & Williams, 1962) a possible exception, have involved responses to stimuli other than recognition responses. Correctly or incorrectly, such responses have not been considered as responses of a first PA task. Instead, it is apparently assumed they do not carry over into the second task (Epstein, Rock, & Zuckerman, 1960) or that they appear in the second task as noninterfering mediating responses (Sheffield, 1946).

When placed within the broader framework of transfer of training, the problem arises of control for possible effects on second-task learning of any nonspecific factors activated and strengthened during first-task learning. Familiarization of irrelevant stimuli has been one approach. Alternatively, subjects might learn partly mixed or mixed lists in which some stimulus members, response members, or both, had been familiarized and others had not.

EFFECTS OF FAMILIARIZATION

Whatever the general technique of familiarization and particular variation thereof employed, the possible designs are complete or incomplete orthogonal with unmixed, partly mixed, or mixed lists. Familiarization may be the only variable; familiarization may be combined with meaningfulness, similarity, or other classes of variables. Findings obtained with complete orthogonal designs are examined before those obtained with various incomplete orthogonal designs. Within each design, results for unmixed lists are examined first; these results are considered the criteria against which those for partly mixed and mixed lists are compared.

Familiarization of response members, it is assumed, increases those correlates of meaningfulness of response members, such as availability and integration of recognition responses, which are the postulated actual bases of the direct relationships between acquisition rate and meaningfulness of response members. Satiation presumably decreases availability and integration or leads to formation of associations between successive occurrences of recognition responses. Familiarization and also satiation of stimulus members are presumed to influence subsequent PA learning through changes in the same postulated bases of the direct relationship between acquisition rate and meaningfulness of stimulus members. Specifically, greater familiarization of stimulus and response members of low meaningfulness is expected to influence acquisition of PA units and lists in manners increasingly similar to effects of stimulus and of response members of high meaningfulness. Within the orientation of Lambert and collaborators, greater amounts of satiation are expected to have effects increasingly similar to those obtained with stimulus and response members of low meaningfulness. Familiarization and satiation interpretations apparently generate opposing predictions.

The simplest complete orthogonal design for testing presumed effects of familiarization or satiation involves pairs or lists representing combinations of stimulus and response members which have been (familiarized, satiated) or have not been (unfamiliarized, unsatiated) familiarized or subjected to satiation experiences. The predicted rank order of these combinations in terms of increasing acquisition rate, corresponding to the low-low, high-low, low-high, and high-high order for combinations of high or low meaningfulness of stimulus and response members, is unfamiliarized-unfamiliarized, familiarized-unfamiliarized, unfamiliarized-familiarized, and familiarized-familiarized. For those experiences conceived as satiation with inhibitory consequences, the order is satiated-satiated, unsatiated-satiated, satiated-unsatiated, and unsatiated-unsatiated.

As mentioned above, with unmixed lists and with some partly mixed lists, regardless of the particular design, familiarization or satiation with irrelevant stimuli may be necessary to control for presumed facilitative or inhibitory effects of changes in nonspecific sources. Also, the familiarization or satiation technique should be the same for relevant and irrelevant stimuli.

Complete Orthogonal Designs

In experiments with complete orthogonal designs reported thus far, stimulus members and response members of low meaningfulness either were or were not familiarized; thus the designs are limited to 2×2. In Morikawa's (1959b) Experiment II, the same eight subjects learned different nine-pair lists. For trials to successive criteria, the order was unfamiliarized-unfamiliarized < familiarized-unfamiliarized < unfamiliarized-familiarized = familiarized-familiarized. Forward recall after reaching a criterion of one perfect trial was poorest for the unfamiliarized-unfamiliarized combination and about equal for the other three combinations; backward recall increased in the order unfamiliarized-unfamiliarized, unfamiliarized-familiarized, familiarized-unfamiliarized, and familiarized-familiarized. Less regular orders were obtained for forward and for backward recall after criteria of six of nine and three successive perfect trials. In a further experiment, using somewhat different methods, these findings were confirmed.

Gannon and Noble (1961) presented lists of 15 dissyllables of low Noble M_n for 20 familiarization trials. These dissyllables were then used to form five-pair lists in which both stimulus and response members, stimulus members, response members, or neither stimulus nor response members had been familiarized. Four groups of 24 subjects each had 17 trials of PA learning with these lists. A control group of 24 subjects who had not had irrelevant familiarization also learned the list. Acquisition rates were in the order unfamiliarized-familiarized < unfamiliarized-unfamiliarized < familiarized-unfamiliarized < familiarized-familiarized with the rate for the control group the same as that for the former two combinations.

With minor changes in the familiarization procedure, and omission of Gannon and Noble's control group, Hakes (1961a) replicated their experiment. Increasing totals of correct responses were obtained with unfamiliarized-unfamiliarized, unfamiliarized-familiarized, familiarized-unfamiliarized, and familiarized-familiarized combinations. As for Gannon and Noble, effects of familiarization of response members were not significant. However, effects of familiarization of stimulus members were just short of .05. The rank of the unfamiliarized-familiarized combination, particularly in Gannon and Noble's experiment, is not consistent with the expectation that a list of unfamiliarized-familiarized pairs would be acquired less rapidly than a list of familiarized-familiarized pairs but more rapidly than lists of familiarized-unfamiliarized and unfamiliarized-unfamiliarized pairs. As noted below, however, these findings may be limited to the particular acquisition procedure of 2 sec. for subjects to pronounce stimulus members out loud and then to anticipate response members.

In Besch's (1961) last three experiments, six familiarization trials were given to different groups which then learned lists representing the combinations of unfamiliarized-unfamiliarized, familiarized-unfamiliarized, unfamiliarized-familiarized and familiarized-familiarized. None of the experiments yielded significant differences among the four combinations.

Cieutat (1960a) used two mixed lists of four pairs of Noble's dissyllables of low M_n with one pair representing each of the unfamiliarized-unfamiliarized, familiarized-unfamiliarized, unfamiliarized-familiarized, and familiarized-familiarized combinations. Familiarization was 60 sec. for subjects to examine the dissyllables. Means of correct responses per trial over 20 trials were 2.16, 2.35, 2.46, and 2.65 for pairs representing the combinations unfamiliarized-familiarized, familiarized-unfamiliarized, unfamiliarized-unfamiliarized, and familiarized-familiarized, respectively. Neither familiarization of stimulus members nor familiarization of response members had a significant effect, but their interaction was significant in the form of familiarization of response members being facilitative with familiarized stimulus members but inhibitory with unfamiliarized stimulus members.

The results of the Morikawa, Gannon and Noble, Hakes, and Cieutat experiments agree to the extent that the familiarized-familiarized combination always yielded the most rapid acquisition. But the unfamiliarized-unfamiliarized and unfamiliarized-familiarized combinations have been at each of the other three ranks at least once, and the familiarized-unfamiliarized combination has been both second and third. Thus, no conclusion about the relative potency of familiarization of stimulus members and of familiarization of response members is possible. Besch's findings, unless dismissed on grounds that six familiarization trials are too few, suggest that familiarization, whether of stimulus members or of response members, may have little or no effects on acquisition.

Noted briefly among experiments involving combinations of both similarity and meaningfulness was Experiment 6 in the Appendix. Familiarization was an additional variable. Each pair of four-pair lists represented different subsets of the 16 possible combinations of stimulus and response members of high or low similarity and high or low M_a. There were 12 trials for familiarization of both stimulus and response members, of stimulus members, of response members, or of neither with appropriate irrelevant familiarization controls. Regardless of lists, familiarization had no significant effects on number of correct responses through 12 acquisition trials. In fact, familiarization occasioned slight but not significant inhibition.

The first phase of Battig's (1964, pp. 5-8) experiment involved familiarization of 12 Turkish words or 12 nonsense dissyllables by the technique of selecting a word from several arranged in a matrix. These words were then paired with each other or with unfamiliarized words of the same type to realize parallel 12-pair lists in which each of the combinations of familiarized and unfamiliarized stimulus and response members was represented by three pairs. These pairs were presented in constant or varied serial order, with pairs representing each familiarization combination occurring one after the other (grouped) or with other pairs interspersed (ungrouped). Loci of overt pronunciation of stimulus and response members were also varied. These three variables proved ineffectual and hence are ignored.

With Turkish words, the means of errors per pair were 4.58 for familiarized-familiarized pairs, 5.50 for unfamiliarized-familiarized pairs, 6.88 for familiarized-unfamiliarized pairs, and 6.94 for unfamiliarized-unfamiliarized pairs. For dissyllables, the corresponding means were 4.74, 6.01, 7.13, and 7.31. Thus, confirming the results of a previous experiment by Battig and a collaborator (1964, p. 5), familiarization of stimulus members and familiarization of response members facilitated acquisition with the latter the more potent variable.

Incomplete Orthogonal Designs

One type of incomplete orthogonal design involves elimination of the unfamiliarized-unfamiliarized or of the familiarized-familiarized combination from the four combinations of stimulus and response members which were or were not familiarized. Another type is a diagonal design involving the unfamiliarized-unfamiliarized and familiarized-familiarized combinations. Only stimulus members or only response members might have been familiarized and then paired with, respectively, unfamiliarized response members or unfamiliarized stimulus members. These might also be combined in a design in which familiarized or unfamiliarized stimulus members are paired with unfamiliarized response members, and unfamiliarized stimulus members are paired with familiarized or unfamiliarized response members.

FAMILIARIZED-FAMILIARIZED OR UNFAMILIARIZED-UNFAMILIARIZED COMBINATION OMITTED

In Underwood and Schulz's (1960a) third experiment on PA learning, their Experiment 4 (pp. 119-126), the familiarized-familiarized combination was omitted from a 2×2 orthogonal design. Acquisition was faster with lists of unfamiliarized-familiarized pairs than with lists of unfamiliarized-unfamiliarized pairs. Pairs whose stimulus members had been familiarized in PA learning with forms were learned no faster than unfamiliarized-unfamiliarized pairs; and pairs whose stimulus members had been familiarized in PA learning with nouns were learned less rapidly than unfamiliarized-unfamiliarized pairs. Thus, familiarization of response members was facilitative but, contingent on prior familiarization with nouns or forms, familiarization of stimulus members either had no effect or was inhibitory.

The results of Hakes's (1961a) second experiment, which are noted below, set the problem of his final experiment: does familiarization of stimulus members influence acquisition only when stimulus and response members of pairs are of the same type, for example, both dissyllables? The three combinations were familiarized stimulus members (20 trials) and unfamiliarized response members, unfamiliarized-familiarized, and unfamiliarized-unfamiliarized. Differences in acquisition rate through 17 trials with these combinations were not significant. Familiarization of stimulus members may have been slightly inhibitory; there was no evidence of facilitation due to familiarization of response members. The finding for familiarization of stimulus members are opposite those obtained by Gannon and Noble and in Hakes's (1961b) own earlier experiment. But the results of all three are consistent with respect to ineffectiveness of familiarization of response members.

In Kanungo and Lambert's (1963) first experiment, stimulus members or response members of lists of 10 pairs of words of high counted frequency, high M_p had been subjected previously to the satiation experience of repeating those members "aloud continuously for 15 sec. at a rate of 3–4 repetitions per sec." Both retest control and different word (irrelevant stimulus) satiation conditions served as the unfamiliarized-unfamiliarized or unsatiated-unsatiated control. The familiarized-familiarized or satiated-satiated combination was absent. Means of trials to three consecutive errorless trials adjusted for differences in learning a practice list were 15.06 for response satiation, 14.66 for stimulus satiation, 9.85 for different word satiation, and 11.18 for retest control. The differences between the former pair of means and the latter pair of means were significant at .05 or less. While response satiation slowed learning slightly more than stimulus satiation, the difference was not significant.

Explanation of the decremental effects of satiation as due entirely to decreased meaning of satiated members was rejected on grounds of a presumed implication of significantly less rapid acquisition after response satiation than after stimulus satiation. Contrary to this implication, the difference was not significant. Then proposed was a two-process explanation: decreased meaning and increased strength of the association between the recognition response and itself. In terms of these processes, the decremental consequence of satiation of response members was attributed entirely to decreased meaning; the decremental consequence of satiation of stimulus meaning was attributed to decreased meaning and increased intra-recognition-response associations.

The increased intra-recognition-response associations were placed within conventional transfer paradigms. Satiation experiences with stimulus members, response members, and with irrelevant stimuli were each viewed as an S_{i1} S_{i2} pairing in which S_{i1} is one occurrence of stimuli produced by the recognition response to the ith stimulus and S_{i2} is a continued or "second" occurrence of that stimulus and recognition response thereto. When the satiated stimulus occurs as a stimulus member, the proffered representation is S_{i1} $S_{i'2}$. The paradigm for the two successive tasks, therefore is S_{i1} S_{i2}, S_{i1} $S_{i'2}$. On the basis of interference of the repeated recognition response with the recognition response to the paired response member which is to be anticipated or recalled, negative transfer was predicted.

When the satiated stimulus occurs as a response member, the proffered representation is $S_{i'1}$ S_{i2} to form a S_{i1} S_{i2}, $S_{i'1}$ S_{i2} paradigm. Positive or no transfer would be predicted on the basis of degree of similarity between S_{i1} and $S_{i'1}$ and hence generalization of the response to S_{i2} to $S_{i'1}$. When an irrelevant stimulus is replaced by two new stimuli as members of a PA unit, the paradigm is S_{i1} S_{i2}, $S_{i'1}$ $S_{i'2}$, with marked dissimilarity between S_{i1} and $S_{i'1}$ and also between S_{i2} and $S_{i'2}$. Therefore, no transfer effects due to specific associations would be predicted.

Predictions from this analysis were tested in a second experiment for which both stimulus members and response members were low frequency, low M_n nouns. Presumably, satiation would not lower the meanings of these stimuli while increasing intra-recognition-response associations. Predicted was negative transfer to PA learning from stimulus satiation and positive transfer from response satiation. Means of trials to three consecutive errorless trials adjusted for rate of learning a practice list were 10.61, 15.91, and 11.56 for response satiation, stimulus satiation, and different word satiation, respectively. The corresponding means for errors were 16.33, 24.42, and 19.00. The F for trials was significant; the F for errors was not. The difference between the conditions of stimulus satiation and different word satiation was significant at less than .05 in agreement with the prediction of negative transfer effects of stimulus satiation. The mean of trials to criterion for response satiation was not significantly lower than the mean for different word satiation. As the authors note, this failure to obtain the predicted positive transfer may be due to dissimilarity between satiated stimuli and stimulus members of the PA lists.

Sheffield's (1946) lists were partly mixed. The baselines for assessment of effects of familiarization of stimulus or response members were "within-subjects" differences between acquisition with pairs whose stimulus and response members represented combinations of meaningfulness of high-high and high-low or of high-high and low-high. The members of these pairs of low meaningfulness were familiarized so that effects of familiarization were reflected in "within-subjects" differences between the high-high and high-low pairs or between the high-high and low-high pairs. Familiarization of the stimulus members of low-high pairs for 10 trials had an inhibitory effect which 20 trials did not entirely overcome. Familiarization of response members of high-low pairs was facilitative, but 20 trials were no more effective than 10.

The inhibitory effect of familiarization of stimulus members may have been the consequence of the particular procedure for familiarization. The same response was conditioned to all 10 stimulus members. Subsequently that common response may have increased similarity among stimulus members to retard acquisition of different response members to those stimulus members. That the inhibition was greater with 10 than with 20 familiarization trials may reflect increasing positive transfer from nonspecific sources. Also, pronunciation of stimulus members may have become faster to lengthen the effective anticipation interval. For familiarization of response members, these factors, relative to greater response integration and response availability, would have been negligible.

Noble (1963) describes the incomplete results of an experiment in which subjects spelled CVCs of low M_r for 0, 1, 2, 4, 8, 16, 32, or 64 exposures.

These trigrams were then the stimulus members of a list whose response members had not been familiarized or the response members of a list whose stimulus members had not been familiarized. Familiarization of response members led to better performances through 50 learning trials than familiarization of stimulus members which, in turn, led to faster acquisition than occurred with pairs whose stimulus and response members were both unfamiliarized.

UNFAMILIARIZED-UNFAMILIARIZED VS. FAMILIARIZED-FAMILIARIZED

The eight different lists of Goss, Nodine, Gregory, Taub, and Kennedy's (1962) second experiment represented combinations of stimulus and response members of high and low similarity and high and low M_a acquired under 25% or 100% ORM. Both stimulus and response members or neither stimulus nor response members were familiarized for four or 12 trials. There was an irrelevant stimulus control for effects of nonspecific factors. Across all combinations of the other variables, the difference between unfamiliarized-unfamiliarized and familiarized-familiarized lists was not significant. Nor did familiarization enter into interactions in patterns suggestive of significant effects. In a subsequent study with a somewhat different familiarization procedure, two lists representing the easiest and the hardest combinations of similarity and M_a of stimulus and response members were acquired under 25% and 100% ORM; again familiarization of both stimulus and response members was not facilitative.

In the first of Epstein, Rock, and Zuckerman's (1960) experiments, subjects had, for practical purposes, one familiarization trial with each of 12 CVCs of 80% Glaze M_a. These trigrams were then used to form a list of six pairs with familiarized stimulus and familiarized response members. The control was a list of six unfamiliarized-unfamiliarized pairs. Following two learning trials in which each pair was presented for 5 sec., there was a 1-min. wait and then a recall trial. More responses were recalled with the familiarized-familiarized list than with the unfamiliarized-unfamiliarized list.

In the fourth of the Epstein, Rock, and Zuckerman experiments, the procedure of the first experiment was modified for group administration. The results of this experiment, combined with findings of their second and third experiments, were interpreted as indicating that familiarization of both stimulus and response members was facilitative.

In contrast to these findings of facilitative effects of familiarization of stimulus and response members, Besch (1961), in her first experiment, found that six familiarization trials with both stimulus and response members produced significant inhibition relative to unfamiliarized-unfamiliarized controls.

The experimental list of Battig, Williams, and Williams' (1962) second experiment contained several subsets of familiarized-familiarized pairs, each with different familiarization histories; familiarization involved verbal-discrimination learning to two errorless trials or 24 trials. Comparisons of acquisition of these subsets were "within subjects." Comparisons of acquisition of these subsets with acquisition of a control list of unfamiliarized-unfamiliarized pairs were "between subjects." The means of correct responses for pairs representing the three major subsets of discriminated and familiarized stimulus and response members were, for one subset, slightly but not significantly larger than the mean for the list of unfamiliarized-unfamiliarized pairs. Means of correct responses for the other two subsets were lower than the mean for the list of unfamiliarized-unfamiliarized pairs. With one error term, these differences were not significant; with another error term, the differences were significant at .05. Thus, familiarization of stimulus and response members was certainly not facilitative and, under some conditions, may have been inhibitory.

Familiarization was a "within-subjects" variable in Battig, Williams, and Williams' first experiment. The 12-pair lists contained four pairs whose stimulus and response members were familiarized and discriminated, four pairs whose stimulus and response members were familiarized, and four control pairs whose stimulus and response members had not been familiarized. Means of correct responses for the familiarized and discriminated pairs and for the control pairs were 9.72 and 9.88, respectively. The mean for the familiarized pairs was 7.67. Thus, familiarization and discrimination made no difference and familiarization may have been inhibitory.

Replication and extension of this experiment by Battig and Brackett (1963) were discussed previously in connection with positively correlated similarity of stimulus and of response members. The variables in addition to similarity and familiarization were %ORM and presentation under both recall and anticipation formats. The over-all F for discriminated, familiarized, and control pairs was significant at less than .025. Correct responses decreased in the order discriminated, control, and familiarized pairs for which the only significant difference was between discriminated and familiarized pairs.

The interaction of familiarization with format of presentation approached significance at .10. The pattern responsible was the discriminated > control > familiarized order under the anticipation format but not under the recall format. Battig, Williams, and Williams had employed the anticipation format so their findings were confirmed. The interaction of familiarization, format, and %ORM was significant for the before-errors measures: more errors occurred with familiarized than with discriminated and control pairs with the anticipation-100% ORM and the recall-50% ORM combinations; familiarization produced no differences with the anticipation-50% ORM and recall-100% ORM combinations. The form of the interaction suggests attributing it to chance fluctuations.

The results of Spear, Ekstrand, and Underwood's (1964) third experiment provide some clarification of the nonsignificant or slight facilitative effects Battig and collaborators obtained with discrimination training, and of the apparent inhibitory effects they obtained with familiarization training. In that experiment, 12 pairs of three- and four-letter words were presented for verbal discrimination to a criterion of two perfect trials. The control condition was the same verbal discrimination task with irrelevant stimuli. For the subsequent PA task, members of these pairs were either kept together (appropriate pairings) or each was paired with a member of another pair (reversed or inappropriate pairings). These pairings correspond to those which Battig and collaborators called discrimination training and familiarization training, respectively. Within both appropriate and inappropriate pairings half of the correct members of pairs during verbal discrimination served as stimulus members and half served as response members, or all correct members served as stimulus members or as response members.

Means of total correct responses during 10 trials of PA learning did not differ among the three arrangements within appropriate pairings or among the three arrangements within inappropriate pairings. The mean of 87.2 for the arrangements within appropriate pairings combined was significantly larger than the mean of 72.0 for the control condition which, in turn, was significantly larger than the mean of 59.6 for the arrangements within inappropriate pairings combined.

Spear, Ekstrand, and Underwood interpreted these results as evidence of the strengthening of bidirectional association between members of pairs presented for verbal discrimination. Contiguity and a requirement for subjects to "learn something" were apparently sufficient conditions. With appropriate pairings such strengthening should be and was facilitative for PA learning; with inappropriate pairings such strengthening should be and was inhibitory. Battig and collaborators had assumed that neither discrimination training nor familiarization training involved formation of associations between members of pairs. The assumption seems incorrect.

Spear, Ekstrand, and Underwood suggest that Battig and collaborators' use of CVCs of relatively low meaningfulness (34–37% Archer M_a), instead of more meaningful words, might have resulted in associations between members of pairs which were, at most, of low strength. When paired for PA learning in the manner of discrimination training, no or only slight facilitation would, therefore, be expected. Indeed, the facilitation which was obtained might have been due to integration of recognition responses rather than to slight initial strength of associations between stimulus and response members. When paired for PA learning in the manner of familiarization training only slight inhibitory effects would then also be expected. The inhibition observed, however, was apparently greater than any facilitation produced by discrimination training. No reason for this asymmetry of effects is immediately evident.

These findings suggest that verbal discrimination is not a satisfactory technique for familiarization in that any integration of recognition responses may also involve formation of bidirectional associations between members of pairs. The technique of familiarization by selection of a stimulus from matrices of stimuli which Battig (1964) employed subsequently seems less likely to result in associations of effective strength between the familiarized stimulus and other stimuli of the matrix. Any facilitative effects of such familiarization, therefore, would be more likely to reflect changes in recognition responses to stimuli alone rather than effects of such changes plus the formation of new associations. Whether or not formation of new associations is minimized can be determined by experiments in which Spear, Ekstrand, and Underwood's design is extended to larger numbers of stimuli.

Goss, Nodine, Gregory, Taub, and Kennedy's (1962) Experiment IV was also with four-pair lists representing the easiest and the hardest combinations of similarity and M_a of stimulus and response members. The lists were acquired under 25% ORM and 100% ORM. Two of the response members had been familiarized for 12 or 60 trials and two of the response members had not been familiarized. Even for such presumably more sensitive "within-subjects" comparisons, familiarization had no apparent effect.

As described in Experiment 3 in the Appendix, two of the four response members of four-pair lists had been presented for 60 familiarization trials; the other two response members had not been familiarized. These lists represented the 16 combinations of stimulus and response members of low or high similarity and of low or high M_a. They were learned by recall under group administration for 48 trials under 25% or 100% ORM. Familiarization had no significant over-all effect, and there were no patterns suggestive of significant interactions with one or more of the other variables.

In Besch, Thompson, and Wetzel's (1962) third experiment, stimuli of List B were familiarized for one set of four groups; another set of four groups had familiarization experiences with irrelevant stimuli beginning with the same letters. Familiarized or unfamiliarized stimuli occurred as both stimulus and response members in D-C pairs and also as response members of A-C and A_1-C pairs. With the D-C pairs, more correct responses occurred with unfamiliarized than with familiarized stimulus and response members. With the A-C and A_1-C pairs combined, familiarization of response members resulted in slightly more correct responses. The D-C comparisons involving familiarized and unfamiliarized stimuli could be regarded as familiarized-familiarized versus unfamiliarized-unfamiliarized. The A-C and A_1-C comparisons could be regarded as familiarized-familiarized and familiarized-unfamiliarized on an assumption of familiarization of A during first-list acquisition. Strictly, the design for this comparison is variations in familiarization of response members. Because of differences in manner of familiarization and extent of transfer from first-list acquisition, the two familiarized-familiarized combinations cannot be pooled and the unfamiliarized-unfamiliarized combinations cannot be compared with the two combinations for the A_1-C and A-C pairs regarded as familiarized-unfamiliarized.

Rock and Heimer (1959) report that "names were first pre-exposed by presenting them individually for three trials in random order. Subsequent learning of pairs formed from these names proved to be no better than of other name pairs" (p. 8). Whether this comparison of acquisition with apparently familiarized-familiarized pairs and with apparently unfamiliarized-unfamiliarized pairs was "within subjects" or "between subjects" is not stated explicitly.

Compared in Battig's (1964, pp. 10-14) experiment were effects of familiarization by recall in any order or in exact order and by a variation on the technique of selection of a stimulus from among those in a matrix. Fourteen stimuli which had been familiarized by means of each of these techniques were paired to form seven familiarized-familiarized pairs; three unfamiliarized-unfamiliarized pairs were added. For each of the three techniques of familiarization, whether expressed in terms of correct reproductions of both trigrams of the pairs or of individual trigrams, familiarized-familiarized pairs were acquired more rapidly than unfamiliarized-unfamiliarized pairs. Acquisition was most rapid following familiarization by recall in exact order and least rapid following familiarization by recall in any order. The magnitudes of differences between familiarized and unfamiliarized pairs were in the same order.

FAMILIARIZATION OF STIMULUS MEMBERS

In Schulz and Tucker's two experiments, familiarized stimulus members were paired with unfamiliarized response members. The first experiment (1962a) involved 2 sec. to anticipate responses to stimulus members familiarized for 0, 20, or 60 trials. Half of the subjects of each familiarization condition learned with instructions to say stimulus members overtly before anticipation; half learned under instructions which did not require overt pronunciation.

Under instructions for overt pronunciation, number of correct responses was a negatively accelerated function of amount of familiarization. Under instructions which did not require overt pronunciation, the fastest learning was by subjects with no prior familiarization with amount of familiarization inversely related to number of correct responses.

Overt anticipation, Schulz and Tucker hypothesized, reduced the interval for anticipation and, therefore, decreased performance. This reduction was only partially overcome by 60 familiarization trials which, because of increasing speeds of evocation and completion of pronouncing the stimulus members, would have lengthened the interval for anticipation. Following overt pronunciation of stimulus members during 20 or 60 familiarization trials, PA learning with no overt pronunciation of stimulus members may have involved conflict between overt and covert pronunciation which was a direct function of amount of familiarization. On the assumption that such conflict would be inhibitory, acquisition rate and amount of familiarization should be related inversely.

Schulz and Tucker's (1962b) test of their explanation of the preceding findings involved lengthening the anticipation interval to 4 sec. which, along with omission of the 20-trial condition, was the only important difference between the two experiments. The longer interval, they hypothesized, would provide sufficient opportunity for overt pronunciation of stimulus members and anticipation of response members; consequently differences due to familiarization and to instructions should be reduced or eliminated. Such was the case: familiarization had no effects and the difference between instructions which did and did not require overt pronunciation was reduced, although learning under instructions for overt pronunciation was slightly inferior to learning without such instructions.

Tucker (1962) replicated the conditions of the first of the Schulz and Tucker experiments. Added was the recording of latency and duration of pronunciations of stimulus members during the 20 or 60 familiarization trials and, for the overt pronunciation condition, during the 15 trials of PA learning. Contrary to the original results, neither familiarization nor overtness of pronunciation influenced rate of acquisition of correct responses. Nor were these variables related to latency and duration of pronunciation of the stimulus members. Noting that the majority of the subjects had already participated in one or more verbal learning experiments, Tucker analyzed the protocols of only those subjects who had not previously participated in such experiments. The results for each of the naive subjects exhibited the expected direct relationship between number of familiarization trials and speeds of evocation and completion of pronunciation of the stimulus members. But too few naive subjects were available to warrant statistical analyses.

Overt or covert pronunciation of stimulus members may influence acquisition at least with anticipation intervals of up to 4 sec. However, even disregarding Tucker's ambiguous results, the evidence is not entirely consistent. For acquisition with and without overt pronunciation of dissyllabic stimulus members during 2-sec. anticipation intervals, but with numbers rather than adjectives as response members, Hakes (1961b) reports overlapping curves. Nonetheless, Schulz and Tucker's results suggest that Gannon and Noble's (1961) original and Hakes's (1961a) replicatory findings of a significant facilitative effect of familiarization of stimulus members may be of limited generality: specifically, such facilitation may be demonstrable only with overt pronunciation of stimulus members and anticipation intervals of up to 4 sec. The findings of the Gannon and Noble, Hakes, and Schulz and Tucker studies together provide indirect support for the notion that the direct relationship between acquisition rate and meaningfulness of stimulus members is due in part to faster evocation and completion of all or some components of recognition responses, with consequent longer effective anticipation intervals.

Children of kindergarten age were the subjects of Staats, Staats, and Schutz's (1962) experiment. "Discrimination pretraining" or familiarizations of four words or of the 12 letters contained in those words was by subjects pointing to "the one that doesn't belong" in triads of two instances of one word or letter and one instance of another word or letter. The words then served as stimulus members for which the experimenter saying the word was the response member. During 10 trials of PA learning, children whose familiarization experiences had been with words made more correct responses than those whose familiarization experiences had been with the letters. Children who had not had familiarization experiences made the smallest number of correct responses. While suggesting facilitation due to familiarization, these differences were of doubtful significance statistically. The importance of the experiment, therefore, is largely in the use of children as subjects rather than adults. That Staats, Staats, and Schutz's term "familiarization" has a different meaning than familiarization as used here should be noted.

The stimulus members of C. J. Martin's (1963) 12-pair lists were nine words of high M_n and three dissyllables of low M_n. Single letters served as response members. After two trials, the dissyllables were retained through trials to a criterion of one perfect trial (C), they were retained but the responses to them were reversed (E-1), or they were replaced by new dissyllables of low M_n (E-2). Only subjects who had not made a correct response to these stimuli were continued through the remaining trials.

The medians of the number of trials to the first correct recall under each of these conditions were 13 for C, 17 for E-1, and 23 for E-2. The differences among these values by the Mann-Whitney U-test were significant at .05 or less. The more rapid acquisition under the C than under the E-1 condition was interpreted as support for an incremental conception of the formation of associations. Were a prediction made only in terms of relationships between the dissyllables and recall of the response members, the re-pairing of the E-1 condition would have been expected to occasion slower acquisition under this than under the E-2 condition. The opposite trend obtained. To account for this, Martin postulated the development of differentiation among the dissyllables during the first two trials. The differentiation presumably in part offset the inhibitory consequences of re-pairing. Alternatively, or perhaps in different words, the experiences with the dissyllables during those trials can be viewed as leading to greater integration of recognition responses to the dissyllables. Thus restated, Martin's results are some evidence of facilitation produced by familiarization of stimulus members.

FAMILIARIZATION OF RESPONSE MEMBERS

In contrast to Gannon and Noble's (1961) and Hakes's (1961a, 1961b) findings, facilitative effects of familiarization of response members were obtained in three other experiments with unmixed lists. The pairs learned in Underwood, Runquist, and Schulz's (1959) two experiments had response members of low or high similarity in terms of common meaning. These response members had or had not been familiarized previously by a procedure which consisted of five learning trials with the response members in different orders with each trial followed by a recall test. In the first experiment, familiarization of response members of low similarity was facilitative only during the first five trials of PA learning. Familiarization of response members of high similarity was facilitative both for response members of low and for response members of high similarity throughout the 15 trials. In neither experiment, however, was the interaction of similarity of response members and familiarization significant.

Saltz (1961) used a familiarization procedure resembling that of Underwood, Runquist, and Schulz. During PA learning, however, Saltz made all relevant responses available on a card on the top of the memory drum. With both similar and dissimilar response members, the lists with familiarized response members were learned faster than those with unfamiliarized response members. In addition, Saltz found that, both for response members of low similarity and response members of high similarity, familiarization reduced oscillation from correct to incorrect responses. Because response members were available, Saltz interprets his findings as favoring an interpretation of familiarization as increasing response differentiation rather than as increasing response availability.

The conclusion advanced by Saltz of facilitation due to differentiation of response members over and above facilitation attributable to response availability has been questioned by Runquist and English (1964). They suggest that Saltz's anticipation interval might have been too short for subjects to use the cards on which the response members appeared as means of selecting and giving the responses. Thus, the responses may not have been equally available. Ignoring response similarity, Runquist and English replicated Saltz's arrangement (paced) and added one in which subjects could select and give responses at their own pace (unpaced). Acquisition of a 10-

pair list under paced or unpaced arrangements was preceded by five familiarization experiences with the response members of the pairs (relevant) or with another set of response members (irrelevant).

During the first eight trials under the unpaced arrangement the curve for relevant familiarization was above that for irrelevant familiarization. Since effects of familiarization should be most evident during the early trials, this difference constitutes some corroboration of Saltz's findings. Surprisingly, under the unpaced arrangement, the curve for irrelevant familiarization was consistently above that for relevant familiarization. A possible explanation is that subjects under the latter condition took longer to respond and hence were able to respond better.

As both Schulz and Lovelace (1964) and Runquist and English have observed, the Schulz and Lovelace finding of an inverse relationship between latency of selection and meaningfulness of stimuli complicates interpretations of results of experiments in which response availability was presumably equalized by presentation of all of the response members for subjects to respond by selection. Unless latency of selection is equated among stimuli which differ in meaningfulness or in extent of familiarization, responses cannot be considered equally available. Schulz (personal communication) has used response members of equal latencies of selection but his results are not in final form.

On the assumption of no similarity between the sets of stimulus members of Crawford and Vanderplas' (1959) first and criterion tasks, the B-C first task might be viewed as familiarizing subjects with the response members of the A-C criterion task. There were two groups which had such first-task experience, C-1 and C-4, for whose criterion task performance the controls were, respectively, C-3 and C-6. C-1 learned less rapidly than C-3, but C-4 learned more rapidly than C-6. Thus, the first difference suggested that familiarization was inhibitory and the second that familiarization was facilitative; but neither difference was significant.

Blanchard (1962) familiarized CVCs by the technique of Underwood and Schulz's (1960a) first experiment for 0, 10, 20, or 40 trials. With adjectives of low similarity as stimulus members and the CVCs as response members, number of correct responses was a negatively accelerated function of familiarization. Performance of a group administered 40 familiarization trials on irrelevant CVCs was between that of the 0 and 10 familiarization groups. One reason for the more pronounced effect of familiarization in this experiment may be Blanchard's use of a list with adjectives as stimulus members and CVCs as response members in contrast to the CVC stimulus and response members of Underwood and Schulz's list.

Hypothesizing that Gannon and Noble's (1961) failure to obtain facilitation from familiarization of response members may have been due to interference from the irrelevant response members of the familiarization experience, Horowitz and Larsen (1963) compared transfer from familiarization of response members to associative matching and to PA learning. Greater interference and hence less transfer was anticipated for PA learning than for associative matching. The four conditions were familiarization with the Japanese words later used as response members of a PA list, familiarization with Japanese words different than those which were the response members of the PA list, familiarization with Russian words in the Roman alphabet, and a no familiarization control.

For correct responses across all five trials of associative matching or of PA learning, no differences in transfer effects occurred which were attributable to familiarization with relevant Japanese words, familiarization with irrelevant Japanese words, or familiarization with irrelevant Russian words. Nor did these conditions differ significantly from the no familiarization control. However, for both associative matching and PA learning, the interactions of conditions and trials were significant. Associative matching was better during the first three trials following familiarization with relevant or with irrelevant Japanese words than following familiarization with Russian words or with no familiarization. Familiarization with relevant Japanese words led to the fastest PA learning during the first three trials; familiarization with irrelevant Japanese words led to the slowest learning. The results were not those predicted in that any facilitative effects of familiarization of response members were with PA learning rather than with associative matching. And familiarization had only a slight effect.

The response words of the lists constructed by Kanungo, Lambert, and Mauer (1962) for their first experiments were of high counted frequency, high M_p; the CVC stimulus members were of low M_a. Prior to learning these lists, subjects of the experimental group had satiation experiences with the response members; subjects of the control group had satiation experiences with irrelevant words. Both in terms of trials and errors, satiation slowed acquisition of the PA lists although only the difference for errors was significant.

Findings of W. Epstein's (1963) experiment were described earlier in terms of M_n of stimulus and of response members. As mentioned there, familiarization was by learning to recall response members. For all combinations of high and low M_n of stimulus and response members, familiarization occasioned fewer trials to mastery of correct anticipations and fewer trials to availability of response members. Familiarization and M_n interacted in the form of a smaller difference in trials to mastery of familiarized response members. But the two variables did not interact in this manner for trials to availability of response members.

Noted earlier were the comparisons involving the A-C and A_1-C pairs of

Besch, Thompson, and Wetzel's (1962) List B, which were considered familiarized-familiarized and familiarized-unfamiliarized. Familiarization of responses was slightly facilitative.

FAMILIARIZATION OF STIMULUS MEMBERS VARIED,
FAMILIARIZATION OF RESPONSE MEMBERS VARIED

R. L. Weiss's (1958) design included 10 of the 16 combinations of stimulus and response members of high or low M_a which were or were not
familiarized. Because these variables were not orthogonal, effects of familiarization of stimulus members and of familiarization of response members were
analyzed separately. Acquisition with familiarized stimulus members for
combinations of high-high, low-high, and low-low M_a was compared with
acquisition with unfamiliarized stimulus members for the same M_a combinations. Means of trials to criterion adjusted for practice performance were
lower with familiarized stimulus members than with unfamiliarized stimulus
members for the high-high and low-high M_a combinations but not for the
low-low combination. The over-all F for familiarization was not significant.
However, familiarization of stimulus members did produce greater over-all
backward recall of stimulus members.

Acquisition with familiarized response members for high-high, high-low,
and low-low M_a combinations was compared with acquisition with unfamiliarized response members for the same combinations of M_a. For all three M_a
combinations, means of trials to criterion adjusted for practice performance
were lower with familiarized response members than with unfamiliarized
response members. However, as expected, the difference for the high-high
combination was the smallest of the three and was not significant. Familiarization of response members did not influence backward recall. Thus, familiarization of stimulus members did not facilitate acquisition but did increase
backward recall of stimulus members; familiarization of response members
facilitated acquisition but had no effect on backward recall.

In Underwood and Schulz's (1960a) first experiment, each pair of eight-
pair unmixed lists consisted of stimulus members with which subjects had
had 1, 10, 20, or 40 familiarization trials paired with unfamiliarized response
members, or the converse. Less than 40 familiarization trials with response
members apparently had no effect, but 40 trials were slightly facilitative.
More correct responses were made with familiarized response members than
with familiarized stimulus members. While less than 40 familiarization trials
with stimulus members had no effect, 40 trials produced some inhibition
which was tentatively attributed to loss of differentiation between stimulus
and response members.

The loss-of-differentiation hypothesis was tested by comparing the difference between rates of acquisition of lists of syllable-syllable and of syllable-

paralog pairs whose stimulus members had been familiarized with the difference between the same lists without familiarization of stimulus members (pp. 110-113). This design might be regarded as one which combines type of response members—syllables or paralogs—which were not familiarized with stimulus members which were and were not familiarized. Loss-of-differentiation would be indicated by interaction of type of response members with familiarized or unfamiliarized stimulus members. The interaction F was nonsignificant; familiarization of stimulus members was neither facilitative nor inhibitory.

The primary concern of Hakes's (1961b) second experiment was whether familiarization of stimulus members had facilitative effects with dissyllabic stimulus members but not with one-syllable stimulus members. One set of conditions was unmixed lists of familiarized (20 trials) or unfamiliarized stimulus or response members of CVC structure with numbers as response or stimulus members, respectively. Another set of conditions was unmixed lists of familiarized (20 trials) or unfamiliarized dissyllabic stimulus or response members of CVCVC structure paired with the same numbers as response or stimulus members, respectively. Neither familiarization of trigram nor familiarization of dissyllabic stimulus members influenced acquisition rate. But familiarization of response members, both trigrams and dissyllables, was facilitative. Whether the familiarized stimulus or response members were trigrams or dissyllables made no difference. Suggested, however, is the additional limitation of Gannon and Noble's and Hakes's results to lists with syllables but not numbers as stimulus or response members.

The design of Kanungo, Lambert and Mauer's (1962) second experiment involved four trials with a list of 12 pairs of words followed by satiation experiences with half the stimulus members for one group and with half the response members for the other group. The remaining stimulus or response members were unsatiated and the response members for the first group and stimulus members for the second group were unsatiated. Subjects were then shown each stimulus member for 3 sec. for recall of its response member. For pairs with satiated stimulus members, correct responses decreased from 3.00 on the fourth acquisition trial to 1.73 on the recall trial; for pairs with unsatiated stimulus members, the decrease was from 2.85 to 2.27. The difference in decrements was significant at less than .001. For pairs with satiated or unsatiated response members, the difference in decrements from 2.65 to 1.96 and from 2.65 to 1.84, respectively, did not even approach significance. Satiation of stimulus members but not of response members proved decremental, a finding which was explained by means of the transfer interpretation described earlier in connection with Kanungo and Lambert's (1963) experiments.

Schulz and Martin's (1964) lists were the eight pairs of CVCs and numbers or of numbers and CVCs employed previously by Martin and Schulz

(1963). Two each of the CVCs had mean pronunciability values of 8.54 (hard), 6.44, 3.34, and 1.93 (easy). Different groups of 30 subjects each had 30 familiarization trials with these CVCs (relevant) or with different but comparable CVCs (irrelevant) or they had no familiarization experiences ("0"). Familiarization consisted of the experimenter spelling the CVCs while subjects listened silently, with recall of the stimuli after 10, 20, and 30 trials. Number of CVCs recalled was a direct function of ease of pronunciation; slope of the acquisition curves was progressively steeper as pronunciability decreased.

The curves for 30 familiarization experiences with relevant and irrelevant stimulus members overlapped. Thus familiarization had no specific facilitative effects. However, both curves were significantly above the curve for "0" familiarization to indicate some facilitative effects of nonspecific changes during the familiarization experiences. Acquisition was faster as pronunciability was easier, with parallel curves for the three conditions. The curve for 30 familiarization experiences with relevant response members was significantly above the curve for 30 familiarization experiences with irrelevant response members which, in turn, was significantly above the curve for "0" experiences. The former difference can be attributed to specific facilitative effects of familiarization; the latter difference to nonspecific facilitative effects. Rate of acquisition was related directly to ease of pronunciation. The greater difference between the curves for relevant and irrelevant familiarization experiences for CVCs difficult to pronounce than for those easy to pronounce suggested that familiarization had a relatively greater facilitative effect on the former CVCs. The curves for variations in pronunciability of response members were consistently steeper than the corresponding curves for variations in pronunciability of stimulus members. Thus, Martin and Schulz's finding for "0" familiarization was replicated and extended.

DeBold (1964) attempted to devise a technique of prior exposure to stimuli which would induce differentiation among or acquired distinctiveness of stimulus or response members over and above any effects of familiarization in terms of sheer frequency of prior experiences with stimuli. The specific technique to induce acquired distinctiveness was for subjects to pronounce members of pairs of CVCs of high formal similarity aloud and then to rate their pronunciability. Why this procedure was presumed to induce acquired distinctiveness is not clear. Familiarization was also accomplished by requiring subjects to pronounce members of the pairs. Both relevant and irrelevant familiarization experiences were administered, with the CVCs then serving as stimulus or response members for which the response members or stimulus members were two-digit numbers. In addition, one group of subjects who had had no familiarization experiences learned the list with CVCs as stimulus members and another group without familiarization experiences learned the list with CVCs as response members.

With CVCs as stimulus members, relevant familiarization by pronunciation or pronunciation plus ratings led to fewer correct responses during 20 trials than did irrelevant familiarization by these techniques. With CVCs as response members, the same relationship held following familiarization by pronunciation, but there was no difference following familiarization by pronunciation plus ratings. Thus, in three of four comparisons of the effects of relevant and irrelevant familiarization, relevant familiarization slowed acquisition; the retardation was greater following familiarization by pronunciation than following familiarization by pronunciation plus ratings. In comparisons of the same three relevant familiarization conditions with groups which had had no familiarization experiences, inhibitory effects of familiarization were also evident. Only for relevant familiarization of response members by pronunciation plus ratings was the mean about equal to the mean for the comparable group which had had no familiarization experiences. The most likely basis of the observed inhibitory effects was interference within the lists arising from associations between members of pairs which had been established during familiarization (Spear, Ekstrand, & Underwood, 1964).

Summary of Results for Familiarization

For summary purposes, satiation experiences are regarded as variations on familiarization. Findings with unmixed and mixed 2×2 complete orthogonal designs supported a tentative conclusion of faster learning of familiarized-familiarized lists or pairs than of unfamiliarized-familiarized, familiarized-unfamiliarized, or unfamiliarized-unfamiliarized lists or pairs. However, the evidence does not unequivocally support a conclusion of greater facilitation due to familiarization of response members than due to familiarization of stimulus members.

The results of experiments involving various incomplete orthogonal designs are less consistent. With respect to familiarization of response members, facilitation has been obtained with unmixed lists by R. L. Weiss (1958), Underwood, Runquist, and Schulz (1959), Underwood and Schulz (1960a), Saltz (1961), Blanchard (1962), and Epstein (1963); with partly mixed lists by Sheffield (1946); and with a mixed list by Noble (1963), Kanungo and Lambert (1963), Schulz and Martin (1964), and perhaps by Besch, Thompson, and Wetzel (1962). But familiarization of response members has not proved facilitative or has been inhibitory in a number of other experiments involving small to considerable amounts of familiarization by several techniques and variations thereof with both unmixed and partly mixed lists (Besch, 1961; Crawford & Vanderplas, 1959; DeBold, 1964; Experiments 3 and 6 in Appendix; Gannon & Noble, 1961; Goss, Nodine, Gregory, Taub, & Kennedy, 1962; Hakes, 1961b; Kanungo & Lambert, 1963; Kanungo, Lambert, & Mauer, 1962). With unmixed lists, Runquist and English (1964) obtained slight facilitation under a paced arrangement and inhibition under an unpaced arrangement.

Findings on effects of familiarization of stimulus members are also contradictory. Some facilitation, though not always significant, has been obtained by Gannon and Noble, Hakes, Noble, and Schulz and Martin. However, Schulz and Tucker's results suggest that familiarization of stimulus members may be facilitative only under relatively special conditions. Both for Schulz and Tucker and for others (Besch, 1961; DeBold, 1964; Experiments 3 and 6 in Appendix; Kanungo & Lambert, 1963; Kanungo, Lambert, & Mauer, 1962; Sheffield, 1946; Underwood & Schulz, 1960a; Weiss, 1958), familiarization of stimulus members has also proved ineffectual or inhibitory.

Comparisons of unfamiliarized-unfamiliarized and familiarized-familiarized combinations do not permit separation of effects of familiarization of stimulus members and of familiarization of response members. While acquisition with familiarized-familiarized lists or pairs has sometimes been faster than with unfamiliarized-unfamiliarized lists or pairs (Battig, 1964, pp. 10-14; Epstein, Rock, & Zuckerman, 1960), the more common outcomes have been no difference or inhibition (Battig & Brackett, 1963; Battig, Williams, & Williams, 1962; Besch, 1961; Besch, Thompson, & Wetzel, 1962; Goss, Nodine, Gregory, Taub, & Kennedy, 1962).

These findings of facilitation, no effects, and of inhibition have been for varying amounts of familiarization by different techniques with unmixed, partly mixed, and mixed lists in both complete and incomplete orthogonal designs. At the present time, therefore, factors responsible for inconsistencies cannot be specified; and their ultimate identification is likely to prove a substantial enterprise.

Until better data on effects of familiarization are available, any interpretations of the bases of direct relationship between acquisition rate and meaningfulness of stimulus members and of meaningfulness of response members must be regarded as speculative at best and possibly premature. Experimental determination of the relative contribution of each of the several possible bases of effects of meaningfulness requires procedures for familiarization which are more certain and more general in their effects, whether facilitative or inhibitory. More and better information about the conditions and course of acquisition of verbal PA tasks may also be necessary.

CHAPTER 7

Meaning and Association

Acquired-distinctiveness training or training to establish response-mediated dissimilarity can be regarded as experiences which alter response hierarchies or meanings of stimuli. Other experiences with stimuli, but also acquired-distinctiveness training, have been explicitly considered means of inducing meaning and meaningfulness. In turn, stimuli produced by recognition responses, association responses, or both to stimulus members, which are altered by acquired-distinctiveness training or by induction of meaning and meaningfulness, may be associated with recognition responses, association responses, or both to response members to introduce the possibility of response mediation of associations between stimulus members and response members.

Integration and availability of recognition responses to stimulus and to response members and the patterning of the hierarchies of such responses should be a function of the number of their components or elements. Moreover, number of elements should influence ease and manner of selection of maximally dissimilar elements, primarily of stimulus members, since recognition responses based on entire response members are usually required. Also considered, therefore, are experiments involving manipulation of number and strength of associations between elements of recognition responses to stimulus and to response members.

ACQUIRED-DISTINCTIVENESS TRAINING

Acquired-distinctiveness training is only one way of manipulating responses to stimuli in manners calculated to influence the occurrence of still additional responses to those stimuli. Shown in Table 6 are 16 paradigms generated by combining binary values of similarity of stimulus members, similarity of mediating responses to those members, similarity of response members

TABLE 6

Paradigms Generated by Binary Values for Similarity of Stimulus Members, of Mediating Responses and Stimuli, and of Response Members and Recognition Responses to Them along with Initial Strengths of Associations between Mediating Stimuli and Recognition Responses to Response Members; Assumed Are Initial Strengths of Associations between Stimulus Members and Mediating Responses Greater than Zero

Conventional label for paradigm	Stimulus member	Mediating responses-stimuli	Response members and recognition responses to them	Strength of initial association
	Similar	Similar[a]	Similar[b]	0
	Similar	Similar	Dissimilar	0
	Similar	Similar	Similar	>0
	Similar	Similar	Dissimilar	>0
Acquired distinctiveness; response-mediated dissimilarity	Similar	Dissimilar	Similar	0
	Similar	Dissimilar	Dissimilar	0
Response-mediated discrimination	Similar	Dissimilar	Similar	>0
Response-mediated discrimination	Similar	Dissimilar	Dissimilar	>0
Acquired equivalence; response-mediated similarity	Dissimilar	Similar	Similar	0
	Dissimilar	Similar	Dissimilar	0
Response-mediated generalization	Dissimilar	Similar	Similar	>0
Response-mediated generalization	Dissimilar	Similar	Dissimilar	>0
	Dissimilar	Dissimilar	Similar	0
	Dissimilar	Dissimilar	Dissimilar	0
Response-mediated association	Dissimilar	Dissimilar	Similar	>0
	Dissimilar	Dissimilar	Dissimilar	>0

[a] The limiting case for similar mediating responses is the same response to two or more similar or dissimilar stimulus members.
[b] Evocation of similar responses by similar stimuli is assumed, but this is not a necessary relationship.

and recognition responses to them, and initial strengths of associations between stimuli produced by mediating responses and recognition responses to response members. Acquired-distinctiveness training presumably establishes dissimilar mediating responses and response-produced stimuli to similar initiating stimuli. The response members and recognition responses to them may be similar or dissimilar. Thus, two paradigms are subsumed by acquired-distinctiveness training. The dissimilar mediating responses which are established may be recognition responses, association responses, or both. Also, one or more than one of such responses may be established. In all cases they are presumably new in the strong sense of no prior relationship to the initiating stimuli or new in the weak sense of increases from initial values in the strength of some responses and decreases in the strength of others.

The relationship between acquired-distinctiveness training and acquired-equivalence training is evident from the table. Both types of training should be distinguished from prior training which has also involved the strengthening of associations between mediating stimuli and recognition responses to response members of which mediate association or response-mediated association is one paradigm. Response-mediated generalization and discrimination are two other types of training each of which also subsumes two of the paradigms of Table 6.

Within the paradigm labeled response-mediated association are the special paradigms which Jenkins (1963a) has labeled simple chains, reverse chains, stimulus equivalence and response equivalence. Jenkins' paradigms are differentiated by functions of the set of stimuli common to the two antecedent tasks, function in the criterion task of the set of stimuli unique to an antecedent task, and order of antecedent tasks. They are important here merely as special paradigms under response-mediated association which should not be confused with any of the other paradigms of Table 6.

As can be seen, some of the paradigms of Table 6 have no conventional label. Of the 16, only the two labeled acquired-distinctiveness training and the two involving dissimilar stimulus members, dissimilar mediating responses-stimuli, and zero strength of initial associations are considered here.

Effects of acquired-distinctiveness training on subsequent acquisition of associations between stimulus members (initiating stimuli) and recognition responses to response members (terminating responses) have been investigated extensively (Arnoult, 1957; Goss, 1955; Goss & Greenfeld, 1958). Unfortunately, however, only a few of the available experiments on effects of acquired-distinctiveness training are pertinent to the present concern of the role of such training in altering the presumed bases of the relationships between acquisition rate and meaningfulness of stimulus members and, perhaps, of response members. One reason for this lack of pertinence is the almost exclusive use of sets of nonverbal stimulus members in such studies in contrast to the almost exclusive use of verbal stimulus members in studies of effects of meaningfulness of stimulus members or of response members on acquisition. An exception is Vanderplas and Garvin's (1959b) investigation of the relationship between acquisition rate and M_a of nonsense forms. Also, except in the Vanderplas and Garvin investigation, meaningfulness of nonverbal stimuli of studies of acquired distinctiveness has not been specified. However, their criterion task was recognition rather than PA learning. Had the meaningfulness of the nonverbal stimuli of other studies of acquired distinctiveness been specified, the resultant findings would have only indirect relevance for interpretations of effects of meaningfulness of verbal stimulus members.

Sheffield (1946), Bailey and Jeffrey (1958), Crawford and Vanderplas (1959), and Saltz, Metzen, and Ernstein (1961) report data which might be regarded as involving acquired-distinctiveness training with verbal stimulus members of known meaningfulness. Sheffield regarded his symbolic training as experimental induction of meaning and meaningfulness. But, since the subjects learned a different response to each of 10 formally dissimilar trigrams, except that the stimulus members were dissimilar rather than similar, the procedure is that of acquired-distinctiveness training. Strictly, the paradigm was the third from the bottom of Table 6. As with familiarization of stimulus members, 10 trials of symbolic training of stimulus members had inhibitory effects which 20 trials did not entirely overcome. Ten trials of symbolic training of response members were slightly but not significantly more facilitative than 20 trials. Although the procedure resembled acquired-distinctiveness training, because the stimulus members were dissimilar, any mediating responses based on such training would not be expected to have appreciable effects on the dissimilarity of stimulus patterns consisting of stimulus members and mediating stimuli. Furthermore, symbolic training probably involved learning discriminative verbal responses as well as discriminative motor responses. Therefore, with verbal responses for both training and test tasks, Sheffield's conditions were those of the traditional A-B, A-C paradigm for negative transfer. And, as implied by this interpretation of symbolic training of stimulus members, inhibition did occur.

Symbolic training of response members, in addition to strengthening recognition responses, might increase the strength of association responses. Unless the presence of association responses increased indirect or response-mediated associations between stimulus and response members—and there was no evidence of this consequence—it seems unlikely that their occurrence per se would be facilitative. Sheffield did not attribute the observed facilitation of symbolic training of response members to response-mediated associations. Instead, symbolic training was interpreted as occasioning integration of perceptual responses to response members or, what are here labeled, recognition responses.

The training series for the "Single S-R Pairs" of Bailey and Jeffrey's (1958) first and third experiments involved the conditioning of different verbal responses to dissimilar and to similar stimulus members, respectively. The test was learning new, different responses to stimulus members which were presumably differentiated by mediating stimuli produced by responses strengthened during the training series. In the first experiment, slightly but not significantly fewer errors were made with pairs whose stimulus members had been in "Single S-R Pairs" during training than with pairs of the separate familiarization control. The paradigm for their training series and test list was A-B, A-C; thus the "B" responses may have interfered with the "C" responses to reduce any facilitation based on acquired distinctiveness. The use of a 3-sec. anticipation interval might have enabled "B" responses to function as mediating responses rather than as sources of interference with the "C" responses. But Bailey and Jeffrey's requirement of pronunciation of stimulus members probably shortened the effective anticipation interval so that the "B" responses remained potential sources of interference.

The other condition of Bailey and Jeffrey's third experiment, what they termed "Multiple R, Single S," was regarded as an arrangement for inducing meaning. There was no difference between mean errors under this condition and under the Single S-R Pairs condition. The criterion for acquisition of the successive training lists was relatively stringent. Consequently, for learning the test list immediately after mastery of the third training list, the associations of the Single S-R Pairs may not have been markedly stronger than associations of the third and last list of the Multiple R, Single S condition. Lack of a control for effects of familiarization and nonspecific sources of transfer precluded determination of whether the two conditions together facilitated or inhibited acquisition of the test list. Thus, the conditions of both experiments were unsatisfactory for determining possible contributions of response-mediated dissirilarity to the direct relationship between acquisition rate and meaningfulness of stimulus members.

Single S-R Pairs was also one of the training conditions of Bailey and Jeffrey's second experiment. Acquisition of pairs with these stimuli as response members of the test list was slightly but not significantly slower than with pairs of stimuli which subjects had not experienced previously. Acquired-distinctiveness training of response members, therefore, had no effect on acquisition rate.

The paradigms for the conditions which Crawford and Vanderplas (1959) labeled C-2 and C-3 were, respectively, D-E, A-B, A-C, and D-E, F-G, A-C. The A-B relationship of the second task of the C-2 paradigm might be regarded as providing acquired distinctiveness for "A" in the A-C task; the F-G relationship of the C-3 paradigm controlled for nonspecific sources of transfer but not for familiarization of "A." The —, A-B, A-C paradigm of C-5 might also be regarded as providing acquired-distinctiveness training. The D-E, —, A-C paradigm of C-6 controlled for nonspecific sources of transfer but not for familiarization of "A." The means of trials to criterion on A-C were 33.3 for C-2 and 28.1 for C-3. The means for C-5 and C-6 were 26.6 and 31.6, respectively. Thus, while the first comparison suggests that A-B training was inhibitory, the second comparison suggests that such training was facilitative. Neither difference was significant. The anticipation interval for the A-C task was 2 sec. which, as suggested above for A-B, A-C paradigms, might produce interference between "B" and "C" rather than chaining in which mediated "B" responses enhanced dissimilarity. The stimulus members of the A-C pairs were dissimilar. Even under more favorable training arrangements, therefore, any further differentiation by response-produced stimuli might have been negligible.

Saltz, Metzen, and Ernstein (1961, pp. 130-131) mention the results of an unpublished experiment by Yelen, Whitman, and Frazier on transfer to PA learning from acquired-distinctiveness training with nonsense-syllable stimulus members. Acquired-distinctiveness training with stimulus members of difficult pairs is described as facilitating acquisition of easy pairs whose stimulus members had not had acquired-distinctiveness training. In contrast, acquired-distinctiveness training with stimulus members of easy pairs is described as slowing acquisition of difficult pairs whose stimulus members had not had acquired-distinctiveness training. An alternative interpretation is facilitation stemming from acquired-distinctiveness training with stimulus members of difficult pairs and inhibition stemming from acquired-distinctiveness training with stimulus members of easy pairs.

An experiment of Staats, Staats, and Schutz (1962) which they described as involving "discrimination pretraining" was discussed previously as an example of effects of familiarization of stimulus members. Their procedure does not fit the paradigm of acquired distinctiveness as here defined. Nor does Martin's (1963) procedure fit the paradigm.

In summary, acquired-distinctiveness training with stimulus members has been slightly but not significantly facilitative, ineffectual, slightly but not significantly inhibitory, and significantly inhibitory. Such training with response members has been ineffectual or facilitative. The new, different responses conditioned to stimulus or response members during training might be considered responses of association hierarchies or as providing extrinsic meaning. However, the inconclusive, present data on transfer from acquired-distinctiveness training with stimulus or response members offer no support for an interpretation of effects of meaningfulness of stimulus members or of response members in terms of dissimilarity produced by responses of association hierarchies.

INDUCTION OF MEANING AND MEANINGFULNESS

Sheffield regarded his symbolic training as inducing meaningfulness in stimulus and response members. But the particular procedure approximated acquired-distinctiveness training; it was so classified. The Multiple R, Single S condition of Bailey and Jeffrey's first and third experiments and, assuming backward associations, the Multiple S, Single R condition of their first experiment might have established a hierarchy of three different responses to each stimulus member. In their second experiment, these same conditions might have established a hierarchy of three different responses to each response member. Instead, however, the A-B, A-C, A-D or the B-A, C-A, D-A sequences of Experiments 1 and 2, respectively, might have involved successive negative transfer from each task to the next. Interference from A-B, A-C or B-A, C-A might have retarded acquisition of A-D or D-A associations. But, as noted previously, the criterion was sufficiently stringent to assure that, at the end of acquisition and for some time thereafter, the associations were probably not three different responses to each stimulus member but rather one different response to each stimulus member. Were only one response to occur to each stimulus member, the relationships of Multiple R, Single S and Multiple S, Single R conditions would not have been markedly different from the relationships of the Single S-R Pairs condition. All three were the limiting case of meaning and meaningfulness, namely a stimulus member and a single association response.

In the first experiment, Multiple R, Single S training led to the poorest performance on the criterion task, even lower than the performance of the familiarization control. While Multiple S, Single R training led to slightly better performance than that of the familiarization control, the best performance was that following Single S-R Pairs training. Differences among these conditions were small and nonsignificant. The results of the third experiment indicated that even with stimulus members of high similarity there was no difference in criterion performance under Multiple R, Single S and under Single S-R Pairs conditions.

Differences among conditions of the second experiment were also nonsignificant, with the best and poorest performances, respectively, by subjects under the Multiple S, Single R condition and under the Multiple R, Single S condition. Thus, disregarding the issue of whether or not the particular training conditions produced variations in the number of responses to the stimulus and response members of the criterion task, there were no significant differences among training conditions or between those conditions and the familiarization control. Induction of meaning and meaningfulness of response members did not influence PA learning.

In the first of two experiments, Parker and Noble (1963) induced meaning and meaningfulness by conditioning 3, 6, or 9 different adjective responses to other adjectives of low Noble M_n (Noble & Parker, 1960). The latter were then the response members of three of the pairs of an eight-pair list; the response members of the other pairs were adjectives to which no responses had been conditioned experimentally. Through 20 learning trials, the percentages of correct responses for pairs with response members to which subjects had learned 3, 6, or 9 different responses were higher than the percentage of correct responses for the five control pairs. In acquiring the 3, 6, or 9 different responses to the adjectives subsequently used as response members, subjects had approximately 60, 120, or 180 experiences in repeating or seeing those adjectives overtly. Therefore, familiarization of response members, rather than induced meaning and meaningfulness, may have been the basis of the observed facilitative effects of prior experiences with response members.

In the second experiment, the conditions of one group (E) were essentially those of the first experiment. The conditions for a second group (E-F) were the same as those for E for stimulus members to which associations were learned; but subjects of E-F also had 32 familiarization experiences with the control response members. Two additional groups had no meaning and meaningfulness training with response members whose normative meaningfulness was equated with experimentally-established meaningfulness, and either no familiarization (C) or 32 familiarization (C-F) experiences with the control response members. For the E condition, number of correct anticipations during Trials 1–20 was a shallow positively accelerated function of number of associations. The curve for the E-F condition was flat; it was significantly above the curve for E at no (2.8) associations but did not differ significantly from that for E at 3 (5.8), 6 (8.7), and 9 (11.4) associations. (The numbers in parentheses are the sums of preexperimentally and experimentally established associations.) Comparisons of response members which had been familiarized under C-F but not familiarized under C yielded a significant t for the better learning of the familiarized response members. The flat curve for E-F indicated that 32 familiarization experiences with response members were sufficient to produce facilitation equal to that brought about by induced meaning and meaningfulness. This finding plus the superiority of C-F to C on familiarized response members suggest that the basis of facilitative effects of induced meaning and meaningfulness training is familiarization rather than number of different association responses.

Other data pertinent to a familiarization interpretation of effects of induced meaning and meaningfulness have been reported by Phipps (1959).

Different groups learned 1, 2, or 4 different CVC responses to stimulus members of 0% Glaze M_a. Regardless of the number of different responses, stimulus members occurred with equal frequency. A fourth group had no previous experience with the stimulus members. All four groups then learned a nine-pair list in which the stimulus members of four pairs were the CVCs to which subjects of the three experimental groups had learned 1, 2, or 4 different responses; the stimulus members of the other pairs were CVCs with which subjects of the experimental groups had had no previous experience. The four groups learned the entire list at the same rate. Nor was there a difference within lists between stimulus members to which subjects had learned 1, 2, or 4 different responses and stimulus members to which they had not been exposed. Thus, with familiarization of the CVCs the same among the three experimental groups, induced meaning and meaningfulness did not affect acquisition rate. Since these groups learned no faster than the control group, familiarization was also ineffectual.

The conclusion at present, therefore, is of no convincing demonstration of either facilitation or inhibition attributable to induction of meaning and meaningfulness of stimulus or of response members. Those effects which have been demonstrated could be accounted for by other processes such as acquired-distinctiveness or acquired-equivalence training and familiarization. And even familiarization is of doubtful potency.

RESPONSE-MEDIATED ASSOCIATIONS

Response-mediated associations are here restricted to associations between stimulus and response members which involve association responses to one or both stimuli. Occurrences of such mediating associations have usually been inferred from subjects' reports of devices, strategies, hypotheses employed to learn a particular association. Occasionally, extra-list or intra-list intrusion errors provide some evidence for inferences about response-mediated associations. But such information has not been analyzed systematically. Nor does information about errors contribute substantially to an understanding of possible effects of response-mediated associations on occurrence of correct responses.

Data on facilitation and inhibition attributable to experimentally induced response-mediated associations (Jenkins, 1963a) offer indirect support for possible effects of such associations linking stimulus and response members. Illustrative of such indirect support are the results of the first two of four experiments reported by Peterson and Blattner (1963). The first task established an association between a stimulus member and potential mediating responses (A-B); the second task established an association between the stimulus for the potential mediating response and the recognition response to a further stimulus (B-C). The pair of stimuli for A-B and the pair of stimuli for B-C were each presented 1, 3, or 6 times. Response-mediated association was tested by presenting the first stimulus accompanied by the third or "C" stimulus and two additional stimuli. Subjects were to choose the one stimulus among the three "that seemed 'to fit best . . . or to be right.' " The stimuli of Experiment I were CCCs of 0–17% Witmer M_a; those of Experiment II were CVCs of 100% Glaze M_a.

In both experiments, subjects of the mediation condition chose the "C" response of the A-B-C chain significantly more often than did subjects of either of the two control conditions. Choice of the "C" response was more frequent for the mediation and control conditions for which the stimuli were CVCs of 100% M_a than for the mediation and control conditions for which they were CCCs of 0–17% M_a. When the stimuli were CVCs rather than CCCs, selection of the "C" response increased for both mediation and control conditions. Thus, the parsimonious explanation of the difference between results for stimuli of high and of low M_a is of greater integration and availability of CVCs than of CCCs during the test for mediation. Number of different association responses to the stimulus member or "A" stimuli was not observed and need not be introduced to explain the findings.

In Peterson and Blattner's Experiments III and IV, meaningfulness of the stimulus member or "A" stimulus was not varied. Nor were the association responses to that stimulus observed. Therefore, while perhaps providing some indirect support for notions of a response-mediation basis of effects of meaningfulness, these four experiments are essentially irrelevant to the present discussion. Indeed, in general, data from experiments on response-mediated association are no substitute for more direct evidence of a positive relationship between number of apparently facilitative response-mediated associations and meaningfulness of stimulus members, of response members, or of both.

The inverse relationships between acquisition rate and similarity of stimulus and of response members in terms of common meaning also provide some support for inferences of the occurrence of response-mediated associations between stimulus and response members. But the inverse relationships may be substantially due to tendencies for stimulus members which have a common meaning to evoke recognition responses to each other which interfere with acquisition of new responses to those stimulus members. Regardless, knowledge of inhibitory effects contributes only indirectly to an understanding of presumed facilitative effects of mediating responses and stimuli.

For the reasons noted, available data on intrusion errors, experimentally induced response-mediated associations, and effects of similarity of stimulus and response members in terms of common meaning offer, at best, indirect support for hypotheses of a direct relationship between meaningfulness of stimulus members, of response members, or of both and occurrence of facilitative response mediation of associations between stimulus and response members.

Experiments by Barclay (1964), Horton (1964), and Dallett (1964) were planned to obtain information pertinent to understanding the possible role of response-mediated associations in the direct relationships between acquisition rate and meaningfulness of stimulus and of response members. Barclay used lists of stimulus members and response members both of 50% or 80% Glaze M_a with what Jenkins (1963a) labeled stimulus equivalence, response equivalence, and simple chaining paradigms of response-mediated association in the forward direction. Across the eight acquisition trials with the criterion list significant mediation was demonstrated, and the list of pairs of high M_a was acquired faster than the list of pairs of low M_a. But expected differences among the paradigms were not obtained. Nor was the interaction of meaningfulness and paradigms significant.

Meaningfulness of the common or "B" term of A-B, B-C, and A-C (simple chaining) and B-A, B-C, A-C (response equivalence) paradigms was the variable of primary interest in Horton's two experiments. The "B" terms were dissyllables of high or low Noble M_n. Ability of the subjects was varied by using those in the upper and lower halves of the Carroll and Sapon (1958) Modern Language Aptitude Test; their awareness of the mediational relationship of "B" was determined by post-experimental inquiry. In both experiments, more correct anticipations occurred with "B" response members of high than of low M_n. In the first experiment, the interaction between meaningfulness and paradigm was not significant. In the second experiment, larger differences obtained between experimental or mediation and control or non-mediation pairs with "B" terms of high than of low M_n. Ability of the subjects did not enter into significant interactions. The greater the awareness of the mediating relationship of the "B" term, the greater the mediation both for "B" terms of high and for those of low meaningfulness.

Interesting though these results are for the phenomenon of response-mediated association, they add little to an understanding of the contribution of such associations to relationships between acquisition rate and meaningfulness of stimuli. The findings of direct relationship between rate of acquisition of the criterion list and meaningfulness of one or more of the component sets of stimuli is simply a further demonstration of the ubiquity of effects of meaningfulness of stimuli rather than a revelation of the manner by which response-mediated associations contribute to those effects. Moveover, no direct information was obtained about the occurrence and consequences of preexperimentally established mediators.

Dallett's approach involved selection and manipulation of potential mediating responses. After obtaining associations to 24 CVCs of high M_a, he was able to select 12 CVCs which evoked two different responses which, in turn, were in a mediating relationship with two different terminating responses. The mediating response and terminating response of one of these sequences were not related to the responses of the other sequence. Two of the experimental conditions involved pre-acquisition presentation of each stimulus member with the stimulus for the mediation response which led to the response which, in acquisition of the PA list, would be correct (relevant) or would be an extra-list intrusion (irrelevant). The three controls were a condition in which an association was given to the stimulus member (association), one in which the stimulus and response members were presented together (practice), and another of no prior exposure to stimuli of the PA list (control). Trials of acquisition of the PA list to a criterion of one perfect trial followed. Subjects then described any mnemonic aid they might have used with each pair after which they learned a second list. Because of ambiguity of interpretation, data on acquisition of the second list were largely ignored.

Acquisition in terms of responses correct on the first trial and trials to criterion was most rapid under the relevant condition and least rapid under the irrelevant condition. Relative to the control condition, the facilitation induced under the relevant condition was less than the inhibition induced by the irrelevant condition. Only the latter difference was significant. Acquisition under the association condition was also slower than under the control condition; there was only a small difference between the control and practice conditions. The largest numbers of all mediators and of relevant mediators were reported by subjects under the relevant condition. Numbers of all mediators decreased under practice, control, irrelevant, and association conditions and numbers of relevant mediators decreased under practice, irrelevant, control, and association conditions. In general, differences among conditions were small. Dallett's results demonstrate the selection and manipulation of presumed mediators with facilitative or inhibitory consequences for PA learning. But, as he notes, "the findings (may) apply only to materials which are specially selected to have exactly those associative properties which the [Underwood and Schulz (1960a, pp. 295-296) associative probability] hypothesis requires" (p. 214). As noted previously, stimuli of different meaningfulness values have usually been paired to minimize direct and indirect associations between stimulus and response members.

Simon and Wood (1964) describe an experiment involving response-mediated associations whose design and procedures they considered pertinent to the interpretation of decremental effects of familiarization of stimulus members obtained by Underwood and Schulz (1960a, Exp. 4). The stimulus members and response members of the lists of their two experimental conditions were paired so that response-mediated associations would presumably facilitate acquisition of one list and retard acquisition of the other. In most or all of the experiments of familiarization described in the preceding chapter, stimulus members and response members were paired in manners designed to minimize both direct and indirect initial associations between them. Because of this and other differences in design and procedure, Simon and Wood's results are of doubtful pertinence to findings of facilitation or inhibition in those experiments.

Analyses of subjects' reports of their manner of forming a particular association in Reed's (1918a, 1918b) investigation of "associative aids" in PA learning provide some data on effects of response mediation of associations. All subjects learned each of four lists, relearned them five times, and were then tested by backward associations, associations between each stimulus member and the stimulus member of the next pair, and associations between each stimulus member and the stimulus member of the preceding pair. Two of the four lists consisted of 10 pairs of English words, the third list consisted of 10 pairs with German words as stimulus members and their English equivalents as response members, and the fourth consisted of 10 pairs of CVCs. The subjects were asked to report "any associations . . . formed between a given pair either after each series was learned or after every response" (1918a, p. 129). The two lists of pairs of English words might be regarded as high-high with respect to meaningfulness of stimulus and response members, the list of pairs of German and English words might be regarded as low-high, and the list of pairs of trigrams as low-low.

If meaningfulness of stimulus members, of response members, or of both influences acquisition through response mediation of associations, successively slower learning and decreasing percentages of associative aids indicative of such mediation should be obtained with lists of pairs of English words, of pairs of German and English words, and of pairs of trigrams. Acquisition rates were in the predicted order. Also, reported percentages of use of all associative aids were higher during learning and relearning for the lists of pairs of English words than for the list of pairs of German and English words for which the percentages were higher than for the list of pairs of trigrams. However, only some of the associative aids could be considered indicative of occurrences of response-mediated associations between stimulus members, recognition responses to stimulus members, or both, on one hand, and recognition responses to response members on the other.

Reed used 15 combinations of second-order and third-order categories to classify associative aids (1918a, p. 148). Assuming the representativeness of his examples of associative aids placed in each combination, seven of the combinations might be regarded as indicating occurrences of response-mediated associations between stimulus and response members. These are similarity in meaning of contrast, of coordination, of prediction; thoughts of patterns like objects; and thoughts of words only, of objects only, of words and objects. The examples cited for the other eight combinations were of three types. One was between components of stimulus and response members or between two events physically similar to stimulus and response members. Another was simply changing the order of stimulus and response members. The third was position of the pair in the series or in a sequence of incorrect responses.

The significance of Reed's findings, however, is reduced by lack of more precise information about meaningfulness of the stimulus and response members of the three lists of pairs of words. More importantly, for the list of pairs of trigrams, no associative aids indicative of occurrences of response-mediated associations were reported. The averages of the Glaze M_a of the stimulus and response members for trigram pairs ranged from 20% to 90% and five pairs had average values greater than 50%. If response mediation of associations facilitates acquisition of trigram pairs, it is puzzling that associative aids indicative of occurrences of such mediation were not reported. About 40% of the associative aids reported for pairs of trigrams referred to position of the pair in the series. Such aids, which were probably due to Reed's use of a fixed order of presentation, could hardly be indicative of preexperimentally established indirect associations between stimulus and response members. On the whole, therefore, for materials comparable to those for which direct relationships have been hypothesized between response mediation of associations and meaningfulness of stimulus members, of response members, or of both, there was no evidence of even the presence of such mediation. Data for successive relearning sessions and the subsequent tests were not presented in a form which permitted replication of the analyses of learning data.

On various grounds Underwood and Schulz (1960a, pp. 294-295) rejected a stimulus integration interpretation of the basis of effects of meaningfulness of stimulus members. Suggested instead was the associative probability interpretation noted earlier: "the greater the number of associates elicited by a stimulus the greater is the probability that one of these will link up with another item" (p. 296). To obtain some information on this proposal, Underwood and Schulz prepared a list of eight pairs with generated trigrams of low meaningfulness as stimulus members and three-letter words of high meaningfulness as response members. Since the response members were integrated, most of the learning was presumably formation of correct associations between stimulus and response members. This list was administered to 35 subjects who learned to a criterion of two successive perfect trials.

Each subject was asked to report on use of associations "to hook up the response with the stimulus." For the 280 pairings of 35 subjects and eight pairs, associations were reported for 205 pairings. Of these, 29 were classified as involving two or more mediating associations. Most of the remaining mediating associations were presumably one-step; a number of examples are cited. Thus, in contrast to the apparent nonoccurrence of mediating associations in the learning of a list of trigram pairs by Reed's subjects, Underwood and Schulz's subjects might have used mediating associations for up to 73% of the pairings.

Of the associative aids reported by Reed's subjects, if all, or all but those referring to position in the series are considered indicative of mediating associations, 39% and 25% of the pairings, respectively, might then have involved such associations. Assuming that Reed's data are also for number of pairings (number of subjects times number of pairs), even by these more generous criteria for occurrences of mediating associations, his subjects made less use of such associations than did those of Underwood and Schulz's experiment. One reason for this difference may have been the nature of the stimulus members. Reed used pronounceable CVCs, while Underwood and Schulz used generated trigrams of several different structures with letter combinations of low pronunciability. In part, probably because of low pronunciability of stimulus members, Underwood and Schulz report that for 62% of the 205 pairings for which subjects reported mediating associations, these associations were to only one letter of the stimulus members.

After eliminating subjects who reported mediating associations for all pairs and those who reported mediating associations for all but a single pair, Underwood and Schulz compared means of correct responses with pairs for which mediating associations were and were not reported. Significantly more correct responses occurred with the former than with the latter pairs. Reed reported higher percentages of occurrence of associative aids with pairs which were forgotten slowly than with pairs which were forgotten quickly. But Reed does not report percentages for those associative aids seemingly indicative of response-mediated associations.

After Bugelski's (1962) subjects had completed their acquisition trials, each was "asked specifically how he happened to learn each pair, what made him think of the correct responses, why some pairs were easy and some difficult" (p. 410). All subjects reported the occurrence of responses other than or more extensive than recognition responses to the stimulus and response members. The responses which Bugelski classified as Group I, Group II and, perhaps, Group III mediators do not constitute unequivocal evidence of the occurrence of such responses in a mediating relationship (Goss, 1964). Instead, they may be evidence of the presence at some strength and of the facilitative consequences of preexperimentally established direct associations. The basis of such direct associations, as suggested in the analysis of relationships between stimulus and response members advanced in Chapter 4 would be generalization from similar sequences of stimuli and responses which had been experienced in extra-experimental contexts. An example is DEPUTIZE for DUP-TEZ. Bugelski classified DEPUTIZE as a Class I mediator.

Under conventional durations of presentation of stimulus and response members, several of the responses given as examples of those classified as Group III and particularly as Group IV were too long to occur readily in a mediating relationship. However, Bugelski's experimental variable was duration of joint presentation of the stimulus and response members. The values ranged from 2 to 15 seconds. As duration increased, responses which he considered mediators occurred more often.

Williams (1962) found no difference between 1-sec. and 4-sec. durations of joint presentation of stimulus and response members in frequency of reports of the use of mnemonic aids. However, use of such aids was associated with significantly more correct responses and, although the difference was not significant, with lower latencies of response. Whether the mnemonic aids functioned as mediators is again conjectural.

In Jensen and Rohwer's (1963a) first experiment, adult retardates were or were not "asked to form a phrase connecting the names of the two pictures." Following these two pre-acquisition experiences, means of errors during 10 trials with the PA list presented in the "fifth week" phase of this experiment were 13.9 and 43.7, respectively. In their second experiment and in another experiment (1963b), mediators were presumably induced by experimenter's verbalizations such as "I threw the SHOE at the CLOCK," where SHOE-CLOCK was one of the pairs of the PA list. In both experiments, subjects who had such pre-acquisition experience learned the PA list faster than subjects whose pre-acquisition experience was limited to seeing and naming the stimuli. Some subjects said the "mediating verbalizations" aloud during the first two trials; they may have continued to do so covertly in subsequent trials. The better acquisition by subjects who were required to provide their own or were exposed to the experimenter's "mediating verbalizations" than of subjects who did not have such experiences constitutes some evidence of facilitative effects of mediators. Not developed, however, is the rationale of Jensen and Rohwer's expectation of facilitative effects of "mediating verbalizations," whether subject- or experimenter-supplied. A complementary or alternative explanation of the facilitation produced by both kinds of pre-acquisition experience is that the verbalizations connecting members of pairs of stimuli simply oriented subjects to the pairwise division of the stimuli.

Subjects' reports of their use of words other than or more extensive than recognition responses to the stimulus and response members and of better learning occasioned by prior experience with such additional responses constitute some, but not unequivocal evidence of response-mediated associations between stimulus and response members. Some possible complementary or alternative interpretations were suggested.

One shortcoming of these data is lack of information about occurrences of mediating responses on as close to a trial-by-trial basis as possible. Reports of response mediation of associations after a pair or a list has been learned only indicate that mediating responses may have been used once or more. During what stage and how frequently constitute important future information which post-learning reports do not provide or for which they provide estimates of unknown validity. In addition to descriptive precision, trial-by-trial information would permit more adequate analyses of relationships between correct and incorrect responses and occurrence and nonoccurrence of response mediation of associations (Goss, 1964).

Another shortcoming of available information is lack of reports for lists whose stimulus and response members represent different combinations of meaningfulness of discrete stimuli and of pairs of stimulus members. Also, lists representing different combinations of similarity of stimulus and response members, particularly for similarity in terms of common meaning, should provide data on effects of mediating responses on intra-list generalization and discrimination. Ultimately, the lists on which subjects report should represent different combinations of meaningfulness and similarity of stimulus and response members.

NUMBER OF AND ASSOCIATIONS AMONG ELEMENTS

Examined here, in addition to experiments on effects of simple variations in the number of elements and associations among them, are investigations of transfer from acquisition with elements to acquisition with those elements in compounds and of transfer from compounds to elements. Some of the latter and additional experiments are then reexamined for information about learning to respond to more discriminable elements of members of sets of complex stimuli.

Simple Variations

The presumed bases of effects on PA learning of meaningfulness of stimulus and response members may be reduced wholly or in part to integration and consequent availability of recognition responses to stimulus members and to response members. Such reduction introduces as potentially significant variables number of elements of stimulus members and of response members and, by inference or observation, number of elements of recognition responses to those stimuli and probability of transition from the recognition response to one element to the recognition response to the next. Probability of transition from the recognition response to the last element of stimulus members to the recognition response to the first element of response members also becomes an important link in the postulated chains of associations of each PA unit.

The first session of experiments on transfer from compounds to elements may involve stimulus members which are compounds and, for subsequent controls, those which are elements. Since the former may be regarded as constituted of more elements than the latter, comparisons between the two just for acquisition during the first session provides information about effects of number of elements. The compounds employed have consisted of two or more words or nonsense syllables, which are treated along with number of verbal elements, and also of words or nonsense syllables and colors.

NUMBER OF ELEMENTS; COMPOUNDS OF SYLLABLES OR WORDS

On the basis of assumptions concerning hierarchies of responses to stimulus and response members and differences among hierarchic levels of responses with respect to integration of elements, Newman (1961) predicted inverse relationships between acquisition rate and number of elements of both stimulus and response members. The further considerations of necessity of overt emission of response members and of time to say response members overtly during recall generated the prediction of greater potency of number of elements of response members than of stimulus members.

In one experiment, stimulus members and response members of one or three elements were combined orthogonally. Transitional probabilities among elements of the trigram stimulus and response members were low. Number of elements of stimulus members was inversely related to acquisition rate, though the relationship was significant only during Trials 1–4 of 17 trials. Number of elements of response members was inversely related to acquisition rate both during Trials 1–4 and through all 17 trials. Thus, in accordance with Newman's hypothesis, number of elements of response members was more potent than number of elements of stimulus members. There was no evidence of a significant interaction of these two variables.

Newman also reported that, with stimulus members of three elements, subjects may have responded increasingly to only one letter of the three, most often the first letter. Such selection would reduce any differences between one-element and three-element stimuli.

Underwood and Schulz's (1960a) GV is a measure of association among elements of trigrams. In general, GV was not as strongly related to acquisition rate as was pronunciability. Nonetheless, correlations between GV of response members and acquisition rate have ranged from .67 to .89 (p. 247); those between GV of stimulus members and acquisition rate have ranged from .39 to .82 (p. 254).

For two later experiments, Underwood and Schulz (1961) constructed lists whose stimulus members were either trigrams of low, medium, or high strengths of associative connections (integration) or bigrams of low or high integration. Formal similarity among these stimulus members was minimal. Single digits served as response members. With the exception of slightly slower learning with trigrams of high than of medium integration under massed practice, total correct responses with both trigrams and bigrams were related directly to strength of integration of stimulus members.

Noted previously was McGuire's (1961) use of lists with stimulus members of low or high similarity along a physical dimension of size. The response members were single digits or three-digit numbers. Stimulus members of high or of low similarity were paired with response members in two ways: stimulus members of increasing size were accompanied by numbers of increasing magnitude or there was no relationship between size of stimulus members and magnitude of paired numbers. In each of three comparisons of pairs of conditions, alike except for response members of one or three digits, significantly more correct anticipations were obtained with response members of one digit than with response members of three digits. In each of two comparisons of pairs of conditions, alike except for the relationship between size of stimulus members and magnitude of paired three-digit numbers, pairs involving the presumed stronger association between increasing size and increasing magnitude of paired numbers were learned faster than pairs without such associations between their stimulus and response members. Thus, strengths of associations between stimulus and response members and within response members were related directly to acquisition rate.

Baddelay's (1961b) finding that predictability but not meaningfulness of trigrams was significantly related to acquisition rate will be recalled. He also constructed pairs with stimulus and response members for which the probability of guessing the first letter of response members following the last letter of stimulus members (compatability) was high in one order and low in the other. Pairs of high compatibility of stimulus and response members were learned more readily than pairs of low compatibility of stimulus and response members. In the experiments in which predictability or meaningfulness were also varied, compatibility between stimulus and response members was also related directly to acquisition rate.

The stimulus members of Newman's (1963b) lists were CVCs of low formal similarity and difficult to pronounce, or they were the first letters of those CVCs. In the first experiment, the response members were three-digit numbers; in the second experiment, they were single digits. With CVC stimulus members the three conditions were information that each member began with a different letter (instructions); first letters red, second and third letters black (isolation), and no information about the first letters; and all three letters black. The first two conditions were to facilitate responding to more discriminable features. Acquisition with all three conditions could be compared to acquisition of lists whose stimulus members were single black or red letters when stimulus and response members were paired and black letters when stimulus members were presented alone during the test phase of trials under a recall format of presentation.

In the first experiment, more correct responses occurred with single letters than with three letters as stimulus members. Whether single letters or first letters were black or red made no difference. The failure to find faster acquisition with red first and black second and third letters than with the three black letters was contrary to Newman's expectations as was the slower acquisition with information about differences among the first letters than without such information about the CVCs of three black letters.

With single-digit response members, from three and one-half to nine and one-half times as many correct responses occurred over 20 trials than were obtained with three-digit response members. However, the F for number of letters in the stimulus members was not significant as it had been with three-digit response members. More correct responses were obtained with black than with red single or first letters and the difference was greater for the single letters. But neither the F for color nor the F for the interaction of color and number of letters was significant. In direct contrast to the results of the first experiment, the mean for the condition of information about the first letters was greater than the means for the other two three-letter conditions and equal to the means for the one-letter conditions.

Combining the results of the two experiments, both number of elements of stimulus members and of response members are seemingly related inversely to acquisition rate, with a stronger relationship for number of elements of stimulus members when response members were of three than of one element. Directing subjects to the first element by isolation had little effect. Doing so by instructions may have had slight inhibitory consequences with three-element response members and slightly facilitative consequences with one-element response members.

In summary, although few in number, these experiments with letters as elements indicate that number of elements and strength of associations among elements of stimulus and of response members are, respectively, related inversely and directly to acquisition rate. Also, there is a positive relationship between acquisition rate and strength of associations between last letters of stimulus members and first letters of response members. More generally, these findings support an analysis of PA learning in terms of concepts and principles governing the formation and consequent effects of chains of elements the strengths of whose successive links may range from all weak to all strong. Similarity of elements both within and among pairs is probably an additional factor. Moreover, some of the elements may be components of mediating responses.

Brown, Battig, and Pearlstein, (1964) compared acquisition of responses to stimulus members with three letters throughout and to stimulus members initially of one letter to which the second and third letters were added upon attainment of criteria for responses to the single letters and to the pairs of letters. More trials were required to reach criterion when stimulus members of three letters were reached by successive addition than when they were presented throughout. However, in total errors the latter condition was slightly but not significantly inferior. Involved in acquisition with stimulus members to which letters are added is an initial advantage of greater ease of selection of and recognition responses to discriminable features which persists when the original letter is to the left of the added letters. Adding letters, particularly to the left of the original letter, entails the disadvantage of further selection and chaining of elements of recognition responses. But adding letters at intermediate stages of acquisition, Brown, Battig, and Pearlstein suggest, may also have the advantage of reducing intra-list interference. Their results contribute to determination of the points in the course of acquisition at which facilitative or inhibitory effects of additional letters in multiletter stimulus members occur. However, their procedure did not permit comparison among rates of acquisition of responses to stimulus members of one, two, or three letters.

In six additional experiments, words rather than letters have been the elements. Thirty words served as the stimulus members of one of Musgrave and Cohen's (1964) lists. Half of these words were stimulus members of the other list; the remaining stimulus members of this list were compounds of two words. Word responses were learned faster with the list whose stimulus members were all words than with the list of half single words and half compounds of two words. Within the latter list, responses to single words were acquired faster than responses to compounds.

The compound stimulus members of Cohen and Musgrave's (1964a) unmixed lists were constituted of two CVCs representing the combinations of high or low M_a of the first element of the compound and of high or low M_a of the second element. The stimulus members of two other lists were single CVCs of high M_a or of low M_a. The list with single elements of high M_a was acquired faster than the list with compounds of two elements both of high M_a. Also, the list with single elements of low M_a was acquired faster than the list with compounds of two elements both of low M_a. But these differences were not significant.

Cohen and Musgrave (1964b) also varied formal similarity among elements of compound stimulus members and among single elements. Acquisition was faster with single elements of high similarity than with compounds whose elements were of high similarity; the advantage of single elements of low similarity to compounds whose members were of low similarity was slight.

The stimulus members of the first task of Horowitz, Lippman, Norman, and McConkie's (1964) Experiment I were nine triads of words. Three of the triads had strong associations among their elements (horizontal); three had weak or no associations among their elements, but strong associations with elements of two other triads (vertical); and three of the triads had weak or no associations among either their elements or the elements of other triads (independent). For the first task of Experiment II, the stimulus members were the first elements of the triads of Experiment I. Dissyllables of low Noble M_n served as response members for both lists.

Faster acquisition through 15 trials occurred with stimulus members of one element than of three elements. With stimulus members of one element, acquisition was slower for stimulus members with strong associations with other stimulus members than for stimulus members with no or weak associations with other stimulus members. With stimulus members of three elements, acquisition rate increased in the order vertical, independent, and horizontal triads. The same results were obtained for the larger subsets of horizontal, vertical, and independent triads of the list of the second task of Experiment II.

For Experiment III, two words were deleted from the vertical triads of the list for the second task of Experiment II and replaced with asterisks. Despite the vertical associations among the single elements of these triads which remained, pairs with these stimulus members were learned somewhat faster than pairs whose stimulus members were horizontal or independent triads. Contrary to the results of Experiments I and II, acquisition rates for the latter two types of triad did not differ. The proffered explanation was that the procedure did not permit perception of the difference between horizontal and independent triads.

The results of these three experiments warrant three conclusions. First, responses are acquired faster to single words than to three words, thus indicating that relationships obtained with stimulus members constituted of different numbers of letter elements also hold for stimulus members in which number of word elements was varied. Second, associations among elements of the same triad and among those of different triads may have facilitative and inhibitory effects, respectively. Third, comparisons of effects of single-element and three-element stimulus members and probably in general for different numbers of elements must allow for associations among elements or among different multi-element stimulus members.

Although Crothers (1962) did not vary the number of response elements, his analysis of conditional probabilities of the second response of the two-response compounds contributes to an understanding of the course of the chaining of response elements. Also, the experiment is instructive with respect to the manner of analysis of chains of responses. Three different schedules of pairings of stimulus and response members (R) and presentation of stimulus members alone (T) were employed (RTT, RRTT, and RTRT). For all three schedules and regardless of whether a list under a particular schedule was first or second, probabilities of correct second responses on both the first and second presentations of stimulus members alone were higher when the first response was correct than when it was incorrect. Accordingly, the findings were interpreted as supporting an hypothesis of separate but not independent conditioning of elements of compound responses. With such separate conditioning, acquisition of response members of one element should be faster than acquisition of those of more than one element.

WORD OR SYLLABLE AND COLOR COMPOUNDS

One concern of Weiss and Margolius' (1954) experiment was effects of added differences in colors (context) on acquisition of word responses to stimulus members whose other elements were hyphenated pairs of CVCs. All five of the groups which learned to respond to the hyphenated CVCs each on a different color reached criterion in fewer trials than the sixth group, which learned to respond to the hyphenated CVCs all on gray cards. One of the explanations proposed for the superiority of the former groups was less intra-list generalization of responses due to dissimilarity of stimulus members based on "distinctly discernible" colors. Alternatively, the common gray background may have reduced the distinctiveness of the hyphenated CVCs to retard learning. Unfortunately, controls for whom the stimulus members were the hyphenated CVCs alone or the colored cards alone were not employed.

In Sundland and Wickens' (1962) Experiment I, conditions in which three-letter word responses were learned to six-letter words alone, to hyphenated pairs of CVCs alone, and to colors alone served as controls for learning those same responses to compounds of words and colors and of hyphenated CVCs and colors. Acquisition was faster with word stimulus members alone or with the word and colors, respectively, than for hyphenated CVCs alone or with hyphenated CVCs and colors. But addition of the colors did not facilitate acquisition.

Stimulus members which were compounds of CVCs ("Y" a vowel) and colors or which were the CVCs or colors alone were three of the conditions of a subsequent experiment by Hill and Wickens (1962). On each of three test trials, more responses were recalled correctly to the compounds than to the elements alone, which is in rough agreement with Weiss and Margolius' but not with Sundland and Wickens' results. The suggested interpretation was "greater opportunity [with compounds] to select as the functional stimulus the dimension of the entire stimulus which was either most compatible with the responses or which reduced interference with other S-R connections in the list" (p. 150).

Saltz (1963) employed lists whose stimulus members were CVCs with or without accompanying colors during the learning and during the test phases of each trial under a recall format. The four combinations were, therefore, colors present in both phases, colors present in the learning phase and absent in the test phase or the converse, and colors absent in both phases. In the first replication of the first experiment, the colors were in the form of squares pasted to the left of the CVCs; in the second and third replications, the colors formed a rectangular border around the CVCs.

The CVCs of the first experiment were nonwords with mean Archer M_a values of about 35% and 45% for the first two and the third replications, respectively. The stimulus members of the second experiment were word CVCs with mean Archer M_a values just short of 100%. The response members of the first experiment were words of from five to eight letters of unspecified and perhaps undetermined meaningfulness; different sets were employed in the first two and the third replications. The response members of the second experiment were the stimulus members of the first two replications of the first experiment. Although not stated explicitly, the phrase that subjects "could indicate the appropriate word" (Saltz, 1963, p. 3) suggests that responses were selected rather than reproduced.

With one exception, in all three of the replications which constituted the first experiment and in the second experiment, increasing numbers of correct responses were obtained for colors absent during both learning and test phases, for colors absent during the learning phase and present during the test phase, for colors present during the learning phase and absent during the test phase, and for colors present during both learning and test phases. The exception was an inversion of the two intermediate combinations in the third replication. The two extremes of colors present or colors absent during both learning and test phases could be regarded as color-word compounds and word elements. Acquisition was faster with compounds than with elements.

Within the framework of Saltz's conception of familiarization and other experiences with stimuli as conditions which occasion differentiation, he interprets the superiority of the combination of colors absent during the learning phase and present during the test phase to the combination of colors absent during both phases as evidence of the occurrence of sensory differentiation. The accompanying colors during the test phase are viewed as increasing differentiation among the CVCs. The superiority of the combination of colors present during the learning phase and absent during the test phase to the combination of colors absent during both phases is attributed to cognitive differentiation. Somehow the presence of colors during the training phase is assumed to increase differentiation among CVCs alone during the test phase. Proposed is the possibility of the additive combination of effects of both types of differentiation to bring about the superiority of the combination of colors present during both learning and test phases to the other three combinations.

The second experiment was executed to check on what Saltz considered a possible alternative interpretation of the results of the first experiment, particularly for combinations of colors absent and colors present and of colors present and colors absent during learning and test phases, respectively. Presumed in this interpretation is the formation of associations between CVCs and recognition responses to colors during the test phase with the former combination or during the learning phase with the latter combination. The responses of saying color names to CVCs might then mediate between CVCs and responses to response members during the learning phase for the combination of colors absent and colors present and during the test phase for the combination of colors present and colors absent.

Saltz questioned that subjects would have time for such chains of responses. As a precaution, however, the verbal element of stimulus members was changed from nonword CVCs to word CVCs. Thereby, he assumed, formation of associations between the verbal elements and recognition responses to response members would be facilitated relative to the formation of associations between stimuli produced by recognition responses to colors and recognition responses to response members.

The stimulus members of the second experiment had a mean Archer M_a of nearly 100% in contrast to the means of 35% and 45% for the stimulus members of the first experiment. As noted, meaningfulness values for word response members of the first experiment were of unspecified and, perhaps, of undetermined values. Therefore, whether the CVC response members of the second experiment were of lower, equal, or higher meaningfulness than the word response members of the first experiment is not known. Whatever the relative meaningfulness values, the response members of the second experiment were pronounceable nonword monosyllables of three letters in contrast to the previously employed word bisyllables of five to eight letters. With these changes, the resultant list of pairs of CVC words and nonwords was considerably easier than the list of CVC and word pairs used for the first two of the replications constituting the first experiment.

Because stimulus members of the second experiment were more meaningful and response members were pronounceable monosyllables, more time may have been available for subjects to form associations not only between the word stimulus members and recognition responses to the response members but also between word stimulus members and recognition responses to the colors. In turn, associations between stimuli produced by those recognition responses and recognition responses to the response members might have been established more rapidly to mediate evocation of recognition responses to response members by word stimulus members when the colors were absent. Thus, contrary to Saltz's interpretation, the list and the results of the second experiment do not preclude the possibility of at least some response mediation by color names of associations between words and recognition responses to response members. However, subjects' retrospective reports of confusion in trying to use color as a cue argues against the formation and use of color names as mediating responses. Elimination of formation and use of such mediating responses leaves the possible bases of the presumably independent concepts of sensory differentiation and of cognitive differentiation obscure except perhaps as specified by the particular experimental arrangements.

The stimulus members of Postman and Phillips' (1964) 10-pair list were compounds of dissyllabic nouns. These compounds were constituted of constant elements of intermediate Thorndike-Lorge frequency and pairs of variable elements which, in one list, were of low frequency and, in the other list, were of high frequency. The elements were arranged in vertical columns with response members opposite the constant elements. The response members were dissyllabic nouns of intermediate frequency. Acquisition was to an 8/10 criterion with recall and relearning after 30 sec. or 7 days.

Due to the difference in numbers of trials between the first trial on which each response had occurred correctly once and attainment of the criterion, correct responses were acquired faster to compounds with variable elements of low than of high frequency. The rationale advanced was that more interfering associations were formed between the responses and contextual or irrelevant stimuli of high frequency than of low frequency. Providing some independent justification of this explanation is Schulz and Lovelace's (1964) finding of an inverse relationship between meaningfulness and latency of selection. Subjects would be expected to select and make recognition responses to variable stimuli of high frequency more often than to the constant stimuli of intermediate frequency. Constant stimuli of intermediate frequency should be responded to more often than the variable stimuli of low frequency. Thus frequency and, by inference, meaningfulness of the contextual stimuli should influence probability of selection and recognition responses to elements of the compounds. In turn, stimuli produced by the recognition responses should be part of the compound or the immediate stimulus to which responses were conditioned.

More responses were recalled correctly following acquisition with contextual stimuli of high than of low frequency. Suggested as an explanation was that "once the appropriate stimuli have been differentiated, however, converging associations serve to 'prime' the prescribed responses at recall" (p. 71). An alternative explanation is that, by the criterion trial of acquisition, subjects had learned to select and recognize the constant elements in contexts of words of high frequency faster than they were able to do so in contexts of words of low frequency.

Elements to Compounds, Compounds to Elements

Stimuli may be presented separately as elements; those same stimuli may then be presented simultaneously as elements of a compound. Alternatively, stimuli may be presented simultaneously as elements of a compound and then be presented separately as elements. On the assumption of changes in integration and availability of recognition responses during acquisition of new responses to elements alone or in compounds, shifts from elements to compounds or from compounds to elements should occasion changes in recognition responses. Such changes, in turn, should influence anticipation or recall of the new responses which had been conditioned to stimulus members and stimuli produced by recognition responses to the stimulus members. Data on transfer from elements to compounds and the converse are, therefore, of some pertinence to interpretations of the role of meaningfulness and familiarization in PA learning.

Elements to Compounds

Among the various experiments reported by Shepard and Fogelsonger (1913) were some concerned with transfer from tasks in which elements were presented separately to tasks in which those elements were presented simultaneously as members of compounds. Lengthened reaction time was the usual outcome of the change from elements to compounds.

In a replication and extension of some aspects of the Shepard and Fogelsonger experiments, Musgrave (1962) trained subjects to respond with the same or different CVC responses to two CVC stimulus members presented separately. When these CVCs were presented simultaneously, faster responding occurred to stimulus members to which the same response had been learned (convergent compound) than to stimulus members to which different responses had been learned (divergent compound). In a third type of compound (associated-nonassociated), one element had been conditioned to a response, the other had not. Speeds of responses to the associated-nonassociated compound were lower than speeds of responses to convergent compounds but higher than speeds of responses to divergent compounds. Response speeds even to the convergent compounds, however, were below those for responses to continued single elements.

Essentially the same relationships obtained in a subsequent experiment which differed only in presenting the stimuli in compounds without rather than with an intervening space (Musgrave, Goss, & Shrader, 1963). One basis for the decrement in speeds for convergent compounds relative to continued singles might be longer time to make recognition responses to compounds than to elements. After learning to respond to some elements of the compound and disregarding others, however, any differences due to this factor should largely disappear. Another basis might be disruption of responses of responding to more or the most distinctive features. And both processes might obtain.

Following 12 training trials, Musgrave and Cohen (1964) combined single-word stimulus members into two-word convergent or divergent compounds. Slightly but not significantly fewer correct responses occurred to convergent compounds than to continued single elements. Markedly and significantly fewer correct responses occurred to divergent compounds than were obtained under either of the two former conditions.

Hill and Wickens (1962) also had a condition in which subjects learned the same response first to CVCs and then to colors or the converse. These elements were then combined. More correct responses occurred to the color-word compounds than to colors alone or to words alone. Application of Hull's summation hypothesis of a larger number of correct responses to compounds than continued elements is rejected on the basis that no more correct responses occurred to the elements alone than to the compounds when no previous responses to the elements had been correct. Instead, the advantage of responding to the compounds is attributed "to having more than one cue available to recall the response" (p. 149).

Formation of two-element compounds of CVCs or of words, whether those compounds are convergent or divergent, seemingly decreases speed of responses and may decrease correctness of responses. In contrast, forming compounds of colors and CVCs increases the number of correct responses relative to continued singles. Speculatively, subjects may be able to respond to words or colors more easily than to one or both of two words. Therefore, recognition responses to word-color compounds might be faster than such responses to word-compounds, and subjects might be able to respond to more distinctive features with greater ease.

Compounds to Elements

Shepard and Fogelsonger (1913) also describe two experiments in which elements were presented simultaneously in compounds and then separately. Again transfer from compounds to elements was not perfect in that reaction times of responses to elements were longer than for those responses to compounds and correct responses may have decreased in

frequency. After an interim of 50 years of virtually no activity, experimentation on transfer from compounds to elements in PA learning has
revived and is here exemplified by six recent experiments. In one experiment,
elements of the compounds were letters; in another they were words; in four
other experiments, one element of the compounds was a word or letter
sequence, the other was a color.

The seven CCC stimulus members of Jenkins' (1963b) list were constituted of 21 different consonants. The response members were single
digits from one through seven which were learned to a criterion of two
consecutive errorless trials. All of the consonants alone were then presented
in counterbalanced order to yield means of numbers of correct responses
to initial, medial, and terminal letters of 3.00, 1.75, and 2.54, respectively.
The over-all F was significant as was the difference between initial and
medial but not the difference between initial and terminal. The decrements
from criterion responding to consonants alone were markedly greater than
the post-criterion decrement of 0.4 correct responses to continued intact
CCCs.

As described previously, Cohen and Musgrave (1964a) constructed
stimulus members whose two CVCs represented each of the four combinations of high or low M_a of the first and second elements. During the first
and across all four transfer trials in which the elements were presented
separately, more correct responses occurred to elements of high M_a than
to elements of low M_a regardless of whether the responses had been acquired
to high-high, high-low, low-high, or low-low compounds. Furthermore,
for elements of low M_a alone, transfer was greater when they had been
in the first position in compounds than when they had been in the second
position. Thus, meaningfulness of elements of compounds and position of
elements, at least those of low M_a, apparently effects strengths of associations
between elements in compounds and responses differentially. A possible
basis is stronger recognition responses to elements of high than to those of
low M_a and to elements of low M_a in the first than in the second position.

Correct responses to elements from compounds were also compared with
correct responses to continued single-element stimulus members and to
continued compounds. Across all four transfer trials, the shift from compounds to elements produced decrements relative both to continued elements
and to continued compounds.

When acquisition was to compounds in which formal similarity of the
elements was varied (Cohen & Musgrave, 1964b), greater transfer occurred
to elements of low than of high similarity and to elements which had been
in the first position in the compounds than in the second. Greater transfer
occurred to continued single-element stimulus members and to continued
compounds than to elements of the compounds.

Two of Sundland and Wickens' (1962) conditions were stimulus members constituted of words and colors or of hyphenated CVCs and colors. Following 15 trials with these compounds, words alone and then colors alone or the converse, and hyphenated CVCs alone and then colors alone or the converse were presented. For word and color compounds, transfer from the compounds to words alone was almost perfect; but only about 11% of the number of responses correct to compounds were correct to colors alone. For hyphenated CVCs and colors, about 75% of the responses correct to compounds were correct to hyphenated CVCs alone compared to about 48% for responses to colors alone.

The outcome of a second experiment was essentially the same to suggest, in accordance with Sundland and Wickens' initial hypothesis, that transfer to colors would be less when colors were in compounds with the presumably more discriminable words than with the less discriminable hyphenated CVCs. Since the hyphenated CVCs were of low Glaze M_a, the basis for the observed difference between words and hyphenated CVCs may be less frequent recognition responses to stimuli of low meaningfulness in compounds than to stimuli of high meaningfulness. But the hyphenated CVCs may also have been of greater formal similarity than the words so that the results could reflect differential responding on the basis of similarity among word elements of the compounds.

In Underwood, Ham, and Ekstrand's (1962) main experiment, as noted previously, single digits from 2 to 8 were associated with compounds of three-letter words and colors or of CCCs and colors. Following acquisition to a criterion of one perfect trial, these compounds were continued for 10 more trials, or colors alone, words alone, or CCCs alone were presented. The shift from CCC and color compounds to colors alone had no influence on the number of correct responses relative to correct responses to continued CCC and color compounds. But the shift to CCCs alone occasioned a marked decline in correct responses which, at the end of 10 trials with the CCCs alone, had not been overcome entirely. In contrast, the shift from compounds to words alone produced some but not a pronounced decrement in correct responses relative to correct responses to continued compounds. The shift to colors produced a somewhat greater decrement, although not as great as that occasioned by the shift from CCC and color compounds to CCCs alone. The same relationships among conditions have been obtained with names of colors substituted for colors and with overt occurrence of recognition responses to trigram elements of the compounds in the form of spelling them aloud (Jenkins & Bailey, 1964). These results, therefore, corroborated those of Sundland and Wickens.

Removal of colors from Newman and Taylor's (1963) compounds of colors and CVCs of low formal similarity reduced the number of correct responses slightly. Removal of colors from their compounds of colors and CVCs of high formal similarity markedly reduced the number of correct responses. Subjects apparently responded to CVCs of low formal similarity relatively more often than they did to CVCs of high formal similarity.

The results of all three experiments suggest that the degree to which color elements of compounds are conditioned to responses is, in part, contingent on characteristics of the word elements or letter-sequence elements of the compounds. The lower the similarity among word or letter sequences, the higher their meaningfulness, or both, the greater the likelihood subjects will later respond primarily to the words or to the letter sequences rather than to the colors. Differences in relative strengths of recognition responses to colors or to word or letter sequences are a presumed basis of the observed relationships.

Two of the conditions of Spear, Ekstrand, and Underwood's (1964) first experiment involved transfer of responses from compounds to elements. The color elements of the compounds were replaced by three-letter words; the other elements were again trigrams. Acquisition of single-digit numbers as responses to the compounds was carried to one perfect trial, after which the word or trigram elements were presented for 10 trials. On the first transfer trial, 6.88 correct responses occurred to the words and 1.92 correct responses to the trigrams; during all 10 trials, 75.8 and 52.1 correct responses occurred to these stimuli, respectively.

Also investigated in this experiment was transfer from acquisition of the compound-number list to acquisition of PA lists with the trigrams as stimulus members and the words as response members. In one condition, the trigram and word which had appeared in a compound were paired (appropriate); in the other condition, the trigram of one compound was paired with the word of another (inappropriate). The pattern of results indicated better acquisition of word responses to trigrams with appropriate than with inappropriate pairings. Better acquisition with appropriate than with inappropriate pairings was also obtained in a second and a third experiment in which transfer to the PA task was from acquisition of a discrimination between words. The methods and findings of the third experiment were described in greater detail in Chapter 6. The transfer to PA learning obtained in these three experiments is significant here as an apparent demonstration of the formation of bidirectional association between members of compounds during PA learning or between members of pairs of stimuli during verbal discrimination learning. Therefore, the possibility exists of the formation of response sequences in which trigrams evoke recognition responses to colors, names of colors, or words which, in turn, evoke correct terminating responses.

Responding to More Discriminable Features

When stimulus members differ in form, in component letters, or in more than one dimension, subjects may learn to orient toward and make recognition responses only or primarily to those features of the forms, those letters, or those dimension(s) which are maximally discriminable. Thus, Miller and Dollard (1941) have suggested that "a cue which would otherwise not be distinctive can acquire greater distinctiveness in two ways: the individual may learn to direct his sense organs toward that cue, or he may learn to react to that obscure cue with a response, such as counting, which produces a more distinctive cue" (p. 74). Mentioned in a subsequent elaboration of Miller and Dollard's (1941, 1950) conceptions of acquired distinctiveness and acquired equivalence of cues was the possibility of altering the number and probabilities of cue-producing (here recognition) responses by "the strengthening of responses of looking for the specific parts or part-characteristics which differentiate complex stimuli" (Goss, 1955, p. 26). More recently, this particular means of enhancing the distinctiveness of cues has been labeled cue-selection (Underwood, Ham, & Ekstrand, 1962).

Familiarization experiences and experiences with elements alone or in compounds may produce greater distinctiveness among stimuli based upon responding to more discriminable elements. Moreover, meaningfulness of elements, their similarity, or both may influence the occurrence of orientation toward and recognition of those elements. Therefore, several of the experiments described above are reexamined for any information they might provide concerning the course and extent of learning to respond to more or the most dissimilar elements of stimuli. Also analyzed are the results for the transfer phases of the Weiss and Margolius and the Horowitz, Lippman, Norman, and McConkie experiments. These experiments might be described as involving transfer from compounds to changed compounds.

The first of the reexamined experiments is Newman's (1936b). The distinctive first letters of trigram stimulus members were emphasized by information about their distinctiveness or by making them red in contrast to black second and third letters. In a third condition all letters were black. During acquisition of responses of three digits when no information had been received about the first letters, reports of the use of red first letters and of black first letters were made by almost exactly the same percentages of subjects. Twenty percent more of the subjects who had been informed about the distinctiveness of the first letters reported that they used them.

During acquisition of responses of a single digit, the percentages of subjects who reported use of the first letters for these three conditions were 68, 44, and 86, respectively. But in terms of correct responses and also of the free recall and backward recall of entire stimulus members, neither information about nor isolation of first letters was facilitative with responses of three digits and only instructions may have been facilitative with responses of a single digit. Thus, emphasis of distinctive elements and reported use of those elements were neither strongly nor consistently related to acquisition measures.

Cohen and Musgrave's (1964a) results could be interpreted as suggesting a direct relationship between M_a of CVC elements of compounds and the likelihood of subjects orienting toward the elements, recognizing them, or both. Also, their finding for transfer from acquisition with compounds of two CVCs of low M_a could be regarded as suggesting orientation and recognition responses to elements in the first position more often than to those in the second position. Since formal similarity among these compounds of CVCs of different M_a was minimal, the Cohen and Musgrave experiment is perhaps the only one which provides relatively unequivocal evidence of a direct relationship between meaningfulness of elements of stimuli and the probability of subjects orienting toward those elements, recognizing them, or both. Except that the relationships are inverse, the results of Cohen and Musgrave's (1964b) later experiment, in which similarity among elements of compounds was varied, can be interpreted in the same way.

The Sundland and Wickens (1962), Underwood, Ham, and Ekstrand (1962), and Newman and Taylor (1963) experiments with compounds of words or CVCs and colors provide additional information on factors influencing subjects' responding to more discriminable elements. Sundland and Wickens, as mentioned earlier, found that subjects were more likely to respond correctly to words of word and color compounds than they were to hyphenated CVCs in compounds of such elements and colors. An analysis of subjects' reports of elements to which they reacted adds support to the inference of more frequent orientation and recognition responses to words than to hyphenated CVCs. Differences in meaningfulness of words and hyphenated CVCs, their meaningfulness, or both may be the basis of the inferred differential orientation and recognition responses.

Whether lower meaningfulness of CCCs than of words or greater similarity among CCCs occasioned the apparently stronger tendency of Underwood, Ham, and Ekstrand's subjects to respond to words than to CCCs is conjectural. Regardless, in color and word compounds it may be inferred that subjects were less likely to make orientation and recognition responses to colors than to words while in CCC and color compounds they apparently responded almost exclusively to colors. Newman and Taylor's findings, as described previously, suggest a greater likelihood of orientation and recognition responses to colors in compounds of colors and CVCs of high similarity than in compounds of colors and CVCs of low formal similarity.

In Weiss and Margolius' (1954) experiment, acquisition with hyphenated pairs of CVCs on colored or gray cards was followed by several changes: the colored cards remained the same or were changed to gray; the hyphenated CVCs remained the same, were changed by replacing the first two letters of the second CVC, or were eliminated. Also, the gray cards were changed to colored ones and the hyphenated CVCs eliminated. As measured by recall and relearning of word responses, the change from colored to gray cards reduced amount retained over 24 hours relatively more than the change in hyphenated CVCs. In fact, removal of the hyphenated CVCs was a less deleterious change. One interpretation of these findings is subjects' preferential recognition responses to colors rather than to hyphenated CVCs. Alternatively, the change from colors to gray may have been relatively greater than the change in CVCs.

Some additional evidence that subjects had learned to respond primarily in terms of differences in color rather than in hyphenated CVCs is provided by the approximate equality of trials to learn with compounds of colors and hyphenated CVCs and of trials to relearn with colors alone following the change from gray to colored cards and elimination of the hyphenated CVCs. Relearning with colors alone might have been facilitated by transfer based on nonspecific factors. Assuming negligible facilitation from this source, this equality suggests that the presence of hyphenated CVCs added little to learning with the color and hyphenated CVC compounds.

The first of Horowitz, Lippman, Norman, and McConkie's (1964) experiments involved acquisition of responses to triad stimulus members, after which the word in the first, second, or third positions was held intact and the other two words were changed. Whether the changes were in horizontal, vertical, or independent triads made no difference in 15 trials of acquisition of old responses to the new triads. But the position in which the word remained the same occasioned a highly significant difference in the form of the largest number of correct responses when the word in the first position remained intact and the smallest number when the word in the second position remained intact. A parallel relationship obtained for post-transfer recall of stimulus members of original triads to response members.

These results for position of elements along with those of Cohen and Musgrave (1964a, 1964b) for position of elements in compounds of CVCs of low M_a or of high similarity may wholly or in part explain Newman's (1963b) failure to find consistent, significant facilitation for instructions and isolation conditions. Possibly because of reading habits, subjects may orient toward and make recognition responses to the initial element of compounds. If so, neither instructions nor isolation provided any appreciable additional emphasis of those elements. Terminal elements may prove to be oriented toward and recognized more often than intermediate ones, perhaps because the white space to the right permits easier isolation.

The stimulus members of Chang and Shepard's (1964) lists were either eight CVC words of high Archer M_a and Noble m' or eight CVC nonwords of low M_a and m'. The members of both sets had two different initial consonants, two different vowels, and two different terminal consonants. In $n:1$ pairings, these CVCs were assigned to the responses "one" or "two" so that only the first, second, or third pairs of letters (Type I) or all three pairs of letters (Type VI) were necessary for perfect differential responding. The remaining lists consisted of members of the two sets of CVCs paired 1:1 with eight different letters.

With Type I assignment, the means of the total number of errors were 16 for word and 23 for nonword stimulus members; with Type VI assignment, the corresponding means were 64 and 74. The faster acquisition with Type I than with Type VI assignment presumably reflected facilitative effects of less time necessary to orient to relatively more distinctive features of the stimuli; of recognition responses of shorter latencies, shorter duration, less variability, and greater distinctiveness; or of both sets of differences in reacting to the stimuli. As expected, acquisition rate varied directly with meaningfulness of the stimulus members. The interaction of type of assignment and meaningfulness was not significant. Thus, type of assignment did not have different effects with more meaningful than with less meaningful stimulus members.

With lists with 1:1 pairings, the direct effect of meaningfulness was more pronounced. A further analysis of errors with both words and nonwords showed a positively accelerated relationship between number of errors and number of common letters.

In an experiment by Bower and Wilkenson (Bower & Trabasso, 1964, pp. 48-49), perfect discrimination was possible in terms of only the pairs of letters in the second position in three-letter stimuli constituted of different pairs of letters in the first, second, and third positions. In post-acquisition tests with three-letter stimuli, combinations of two letters, and single letters, when one or the other of the second pair of letters in the second position was present, subjects responded to combinations of component pairs of letters or to the single letters nearly as well as to the three-letter stimuli. When one of the pairs of letters in the second position was not present, responses were on a chance basis.

In summary, with respect to learning to orient toward and recognize more or the most discriminable features of complex stimuli, some evidence for the occurrence of these changes can be derived from, particularly, results of experiments on transfer from compounds to elements. One interpretation is that elements of high rather than of low meaningfulness, and of low rather than of high similarity are likely to be oriented toward and recognized more often. In compounds of two elements the initial position may be favored; in compounds of three elements the initial and then the terminal position may be favored.

SUMMARY

Considered here were findings from experiments which involved acquired-distinctiveness training, induction of meaning and meaningfulness, response-mediated association, and manipulation of the number and strength of associations among elements of recognition responses to stimuli and to response members. The conditions of all four types of experiments presumably entail or occasion changes in hierarchies of recognition responses to stimuli, of association responses, or of both. Therefore, relationships observed in these experiments may contribute to an understanding of the role of meaningfulness of stimulus and of response members in PA learning and also, perhaps, of the role of their similarity.

Because of the infrequent use of verbal stimuli, and, when such stimuli were employed, failure to vary their meaningfulness, only a few of the experiments involving acquired-distinctiveness training are pertinent. Unfortunately, the results of these few experiments are inconclusive: acquired-distinctiveness training with stimuli has not had consistent effects on subsequent acquisition of lists in which those stimuli were stimulus members or response members.

The overlap between acquired-distinctiveness training and induction of meaning and meaningfulness was noted. Regardless of this issue, procedures which were presumed to alter the meaning and meaningfulness of stimuli have also failed to produce consistent transfer to tasks in which those stimuli then served as stimulus or response members.

Most of the available data on response-mediated associations were considered irrelevant to understanding their possible role in relationships between acquisition rate and meaningfulness. Moreover, information of seeming pertinence had two serious shortcomings: occurrences of mediating responses were not observed on a trial-to-trial basis or approximations thereto; and the lists employed did not represent adequately different combinations of meaningfulness, of similarity, or of both.

In experiments whose procedures involved simple variations in number and strength of associations among elements of recognition responses, the larger the number of elements and the weaker the associations among them, the slower the acquisition. These relationships are consistent with an interpretation of effects of meaningfulness at least partly in terms of integration and availability of recognition responses to stimulus and to response members.

Number of and associations among elements also appear as variables in experiments on transfer from elements presented separately to those same elements presented simultaneously in compounds and on transfer from compounds to elements. The apparent direct relationship between extent of transfer and meaningfulness and the inverse relationship between extent of transfer and similarity of elements in compounds can be interpreted as due to differential strengths of occurrence of recognition responses to those elements. For stimulus members of three and possibly more elements, the relationship between extent of transfer and position of elements may be U-shaped. The advantage of the first position can be attributed to initial orientation toward and hence stronger recognition responses to elements in that position; on a *post factum* basis, the advantage of the last position was also attributed to stronger recognition responses.

Aspects of experiments on transfer from compounds to elements and of two other experiments involving transfer from compounds to compounds were reexamined in terms of the notion that effects of meaningfulness, familiarization, and similarity may be in part attributable to differential ease and extent of orientation toward and recognition responses to more or the most discriminable elements of complex stimuli. The relationships observed in several experiments could be interpreted as reflecting such differential changes.

CHAPTER 8

Summary, Significance,

and Suggestions

Presented first is an over-all summary of findings and suggested conclusions regarding effects of meaningfulness, similarity, familiarization, and meaning and association in PA learning, as described in the chapters devoted primarily to normative and experimental studies. The theoretical analyses which have been proposed are then summarized preliminary to consideration of the significance for these analyses of the empirical findings and conclusions. Such consideration has the dual function of bringing data and theory together and of preparing the way for suggestions about future experimentation on meaningfulness, similarity, familiarization, and meaning and association in PA learning. These suggestions were deferred for development here rather than separately in the chapters on effects of these variables on PA learning.

SUMMARY

The first chapter devoted primarily to data was on scaling of meaningfulness and related attributes. Subsequent chapters were concerned with meaningfulness in PA learning and then with effects of similarity, familiarization, and meaning and association.

Scalings of Meaningfulness and Related Attributes

Three general techniques for the scaling of meaningfulness and related attributes of discrete stimuli and of pairs of stimuli were distinguished: requiring subjects to produce associations, stimuli for responses supplied by experimenters, and counts of frequency of occurrence or of use. The first of these general techniques was divided into single associations and multiple associations. The second general technique was divided into experimenter-

217

supplied discrete stimuli or continuous stimuli either of which might be used to obtain single or multiple associations. The semantic differential format was viewed as the special case of multiple associations to experimenter-supplied continuous stimuli whose extremes are defined by bipolar adjectives.

Meaningfulness of members of sets of discrete stimuli has been scaled by different general and more specific techniques using the same and different groups of subjects at different times under the same and different instructional and other conditions. The stimuli have been primarily verbal, but some have been nonverbal; the most extensive norms are for words and nonwords of CVC structure. Significant coefficients of correlation from .52 to .99 have been obtained for pairs of values for the same sets of stimuli which have ranged in number from 10 to 1933.

Meaningfulness values of discrete verbal stimuli as obtained by different techniques are related directly to additional attributes of stimuli which include counted frequency of occurrence of stimuli; ratings of stimuli for familiarity, ease of learning, emotionality and social values; and their short-term retention by recognition. Meaningfulness and word-recognition thresholds of stimuli may be related inversely, with some uncertainty about this relationship for nonword CVCs. Values for each of the additional attributes proved, in general, to be related to values for one or more of the other additional attributes. For example, counted and rated frequencies of use have correlated highly.

Pairs of stimuli have been scaled for attributes such as estimated strength of the association between members of the pair, estimated co-occurrence of referents of members of pairs, similarity of their meaning, and vividness of connotation. Values for meaningfulness of pairs have apparently not been reported. Correlations among these attributes of pairs of stimuli have usually been significant, but not always. For example, in one investigation the coefficient of correlation for strength of association and similarity of meaning was .90; but the coefficients for each of these variables and vividness of connotation were only .17 and .09. Meaningfulness and other attributes of discrete stimuli have sometimes proved predictive of values of attributes of pairs constituted of those stimuli.

Among the areas in which further research with discrete stimuli was viewed as desirable were counts of frequencies of phoneme-sequences of various lengths and also counts of frequencies of words in both written and spoken protocols which reflect more contemporary exposure and use. These protocols should allow for differences in various personal and social factors. Semantic counts based on these protocols were viewed as a related need.

Using meaningfulness based on multiple associations, further scalings of bigrams, of CVCs, and of samples of trigrams of other structures as well as words from English and from other languages were proposed. Ratings for pronunciability and, perhaps, for familiarity were considered important supplementary information. Moreover, these scalings should also be by subjects other than college undergraduates, including children and adolescents. These suggestions for scalings of discrete stimuli were extended to pairs of stimuli.

Viewed as requiring detailed attention was the extent of congruence between hierarchies of associations to individual stimuli based on groups and for individual subjects.

Meaningfulness in PA Learning

Construction and use of lists of PA units whose stimulus members, response members, or both represent different values of meaningfulness or related attributes were discussed in terms of various complete and incomplete orthogonal combinations of those values. Assignment of combinations of values or designs to lists was described in terms of unmixed, mixed, and partly mixed lists. Lists are unmixed when all PA units of each different list represent a different one of the combinations of values. Lists are mixed when one or more pairs representing all of the combinations are presented as a single list. Lists are partly mixed when PA units representing two or more but not all combinations of values are assigned to one list and the remaining PA units are assigned to one or more other lists. All, more than one but not all, or only one of unmixed or partly mixed lists can be administered to the same subjects.

Complete orthogonal designs permit assessment of the relative potency and interaction between or among two or more component variables. Findings for meaningfulness of discrete stimuli by means of such designs for unmixed, partly mixed, and mixed lists of PA units have indicated frequently, but not without exception, that acquisition rate and meaningfulness of stimulus members and of response members are related directly. Meaningfulness of response members has usually but not always proved more potent than meaningfulness of stimulus members. With greater potency of response members, acquisition rates for the four combinations of a 2×2 design increase in the order low-low, high-low, low-high, and high-high meaningfulness of stimulus and response members. Significant interactions between meaningfulness of stimulus and of response members do occur but exceptions are common. The significant interactions are typically but not always in the form of greater effects of meaningfulness of stimulus members for decreasing values of meaningfulness of response members and the converse.

Findings of experiments employing various incomplete orthogonal designs have been reasonably consistent with expectations based on results for the same combinations of meaningfulness within complete orthogonal designs. Also, findings with both complete and incomplete orthogonal designs have usually held up over various other conditions such as anticipation or recall formats of presentation, administration to subjects individually or in groups, and %ORM.

Data on effects of attributes of discrete stimuli other than meaningfulness are scarce. However, differences in such attributes of response members have typically proved more potent than comparable differences in stimulus members.

Backward recall of stimulus members is related directly to meaningfulness of stimulus and of response members. The former has often been the more potent variable. Data on effects of meaningfulness on retention and transfer were noted; at present they are too limited to warrant any conclusions about direction and extent of effects of meaningfulness and related attributes either without or with adjustments for differences in acquisition rate.

Attributes of pairs of stimuli have usually been employed to specify initial strengths of relationships between stimulus members and response members of the same or different units. For relationships between the stimulus member and response member of the same unit, greater initial strengths of association occasion faster acquisition. For relationships involving stimulus members, response members, or both of different units, the usual outcome has been retardation in rates relative to rates for pairs in which initial associations between stimulus and response members of the same unit are varied and other intra-list associations are weak.

Similarity

Relative distance(s) along physical dimensions, common letters or phonemes, common meaning, and subjects' reactions in the form of judgments or interstimulus generalization errors were mentioned as the bases for scalings of similarity between or among stimuli. After noting specific techniques for defining similarity for each of these kinds of information about stimuli or about stimuli and subjects' reactions to them, the stimuli, techniques and outcomes of various scalings were summarized. Similarity among the same stimuli has occasionally been determined by two or more different techniques and resultant values correlated. The values of the coefficients thus obtained have not always been significant. However, they have been significant with sufficient frequency to justify a conclusion of direct relationships between values of similarity among members of sets of stimuli, particularly when the values have been obtained by different techniques applied to the same basis for scaling similarity.

Experiments concerned with similarity of verbal stimuli were divided into those in which similarity alone was varied and those in which both similarity and meaningfulness were varied. The former were divided further into those with verbal and with nonverbal stimuli. Most of the experiments with similarity alone have been with incomplete orthogonal designs. However, 2×2 orthogonal designs have been realized in unmixed lists. In general, acquisition rate and similarity of stimulus members and similarity of response members have been related inversely with similarity of stimulus members the more potent variable. The apparent order of increasing rates is high-high, high-low, low-high, and low-low. Nothing in the outcomes of experiments in which incomplete orthogonal designs have been employed seems seriously contrary to this conclusion. Moreover, findings with both complete and incomplete orthogonal designs suggest that the inverse relationships hold for similarity specified in several ways and across conditions such as massed or distributed trials, %ORM, and recall or anticipation formats of presentation. Similarity of stimulus members and of response members have also been related inversely to backward recall of stimulus members. Whether or not these variables differ in potency is uncertain.

Similarity and meaningfulness of stimulus and response members have been combined in both complete and incomplete orthogonal designs realized in unmixed, partly mixed, and mixed lists. The relationships which have obtained for similarity of stimulus and of response members disregarding meaningfulness, and for meaningfulness of stimulus and response members disregarding similarity, have proved essentially the same as those obtained with comparable differences in similarity alone or in meaningfulness alone. With complete orthogonal designs realized in unmixed and mixed lists, interactions involving similarity and meaningfulness have not generally been significant. Thus, relationships for similarity hold for different combinations of meaningfulness, and conversely.

Again, findings of effects on acquisition rate of similarity and meaningfulness combined in incomplete orthogonal designs appear consistent with findings obtained with complete orthogonal designs. Also, observed direct relationships for meaningfulness and inverse relationships for similarity have held generally over various other conditions such as %ORM, format of presentation, individual or group administration, and durations of stimulus members alone and with response members. Similarity alone or with meaningfulness has rarely been combined with other variables in designs which are orthogonal for all variables.

Familiarization

Familiarization of stimuli has been accomplished by three different general techniques. One technique is repeated elicitation of recognition responses to stimuli on the supposition of thereby increasing their integration and availability. Some variations of this technique have been regarded as familiarization by some investigators and as satiation by others. The expectations of facilitative and inhibitory consequences for subsequent acquisition are diametrically opposed. Two other techniques are presentation of stimuli to be familiarized in other learning tasks and strengthening of responses other than recognition responses. Both may also involve incidental strengthening or weakening of recognition responses.

When placed within the broader framework of paradigms for experiments on transfer, familiarization or satiation was viewed as involving changes in responses to stimuli alone rather than paired. Noted for comparison were conventional paradigms of transfer in which one or both members of pairs of stimuli are changed from the first task to the second task.

Effects of familiarization have been investigated by means of both complete and incomplete orthogonal designs. In the simplest complete orthogonal design, stimulus members which have or have not been familiarized or satiated are combined with response members which have or have not been familiarized or satiated. Familiarization of stimulus members and also of response members have had facilitative, no, and inhibitory effects on acquisition rate. These contradictory findings have often been for familiarization by the same or similar variations within the same general technique.

One of the explanations offered for inhibitory effects of satiation, and familiarization might be included, is decreased meaning of stimuli. Response interference arising from at least three different sources is an alternative or supplementary explanation. Recognition responses to other familiarized stimuli of the list is one of the proposed sources. Another is recognition responses to irrelevant stimuli of familiarization lists. The third source is repetitions of the recognition response to each stimulus as a consequence of the formation of chains of recognition responses during at least some familiarization experiences.

Meaning and Association

Discussed under meaning and association were acquired-distinctiveness training, induction of meaning and meaningfulness, response mediation of associations between stimulus members and response members, and manipulation of number of and associations among elements of recognition responses to stimulus and to response members.

ACQUIRED-DISTINCTIVENESS TRAINING

Acquired-distinctiveness training was regarded as establishing or strengthening dissimilar recognition responses, association responses, or both to similar stimuli. Noted were the relationships between acquired-distinctiveness training and other paradigms generated by combining binary values of similarity of stimulus members, similarity of mediating responses to those members, similarity of response members and recognition responses to them, and initial strengths of associations between stimuli produced by mediating responses and recognition responses to response members.

The use of nonverbal stimuli in most experiments on acquired distinctiveness and lack of information about the meaningfulness of those stimuli were viewed as rendering the outcomes of most experiments on acquired-distinctiveness training of little or no pertinence to possible interpretation of effects of meaningfulness of stimuli in terms of acquired distinctiveness. In the few, possibly pertinent experiments, acquired-distinctiveness training of stimulus members had facilitative, no, or inhibitory effects on acquisition of PA lists. Acquired-distinctiveness training of response members had no or facilitative effects.

Induction of Meaning and Meaningfulness

Acquired-distinctiveness training and induction of meaning and meaningfulness overlap. The latter was viewed as primarily the formation or strengthening of associations between a stimulus and from one to several different association responses. Only a few experiments are available on transfer from induction of meaning and meaningfulness of stimuli to acquisition of lists in which those stimuli appear as stimulus and response members. Again the outcomes are not sufficiently consistent to permit conclusions either about occurrence of transfer or about those conditions which might influence direction and extent of transfer.

Response-Mediated Associations

Associations between stimulus members and recognition responses to response members may be mediated by association responses. Considered, at best, as indirect evidence of response mediation of associations were intralist or extra-list intrusion errors, and also findings of experiments on mediate or response-mediated associations and of those involving similarity specified by common meaning. Then considered were subjects' reports of their manner of forming a particular association. These reports seemingly offer some support for inferences of response mediation of associations between stimulus members and recognition responses to response members. Extent of subjects' use of mediating responses, however, has not yet been related satisfactorily to meaningfulness of stimulus and response members; and such relationships are requisite to interpretations of effects of meaningfulness of stimulus and response members through facilitative mediating responses.

Number of and Associations among Elements

Discussed in connection with number of and associations among elements were simple variations, transfer from elements to compounds and the converse, and responding to more discriminable features of stimuli. Simple variations were divided into experiments in which number of letter, syllable, or word elements were varied and experiments involving compounds of syllables or words and colors. With the former variations, acquisition rate was related inversely to number of elements of stimulus and response members. Also, available data suggest direct effects on acquisition rate of strength of associations between elements of stimulus and of response members and between the last element of stimulus members and the first element of response members. Although not without exception, acquisition is apparently faster with stimulus members which are compounds of words or syllables and colors than with stimulus members which are words or colors alone.

Letters, syllables, words, or other stimuli can be presented alone as elements and then together as elements in compounds. Conversely, two or more of such stimuli can be presented together in compounds and then alone as elements. For changes from letter, syllable, or word elements alone to those elements in compounds, the data are consistent in showing longer latencies and fewer correct responses. Extent of such decrements, however, is apparently contingent on the pattern of relationships between stimuli in compounds and the responses they elicit when presented alone. Thus, decrements are smaller for compounds in which both elements have been associated with the same response (convergent) than for compounds in which each of two elements was associated with different responses (divergent).

Changes from compounds of letters, syllables, or words to component stimuli alone as elements occasion longer latencies and fewer correct responses. However, the more meaningful the elements the smaller the decrements. Also, the decrements are smaller for elements in the first of two positions and in the first and last of three positions.

Whether or not changes from compounds of syllables or words and colors to those elements alone produce decrements depends, in part, on whether syllables or words were elements of the compounds. With syllables of low meaningfulness and, perhaps, of high similarity combined with dissimilar colors, a change to syllables alone may occasion a considerable decrement but a change to colors alone may occasion no or smaller decrements. With words of high meaningfulness and, perhaps, of low similarity combined with dissimilar colors, a change to words alone may occasion little or no decrement. A change to colors may occasion somewhat larger decrements, but not as large as those occasioned by a change from syllable and color compounds to syllables alone.

Learning to orient toward and make recognition responses to more or the most discriminable features of complex stimuli is another of the changes in stimulus-response relationships which may be brought about by familiarization and hence may be of some significance for the interpretation of the role of meaningfulness in acquisition. Such changes are also pertinent to interpretations of the role of similarity. Accordingly, some of the experiments involving simple variations and transfer from elements to compounds and from compounds to elements were reexamined for evidence of subjects' learning to orient toward and recognize more or the most discriminable features of complex stimuli. Examined also were two experiments on transfer from compounds to other compounds.

Considered as evidence for the presumed changes in orientation and recognition responses were subjects' reports of their responses in terms of elements of compounds of words or syllables and colors. Mentioned earlier were differential effects of attributes of members of compounds and their position on transfer from compounds to elements. Position apparently also influences transfer from compounds to other compounds. These differential effects may be interpreted as reflecting stronger tendencies for subjects to orient toward and to make recognition responses to some elements of complex stimuli than to other elements. Presumably the preferred elements are those which maximize the distinctiveness of the stimuli which is, of course, acquired distinctiveness of cues or response-mediated dissimilarity.

THEORETICAL ANALYSES AND SIGNIFICANCE OF EMPIRICAL FINDINGS AND CONCLUSIONS

Theoretical Analyses

Preceding the theoretical analyses was a description of attributes of stimuli and stimulus-response relationships in terms of verbal repertoires of stimuli and of their similarity. The former were viewed as constituted of hierarchies of recognition responses and of association responses. Latency, duration, and form were distinguished as measures of recognition responses which, it was proposed, are reflected in ratings of pronunciability and, conceivably, of familiarity, emotionality, and other attributes. Number of different forms of association responses and latency and duration of each response were distinguished as attributes of association hierarchies. Specifications of meaningfulness by M_a, M_n, and M_r were regarded as defined by or related to latency and form of association responses and, perhaps, to their duration.

The specific theoretical analyses were in terms of attributes of stimulus members, response members, and relationships between them. The general theme of proposals with respect to attributes of stimulus and of response members was reduction of ostensibly different attributes to integration of recognition responses to those members and, consequently, to their greater availability. Integration of recognition responses was specified in terms of speeds of evocation and completion and stability of form. Association hierarchies of stimulus and response members as reflected in measures of meaningfulness were viewed as significant primarily as correlates of speed and stability of recognition responses.

The important consequences of faster and more stable recognition responses were conceived as more time for rehearsal of those responses and of association responses as well as for anticipation or recall of recognition responses to response members. Also, identification of stimuli as belonging to particular lists and as stimulus members or response members was presumably facilitated. Finally, dissimilar recognition responses to stimulus members were conceived as providing response-mediated similarity among stimulus members.

Direct and indirect relationships between stimulus members and response members were distinguished. Direct relationships include those between stimulus members as a whole or the last elements thereof and recognition responses to response members as a whole or the first elements thereof. These relationships might be based on similarity of members of pairs to two previously associated stimuli.

Distinguished as one form of indirect relationship was mediation of associations between stimulus members and response members by association responses to stimulus members, response members, or both. Also noted were possible indirect relationships by means of principles.

Significance of Empirical Findings and Conclusions

Empirical findings and conclusions of significance for the theoretical analyses of effects of attributes of stimulus and of response members are evaluated. Then considered is information on relationships between stimulus members and response members.

STIMULUS MEMBERS

Were meaningfulness of stimulus members a direct indicant of differentiation of or dissimilarity among stimulus members, the inverse relationship between acquisition rate and similarity for stimulus members of high meaningfulness should be less pronounced than the inverse relationship for stimulus members of low meaningfulness. In general, no such interaction has been observed. Therefore, this interpretation of meaningfulness might be questioned.

Familiarization has been conceived as bringing about faster and more stable recognition responses. These changes, supplemented perhaps by dissimilar association responses established by acquired-distinctiveness training and by induction of meaning and meaningfulness, might also increase acquired distinctiveness or response-mediated dissimilarity of stimulus members. Under appropriate conditions of presentation, greater response-mediated dissimilarity might lead to faster acquisition of the further new responses. However, no consistent results of sufficient generality have yet been reported to warrant conclusions of consistent effects of familiarization, acquired-distinctiveness training, or induction of meaning and meaningfulness of stimuli on subsequent acquisition of PA lists in which those stimuli are stimulus members. Replicable, general effects are requisite to any conclusions about the adequacy of theoretical analyses of the bases of the direct relationship between acquisition rate and meaningfulness of stimulus members.

Strength of associations between and among elements of stimulus members are related directly to acquisition rate. On some evidence, this relationship may be stronger than that between acquisition rate and meaningfulness. These findings, in conjunction with indications of an inverse relationship between acquisition rate and number of elements of stimulus members, constitute additional support for the reduction of meaningfulness to attributes of recognition responses. Consistent with the notion of such reduction, but presently quite indirect evidence, are the indications of stronger associations to more meaningful and, perhaps, less similar elements of compounds.

RESPONSE MEMBERS

The expected interaction of a less pronounced effect of similarity of response members for response members of high meaningfulness than for response members of low meaningfulness has yet to be obtained. The expected facilitative effects of familiarization of response members on subsequent PA learning may have been obtained relatively more often than facilitative effects of familiarization of stimulus members. But the findings for response members are not yet sufficient and consistent to support the proposal that familiarization brings about greater integration and hence availability of recognition responses which, in turn, occasion the direct relationship between acquisition rate and meaningfulness of response members. However, the inverse relationship between acquisition rate and number of elements and the direct relationship between acquisition rate and strength of associations between and among elements of response members support the proposals regarding integration and availability.

Induction of meaning and meaningfulness of response members may lead to faster acquisition; but present data do not warrant a conclusion of facilitation due to induced meaning and meaningfulness of response members per se. Instead, the more parsimonious interpretation is that any facilitation due to induction of meaning and meaningfulness reflects greater integration and availability of recognition responses. Thus, induction of meaning and meaningfulness may have functioned as an indirect means of increasing familiarization. Often, acquired-distinctiveness training can be interpreted in the same way.

RELATIONSHIPS BETWEEN STIMULUS MEMBERS AND RESPONSE MEMBERS

Strengths of associations between stimulus members and response members as specified by ratings for pairs of stimuli and acquisition rate are related directly. Such ratings for pairs of stimuli and meaningfulness of the discrete stimuli constituting those pairs may sometimes be related positively. Except when ratings of attributes of pairs are among the experimental variables, however, stimulus and response members of PA units are selected with the intention of precluding associations between members of a unit. Assuming the achievement of this intention, data on relationships between acquisition rate and attributes of pairs may supplement but add little directly to explanation of the role of meaningfulness of discrete members in acquisition. At most, such data support an analysis of PA learning in terms of a chain of responses within each PA unit of which the association between all or parts of stimulus and of response members is one link. The same conclusion holds for the significance of available data on strength of associations between stimulus members and response members specified by association norms and for strength of associations between the last letter of stimulus members and the first letter of response members.

Some shortcomings of available data on response mediation of associations between stimulus members and recognition responses to response members were noted earlier. Until strengths of possible mediating responses can be specified a priori and in relationship to meaningfulness of stimulus members and response members, response mediation must remain a plausible but conjectural basis for explaining the effects of meaningfulness of discrete stimuli.

SUGGESTIONS

The shortcomings of experiments on acquired-distinctiveness training, induction of meaning and meaningfulness, response-mediated associations, and number of and associations among elements noted previously constitute implicit suggestions of problems requiring further experimentation. Some but not all of these suggestions are made explicit here along with additional suggestions. Advanced first are suggestions which concern attributes of and experiences with stimuli prior to acquisition of PA lists consisting of such stimuli whether the prior experiences were in extra-experimental or experimental situations. Then mentioned are suggestions for experiments on acquisition of PA tasks for which meaningfulness of stimulus members, response members, or both are variables along with, perhaps, their similarity.

Prior to Acquisition

Execution of the further normative studies suggested in Chapter 2 should provide all or a substantial part of the information about verbal repertoires of verbal and nonverbal stimuli necessary to specify initial relationships of and among stimulus members and response members in greater detail and with greater precision. Required specifically are estimates of strengths of all initial direct and indirect associations among stimulus members, among response members, between stimulus members and paired response members and the converse, and between stimulus members and other response members and the converse. Required also are estimates of the strengths of all other responses evoked by stimuli of a list. To achieve such specifications of initial relationships without overwhelming complexity, lists may have to be shortened from the typical of eight to 12 units to, at most, four to six units.

Strengths of initial relationships may be estimated for groups or for individuals by means of norms for the same or different groups or individuals. Ultimately, for final critical tests of implications of theoretical analyses, estimation of initial relationships for individual subjects may be necessary. At present such specification is probably premature. A reasonable compromise may be to use relatively homogeneous groups of subjects (Spence, 1956) of which an example is Shapiro 's (1963b) use of subgroups of children with high and low commonality scores who, respectively, deviated least and most from norms based on the entire group.

Initial relationships may also be established by means of prior experiences in experimental situations. These experiences include familiarization and satiation, acquired-distinctiveness training, induction of meaning and meaningfulness, formation of the associations presumed for response-mediated association, and training with compounds or with elements. Some or all of these experiences presumably involve learning to orient toward and recognize more or the most discriminable features of complex stimuli. Thus far, findings and conclusions regarding direction and extent of transfer from most or all of these experiences are equivocal both for subsequent PA learning in general and as evidence for assessing the adequacy of theoretical analyses of effects of meaningfulness and similarity. In view of this equivocality, use of these experiences might be abandoned.

More constructively, further research might be undertaken. Such research has at least three facets. The first is more detailed assessment of the changes in stimulus-response relationships during familiarization and other experiences with stimuli in experimental situations. The resultant information is important per se. It might also clarify similarities and differences among experiences often assumed to be different but which may overlap, as was suggested, for example, with respect to acquired-distinctiveness training and induction of meaning and meaningfulness as means of bringing about response-mediated dissimilarity.

The second facet is determination of the direction and extent of transfer from such experiences with stimuli not to the entire course of acquisition of further tasks but rather to initial stimulus-response relationships of those tasks. Better information than is now available must be obtained about conditions which assure or preclude transfer from terminal relationships of the prior task to initial relationships of the next task. Further acquisition begins from the latter relationships.

The third facet is assessments of changes in initial stimulus-response relationships during subsequent acquisition of PA lists. Changes in initial stimulus-response relationships specified by means of norms should also be followed. The suggestion of these assessments might be regarded as the transition to proposals concerning the acquisition of PA lists. Before discussing additional proposals concerning acquisition of PA lists, however, the possible problem of successive regression of initial stimulus-response relationships should be discussed.

Experiences designed to establish initial stimulus-response relationships of subsequent PA tasks represent, in turn, modifications of the stimulus-response relationships which obtain at the beginning of those experiences. In order to hold the scope of experiments within reasonable limits in terms of time per subject and number of conditions, if for no other reasons, the regressive specification of initial stimulus-response relationships cannot be pursued profitably. Alternatively, different experiences in experimental situations such as familiarization can be imposed on diverse patterns of initial stimulus-response relationships, particularly patterns in which most intra-task and extra-task relationships are at low strengths. Whether or not achieved, the use of nonword syllables and bisyllables represents an attempt to assure low levels of initial strengths of intra-task and extra-task relationships.

During Acquisition

Often ignored are two classes of variables which may have considerable influence on direction and extent of transfer to acquisition of PA lists from familiarization and other experiences. These are instructions to subjects and temporal parameters. Despite some relatively unpromising available data (e.g., Newman, 1963b), component aspects of instructions might be varied. Thus, when familiarization and other experiences have preceded the PA task, extent to which subjects are instructed to use those experiences and the nature of these instructions could be manipulated. The "unconscious" transfer of such experiences to acquisition of the PA task which is usually assumed is but one possible condition. Also, this assumption may be incorrect as transfer may occur only for those subjects who, somehow, manage to give themselves the "proper" instructions.

Most experiments on response-mediated phenomena have been executed with little or no consideration of the time necessary for the occurrence of chains of two or more responses. The acquisition of correct responses of PA tasks almost certainly entails a third stage or set of changes, achievement of the speeds of evocation and completion necessary to anticipate or to recall recognition responses to response members within the usual short anticipation or short recall intervals. That correct associations between stimulus members and recognition responses to response members have reached levels of strength which are not demonstrated completely in short intervals is shown by recent findings (Nodine, 1963; Price, 1963). Necessary in order to provide optimal intervals for anticipation or recall and for the formation and use of direct and indirect associations are more extensive parametric investigations of effects on acquisition of temporal parameters such as duration of stimulus members alone and duration of stimulus members and response members together.

Presuming attempts to obtain prior or concurrent information on effects of instructional and temporal parameters, several kinds of additional data are necessary. One kind are data on essentially trial-by-trial changes not only in responses anticipated or recalled correctly but also about subjects' recognition and association responses to stimulus members and to response members. Included here would be the changes in initial stimulus-response relationships mentioned earlier. These changes might be determined by requiring subjects to make recognition and any association responses overtly during trials or after each trial without, however, specification of the forms of those responses. Recall of stimulus members and of response members, perhaps after each trial, might provide supplementary or corroborative information. Assumed is observation of these changes for lists and pairs representing different combinations of meaningfulness and similarity. Concurrently or subsequently the lists and pairs should represent different combinations of prior experiences in experimental situations such as familiarization and acquired-distinctiveness training.

Another kind of desirable additional data concerns the influence of number and strengths of associations among elements, particularly when these variables are manipulated independently of meaningfulness and similarity (Baddelay, 1961b). Before some critical experiments can be undertaken, however, better data on letter and phoneme sequences and on associations of "n" letters or phonemes to stimuli of "n" letters or phonemes may be required.

Still another kind of additional data is for subjects known to differ in initial stimulus-response relationships. These may be approached as more molecular differences within differences specified by means of norms for groups from which those individuals were selected. To carry out these experiments, subjects at ages and educational achievements less than those of college students may be necessary. In all of the experiments undertaken to obtain these kinds of data, use of two values of variables must be extended to use of three and more values.

Of possible value in many experiments are response measures in addition to such conventional measures as trials to criterion, correct responses or errors per trial to criterion, and correct responses during each or blocks of fixed number of trials (Cook, 1962). Included are measures such as frequencies of partially correct responses and of completely and partially incorrect responses. Distinction of responses as originating within and outside of a list may be useful. Refinement of many of these measures is possible, including lengths of runs of correct and of various types of incorrect responses and also trials and correct responses or errors per trial to increasingly stringent criteria. Post-criterion occurrences of correct and incorrect responses might be reported.

The conclusion, in short, is that experimentation on meaningfulness, similarity, and familiarization in acquisition of PA lists has just begun. Available data identify some variables and show the contours of their effects but little more. Until better data on acquisition are available, certain endeavors can be of only limited significance. Illustrative are critical tests of theoretical proposals regarding the bases of effects of meaningfulness, development of more precise mathematical representations of PA learning of interesting generality, and evaluation of hypotheses of the manner of formation of associations.

Appendix

The groupings of the 12 experiments reported here and the rationale for those groups were described in Chapter 1. Accordingly, they are here described one-by-one in approximately the order in which they were executed. Each experiment is reported in terms of its purpose and design, method, and results. The results are then discussed and the experiment summarized. Coauthors of each experiment are noted immediately below its title.

EXPERIMENT 1

Acquisition and Retention of Unmixed Lists as Functions of Similarity of Stimulus Members, Meaningfulness and Similarity of Response Members, and %ORM

WITH *Nancy J. Cobb, Nancy C. Farrick,*
Nancy A. Mello, AND *Sally L. Perry*

PURPOSE AND DESIGN

In Goss, Nodine, Gregory, Taub, and Kennedy's (1962) Experiments IA and IB, acquisition of four-unit PA lists and performance under postacquisition 0% ORM were investigated as functions of meaningfulness and similarity of stimulus and of response members combined orthogonally with %ORM. Four of these five variables were incorporated in the present investigation of acquisition and then retention under postacquisition 0% ORM. The variable eliminated was meaningfulness of stimulus members which, in the earlier experiments, was the least potent of the five variables. The resultant design is shown by the column headings and values of the four variables in the left half of Table A1.

Both for Experiment 1 and the earlier experiments, the rationale for investigating acquisition and then performance under postacquisition 0% ORM with lists representing different combinations of meaningfulness and simi-

TABLE A1

Design of Experiment 1 with Means of Trials to Criterion and of Correct Responses per Trial for 16 Postacquisition Trials under 0% ORM for Experiment 1 and for the Same Combinations of Conditions of Goss, Nodine, Gregory, Taub, and Kennedy's (1962) Experiments IA and IB; in Experiment 1 the Change to 0% ORM Was 24 Hours after Acquisition, in Experiments IA and IB the Change Was Immediate

Stimulus simi- larity	Response		%ORM	Trials		Correct responses[c]	
	Simi- larity	Meaning- fulness		Exp. 1[a]	Exps. IA, IB	Exp. 1[b]	Exps. IA, IB
Low	Low	High	100	3.8	11.1	3.0	3.1
			25	12.2	15.1	3.4	3.8
		Low	100	12.4	13.5	2.0	2.9
			25	18.4	26.4	3.0	3.4
	High	High	100	8.8	18.8	1.9	2.7
			25	19.2	26.7	2.4	3.2
		Low	100	18.0	17.2	2.1	2.2
			25	28.2	30.6	2.3	2.7
High	Low	High	100	12.6	21.2	2.3	2.2
			25	22.1	31.2	3.2	3.0
		Low	100	14.6	28.9	2.4	2.6
			25	28.0	40.8	2.7	3.2
	High	High	100	24.2	30.2	2.5	2.2
			25	28.9	41.9	2.8	2.8
		Low	100	28.6	42.4	0.8	1.9
			25	47.2	65.1	1.6	3.1

[a]The rho between means of trials to criterion for Exp. 1 and for Exps. IA, IB is .93 ($p < .01$).
[b]The rho between means of correct responses per trial for Exp. 1 and for Exps. IA, IB is .58 ($p = .02$).
[c]The rhos between means of trials to criterion and of correct responses per trial were .20 for Exp. 1 and .15 for Exps. IA, IB.

larity acquired under different levels of %ORM is developed in greater detail in the general introduction to the earlier experiments (Goss, Nodine, Gregory, Taub, and Kennedy, pp. 1-5). Briefly, one concern was the direction and relative potency of effects of each of the stimulus attributes separately. A second concern was the modes of combination of these variables. Crosscutting these concerns was an interest in whether %ORM would have differential effects for each of the stimulus attributes separately and for different combinations of those variables. Implied by the theoretical analysis were less pronounced effects of %ORM as meaningfulness of stimulus and response members increased, and as their similarity decreased.

In Experiments IA and IB, for trials to an acquisition criterion of one perfect trial, only a few of the interactions involving meaningfulness and similarity of stimulus and response members were significant. Thus, for the particular manners of varying these attributes, they combined additively. Also, the stimulus attributes entered into only a few significant interactions with %ORM. Apparently %ORM had essentially the same effects at each level and combination of levels of the stimulus attributes. Substantially the same conclusions were drawn for combined effects of the stimulus attributes with each other and with %ORM on performance under postacquisition 0% ORM. However, for performance under postacquisition 0% ORM 24 hours rather than immediately after acquisition, a different pattern of effects of stimulus attributes and %ORM might occur.

One reason for undertaking Experiment 1 was to determine the stability of the findings of Experiments IA and IB for acquisition. Another reason was to determine whether or not the stimulus attributes and %ORM had the same or a different pattern of effects on performance under postacquisition 0% ORM 24 hours after rather than immediately after acquisition.

METHOD

Lists. The eight lists which were employed are reproduced in Table A2. They were half of the 16 unmixed lists constructed previously (Goss, Nodine, Gregory, Taub & Kennedy) to represent the 16 combinations of high or low M_a and similarity of stimulus and of response members. By using only those lists whose stimulus members were of high meaningfulness, meaningfulness of stimulus members was eliminated as a variable.

The entire set of 16 lists had been constructed on the basis of Glaze M_a values for the CVCs before Archer M_a values were reported. In parentheses after each CVC are first its Glaze M_a value and then its more recent Archer M_a value. The former values are generally higher than the latter values. Regardless of scaling, means for the high M_a lists are relatively similar as are those for the low M_a lists. Sizable differences obtain between the four means of Glaze or Archer values for the sets of high M_a and those for the sets of low M_a.

The sets of stimulus members and response members of high similarity were constituted of four different letters, the minimum possible for four CVCs. The sets of stimulus members and response members of low similarity were each constituted of 12 different letters, the maximum possible for four CVCs. Formal similarity between stimulus members of a list and any of the response members of that list was minimal. The four different random orders for presentation of the pairs of each list formed a Latin Square.

Apparatus. The tapes of Experiments IA and IB were used again, as was the memory drum. The CVCs had been typed on the tapes in elite capitals. Presentation was at a 2:2-sec. rate with an intertrial interval of about 12 sec.

Acquisition. The procedure for acquisition is described in greater detail by Goss, Nodine, Gregory, Taub, and Kennedy. Under 100% ORM, each stimulus member was presented for 2 sec. within which interval subjects were instructed to spell the anticipated response member. That stimulus member and its paired response member then always appeared together for 2 sec. Under 25% ORM, stimulus members always appeared alone for 2 sec., but on only 25% of these occurrences was the stimulus member then accompanied by its response member. The particular schedule of occurrences of response members imposed in Experiments IA and IB and in Experiment 1 was occurrence of one of the four response members on a given trial and of each of them once within each block of four trials.

TABLE A2

PA Lists Representing the 16 Combinations of Stimulus and Response Members of Low or High Similarity and of Low or High Meaningfulness of Experiments 2 and 3 and from Which the Lists of Experiment 1 Were Selected

Stimulus Members			Similarity of response members			
Attribute		CVC	High		Low	
Simi-larity	Meaning-fulness		Meaningfulness			
			Low	High	Low	High
Low	High[a]	GOB (93, 97)[b]	JEX(0, 23)	RAV(100, 80)	JID (0, 35)	KEN(100, 100)
		FAM(100, 82)	XEZ(7, 7)	VAR (93, 83)	YOV (0, 22)	TIR (93, 67)
		PIL (100, 93)	ZEX(0, 35)	RAD(100, 80)	KEZ (7, 29)	DOV(100, 90)
		CUS(100, 93)	XEJ(0,3)	DAR(100, 88)	NAX(13, 27)	JAZ (93, 95)
		Mean (98, 91)	(2, 17)	(98, 83)	(5, 28)	(96, 88)
	Low	GEC (7, 17)	JEX	RAD	YOV	JAZ
		BOF (7, 31)	XEJ	DAR	NAX	KEN
		WUH (0, 30)	ZEX	RAV	JID	TIR
		QAS (7, 17)	XEZ	VAR	KEZ	DOV
		Mean (5, 24)				
High	High[a]	LIK (100, 91)	JEX	RAD	YOV	JAZ
		KIL (93, 92)	ZEX	RAV	JID	TIR
		LIF (100, 64)	XEZ	VAR	KEZ	DOV
		FIL (80, 93)	XEJ	DAR	NAX	KEN
		Mean (93, 85)				
	Low	WUQ (0, 8)	JEX	RAD	YOV	JAZ
		QUW (7, 13)	XEZ	VAR	KEZ	DOV
		WUH (0, 30)	ZEX	RAV	JID	TIR
		HUW (13, 41)	XEJ	DAR	NAX	KEN
		Mean (5, 23)				

[a]The eight lists of Exp. 1 with stimulus members of high meaningfulness, and of high or low similarity.

[b]Glaze M_a and Archer M_a Values are in parentheses.

Acquisition was carried to a criterion of one perfect trial. Upon attainment of criterion, subjects were asked to come back the next day at times which averaged about 24 hours later. All subjects run on one morning came back the next morning; all subjects run on one afternoon came back the next afternoon.

Retention under postacquisition 0% ORM. When subjects returned for the retention session, each was administered 16 trials in which only the stimulus members of the list learned previously were presented. Only when anticipations occurred within 2 sec. after the appearance of stimulus members were they scored correct.

Subjects. The 144 subjects were assigned in order of their appearance to each of the 16 combinations in counterbalanced cycles in which experimenters ran one subject in each combination before running another subject in that combination. The cycles continued until there were eight subjects in each combination.

RESULTS

Acquisition. The first column of values in Table A1 is for trials to the criterion of one perfect trial for each of the 16 combinations of stimulus attributes and %ORM of Experiment 1. The second column of values is for means of trials to criterion for those same combinations in Experiments IA and IB. Results of the analysis of variance on trials to criterion in Experiment 1 are summarized in Table A3. The *F*s for each of four variables separately, disregarding the other three, were significant at <.01. Rate of acquisition was related directly to %ORM and to meaningfulness of response members. An inverse relationship obtained between acquisition rate and similarity of stimulus and of response members. Similarity of stimulus members was slightly more potent than similarity of response members, which in turn was more potent than meaningfulness of response members.

None of the interactions between any two, among any three, or among the four variables reached 2.50, the arbitrary value for inclusion of exact values for interaction *F*s. Examination of the relationships among means reflected in these interactions revealed the existence of only small differences between or among differences.

Retention under postacquisition 0% ORM. Correct responses per trial across all 16 trials under postacquisition 0% ORM are also shown in Table A1 for Experiment 1 and for Experiments IA and IB. Three of the four *F*s (Table A3) for effects of each of the stimulus attributes and %ORM separately in Experiment 1, disregarding the other variables, were significant at <.01. More correct responses occurred following acquisition under 25% ORM than under 100% ORM, with response members of low than of high similarity, and with response members of high than of low meaningfulness. Although more correct responses occurred with stimulus members of low than of high similarity, the difference was not significant.

Only one of the interactions involving these four variables equaled or exceeded 2.50. The significant interaction of similarity of stimulus members, similarity of response members, and meaningfulness of response members is attributable to different effects of similarity of stimulus and response members for response members of low meaningfulness than for those of high meaningfulness. The rank orders for increasing numbers of correct responses for combinations of similarity were, respectively, high-high $<$ low-high $<$ low-low $<$ high-low and low-high $<$ high-high $<$ high-low $<$ low-low. Across meaningfulness of response members, the rank order for similarity of stimulus and response members was high-high $<$ low-high $<$ high-low $<$ low-low. But the interaction of similarity of stimulus and of response members was not significant.

TABLE A3

Analyses of Variance on Trials to Criterion and on Correct Responses in Successive Four-Trial Blocks under Postacquisition 0% ORM for Experiment 1; Interactions Yielding Fs <2.50 Omitted

Source	df	Trials		Correct responses	
		MS	F	MS	F
%ORM	1	3310.94	19.67**	619.08	10.62**
Similarity of stimulus members (SS)	1	3644.44	21.66**	100.64	1.72
Similarity of response members (SR)	1	3130.38	18.60**	1060.88	18.19**
Meaningfulness of response members (MR)	1	2024.07	12.03**	605.96	10.39**
SS×SR×MR	1			502.05	8.61**
Error (b)	112	168.28		58.32	
Trials (T)	3			382.19	131.74**
T×SR	3			12.01	4.14**
T×MR	3			8.65	2.98*
T×%ORM×SS	3			33.12	11.42**
T×%ORM×SR	3			9.77	3.37*
T×%ORM×MR	3			12.02	4.14**
T×SS×SR	3			8.74	3.01*
T×SS×MR	3			7.76	2.67*
T×%ORM×SR×MR	3			20.72	7.14**
T×%ORM×SS×SR×MR	3			30.41	10.48**
Error (w)	336			2.90	

*$p<.05$.
**$p<.01$.

For all combinations, correct responses per trial during Trials 1–4 decreased from the criterion of all four anticipations correct on one trial to means of from 0.7 to 3.2. Both across all combinations and for each combination, correct responses increased through successive blocks of four trials to means for Trials 13–16 of from 0.9 to 3.6. The F for trials was significant at $<.01$.

Nine of the interactions of trials with stimulus attributes and %ORM separately or combined were significant at from .05 to <.01. Differences between levels of a variable or among combinations of levels of variables decreased over trials for similarity of response members, for %ORM and similarity of stimulus members, for %ORM and similarity of response members, and for similarity of stimulus and response members. Differences increased over trials for meaningfulness of response members, %ORM and meaningfulness of response members, and for similarity of stimulus members and meaningfulness of response members.

The interaction of trials, %ORM, similarity of response members, and meaningfulness of response members reflected two features of the relationships among means. One was a more rapid increase in correct responses through the four blocks of trials following acquisition under 25% ORM than under 100% ORM; the other was a decrease in the dispersion of means for the four combinations of similarity and meaningfulness of response members through the four blocks of trials following acquisition under 25% ORM and an increase and then a decrease in their dispersions following acquisition under 100% ORM. The significant interaction among trials, all three stimulus attributes, and %ORM, in large measure, can also be described in terms of differences in dispersions of means, in this case for the four combinations of similarity of stimulus and response members within the four combinations of %ORM and meaningfulness. For response members of high meaningfulness, dispersions of means for the combinations of similarity were relatively equal through blocks of trials and for 25% and 100% ORM. Greater dispersions of the means for combinations of similarity occurred with response members of low meaningfulness. Also, the dispersions were greater for 25% than for 100% ORM during Trials 1–4 and the opposite during Trials 5–8, 9–12, and 13–16.

DISCUSSION

Results for Experiment 1 for acquisition are examined and then compared with findings for the same combinations of stimulus attributes and %ORM in Experiments IA and IB. Results for retention of correct responses under postacquisition 0% ORM are considered in the same way.

Acquisition. The most important finding of Experiment 1 is the absence of interactions between and among the three stimulus variables and also between %ORM and the stimulus variables alone or in combination. Thus, generalizations of direct relationships to acquisition rate for %ORM and meaningfulness of response members and of inverse relationships for similarity of stimulus and of response members hold at each level and combination of levels of the other variables.

In terms of directions of effects of variables separately, the results of Experiment 1 were consistent with those of the earlier experiments. Also, except for slightly greater potency of similarity of stimulus members than of %ORM in Experiment 1 and the converse in Experiments IA and IB, the rank orders of the relative effects of the variables were the same. For all 16 combinations of stimulus attributes and %ORM, the rho for the rank orders of the means obtained in Experiment 1 and in Experiments IA and IB was .93.

With the five variables of Experiments IA and IB, only five of 26 interactions were significant, four of which involved only two variables. Nonetheless, five of 26 significant interactions is a somewhat higher proportion than no significant interaction among 11 interactions for the four variables of Experiment 1. But the results of the earlier experiments were not reanalyzed just for the 16 combinations common to both those experiments and Experiment 1.

One reason for not undertaking this analysis was the marked agreement between the rank orders of means of trials to criterion for the same combinations of conditions in Experiment 1 and Experiments IA and IB. Despite high or perfect correlations, the patterns of differences among means might be dissimilar. The presence of another factor, however, precluded unequivocal interpretation of any results of more detailed comparison of findings of Experiment 1 and Experiments IA and IB for possible differences in patterns of interactions. That factor was generally faster learning in Experiment 1 than in Experiments IA and IB. Whether the difference in acquisition rates was due to differences in subjects, in experimenters, both, or some other factor is not known.

One concomitant of the difference in acquisition rates was greater dispersion of absolute values of means in Experiments IA and IB than in Experiment 1. Such greater dispersion is to be expected with less rapid acquisition. This difference in dispersions was the only marked difference in the patterns of interactions in Experiment 1 and in Experiments IA and IB. It seems reasonable to conclude, therefore, that the present results agree with those obtained earlier.

Retention under postacquisition 0% ORM. Disregarding trials, only one of the interactions between and among stimulus attributes and %ORM for correct responses under postacquisition 0% ORM was significant. Thus, as in acquisition, with perhaps the one exception, the direct relationship between correct responses and meaningfulness of response members and the inverse relationships between correct responses and each of the other three variables seemingly held not only across but also at each level and combination of levels of the other variables.

Seven of the interactions involving trials and one or more of the stimulus attributes and %ORM could each be interpreted as convergence or divergence over trials for different levels or combinations of levels of the other variables. Across all and within each combination of stimulus attributes and %ORM, correct responses increased over trials. The patterns producing the two significant interactions involving three of the variables and all four along with trials are not amenable to clearcut interpretation.

The more important differences between the results for Experiment 1 and for Experiments IA and IB were in effects of similarity of stimulus members, and in the interactions of trials with the other variables. The F for similarity of stimulus members was very significant in the earlier experiments; it was not significant in Experiment 1. But the relationships are consistently inverse. In Experiments IA and IB, only four of 31 interactions involving trials were significant. In Experiment 1, nine of 15 interactions involving trials were significant.

These and other differences in correct responses under postacquisition 0% ORM immediately and 24 hours after acquisition might reflect interactions of stimulus attributes, %ORM, and trials with retention interval. Also indicating a difference in the pattern of effects obtained in Experiment 1 and Experiments IA and IB is the rho of .58 between rank orders of means of correct responses for the same 16 combinations of attributes and %ORM. While significant ($p = .02$), this value is considerably lower than the .93 obtained for trials to criterion.

Again, the faster learning in Experiment 1 than in Experiments IA and IB precludes unequivocal interpretation of differences in findings for performance under postacquisition 0% ORM. Analysis of covariance involving adjustment for differences in trials to criterion was ruled out because of low correlations between means of trials to criterion and correct responses under postacquisition 0% ORM and between trials to criterion and correct responses for subjects within each of the 16 combinations. The rho between means was .20 for Experiment 1. For Experiments IA and IB, the rho was .15. For Experiment 1, rhos for subjects within combinations ranged from .33 to $-.81$; only the latter was significant at .05. The mean of the 16 rhos was .22. Thus, any relationship between trials to criterion and correct responses under postacquisition 0% ORM was, at most, so slight as to preclude covariance adjustments. Despite these low values, it was decided to forego more detailed comparison of patterns of effects of the variables.

Because trials to criterion and correct responses under postacquisition 0% ORM are not or are but slightly related, one conclusion suggested by the present and earlier results can be advanced with greater confidence: fewer correct responses occurred 24 hours after than immediately after acquisition. In 13 of 16 comparisons, from 0.1 to 1.5 more correct responses per trial occurred immediately after than 24 hours after acquisition. In one of the other three comparisons, the means were the same; in the remaining two, the differences in favor of retention after 24 hours were 0.1 and 0.3. Another conclusion suggested by the results of Experiment 1 and Experiments IA and IB also appears more tenable. For correct responses under postacquisition 0% ORM, irrespective of differences in acquisition rate, there is little evidence of interactions between and among stimulus attributes and %ORM except when trials are also involved.

SUMMARY

Lists representing the eight combinations of stimulus members of low and high similarity and response members of low and high similarity and meaningfulness were acquired under 25% and 100% ORM to a criterion of one perfect trial. In a retention session 24 hours later, stimulus members alone were presented for 16 trials.

Fewer trials to criterion were required under 100% than under 25% ORM but more correct responses occurred under postacquisition 0% ORM following acquisition under 25% than under 100% ORM. Fewer trials to criterion were required and more correct responses occurred under postacquisition 0% ORM for stimulus members and for response members of low than of high similarity and for response members of high than of low meaningfulness. Relatively few of the interactions between and among these variables were significant either for acquisition or for performance under postacquisition 0% ORM. These results were considered reasonably consistent with those for the same combinations of stimulus attributes and %ORM in two previous experiments.

EXPERIMENT 2

Acquisition of Unmixed Lists Administered to Subjects in Groups as Functions of Meaningfulness and Similarity of Stimulus and Response Members and of %ORM

WITH *Sally L. Perry*

PURPOSE AND DESIGN

All 16 of the lists reproduced in Table A2 were employed in Experiment 2. Each was presented under 25% and 100% ORM. The five variables of similarity and meaningfulness of stimulus and of response members and %ORM were, therefore, those of Goss, Nodine, Gregory, Taub, and Kennedy's (1962) Experiments IA and IB. But, Experiments IA and IB and Experiment 2 differed in at least three important ways. In Experiments IA and IB, the anticipation format was used for presentation of the lists to subjects run individually to a criterion of one perfect trial. In Experiment 2, the recall format was used for presentation of the lists to subjects run in groups for a fixed number of trials.

The changes in format of presentation, administration of lists to subjects, and manner of defining an acquisition session from Experiments IA and IB to Experiment 2 were to test the generality of findings obtained in the former experiments. Were the effects of stimulus attributes and %ORM separately and their modes of combination obtained in Experiment 2 reasonably parallel to those obtained in Experiments IA and IB, greater confidence could be placed in the earlier findings and in their generality. Were different effects obtained in Experiment 2 than in Experiments IA and IB, more analytical experiments could be initiated to determine the source or sources of the different effects: recall or anticipation formats, administration to subjects in groups or individually, and acquisition for a fixed number of trials or to a criterion.

The five variables of Experiments IA and IB and of Experiment 2 were also incorporated in the design of Experiment 3. Accordingly, comparisons between Experiments IA and IB and Experiment 2 are deferred until results of Experiment 3 have been described. The results of Experiments 2 and 3 are then compared with each other and with those of Experiments IA and IB.

METHOD

Lists. The 16 lists of Table A2 are described briefly in Experiment 1; they are described in greater detail in Goss, Nodine, Gregory, Taub, and Kennedy (pp. 6-7).

These lists were prepared for administration to subjects in groups by the procedure developed by Saltz and Myers (1955). With minor variations, the same procedure was also used in Experiments 3, 4, 5, and 6. With this procedure, each trial had a learning phase and a recall phase. Each booklet for the learning phase consisted of a cover page and four additional pages. On each of the additional pages, one of the four stimulus members of the pairs of a list appeared alone or with its response member. Whether alone or with response members, stimulus members were always to the left of the center of the one-inch by two-inch pages. Both stimulus members and response members were typed in elite capitals.

For 100% ORM, the four PA units of each list appeared in four different orders which formed a Latin Square. For 25% ORM, the stimulus members of each list, either alone or with their response members, appeared in the same four orders. On each trial, only one of the four stimulus members was accompanied by its response member; which response member was determined randomly within the constraint that all four response members would occur within successive blocks of four trials each. To accomplish this, 16 combinations of orders of stimulus members and occurrence of a particular response member were necessary. The booklets containing these combinations were stapled onto a nine-inch by 11-inch piece of posterboard in four rows and four columns.

The booklets containing the four different orders of pairs for 100% ORM were also stapled onto the posterboard in four rows and four columns. The positions on the posterboard of the 16 combinations for 25% ORM and of the four orders for 100% ORM were determined randomly within the constraint that each of the four orders of stimulus members appear once within each column. In all, 32 different sets of learning booklets were prepared, one for each of the 32 combinations of stimulus attributes and %ORM.

For the recall phase, only one booklet was used. On each page of this booklet the four stimulus members alone appeared in a single column at about the middle of the one-and-one-half-inch by two-inch pages. There were six different orders of the stimulus members alone, all different than the orders of occurrence of the stimulus members either alone or with response members during the learning phase. In turn, these orders occurred in a random sequence within the constraint that each order appear once before any other order was repeated. Blank pages alternated with pages on which the stimulus member alone appeared. The blank pages concealed the pages with stimulus members alone until subjects actually began to write on those pages. The booklet for the recall phase was on a metal ring attached to the upper part of the posterboard. One of these booklets was used by a subject and was then replaced by another booklet for use by the next subject.

Procedure. In so far as possible, subjects were run in groups of 64, two subjects in each of the 32 combinations. Because from a few to many of the subjects scheduled to appear for a given session failed to come, actual groups were usually smaller. The posterboard containing the learning booklets and test booklet for a particular combination was placed on the arm of an ordinary classroom chair and covered by the instructions face down. From session to session the position of each posterboard was systematically rotated through the experimental room.

After all subjects were seated, one experimenter read the instructions aloud as subjects read them to themselves. Explained in the instructions were the nature and use of the learning booklets and the booklet for the recall phase. The original instructions were clear to subjects learning under 100% ORM. However, they were not clear to some of those learning under 25% ORM who, on each test trial, wrote only the response member that had occurred in the learning booklet of the particular trial. All subjects who answered in this fashion were discarded and replaced by others. After the first two sessions, to minimize the number of such subjects, the instructions were changed slightly to emphasize that the task of the recall phase of each trial was to write down the correct response member for all four stimulus members. Following this change, only a few subjects under 25% ORM failed to answer as instructed.

Each trial began by one experimenter telling subjects the number of the learning booklet for that trial. The booklets had numbers from 1 through 16 on their cover pages. Subjects then waited for the experimenter to tell them to "Start," whereupon they opened the cover sheet to examine the pair of stimuli or the stimulus member alone on the first page for 2 sec.; they had 2 sec. to examine the pair of stimuli or stimulus member alone on each of the subsequent three pages of a booklet. Subjects examined each pair or stimulus member alone with the intention of later, in the booklet for recall, writing each of the right-hand syllables or response members to the right of the stimulus member with which it had been paired.

After each 2 sec., subjects were told to "Turn"; when the last page of a booklet had been examined, they were told to "Turn to the test (or answer) booklet." Upon being told to write in the answer booklet, subjects lifted the blank page and began trying to write each response member to the right of the stimulus member with which it had been paired. Eight sec. were allowed for this, after which subjects were told to stop and were given the number of the trial to write on that page of the recall booklet. The page was then turned on the ring to expose a blank page. The next trial began when subjects were told the number of the learning booklet for that trial and to "Start" on that booklet.

Forty-eight trials were administered to subjects in all combinations. Time intervals between the learning and test phases of each trial and between trials were not controlled. Except for interruptions for the experimenter to answer questions or for subjects to catch up or rearrange their materials, these intervals were from 4 to 6 sec.

From one to three additional experimenters or proctors were present to explain the task further to any subjects who raised questions or who seemed confused, to reassemble task booklets of subjects whose rings opened inadvertently, and to prevent subjects from cheating.

Subjects. All subjects were from classes in introductory psychology at the University of Massachusetts. Data are reported on 318, two short of the intended 10 subjects in each of the 32 combinations. Because not all subjects scheduled for the planned last session appeared, two combinations were short one subject each. Rather than run an additional session, values for these missing subjects were estimated from those for the other nine subjects. Data on an additional 52 subjects were discarded from combinations under 25% ORM for the reason noted above: recalling only the response member which appeared during the acquisition phase of that trial. There is no reason to believe that these subjects differed systematically from the other subjects in ability to learn. Data on another 15 subjects were also discarded: two cheated, and one wrote so illegibly that responses could not be scored. The remainder were eliminated for a variety of other reasons, such as getting hopelessly behind, writing the stimulus member rather than the response member, and stopping in the middle of the task. These 15 subjects were distributed widely among combinations.

RESULTS

Means of numbers of correct responses during Trials 1–48 for the 16 combinations under 100% and under 25% ORM are presented in Table A4. Differences among these means and among means for the 32 combinations for Trials 1–24 and Trials 25–48 were assessed by the analysis of variance summarized in Table A5. Similarity of stimulus members, similarity of response members, meaningfulness of stimulus members, meaningfulness of response members, %ORM, and trials all had effects significant at <.01. There were 8% more correct responses under 100% than under 25% ORM, 23% more correct responses with stimulus members of low similarity than with those of high similarity, 11% more correct responses with stimulus members of high meaningfulness than with those of low meaningfulness, 23% more correct responses with response members of low similarity than with those of high similarity, 22% more correct responses with response members of high meaningfulness than with those of low meaningfulness, and 30% more correct responses during Trials 25–48 than during Trials 1–24.

Of 31 interactions between and among stimulus attributes and %ORM, only two were significant. The interaction of similarity of stimulus members and meaningfulness of response members was due to a greater effect of similarity of stimulus members with response members of low meaningfulness than with those of high meaningfulness. The interaction of similarity of stimulus members and of response members with meaningfulness of response members were significant primarily because of a reversal in the rank orders of means in the matrix formed by high and low similarity of stimulus and response members for stimulus members of high and of low meaningfulness. With stimulus members of low meaningfulness, the rank order of increasing numbers of correct responses for the combinations of similarity was high-high < low-high < high-low < low-low. With stimulus members of high meaningfulness, the order was high-high < high-low < low-high < low-low.

Four interactions involving trials were significant at from .05 to <.01. All could be interpreted as partly due to differences in increments from Trials 1–24 to Trials 25–48. The interaction of trials with similarity of stimulus and response members reflected a greater increment from Trials 1–24 to

TABLE A4

Means of Correct Responses during Trials 1–48 for Each of the Combinations
of Stimulus Attributes and %ORM of Experiments 2 and 3

| Stimulus members | | Response members | | %ORM | Exp. 2 | Exp. 3 | | |
Simi-larity	Meaning-fulness	Simi-larity	Meaning-fulness			Famil-iarized	Not Famil-iarized	Both
Low	High	Low	High	100	178.6	94.2	93.0	187.2
				25	169.1	91.5	91.0	182.5
			Low	100	157.8	88.0	85.2	173.2
				25	148.6	90.7	88.0	178.7
		High	High	100	146.7	90.5	91.3	181.8
				25	118.0	87.2	84.3	171.5
			Low	100	135.6	68.3	72.7	141.0
				25	118.4	82.0	80.7	162.7
	Low	Low	High	100	174.7	93.0	92.7	185.7
				25	157.3	91.3	89.8	181.2
			Low	100	115.0	90.0	84.7	174.7
				25	125.2	87.7	83.7	171.3
		High	High	100	132.2	78.0	78.0	156.0
				25	134.5	83.7	83.5	167.2
			Low	100	123.2	64.7	68.3	133.0
				25	100.3	72.8	68.2	141.0
High	High	Low	High	100	149.8	81.0	80.7	161.7
				25	156.9	72.2	67.8	140.0
			Low	100	126.9	83.2	79.3	162.5
				25	115.5	67.5	77.3	144.8
		High	High	100	128.1	85.2	82.5	167.7
				25	109.8	80.2	75.8	156.0
			Low	100	82.7	72.8	76.6	149.5
				25	58.3	53.3	47.2	100.5
	Low	Low	High	100	138.9	72.8	77.2	150.0
				25	133.1	65.5	71.5	137.0
			Low	100	101.6	79.3	76.2	155.5
				25	96.3	71.8	71.0	142.8
		High	High	100	101.3	66.2	65.2	131.3
				25	101.0	51.3	45.2	96.5
			Low	100	73.6	53.5	58.0	111.5
				25	54.7	51.3	52.0	103.3

Trials 25–48 with response members of low similarity than with those of high
similarity for stimulus members of high similarity and the opposite for
stimulus members of low similarity. The interaction of trials, similarity of
stimulus members, and meaningfulness of response members reflected a
greater increment through trials with response members of high meaningfulness than with those of low meaningfulness for stimulus members of high
similarity and the opposite for stimulus members of low similarity. The

average increment for stimulus members of low similarity was greater than that for stimulus members of high similarity; thus, the interaction of trials and similarity of stimulus members was significant.

TABLE A5

Analyses of Variance on Correct Responses in Experiments 2 and 3;
Interactions Yielding Fs < 2.50 Omitted

Source	Exp. 2			Exp. 3		
	df	MS	F	df	MS	F
%ORM	1	4499.70	9.00**	1	579.29	3.07
SS	1	40116.39	80.19**	1	9095.64	48.25**
Meaningfulness of stimulus members (MS)	1	8843.19	17.68**	1	3180.96	16.87**
SR	1	43378.69	86.71**	1	7988.98	42.38**
MR	1	38486.51	76.93**	1	2418.98	12.83**
%ORM×SS				1	1172.65	6.22**
SS×MS				1	714.94	3.79
SS×MR	1	2337.08	4.67*			
SR×MR				1	750.09	3.99*
%ORM×SS×SR				1	762.01	4.04*
SS×MS×MR				1	714.96	3.79
SS×SR×MR	1	1949.51	3.90*			
%ORM×SS×MS×MR				1	688.17	3.65
Error (b)	286[a]	500.23		158[a]	188.51	
T	1	78654.73	545.72**	3	9592.16	391.68**
T×SS	1	733.16	5.09*	3	299.12	12.21**
T×MS				3	117.91	4.81**
T×SR				3	249.73	10.19**
T×MR				3	66.61	2.72*
T×%ORM×SS				3	67.23	2.75*
T×SS×SR	1	1571.90	10.91**	3	126.82	5.18**
T×SS×MR	1	1073.82	7.45**			
T×MS×SR				3	73.36	2.99*
T×%ORM×SS×MS×SR×MR	1	564.11	3.91*			
Error (w)	286[a]	144.13		474[b]	24.49	

[a] Two df for estimated values subtracted.
[b] Six df for estimated values subtracted.
*$p \leq .05$.
**$p \leq .01$.

The interaction involving trials, the four stimulus attributes, and %ORM probably reflected at least three factors. First, there was a slightly greater dispersion of means of correct responses for the 16 combinations of stimulus characteristics under 25% ORM than under 100% ORM. Second, there were differences in the rank orders of the 16 combinations under the two schedules. Such differences, however, were negligible since the rho for the ranks of comparable combinations under 100% and 25% ORM was .90. Third, there were differences in increments from Trials 1–24 to Trials 25–48 both among combinations of stimulus attributes and between the same attributes under 100% ORM and under 25% ORM.

DISCUSSION

Discussion is deferred until Experiment 3 has been reported. As mentioned previously, the results of Experiments 2 and 3 are compared with each other and with those of Experiments IA and IB.

SUMMARY

Lists representing the 16 combinations of high or low meaningfulness and similarity of stimulus and of response members were presented under a recall format for 48 trials under 25% or 100% ORM. Subjects were run in groups. Acquisition rate was related directly to %ORM and meaningfulness of both stimulus and response members; an inverse relationship obtained between acquisition rate and similarity of both stimulus and response members. Only two of the interactions involving these five variables were significant.

EXPERIMENT 3

Acquisition of Unmixed Lists Administered to Subjects in Groups as Functions of Meaningfulness and Similarity of Stimulus and Response Members, Familiarization of Response Members, and %ORM

WITH *Sally L. Perry* AND *Barbara Jaffarian Dunham*

PURPOSE AND DESIGN

In Experiment 3, familiarization of response members was added to the five variables of Experiment 2. A further change in Experiment 3 was two presentations rather than one presentation of each of the stimulus members alone during the recall phase of each trial.

One purpose of Experiment 3 was to serve as a partial replication of Experiment 2. Another more important purpose was to determine whether or not familiarization of response members had two possible consequences: generally better learning of familiarized than of unfamiliarized response members; and interactions in which differences between rates of acquisition of familiarized and unfamiliarized response members were greater at the more difficult level and the progressively more difficult combinations of levels of stimulus attributes and %ORM.

The rationale for the latter consequence was greater gains from familiarization of response members of high than of low similarity, of those of low than of high meaningfulness, and, even more so, of those of high similarity, low meaningfulness than of low similarity, high meaningfulness. Also, the greater response availability presumably brought about by familiarization was expected to be more advantageous for acquisition under 25% than under 100% ORM.

Only response members were familiarized. To avoid additional groups which controlled for transfer from nonspecific sources by familiarization on irrelevant stimuli, all subjects had familiarization experiences with two of the four response members of a list and no such experiences with the other two. Thus, subjects were their own control in comparisons of rate of acquisition of familiarized and unfamiliarized response members.

Previous investigations of effects of familiarization of stimuli of some of the same lists (Goss, Nodine, Gregory, Taub, & Kennedy, 1962, Experiments II and III) had not yielded findings either of over-all facilitation or of greater facilitation with more difficult combinations of stimulus and of response members. At the time Experiment 3 was planned, a possible explanation of these failures to obtain evidence of facilitation was too few familiarization trials, independent groups of subjects rather than the same subjects with and without familiarization experiences, or both.[5] Consequently, subjects in Experiment 3 were administered a markedly larger number of experiences with each of the two familiarized stimuli than had been administered with those same stimuli previously, and they also served as their own controls.

A third, incidental purpose of Experiment 3 was to determine effects of stimulus attributes and·%ORM on changes from correct or incorrect responses on the first presentation of stimulus members alone in the recall phase to, respectively, incorrect or correct responses on the second presentation of stimulus members alone. The only data available when this experiment was executed were those mentioned by Estes (1960), some of which were described in greater detail later by Estes, Hopkins, and Crothers (1960). These data suggested that changes in correctness were relatively infrequent. The response members of their lists were digits from 1 to 8 or familiar one-syllable words; the stimulus members were CCCs of indeterminate but probably low similarity. The CCCs, particularly, differed from the CVC or adjective stimuli employed in most recent studies of PA learning. Also, CCCs and single digits or familiar one-syllable words represented but one or two of many possible combinations of similarity and meaningfulness of stimulus and response members. That any one or more of these stimulus attributes and also %ORM might influence direction and degree of changes from correct to incorrect responses and from incorrect to correct responses seemed entirely possible. Accordingly, in order to obtain data on such

---

[5]In a subsequent experiment (Goss, Nodine, Gregory, Taub and Kennedy, Experiment IV), even 60 familiarization trials with subjects as their own control did not yield evidence of facilitation based on familiarization of response members.

changes, the recall phase of each trial was altered from the one presentation of the stimulus members alone in Experiment 2 to two presentations.

METHOD

Lists for acquisition and familiarization. The 16 lists and the booklets for the learning phase of each trial were those of Experiment 2. For the recall phase, each blank page was followed by two pages on each of which the stimulus members alone appeared.

The prior familiarization experiences for each subject were with two of the four response members of each list. To counterbalance for the particular pair of response members familiarized, six different familiarization lists were prepared, one for each of the six different combinations of two of four response members. Thus, six subjects were necessary for complete counterbalancing of familiarized response members. Each of the two CVCs of a familiarization list appeared 60 times in random order. The 120 instances were arranged in four columns of 30 each.

Procedure for familiarization. Familiarization of the two response members of each of the six familiarization lists consisted of writing each response member rapidly and completely each of the 60 times it occurred. Subjects were paced through each of the four columns of 30 instances at a 2-sec. rate with about 10 sec. between successive columns.

Procedure for acquisition. Except for the two presentations of stimulus members alone during the recall phase of each trial, the procedure was that employed in Experiment 2. For each session, two subjects were scheduled for each of the 32 combinations of similarity and meaningfulness of stimulus and response members and %ORM. Familiarization was with two of the six combinations of pairs of response members from each list. As previously, failure of subjects to appear reduced the actual sizes of these groups.

Subjects. Data on 190 subjects were analyzed. By mistake, two of the combinations of response members were repeated. The extra subjects for these combinations were eliminated randomly. Data on an additional 14 subjects were discarded: the answers of two subjects were illegible; two others had been in Experiment 2; one subject under 25% ORM responded with only the particular response member of the acquisition phase of each trial; and the remaining subjects didn't finish, skipped pages, or otherwise failed to meet procedural requirements. Two of these subjects were discarded after the experiment had been completed, so they could not be conveniently replaced. Although the familiarized response members of the combination in which each appeared were not completely counterbalanced, values for each missing subject were estimated from those available for the other subjects of each of the two combinations. Thus, in 30 combinations there were six subjects each, and in two others there were five subjects each.

RESULTS

Correct responses on first recall test. Shown in Table A4 for Experiment 3 also are means of correct responses on the first presentation of stimulus members alone during the recall phase of Trials 1–48. The means for each of the 32 combinations are for familiarized and unfamiliarized response members both separately and combined.

Familiarization had no significant over-all effect. Nor was there any indication of significant interactions involving familiarization. For these reasons and for easier comparison with the results of Experiment 2, familiarization was not included in the analysis of variance for Experiment 3 summarized in Table A5. The F for %ORM did not reach significance at .05; the Fs for similarity of stimulus members, meaningfulness of stimulus members, similarity of response members, meaningfulness of response members, and trials were significant at < .01. The advantages of 100% ORM to 25% ORM, of low similarity of stimulus members to high, of high meaningfulness of stimulus members to low, of low similarity of response members to high, and of high meaningfulness of response members to low were, respectively, about 6%, 22%, 10%, 17% and 11%.

Only three interactions between and among similarity and meaningfulness of stimulus and response members and %ORM were significant at .05 or less. The interaction of %ORM and similarity of stimulus members was due to a greater difference between stimulus members of high and low similarity under 25% ORM than under 100% ORM. The difference between response members of low and high similarity was sufficiently greater with response members of low than of high meaningfulness to produce an interaction of these two variables. The interaction of %ORM with similarity of stimulus and of response members was largely attributable to faster acquisition with the high-low than with the low-high combination under 100% ORM and the opposite under 25% ORM.

As noted below, the analysis of changes in responses from the first presentation of stimulus members alone to the second was limited to the first 12 trials. For this reason, trials were divided into blocks of 12 rather than of 24 as in Experiment 2. Four of the seven significant interactions involving trials were with the stimulus attributes separately. Each of these interactions could be interpreted as reflecting a convergence of curves for low and high values of each variable through the 48 trials. The interaction of trials, %ORM, and similarity of stimulus members was due to more rapid convergence of the curves for stimulus members of high or low similarity under 100% than under 25% ORM. The interaction of trials, similarity of stimulus members, and similarity of response members and that of trials, meaningfulness of stimulus members, and similarity of response members could be attributed to more rapid convergence of the curves for low and high similarity of response members for stimulus members of low than of high similarity and for stimulus members of high than of low meaningfulness.

Changes during recall. During each of the two presentations of stimulus members alone in the recall phase of each trial, responses were scored as correct or as incorrect in the form of intrusions or omissions. Almost all of the intrusions were clearly or seemingly intralist. Within Estes' (1960) original all-or-none conception, a response correct on the first presentation of stimulus members should be correct on the second presentation; and the intrusion or omission responses to each stimulus member should be repeated. In more sophisticated later analyses, Estes' original views were elaborated to allow for guessing and retention factors (Estes, Hopkins, & Crothers, 1960). But the all-or-none view had not and has not yet been developed to allow for possible differences in direction and extent of changes due to stimulus attributes and %ORM. Were changes from correct responses to incorrect responses not affected by stimulus attributes and %ORM, further development would be unnecessary. Were such changes affected by one or more of these variables, in order to achieve greater generality, further and perhaps complicated development of an all-or-none conception would be necessary.

With only six subjects per cell and lists of four pairs, two with familiarized and two with unfamiliarized response members, the number of possible instances of changes available for the recall phase of a single trial was too few for satisfactory analysis. Accordingly, the plan was to pool instances of changes from as many trials as possible, stopping at the trial in which most subjects in several combinations had reached criterion. As indicated above, 12 trials proved a convenient stopping point. Also, since frequencies of changes were essentially the same for familiarized and unfamiliarized response members, familiarization was disregarded. Therefore, by pooling across six subjects in each combination of stimulus attributes and %ORM, four PA units, and 12 trials, the maximum of possible instances of change was increased to 288.

Summarized in Table A6 are the means of numbers of changes per trial for changes from correct to incorrect responses and from incorrect to correct responses during the recall phase of Trials 1–12. The means for changes from correct to incorrect were from 0.07 to 0.82; those for changes from incorrect to correct were from 0.06 to 0.38. In 31 of 32 comparisons, the means for correct-incorrect were from 0.01 (17%) to 0.72 (700%) higher than the corresponding means for incorrect-correct.

The analyses of variance on correct-incorrect and incorrect-correct changes separately are summarized in Table A7. More changes occurred with stimulus members of high than of low similarity and with 100% ORM than with 25% ORM. Similarity of stimulus members produced significant *F*s in both analyses. The F for %ORM was significant at $<.05$ for correct-incorrect but short of .05 for incorrect-correct. More changes occurred both from

TABLE A6

Means of Numbers of Changes per Trial from Correct to Incorrect (Intralist Intrusions and Omissions) Responses and from Incorrect to Correct Responses during the Two Test Phases of Trials 1–12 in Experiment 3 for %ORM and All Combinations of Stimulus Attributes except Familiarization

Stimulus members		Response members		%ORM	Correct-incorrect	Incorrect-correct
Simi-larity	Meaning-fulness	Simi-larity	Meaning-fulness			
Low	High	Low	High	100	.18	.10
				25	.07	.06
			Low	100	.21	.14
				25	.82	.10
		High	High	100	.39	.28
				25	.12	.10
			Low	100	.68	.24
				25	.29	.22
	Low	Low	High	100	.29	.25
				25	.24	.12
			Low	100	.29	.11
				25	.29	.17
		High	High	100	.72	.36
				25	.29	.14
			Low	100	.74	.25
				25	.39	.21
High	High	Low	High	100	.46	.38
				25	.38	.17
			Low	100	.64	.11
				25	.47	.19
		High	High	100	.54	.12
				25	.36	.17
			Low	100	.58	.35
				25	.22	.24
	Low	Low	High	100	.54	.35
				25	.62	.26
			Low	100	.50	.24
				25	.36	.28
		High	High	100	.47	.21
				25	.43	.21
			Low	100	.51	.29
				25	.51	.29

TABLE A7

Analyses of Variance on Changes from Correct to Incorrect and from
Incorrect to Correct Responses during the Two Test Phases of Trials 1–12
In Experiment 3; Interactions Yielding $Fs < 2.50$ Omitted

Source	df	Correct-incorrect		Incorrect-correct	
		MS	F	MS	F
%ORM	1	94.92	5.36*	19.38	3.58
SS	1	68.88	3.89*	27.75	5.13*
MS	1	16.92		16.92	3.13
SR	1	22.00		11.50	
MR	1	53.13	3.00	0.63	
%ORM×SR	1	125.13	7.06**		
%ORM×MR	1			16.92	3.13
SS×SR	1	66.51	3.75	19.39	3.58
SS×MR	1	53.13	3.00		
MS×MR	1	55.25	3.12		
SR×MR	1			19.38	3.58
%ORM×SS×MS	1	51.05	2.88		
%ORM×SS×MR	1	68.79	3.88		
SS×SR×MR	1			14.62	2.70
%ORM×SS×SR×MR	1			15.52	2.87
Error	158[a]	17.72		5.41	

[a]Two df subtracted for estimated values.
*$p \leq .05$.
**$p. \leq 01$.

correct to incorrect and from incorrect to correct with stimulus members of
low than of high meaningfulness, with response members of high than of
low similarity and with response members of low than of high meaningfulness.
Thus, changes occurred more often with the level of the stimulus variables
associated with slower acquisition than with the level associated with faster
acquisition. But none of the Fs for these variables was significant.

With some exceptions, the generalization of more changes with the level
associated with slower acquisition held for combinations of levels of the
variables. One exception produced the significant interaction of similarity
of responses and %ORM. Under 100% ORM, more changes occurred with
response members of high than of low similarity. Under 25% ORM, although
the difference was less pronounced, more changes occurred with response
members of low than of high similarity.

DISCUSSION

Acquisition. Patterns of effects on acquisition of similarity and meaningfulness of stimulus members and response members under 100% ORM or
under 25% ORM can be compared by noting significant and nonsignificant

sources of variance and their relative magnitudes. Also, rates of acquisition in terms of trials to criterion or correct responses in fixed numbers of trials for particular combinations of stimulus attributes and %ORM in one experiment can be correlated with rates of acquisition for the same combinations in other experiments. Experiment 1 was not considered here because it involved only 16 of the 32 combinations of stimulus attributes and %ORM.

With respect to sources of variance for Experiments IA and IB (Goss, Nodine, Gregory, Taub, & Kennedy, 1962) and also for Experiments 2 and 3, similarity of stimulus and of response members had significant inverse effects and meaningfulness of stimulus and of response members had significant direct effects, usually at less than .01. %ORM had a direct effect in all three experiments which was significant in Experiments IA and IB and Experiment 2 but not in Experiment 3. At the level of gross effects, therefore, there is little doubt of the general potency of all four stimulus attributes and of %ORM across a wide range of differences in conditions.

In Experiments IA and IB, %ORM entered into significant interactions with similarity of stimulus members, similarity of response members, and meaningfulness of response members. The interaction of %ORM and meaningfulness of stimulus members, although not significant, was larger than most of the nonsignificant interactions of Experiments 2 and 3. In Experiment 2, none of these interactions was significant. In Experiment 3, only the interaction of %ORM and similarity of stimulus members was significant.

The use of a fixed number of trials rather than of trials to criterion or differences in aspects of administration of the lists to subjects individually or in groups may account for the failure to obtain significant first-order interactions of %ORM and the stimulus attributes. However, use of the recall format rather than the anticipation format seems a more likely basis of any differences in the patterns of interactions in Experiments IA and IB and in Experiments 2 and 3.

In Experiment 2, presentation of stimulus members and response members together alternated with presentation of stimulus members alone. Thus, under 100% ORM, each trial could be regarded as essentially two trials under 50% ORM. That is, 100% ORM under a recall format might have approximated a 50% single-alternation schedule under an anticipation format. And 25% ORM under a recall format might have approximated a 12½% single-alternation schedule under an anticipation format.

Little is known of the form of the function or functions relating %ORM to learning measures under various conditions. However, for four pairs of CVCs presented at a 2:2-sec. rate, Wilcoxon, Wilson, and Wise (1961, Experiment III) found an approximately linear relationship between trials to one perfect performance and 25%, 50%, and 100% ORM. Should the function for these and similar conditions of lists and conditions of presentation be nearly linear down to 12½% ORM or even less, the difference between 100% and 25% ORM would produce twice as large a difference in learning as the difference between 50% and 12½% ORM. Therefore, assuming approximate equivalence of 100% or 25% ORM under the recall format and 50% or 12½% ORM under the anticipation format, the failure to obtain more significant first-order interactions of %ORM with stimulus attributes in Experiment 2 might be ascribed to a difference in %ORM not sufficient to occasion such interactions.

In Experiment 3, the recall phase of trials involved two presentations of stimulus members alone. Thus, 100% ORM and 25% ORM under this recall format might have approximated 33⅓% and 8⅓% ORM under an anticipation format, respectively, which represents an even smaller difference in %ORM. That %ORM was less potent in Experiment 3 is suggested by an F of 3.07 compared to the F of 9.00 in Experiment 2. Neither in Experiment 2 nor in Experiment 3 did %ORM account for an appreciable proportion of the "between subjects" variance; and in both experiments %ORM accounted for a smaller proportion of the variance than did any of the stimulus attributes. Disregarding the difference in response measures, in Experiments IA and IB %ORM had the largest mean square, which accounted for a large proportion of the total variance and was from about 15% to nearly 1900% larger than the mean squares for the stimulus attributes.

In Experiments IA and IB, interactions of similarity and meaningfulness of stimulus members and of these two variables and meaningfulness of response members were significant, and there was the suggestion of an interaction of similarity of stimulus and response members. Of these, the latter approached significance in Experiment 2 but not in Experiment 3. Thus, the significant or suggested interactions of Experiments IA and IB, even if reliable for the conditions under which they were obtained, apparently do not extend to the different conditions of Experiments 2 and 3. Furthermore, since none of the few significant interactions involving only stimulus attributes was again significant in Experiment 3, any such interactions, if reliable, are relatively weak. Actually, most of the first-order and higher-order interactions of Experiments IA and IB were not significant. Therefore, for at least the particular lists of these experiments, similarity and meaning-fulness of stimulus members and similarity and meaningfulness of response members seemingly combined additively.

One difference between Experiments 2 and 3 was from slight to considerably larger means of correct responses in Experiment 3 than in Experiment 2 for 30 of the 32 combinations. This difference might be due to two presentations rather than one presentation of stimulus members alone, or to a general facilitative effect of familiarization of some response members despite the lack of differences between familiarized and unfamiliarized response members. Differences in subjects is another possible factor. Experiment 2 was carried out toward the end of the fall semester and Experiment 3 was carried out at the beginning of the spring semester. Subjects at the beginning of the semester are usually more eager to participate in experiments. Which among these or possible other factors was the actual source of the difference could not be determined from the information available.

Table A8 summarizes intercorrelations among ranks of means of trials to criterion in Experiments IA and IB and of means of correct responses in Trials 1–48 of Experiments 2 and 3. These correlations were for all 32 combinations of stimulus attributes and %ORM, for the 16 combinations of similarity and meaningfulness of stimulus members and response members under 100% ORM, for the 16 combinations under 25% ORM, and for the 16 combinations of stimulus attributes, disregarding 100% and 25% ORM.

TABLE A8

Coefficients of Correlations between Correct Responses during Trials 1–48 in Experiments 2 and 3 for Different Combinations of Stimulus Attributes and %ORM and between Correct Responses in these Experiments and Trials to Criterion for Goss, Nodine, Gregory, Taub, and Kennedy's Experiments IA and IB

Combinations correlated	Exp. 2-Exp. 3	Exp. 2-Exps. IA, IB	Exp. 3-Exps. IA, IB
All 32	.70	.76	.71
16 under 100% ORM	.72	.83	.65
16 under 25% ORM	.69	.67	.51
16 disregarding %ORM	.73	.86	.84

Decreasing ranks were assigned to decreasing means of correct responses in Experiments 2 and 3 and to increasing means of trials to criterion in Experiments IA and IB. The rho of .51 for the 16 combinations under 25% ORM for Experiments IA and IB and Experiment 2 is significant at .05; the remaining 11 rhos are significant at <.01. The rhos for Experiments IA and IB and Experiment 2 are larger than the corresponding rhos for Experiments IA and IB and Experiment 3. Three of the rhos for Experiments IA and IB and Experiment 2 are larger than the corresponding rhos for Experiments 2 and 3. The rhos for Experiments IA and IB and Experiment 3 and for Experiments 2 and 3 do not differ consistently.

Within Experiments IA and IB, Experiment 2, and Experiment 3, the rhos for the means of the 16 combinations under 100% ORM and those under 25% ORM were .91, .90, and .83, respectively. Despite these high internal consistencies of ranks for the combinations of stimulus attributes under 100% and 25% ORM, correlations for the 16 combinations under 100% ORM were higher than the corresponding correlations for the 16 combinations under 25% ORM. Thus, while the relatively high rhos for all 32 combinations suggest some congruence of the patterns of these effects, the congruence is probably stronger for acquisition under 100% ORM than under 25% ORM.

In Experiments IA and IB, 100% ORM produced better learning than 25% ORM for all 16 combinations of similarity and meaningfulness of stimulus members and response members. In Experiment 2, and also in Experiment 3, 100% ORM was superior to 25% ORM for 13 of the 16 combinations and inferior for the other three. One of the three was the same in both experiments, the combination of stimulus members of low similarity and low meaningfulness with response members of high similarity and high meaningfulness. The other two combinations in Experiment 2 were not the same as the other two in Experiment 3. With only one exception for both Experiments 2 and 3, therefore, 100% ORM apparently occasioned faster acquisition than 25% ORM. But this superiority was neither as consistent nor as marked under the recall format for a fixed number of trials with group administration as under an anticipation format to a criterion with individual administration. The relatively consistent and marked superiority of 100% ORM to 25% ORM under the former conditions is reflected in the higher values for correlations among Experiments IA and IB, 2, and 3 for the 16 combinations, disregarding %ORM, than for the correlations in which %ORM was involved.

Changes in responses. The results for changes from incorrect to correct responses and from correct to incorrect responses were, unfortunately, inconclusive. That such changes may be influenced by some stimulus attributes and %ORM is suggested by the significant Fs for similarity of stimulus members and by the significant and near-significant Fs for %ORM. Supporting this conclusion is the consistent outcome for the other three variables of more frequent changes both from correct to incorrect and from incorrect to correct for the level of each variable accompanied by slower acquisition. But the Fs for these differences were not significant, nor did they approach significance.

Complicating any interpretation of these results are the questionable assumptions of the homogeneity and of the independence of pairs within a list and within a trial and the even more questionable assumption of the independence of pairs from trial-to-trial. The former assumptions are no different than those of most attempts to assess original and elaborated all-or-none conceptions, and nonindependence from trial-to-trial should operate in a direction favorable to the all-or-none conception. Therefore, the results for changes do not support implications even of the elaborated all-or-none conceptions. The more frequent changes from correct to incorrect responses than for incorrect to correct responses are also inconsistent with initial all-or-none conceptions. But some later elaborations do permit prediction of such inequalities.

SUMMARY

Experiment 3 differed from Experiment 2 in two ways. One was the addition of familiarization as a variable in the form of 60 familiarization experiences with two of the four response members and no familiarization of the other two. The other was presentation of each stimulus member alone twice during the recall phase of each trial rather than once. The direct effect of %ORM on number of correct responses during the first presentation of stimulus members alone was not significant. The inverse effects of similarity of stimulus and of response members and the direct effects of their meaningfulness were significant. Familiarization had no apparent effects. Most of the interactions involving stimulus attributes and %ORM were not significant but some involving trials and these variables were significant.

Changes from correct to incorrect responses and from incorrect to correct responses between the first and second presentations of stimulus members alone during Trials 1–12 were related directly to %ORM and to meaningfulness of stimulus and of response members; they were related inversely to similarity of stimulus and of response members. Only for similarity of stimulus members and %ORM, however, were these relationships significant or nearly so.

Across Experiments IA and IB, 2, and 3, there was reasonable agreement with respect to effects of stimulus attributes and %ORM separately and combined. Also, rank orders of means of trials to criterion and of correct responses for the same combinations of variables were in reasonable agreement. The conclusions suggested by the results of all three experiments were, therefore, direct effects of %ORM and meaningfulness of stimulus and response members and inverse effects of similarity of stimulus and response members. At most, only a few interactions of these variables were significant. Thus, most of these relationships for stimulus attributes and %ORM separately held at each level and combination of levels of the other variables.

EXPERIMENT 4

Acquisition of Unmixed Lists Administered to Subjects in Groups as Functions of Meaningfulness of Stimulus and Response Members and of Similarity of Meaning-Ease of Learning of Pairs of Stimuli

PURPOSE AND DESIGN

In 1958, Richardson and Erlebacher obtained ratings of ease of learning and similarity of meaning (common meaning) of pairs of CCCs, CVCs, and adjectives. Advanced in their discussion of the significance of these ratings was the view that: "It is possible that the facilitation of learning by meaningfulness is not the result of association value per se but of the increase in associative connection resulting from the increase in meaningfulness. The important thing may not be the number of associations which can be given to the stimulus and response items independently but the relationship between the two" (p. 68).

The Richardson and Erlebacher proposal can be tested by comparing rates of acquisition of lists in which meaningfulness of stimulus members and meaningfulness of response members are orthogonal to each other and to ease of learning and common meaning of pairs constituted of those stimuli. Unfortunately, this design can probably be realized only approximately in lists constructed from Richardson and Erlebacher's sets of pairs of CVCs. The major difficulty is strong relationships between meaningfulness of the discrete CVCs comprising the pairs and ratings of ease of learning and common meaning of the pairs. But another difficulty is a correlation between ratings of ease of learning and common meaning sufficiently high to preclude independent variation of these two attributes. For CVCs, the r was .81.

METHOD

Lists. Table A9 shows both the design of Experiment 4 and the lists of four pairs of CVCs selected to meet the requirement of stimulus members of low or high meaningfulness, response members of low or high meaningfulness, and pairs of low or high ease of learning and common meaning. Glaze M_a values of each CVC are in parentheses; to the right of each pair are its mean ratings for ease of learning and common meaning. Because of the correlation between values for ease of learning and common meaning, except in the correlational analyses, they are treated as a single variable designated ease of learning-common meaning.

The levels of meaningfulness of stimulus members and of response members were orthogonal. But these levels of both variables were related positively, although not perfectly, to the levels for ease of learning and common meaning of the pairs of which they were members. Thus, the desired design was not realized completely. In all likelihood, however, the design was realized as completely as possible with pairs selected from the particular set of pairs within the further constraint of minimal differences among the lists in similarity among stimulus members, among response members, and between stimulus and response members.

With one exception, stimulus members of the lists had no or one letter in common as did response members, and stimulus and response members of each pair had no or one letter in common. Thus, similarity among stimulus members, among response members, and between stimulus and response members of pairs were low and approximately equal for all lists. In one list, however, the stimulus member of one pair had two letters in common with the response member of another pair.

TABLE A9

Lists of Pairs of CVCs for Experiment 4 Representing High and Low Meaningfulness of Stimulus and of Response Members Combined with High and Low Ease of Learning-Common Meaning of the Paired CVCs together with Means of Correct Responses for Each List during Trials 1–12

Stimulus members	Response members	Ease of learning (EL)—Common meaning (CM)							
		High				Low			
		Stimulus members	Response members	EL[a]	CM[a]	Stimulus members	Response members	EL	CM
High	High	FEM (93)[b]	HOS (93)	8.22	6.47	PAV (93)	KOF (80)	7.59	4.28
		TEL (93)	CUM (93)	8.89	6.39	TEP (87)	LAZ (93)	7.44	4.06
		WIZ (87)	SEC (93)	6.99	5.94	LAN (93)	KUC (87)	6.80	3.85
		VOL (93)	DET (93)	7.96	5.20	BEL (100)	VIF (100)	6.99	3.75
		Mean (91.5)	(93)	8.02	6.00	(93)	(90)	7.20	3.98
			Mean = 41.0				Mean = 29.7		
Low	High	BEP (13)	LIS (100)	7.16	4.54	VAK (20)	JEN (87)	6.47	3.98
		POH (20)	SAV (93)	7.03	4.42	CIJ (0)	DUL (100)	5.07	3.39
		GIC (13)	WIP (87)	7.11	4.25	XEJ (0)	FON (93)	4.33	3.11
		WUC (20)	HOV (87)	6.45	4.24	BIP (20)	QES (87)	5.81	3.07
		Mean (16.5)	(92)	6.94	4.36	(10)	(92)	5.42	3.39
			Mean = 39.3				Mean = 35.6		
High	Low	HOD (87)	BOF (7)	6.75	4.96	HUR (100)	MUK (20)	5.90	3.85
		NAV (100)	RUQ (13)	6.45	4.75	YEG (80)	MEC (7)	5.63	3.70
		BES (93)	CEH (13)	5.91	4.43	TES (100)	JIQ (7)	5.26	3.19
		REG (100)	KIH (13)	5.59	4.17	PAC (100)	QIH (0)	5.74	2.96
		Mean (95)	(11.5)	6.18	4.58	(95)	(8.5)	5.63	3.42
			Mean = 34.3				Mean = 33.1		
Low	Low	GOV (0)	NUB (13)	6.68	4.24	LAJ (0)	VUX (7)	4.77	3.24
		JAT (20)	LEQ (20)	5.98	3.91	KUQ (13)	XAT (0)	4.91	3.09
		VAF (0)	QAP (0)	5.87	3.85	TEV (13)	XEF (0)	5.02	2.68
		KEX (13)	BEH (20)	6.53	3.59	XEQ (0)	GID (7)	4.44	2.61
		Mean (8)	(13)	6.26	3.90	(6.5)	(3.5)	4.78	2.90
			Mean = 33.1				Mean = 24.7		

[a] Mean ratings of ease of learning and common meaning of pairs. [b] Glaze M_a values are in parentheses.

The four different random orders of the pairs were presented in a random order within the restriction of presentation of all four orders before any one was repeated.

Procedure. Subjects were paced through the four pairs of a particular list at a 3-sec. rate. They then had 12 sec. in which to write the response member to the right of the stimulus member alone. There were 12 acquisition trials.

Subjects. The 144 undergraduate men and women who served as subjects were drawn from the course in introductory psychology. Eighteen subjects were assigned randomly to each of the eight lists.

RESULTS

Shown below each of the lists of Table A9 are means of correct responses for that list for Trials 1–12. The maximum possible is 48 correct responses. The analysis of variance on correct responses for Trials 1–12 and for successive blocks of four trials each is summarized in Table A10. The significant Fs for ease of learning-common meaning of pairs and for meaningfulness of response members reflect more rapid acquisition of lists with pairs of high than of low ease of learning-common meaning, and of lists with response members of high than of low meaningfulness.

The F for meaningfulness of stimulus members was not significant. However, from slightly to considerably more correct responses were made with stimulus members of high than of low meaningfulness in three of four comparisons of pairs of lists which were otherwise alike in levels of the other two variables. The exception was the two lists which differed in meaningfulness of stimulus members but were both of low ease of learning-common meaning, high meaningfulness of response members. The list with stimulus members of high meaningfulness was learned less rapidly than the list with stimulus members of low meaningfulness. The mean of 29.7 for the former list, when examined in relationship to the other seven means, was lower than would be expected. A possible explanation is greater similarity between stimulus and response members in this list than in the others in the form of LAN as the stimulus member of one pair and LAZ as the response member of another pair. Regardless of the basis for the observed difference, were it not for this reversal in means, the over-all F for meaningfulness of stimulus members would, very likely, also have been significant.

The F for the interaction of meaningfulness of stimulus and of response members could be interpreted in terms of a stronger effect of meaningfulness of response members with stimulus members of low than of high meaningfulness. The interaction of both of these variables with ease of learning-common meaning reflected primarily the slow learning of the list noted above which represented the combination of high meaningfulness of both stimulus and response members, low ease of learning-common meaning.

TABLE A10

Analysis of Variance on Correct Responses during Trials 1–12 in Experiment 4;
Interactions Yielding $Fs < 2.50$ Omitted

Source	df	MS	F
EL—CM	1	454.28	18.33**
MS	1	22.69	
MR	1	311.78	12.58**
MS×MR	1	146.74	5.92*
EL—CM×MS×MR	1	164.11	6.62*
Error (b)	136	24.77	
T	2	1645.38	386.23**
T×MR	2	16.43	3.85*
T×MS×MR	2	18.31	4.29*
Error (w)	272	4.26	

*$p \leq .05$.
**$p \leq .01$.

Correct responses increased significantly through the three blocks of trials. The significant interactions of trials with meaningfulness of response members and with this variable and meaningfulness of stimulus members could be described in terms of a greater increment over trials with response members of low than of high meaningfulness and of progressively larger increments for the high-high, low-high, low-low, and high-low combinations of meaningfulness of stimulus and response members.

Because of the correlations between meaningfulness of discrete stimuli and ratings of ease of learning and common meaning, relationships between acquisition rate and the three stimulus variables were also analyzed by means of zero-order and first-order partial rank-difference coefficients of correlation. The values correlated were means of trials to criterion with the lists representing the eight combinations and means of the values of the lists with respect to each of the three stimulus variables. Both the zero-order and first-

TABLE A11

Coefficients for Zero-Order Correlations[a] and for First-Order Partial Correlations between Correct Responses in Experiment 4 and M_a of Stimulus Members, M_a of Response Members, Ease of Learning of Pairs and Their Common Meaning

Predictor	Variable partialled out			
	M_a of stimulus members	M_a of response members	Ease of learning	Common meaning
M_a of stimulus members	.09	—.04	—.17	—.38
M_a of response members	.70*	.70*	.62	.50
Ease of learning	.02	—.21	.46	—.17
Common meaning	.70*	.37	.52	.64*

[a]Along the diagonal downward from left to right.
*$p \leq .05$.

order partial coefficients which were obtained are presented in Table A11. Ratings of ease of learning and common meaning were used separately here. Thus, the third variable of attributes of the pairs was represented by two different measures.

The values along the diagonal downward from left to right are the zero-order coefficients for the correlations between correct responses and values for meaningfulness of stimulus members, meaningfulness of response members, ease of learning, and common meaning. Only the second and fourth were significant at .05 or less. The coefficient of .70 for correct responses and meaningfulness of response members was slightly but not significantly higher than the coefficient of .64 for correct responses and common meaning.

The remaining coefficients are for the first-order partial correlations. The coefficients for meaningfulness of stimulus members became increasingly negative when meaningfulness of response members, ease of learning, and common meaning were each partialled out. The zero-order coefficient for meaningfulness of response members was unaffected by partialling out meaningfulness of stimulus members and was reduced only to .62 and .50 by partialling out ease of learning and common meaning. Partialling out the other three variables reduced the coefficient of .46 for ease of learning to coefficients of .02, −.21, and −.17. Partialling out meaningfulness of stimulus members increased the strength of the relationship for common meaning from the zero-order coefficient of .64 to the partial coefficient of .70. Partialling out the effects of the other two variables reduced the coefficient of .64 to coefficients of .37 and .52.

Partialling out meaningfulness of response members from the relationship between acquisition rate and common meaning reduced the zero-order coefficient to a greater degree than partialling out common meaning from the relationship between acquisition rate and meaningfulness of response members. Thus, on the basis of a slightly higher zero-order coefficient and this difference in shrinkage, meaningfulness of response members proved a better predictor than common meaning. Meaningfulness of response members was even more clearly a better predictor than ease of learning.

DISCUSSION

In the eight lists of Experiment 4, levels of meaningfulness of stimulus members and of response members were orthogonal. But both were related positively to ratings of ease of learning and common meaning of pairs constituted of those stimuli. The positive relationships between attributes of the discrete stimuli and ratings of pairs in the set of pairs of CVCs from which the pairs of these lists were selected precluded complete realization of the desired orthogonality of levels of attributes of the discrete stimuli and of the pairs.

Within the limitation of lack of complete independence between meaningfulness of discrete stimuli and attributes of pairs of those stimuli, the results of Experiment 4 offer little or no support for Richardson and Erlebacher's suggestion that the direct relationships between acquisition rate and meaningfulness of discrete stimulus and response members might reduce to a common and more general variable of strength of associations between the two. Over and above the direct relationship between acquisition rate and ease of learning-common meaning of pairs, meaningfulness of response members was related directly to acquisition rate. Although the former variable accounted for more of the variance in the analysis of variance than did the latter, in the correlational analyses meaningfulness of response members was the better predictor. The zero-order coefficient for the relationship between correct responses and meaningfulness of response members was higher than the zero-order coefficients for ease of learning and common meaning. Also, partialling out meaningfulness of response members from the correlation between acquisition rate and the latter two variables reduced the correlations more than did partialling out ease of learning and common meaning from the correlation between acquisition rate and meaningfulness of response members.

The direct relationship between acquisition rate and meaningfulness of stimulus members was not significant, disregarding the other two variables. The failure to obtain a significant over-all effect of meaningfulness of stimulus members was attributed to a typically slow acquisition of the list representing the combination of high meaningfulness of stimulus and response members, low ease of learning-common meaning. This list was learned less rapidly than the list representing the combination of low meaningfulness of stimulus members, high meaningfulness of response members, and low ease of learning-common meaning. In the other three comparisons in which meaningfulness of stimulus members varied and levels of the other two variables were the same, the relationship between acquisition rate and meaningfulness of stimulus members was direct. Thus, these comparisons support a conclusion that meaningfulness of stimulus members also influenced acquisition rate over and above any effects of ease of learning-common meaning of pairs.

More generally, the results of Experiment 4 suggest that acquisition rate is a direct function of meaningfulness of stimulus members, meaningfulness of response members, and ease of learning-common meaning of pairs. The apparently atypical acquisition rate for the list representing high meaningfulness of stimulus and response members, low ease of learning-common meaning largely vitiates any conclusions about the modes of combination of these variables.

Ratings of ease of learning and common meaning of pairs can be interpreted as estimates of preexperimentally-established associations between stimulus members and responses to response members. The present results, therefore, constitute further evidence of the importance of initial strengths of pre-established associations in the further strengthening of those associations. The correlational analyses suggest that ratings of ease of learning may provide better estimates of initial strengths than do ratings of common meaning.

SUMMARY

Tested in Experiment 4 was Richardson and Erlebacher's proposal that the direct relationships between acquisition rate and meaningfulness of stimulus and response members might be indirect manifestations of effects of strength of associations between members of pairs. Their set of pairs of CVCs was the source of the pairs selected for the eight four-pair lists of Experiment 4. In that set of pairs, meaningfulness of stimulus members and of response members were related positively to ratings of ease of learning and common meaning of the pairs. As a consequence, in the eight lists, while levels of the former two variables were independent, they were not completely independent of levels of ease of learning and common meaning. Each of the lists was administered to different groups of 18 subjects. There were 12 trials under a recall format.

In the analysis of variance, acquisition rate was related directly and significantly to ease of learning-common meaning and to meaningfulness of response members. In three of four comparisons involving pairs of lists in which levels of meaningfulness of response members and ease of learning-common meaning were the same, a direct relationship between acquisition rate and meaningfulness of stimulus members was also obtained. The inversion of this relationship in the fourth comparison was attributed to an atypically difficult list for the combination of high meaningfulness of stimulus and response members, low ease of learning-common meaning.

In correlational analyses involving zero-order and first-order partial rank-difference coefficients of correlation, meaningfulness of response members proved a better predictor of acquisition rate than did ratings of ease of learning or of common meaning. This outcome, and the apparent effects on acquisition rate of meaningfulness of stimulus and of response members over and above effects of ease of learning-common meaning, are not consistent with implications of the proposed reduction of effects of the former two variables to differences in associative strength of pairs as estimated by ratings of ease of learning and common meaning.

EXPERIMENT 5

Acquisition of Partly Mixed Lists Administered to Subjects in Groups
as Functions of Meaningfulness-Similarity of Stimulus Members and
Meaningfulness and Similarity of Response Members

WITH *Herbert Levitt*

PURPOSE AND DESIGN

In contrast to the unmixed lists of the four preceding experiments, the
lists of Experiment 5 were partly mixed. The units of each list of partly
mixed lists represent some but not all of the combinations of values or levels
of stimulus attributes. One reason for using partly mixed lists was to determine whether or not differences in acquisition rate among lists representing
different combinations of levels of meaningfulness and similarity of stimulus
and response members would also be obtained with individual PA units each
of which represented different combinations of levels of those stimulus attributes. Another reason was to determine whether or not the modes of combinations of those variables in partly mixed lists were the same as in unmixed
lists.

The lists of most experiments concerned with effects of stimulus attributes
on PA learning have been unmixed. All units of an unmixed list represent
a particular combination of levels of stimulus attributes. Eliminated, therefore,
are possible effects on a unit representing a particular combination of levels
of stimulus attributes of units representing one or more other combinations
of levels. Also, unmixed lists of a particular number of units include the
maximum possible number of units representing a particular combination of
levels of stimulus attributes. Thus, unmixed lists are a better sample of units
representing a particular combination of levels.

Unmixed lists also have disadvantages. One disadvantage is lack of representativeness with respect to the lists of most extra-experimental tasks. For
example, the units of lists of pairs of words with stimulus members in one
language and response members in another language are not likely to be
homogeneous in meaningfulness. Precisely what is required is information
about acquisition of a unit representing a particular combination of levels
of stimulus attributes as influenced by the presence in the lists of units
representing other combinations of levels of those attributes. A second disadvantage of unmixed lists is, for any one task, inter-subject differences in
difficulty, rather than intra-subject differences. By controlling for individual
differences, intra-subject comparisons usually provide a more precise test of
possible differences in effects of different levels of a variable or combination
of levels.

The particular design of Experiment 5 is shown in Table A12. Stimulus members labeled "easy" represented the combination of stimulus members of high meaningfulness, low similarity; stimulus members labeled "hard" were of low meaningfulness, high similarity. The response members represented the four combinations of high or low meaningfulness and high or low similarity.

METHOD

Lists. The lists of pairs of CVCs used to realize the design are also shown in Table A12. The CVCs for these lists were selected on the basis of Glaze M_a values before Archer M_a values were available. However, both Glaze M_a and Archer M_a values of each CVC are in parentheses. The easy stimulus members were all of 100% Glaze M_a values and had no letters in common. The hard stimulus members were of 0% or 7% Glaze M_a values and each one had two or three letters in common with the other three.

In all, 16 different lists with easy stimulus members and 16 different lists with hard stimulus members were prepared. Four of those lists for both easy and hard stimulus members are shown. The response members of these four lists were obtained by combining four sets of CVCs. The CVCs of two of the sets (SUT, YIG and CIN, WUB) had no letters common to each other or to the CVCs of the other two sets. The CVCs of each of the other two sets (FAV, VAF and JOK, KOJ) were constituted of the same letters in opposite order. The former sets were considered of low similarity and the latter of high similarity. Each of the former was combined with each of the latter. The other 12 lists for each level of stimulus members were different pairings of stimulus and response members so that each of the four response members was paired once with each stimulus member. The four different random orders of the units of each list were presented in random order within the restriction of the presentation of all four orders before any one was repeated.

Procedure. Subjects were paced through 10 trials at a rate of 3.5 sec. to examine each pair in the learning booklets and 12 sec. to write the response members to the right of the stimulus members on each page of the booklet used for the recall phase of each trial.

Subjects. Two subjects were assigned to each of the 16 different lists with easy stimulus members and two were assigned to each of the 16 different lists with hard stimulus members. The requisite 64 men and women were all drawn from the course in introductory psychology and assigned at random to the particular combination of stimulus attributes and pairings.

TABLE A12

Lists of Pairs of CVCs for Experiment 5 Representing Stimulus Members of Low Similarity, High Meaningfulness (Easy) or High Similarity, Low Meaningfulness (Hard) Combined with Response Members of High or Low Similarity and Meaningfulness Together with Means of Correct Responses for Pairs Representing Each Combination during Trials 1–10

| Stimulus members | | Response members | | List | | | | Mean |
Attribute	CVC	Similarity	Meaningfulness	1	2	3	4	
Easy	MEX (100, 67)[a]	Low	High	SUT (100, 70)	CIN (100, 89)	CIN	SUT	8.81
	DOZ (100, 98)		Low	YIG (7, 10)	WUB (0, 21)	WUB	YIG	7.12
	QIL (100, 58)	High	High	JOK (93, 80)	FAV (93, 57)	JOK	FAV	7.22
	HUR (100, 84)		Low	KOJ (7, 12)	VAF (0, 22)	KOJ	VAF	7.03
	Mean (100, 77)			(52, 43)	(48, 47)			
Hard	XEZ (7, 7)	Low	High	SUT	CIN	CIN	SUT	5.44
	ZEQ (0, 15)		Low	YIG	WUB	WUB	YIG	4.41
	ZEX (0, 35)	High	High	JOK	FAV	JOK	FAV	4.69
	XEQ (0, 6)		Low	KOJ	VAF	KOJ	VAF	4.00
	Mean (2, 16)							

[a] Glaze M_a and Archer M_a values are in parentheses.

RESULTS

Shown in the last column of Table A12 are the means of correct responses in 10 trials for pairs representing each of the eight combinations of levels of the three stimulus attributes across all 16 lists. The analysis of variance on correct responses (Table A13) involved the additional variable of the four combinations of the two sets of response members of low similarity and the two sets of high similarity. This variable is labeled "Pairings."

TABLE A13

Analysis of Variance on Correct Responses during Trials 1–10
in Experiment 5; Interactions Yielding Fs <2.50 Omitted

Source	df	MS	F
Easy or hard stimulus members (St)	1	543.47	44.08**
Pairings (P)	3	36.68	2.97*
Error	56	12.33	
MR	1	51.66	22.66**
/MR $\times$ Ss	56	2.28	
SR	1	32.34	6.72*
/SR $\times$ Ss	56	4.81	
MR $\times$ SR	1	13.60	4.10*
/MR $\times$ SR $\times$ Ss	56	3.32	

*$p \leq .05$.
**$p \leq .01$.

The Fs for easy or hard stimulus members, meaningfulness of response members, and similarity of response members were significant at from .05 to $<.01$. Thus, lists with easy stimulus members were acquired significantly faster than those with hard stimulus members. About 70% more correct responses occurred with the former than with the latter. Response members of high meaningfulness were acquired faster than those of low meaningfulness and response members of low similarity were acquired faster than those of high similarity. Meaningfulness of response members was more potent than their similarity. Both for easy and for hard stimulus members, acquisition was increasingly more rapid for the high-low, low-low, high-high, and low-high combinations of similarity and meaningfulness of response members.

Only one of the interactions involving stimulus attributes was significant. The interaction of meaningfulness and similarity of response members could be described in terms of a greater effect of similarity with response members of high than of low meaningfulness.

The significant F for pairings was due to more correct responses with the combination of response members of List 3 (CIN, WUB, JOK, KOJ) than with the other three combinations. Across stimulus attributes, the means for the combinations of CVCs in Lists 1, 2, 3, and 4 were 5.64, 5.83, 7.22, and 5.67. None of the interactions involving pairings was significant. Thus, despite this difference between the combination of CVCs in List 3 and the combinations in the other three lists, the three stimulus variables separately and combined seemingly had the same pattern of effects with each of the four combinations.

DISCUSSION

One important feature of the results is the demonstration of differences in rate of acquisition of individual PA units in partly mixed lists as functions of easy or hard stimulus members, meaningfulness of response members, and similarity of response members. Differences in rate of acquisition of individual PA units whose stimulus members, response members, or both differed in meaningfulness have been obtained in other experiments (Baddelay, 1961b; Glanzer, 1962; Johnson, 1962; Keppel, 1963; Kimble & Dufort, 1955; Mandler & Huttenlocher, 1956; Noble & McNeely, 1957; Terwilliger, 1962; Underwood & Schulz, 1960a, Experiments 6–13, 15, 16). In none of these, however, were different levels of one attribute orthogonal to different levels of one or more other attributes. Instead, meaningfulness or related attributes of stimulus members or of response members were varied but meaningfulness of response members or stimulus members was at a fixed level. Alternatively, meaningfulness of both stimulus and response members were varied simultaneously in a positively-correlated design. Thus, Experiment 5 extends previous findings by demonstrating differences in acquisition rate among orthogonal combinations of levels of three stimulus attributes.

Similarity is specified by relationships between and among stimuli. Consequently, an individual PA unit at some particular level of similarity can only be approximated by pairs of PA units at that level of similarity each of whose members also differ with respect to some other attribute. The inverse relationship between acquisition rate and similarity of response members obtained in Experiment 5 is apparently the first evidence of the influence of similarity on acquisition of what are, as closely as possible, individual PA units.

Another feature of importance is the modes of combination of the three stimulus attributes. Of the four possible interactions between and among stimulus attributes, only that between meaningfulness and similarity of response members was significant and then only at .05. In partly mixed lists as well as unmixed lists, the stimulus attributes seem to combine additively. Consequently, effects of each variable can be considered to hold at each level and combination of levels of the other variables.

SUMMARY

The partly mixed lists of four pairs of CVCs of Experiment 5 realized a design in which stimulus members were of high meaningfulness, low similarity (easy) or low meaningfulness, high similarity (hard) and response members represented combinations of high or low meaningfulness and low or high similarity. Lists had one or the other set of stimulus members but common sets of response members. The lists were presented under a recall format for 10 trials.

More correct responses occurred with easy than with hard stimulus members, with response members of high than of low meaningfulness, and with response members of low than of high similarity. Thus, differences were obtained between and among individual PA units representing different combinations of meaningfulness and similarity of stimulus and response members. Moreover, the pattern of these differences was reasonably consistent with the patterns obtained between and among lists of unmixed PA units representing different combinations of the same stimulus attributes.

EXPERIMENT 6

Acquisition of Partly Mixed Lists Administered to Subjects in Groups as Functions of Meaningfulness, Similarity, and Familiarization of Stimulus and Response Members

PURPOSE AND DESIGN

The results of Experiment 5 indicated that rate of acquisition of individual PA units within partly mixed lists was influenced by stimulus attributes in patterns resembling those obtained with unmixed lists. Experiment 6 extended Experiment 5 in three ways. First, the combinations of stimulus members of low meaningfulness, low similarity and high meaningfulness, high similarity were added to the combinations of high meaningfulness, low similarity and low meaningfulness, high similarity. Thus, both meaningfulness and similarity of stimulus members were varied along with meaningfulness and similarity of response members to yield 16 different combinations of high and low levels of these variables. Second, instead of lists in which stimulus members were all of high meaningfulness, low similarity or of low meaningfulness, high similarity, stimulus members of each list represented all four of the combinations of high or low meaningfulness and similarity. Third, the variables of familiarization of stimulus and of response members were added. Stimulus members were or were not familiarized and response members were or were not familiarized to yield combinations of unfamiliarized-unfamiliarized, familiarized-unfamiliarized, unfamiliarized-familiarized and familiarized-familiarized.

Details of the experimental design, excluding the familiarization variables, are shown in the first five columns of Table A14. The eight different partly mixed lists were constructed to represent different subsets of four of the 16 combinations of high or low meaningfulness and similarity of stimulus and of response members. Each of the 16 combinations of stimulus attributes was represented in two lists. In these two lists, another combination of attributes was the same and two others were different.

METHOD

Lists for acquisition and familiarization. The specific CVCs selected and paired to realize the design of Experiment 6 are reproduced in the center columns of Table A14. Their Glaze M_a and Archer M_a values are given in Table A12. Form 1 lists were reversed to obtain Form 2 lists. Such reversal counterbalances for any differences between specific CVCs as stimulus members and as response members.

As in Experiment 5, the two stimulus members and two response members of low similarity in each list had no letters in common with each other or with the two stimulus members and two response members of high similarity. High similarity was obtained by selecting CVCs of the same letters in opposite orders. Similarity between stimulus members and paired or other response members was low. There were no common consonants and only one common vowel. Four different random orders of the pairs of each list were prepared; they were presented in a random sequence within the restriction of no repetition of one order before the other orders had been presented.

An index of expected ease of learning was computed for each pair of the lists. High meaningfulness and low similarity were arbitrarily scored "1"; low meaningfulness and high similarity were arbitrarily scored "0." These four scores for each combination were summed to obtain the values in the column designated Predicted—Σ. Thus, the first pair of List A has a sum of "2" for scores of 0,1,0,1; the second pair has a sum of "0" for scores of 0,0,0,0; and the third pair has a sum of "4" for scores of 1,1,1,1. The sums range from 0 to 4. Those for each pair of each list are also expressed as ranks. A more sophisticated index of ease of learning could be obtained by differential weighting of the variables in terms of their relative influence on acquisition rate. To do so here was considered premature.

Stimulus members were and were not familiarized and response members were and were not familiarized. The lists for their familiarization contained 16 CVCs, of which at least eight CVCs were buffer items. Buffer items were included to reduce differences among familiarization conditions with respect to response availability and to emphasize possible effects of response integration. For the familiarized-familiarized combination, the remaining eight CVCs were those of the PA lists. For the familiarized-unfamiliarized and unfamiliarized-familiarized combinations, four of the remaining eight CVCs were, respectively, stimulus members or response members of the lists; the other four were buffer items. For the unfamiliarized-unfamiliarized combination, none of the 16 CVCs appeared later in the PA lists. The buffer CVCs were of 47% or 53% Glaze M_a and had no consonants in common with the CVCs of the PA lists. Twelve different random orders of the 16 CVCs of each familiarization list were prepared.

Procedure for familiarization. Familiarization involved examining and reciting CVCs as they were exposed successively at a 3-sec. rate by moving a card down columns of the 16 stimuli of a familiarization list. There were 12 such columns, one for each familiarization trial.[6]

Procedure for acquisition. Paired stimulus and response members were exposed at a 3-sec. rate with 12 sec. allowed for the recall phase of each trial. There were 12 acquisition trials.

Subjects. Sixteen men and women currently enrolled in the course in introductory psychology were assigned randomly to each of the 16 combinations of Lists A to H in Forms 1 and 2. Within each of these combinations, there were four subjects in each of the further combinations of familiarized-familiarized, familiarized-unfamiliarized, unfamiliarized-familiarized, and unfamiliarized-unfamiliarized stimulus and response members. The total was 256 subjects. Had there been any suggestion of significant effects of facilitation, the number of subjects would have been doubled.

RESULTS

Means of correct responses during Trials 1–12 for each pair of each list, disregarding forms, and ranks of those means within each list are also shown in Table A14. Differences among means of correct responses for combinations within each of the eight lists were assessed by analyses of variance for which the variables were familiarization, replication by means of Form 1 and Form 2, and combinations of meaningfulness and similarity of stimulus and response members. Table A15 shows those sources of variance for each list for which at least one F significant at .05 was obtained.

For combinations, six Fs were significant at .01, one F was significant at .05, and one F was not significant. The next-to-the-last column of Table A14 shows differences between pairs of means representing different combinations significant at .05 by the criterion of least significant differences. Within every list but List H, at least one of the differences between combinations was significant. Parenthetically, List H was the one list in which the index of ease of learning was the same for all combinations.

[6]Experiments 5 and 6 are exceptions to the parallelism between order of execution and order of description here. They were done before evidence of the desirability of more than 12 trials had been reported.

TABLE A14

Lists of Pairs of CVCs for Experiment 6 Representing Different Combinations of Similarity and Meaningfulness of Stimulus and Response Members Together with Predicted and Obtained Ranks of Pairs in Each List, Means of Correct Responses during Trials 1–12, Differences between Means Significant at .01, and Rhos for Predicted and Obtained Ranks

List	Stimulus members Similarity	Meaningfulness	Response members Similarity	Meaningfulness	Specific CVCs Form 1		Form 2		Predicted Σ	Rank	Obtained Mean	Rank	Difference significant at .01	Rho
A	High	High	High	High	JOK	FAV	FAV	JOK	2	2.5	10.19	3	1.19	.95
		Low		Low	KOJ	VAF	VAF	KOJ	0	4	9.59	4		
	Low	High	Low	High	MEX	CIN	CIN	MEX	4	1	11.56	1		
		Low		Low	YIG	WUB	WUB	YIG	2	2.5	10.22	2		
											(41.56)			
B	High	High	High	Low	JOK	VAF	FAV	KOJ	1	3.5	9.31	3	1.03	.95
		Low		High	KOJ	FAV	VAF	JOK	1	3.5	9.56	4		
	Low	High	Low	Low	MEX	CIN	CIN	MEX	4	1	11.81	1		
		Low			YIG	WUB	WUB	YIG	2	2	9.91	2		
											(40.59)			
C	High	High	High	High	JOK	FAV	FAV	JOK	2	3	10.06	3	0.79	.95
		Low		Low	KOJ	VAF	VAF	KOJ	0	4	9.38	4		
	Low	High	Low	High	MEX	WUB	CIN	YIG	3	1.5	10.94	2		
		Low			YIG	CIN	WUB	MEX	3	1.5	11.03	1		
											(41.41)			

TABLE A14 (Continued)

Group														
D	High	High	High	Low	JOK	VAF	FAV	KOJ	1	3.5	9.38	4	0.99	.90
	High	Low	High	High	KOJ	FAV	VAF	JOK	1	3.5	9.66	3		
	Low	High	Low	Low	MEX	WUB	CIN	YIG	3	1.5	10.19	2		
	Low	Low	Low	High	YIG	CIN	WUB	MEX	3	1.5	11.09	1		
											(40.32)			
E	High	High	Low	High	JOK	CIN	FAV	MEX	3	1.5	10.78	1	0.86	.90
	High	Low	Low	Low	KOJ	WUB	VAF	YIG	1	3.5	8.88	3		
	Low	High	High	High	MEX	FAV	CIN	JOK	3	1.5	10.41	2		
	Low	Low	High	Low	YIG	VAF	WUB	KOJ	1	3.5	8.75	4		
											(38.82)			
F	High	High	Low	Low	JOK	WUB	FAV	YIG	2	2.5	8.06	3	1.57	.95
	High	Low	Low	High	KOJ	CIN	VAF	MEX	2	2.5	9.28	2		
	Low	High	High	Low	MEX	FAV	CIN	JOK	3	1	9.56	1		
	Low	Low	High	High	YIG	VAF	WUB	KOJ	1	4	7.38	4		
											(34.28)			
G	High	High	Low	High	JOK	CIN	FAV	MEX	3	1	10.00	1	1.43	.95
	High	Low	Low	Low	KOJ	WUB	VAF	YIG	1	4	8.19	4		
	Low	High	High	High	MEX	VAF	CIN	KOJ	2	2.5	8.75	2		
	Low	Low	High	Low	YIG	FAV	WUB	JOK	2	2.5	8.69	3		
											(35.63)			
H	High	High	Low	Low	JOK	WUB	FAV	YIG	2	2.5	8.16	3.5	1.34	
	High	Low	Low	High	KOJ	CIN	VAF	MEX	2	2.5	8.97	1		
	Low	High	High	Low	MEX	VAF	CIN	KOJ	2	2.5	8.16	3.5		
	Low	Low	High	High	YIG	FAV	WUB	JOK	2	2.5	8.50	2		
											(33.79)			

TABLE A15

Significant Sources of Variance for Lists of Experiment 6

List	Source			
	Familiarization (F)	Combination (C)	F×C	C×Replication
A		.01		
B		.01		
C		.01		.05
D		.01		
E		.01	.01	
F		.01		
G	.05	.05		
H				

That the differences among combinations were not only significant but in predictable order is indicated by the close agreement between predicted ranks for each combination of a list based on the index of ease of learning and observed ranks based on number of correct responses. The rhos for the differences between predicted and observed ranks are reported in the last column of Table A14. Although a rho of 1.00 is required for significance at .05, occurrence of seven rhos out of eight of .90 and above is an outcome significant at $<.01$.

Each pair representing one of the 16 combinations of meaningfulness and similarity of stimulus and response members appeared in two different lists. The differences between the two means for correct responses for each pair ranged from .07 to 1.37 above a mean difference of .42. Thus, there was close agreement in absolute values of correct responses for each appearance of a pair. The two means for each pair were arbitrarily assigned to two separate distributions, one for the means for the first time and another for the second time each particular pair occurred moving downward by rows in Table A14. The rho for the ranks of the pairs in these two distributions was .93. Both the close agreement in absolute values and this high relationship between ranks suggest that rate of acquisition of particular pairs was determined more by the combination of levels of meaningfulness and similarity of stimulus and response members represented by a pair than by the combinations of attributes represented by other pairs of a list.

Familiarization produced only one F significant at .05. One significant F out of eight cannot be considered indicative of any influence of familiarization of stimulus and response members. None of the Fs for differences between Form 1 and Form 2 was significant. Both of the significant interactions were also obtained in only one of eight analyses. It is unlikely, therefore, that combinations entered into interactions either with familiarization or with replications.

An analysis of variance was also carried out on differences among means of correct responses for entire lists. The means for each list, disregarding familiarization and replications, are in parentheses below the means for each combination of that list. In this analysis, familiarization and replication by means of the two forms were additional variables. The only significant F was for differences among lists with which the difference between pairs of means for the lists significant at .01 was 5.14. For simplicity, therefore, means for all 64 combinations of lists, familiarization of stimulus members and of response members, and forms are not shown.

In this analysis, too, no evidence of any facilitation due to familiarization was obtained. Indeed, over-all means increased in the order familiarized-unfamiliarized, unfamiliarized-familiarized, familiarized-familiarized, unfamiliarized-unfamiliarized. But the suggested inhibitory effects of familiarization were not significant.

Familiarization and replications did not have significant effects and means for the same pairs in two different lists were essentially the same. Accordingly, correct responses were pooled across lists, familiarization variables, and replications to obtain means for the 16 combinations of meaningfulness and similarity of stimulus and response members. These combinations are here coded by a sequence of combinations of high or low for similarity of stimulus members, meaningfulness of stimulus members, similarity of response members, and meaningfulness of response members. The means for these combinations and their ranks, which are shown in parentheses, were: low-high-low-high (11.69,1); low-high-low-low (10.91,2); low-high-high-high (9.98, 6); low-high-high-low (8.45,14); low-low-low-high (10.72,3); low-low-low-low (10.06,5); low-low-high-high (8.59,12); low-low-high-low (8.06,16); high-high-low-high (10.39,4); high-high-low-low (8.11,15); high-high-high-high (9.97,7); high-high-high-low (9.56,8); high-low-low-high (9.12,11); high-low-low-low (8.53,13); high-low-high-high (9.39,10); and high-low-high-low (9.48,9).

Disregarding similarity, increasing numbers of correct responses were obtained in the order low-low, high-low, low-high, high-high meaningfulness of stimulus and response members. Meaningfulness of response members produced a greater difference than meaningfulness of stimulus members. Disregarding meaningfulness, increasing numbers of correct responses were obtained in the order low-high, high-low, high-high, low-low similarity of stimulus and response members. Similarity of response members was more potent than similarity of stimulus members.

DISCUSSION

Discussed first is the significance of the results of Experiment 6 as a further demonstration of effects of stimulus attributes on acquisition of individual PA units. These results are then compared with those obtained in Experiments IA and IB, 2, 3, and 5.

Acquisition of individual PA units. Each of the eight lists represented different sets of four of the 16 combinations of high or low similarity and meaningfulness of stimulus members and response members. Each list appeared in two forms which were regarded as replications. In all of the lists but one, differences were obtained between or among individual PA units. The ranks of means of correct responses for individual units in each list were those predicted by an index of ease of learning obtained by summing scores of 0 or 1 for, respectively, low or high meaningfulness and for high or low similarity. Thus, combinations of levels of stimulus attributes represented by particular units served to predict differences among rates of acquisition of those units.

Each pair representing a particular combination appeared in two different lists. One other combination was common to the two lists, two other combinations were different. Absolute values and ranks of the means for the same pair in different lists were about the same. Thus, rate of acquisition of an individual PA unit representing a particular combination of levels of attributes is apparently determined largely by the particular combination of levels of the attributes and not by other combinations of levels represented by other units of a list. Such invariance in rates of acquisition of pairs representing particular combinations through different lists implies no difference in patterns of effects of combinations of stimulus attributes within unmixed and partly mixed lists. The invariance might extend to mixed lists.

Familiarization of stimulus and of response members were additional variables. No evidence of facilitation was obtained. In fact, fewer correct responses were obtained with all three combinations involving some familiarization. Thus, although the F was not significant, there was some suggestion of inhibition. Only 12 trials of familiarization were administered. However, in view of various failures to find significant facilitation with up to 60 familiarization trials, it is unlikely that the failure for familiarization to facilitate is due to too few familiarization trials.

Relationship to other experiments. Experiment 5 involved eight of the 16 combinations of similarity and meaningfulness of stimulus and of response members of Experiment 6. Correlation of the ranks for means of correct responses for the eight combinations common to the two experiments yielded a rho of only .57, which falls short of significance at .05.

The ranks for the 16 combinations of Experiment 6 were also correlated with the ranks for those combinations for acquisition under 100% ORM in Experiments IA and IB, 2, and 3. The resultant rhos were .54, .54, and .71, respectively. While significant at .05 and .01, two are lower than the rhos of .72 for Experiments 2 and 3, .83 for Experiment 2 and Experiments IA and IB, and .65 for Experiment 3 and Experiments IA and IB for the 16 combinations under 100% ORM (Table A8). Accordingly, relationships among means for combinations of stimulus attributes in Experiment 6 were examined to determine whether or not some systematic basis existed for the lower correlations involving this experiment.

As noted before, the invariance for the same combination of stimulus attributes in lists involving different combinations of those attributes implied no differences in patterns of effects of the same combinations in unmixed and partly mixed lists. Hence, means obtained with the partly mixed lists of Experiment 6 should correlate significantly with those obtained with the unmixed lists of Experiments IA and IB, 2, and 3. Means based on only one unit representing a particular combination should be less reliable than those based on four units. Lower reliability might have attenuated the correlations involving Experiment 6 to some unknown degree. But another, systematic basis for the lower values could be identified.

Stimulus and response members were both of high similarity in four of the 16 combinations of stimulus attributes in Experiments IA and IB, 2, 3, and 6. In Experiment 6, the ranks of those four combinations were 7, 8, 9, and 10. In Experiments IA and IB their ranks were 13, 16, 11, and 15, respectively; in Experiment 2 their ranks were 9, 15, 16, and 14; and in Experiment 3 their ranks were 6, 12, 16, and 15. Thus, in Experiment 6, combinations in which stimulus and response members were both of high similarity were acquired faster than was expected on the basis of findings in earlier experiments. Furthermore, disregarding meaningfulness, means of correct responses for the combinations of similarity in Experiment 6 increased in the order low-high, high-low, high-high, low-low. The expected order was high-high, high-low, low-high, low-low. Thus, ranks of the high-high and low-high combinations were interchanged.

Examination of the lists reproduced in Table A14 suggested a possible basis for the relatively more rapid acquisition of combinations in which stimulus and response members were both of high similarity. Pairs of stimulus members of high similarity were formed of CVCs of the same letters in opposite orders. Pairs of response members of high similarity were formed in the same manner. Consequently, given sufficient time, once the response to one stimulus member of the two of high similarity had been learned, the response to the other stimulus member could be "deduced" by the principle of "reverse the response given to the stimulus member with the same letters in opposite order." Subjects could allocate the 12 sec. for the recall phase to stimulus members unequally. Therefore, on the average, some or all subjects might have taken even more than 3 sec. per trial to apply this principle in responding to one of the stimulus members of high similarity. In the earlier experiments, because of the manner of pairings and because of shorter fixed or average intervals in which to respond, no such principle could be used.[7]

Extent of the suggested attenuation in rhos attributable to relatively more rapid learning in Experiment 6 of combinations with stimulus and response members both of high similarity was assessed by removing the means for those combinations in all of the experiments and computing rhos between ranks of means for the remaining 12 combinations. The rhos for Experiment 6 and Experiments IA and IB, 2, and 3, respectively, were .80, .77, and .84. All were significant at .01 and were from .13 to .26 higher than the rhos based on all 16 combinations. These rhos suggest quite reasonable agreement between the patterns for rate of acquisition of individual PA units representing different combinations of stimulus attributes and those for acquisition of lists representing the same combinations of attributes.

SUMMARY

The four pairs of each of the eight lists of Experiment 6 represented different sets of four of the 16 combinations of high or low meaningfulness and similarity of stimulus and response members. In addition, stimulus members of the pairs and response members were or were not familiarized. During each of 10 trials, paired stimulus and response members were presented at a 3-sec. rate with 12 sec. to recall the response members.

In seven of the eight lists, differences between and among the pairs representing different combinations of stimulus attributes were significant. Furthermore, these differences agreed with those predicted by an index of ease of learning based on meaningfulness and similarity of stimulus and response members. Thus, observed differences between and among pairs representing different combinations of stimulus attributes were predictable from prior knowledge of the combination of attributes. No facilitative effects were obtained with familiarization of stimulus members, response members, or both.

Means for individual PA units representing the 16 combinations of meaningfulness and similarity of stimulus and response members, disregarding the other variables, were related to means for those same combinations of attributes obtained with unmixed lists under 100% ORM in three other experiments. For all 16 combinations, the rhos between the ranks of means in Experiment 6 and in each of the other experiments were .54, .54, and .71. The four combinations involving similarity of both stimulus and response members, presumably because subjects were able to use a principle, were learned more rapidly than expected. Upon elimination of these four combinations, the rhos increased to .80, .77, and .84. These values were sufficiently

[7]In a subsequent experiment, stimulus and response members both of high similarity were obtained in the same manner. Acquisition with the high-high combination was also faster than expected (unpublished data, Miriam Witkin Smith).

high to suggest that the patterns of effects of meaningfulness and similarity of stimulus and response members obtained with individual PA units in partly mixed lists resembled those obtained with unmixed lists representing the same combinations.

EXPERIMENT 7

Acquisition of Unmixed Lists Presented under Recall and Anticipation Formats as Functions of Meaningfulness of Stimulus and Response Members

WITH *Nancy J. Cobb*

PURPOSE AND DESIGN

In Experiment 1, and in the earlier experiments (Goss, Nodine, Gregory, Taub, & Kennedy, 1962) which it extended, PA lists were presented under an anticipation format. Format of presentation was one of three important differences between the conditions of this set of experiments and those of Experiments 2–6. The results of the latter experiments led to no important conclusions regarding effects of meaningfulness and similarity of response members contrary to those based on the results of Experiment 1 and the earlier experiments. Nonetheless, it seemed desirable to compare acquisition of the same lists presented under anticipation and under recall formats. Should formats have no differential effects over combinations of levels of other pertinent variables, experimenters could use whichever was the more convenient, with the knowledge that findings obtained under one format would probably hold for the other format. Should formats have consistent differential effects over combinations of levels of other pertinent variables, experimenters would then have the advantage of use of the format which occasioned faster acquisition.

Experiment 7 and Experiments 8–10 were designed at the same time as an interrelated set of investigations of acquisition under anticipation and recall formats. The designs of these experiments are described briefly. Then considered are further reasons for comparing acquisition under anticipation and recall formats.

Designs. In Experiment 7, formats were combined with meaningfulness of stimulus and of response members realized in unmixed lists. Because of inconclusive results, this experiment was replicated as Experiment 11. In Experiment 8, formats were combined with similarity of stimulus and of response members also realized in unmixed lists. In Experiments 9 and 10, formats were combined with, respectively, meaningfulness of stimulus and response members, and their similarity. But the lists used in these experiments were mixed and there were additional variables of number of units in a list or its length and of whole versus part-whole modes of presentation.

Further reasons. Until some time within the past 25 years, the recall format of presentation may have been used more often than the anticipation format. Other labels for the recall format are the *treffermethode*, the method of correct or right associates, the study-test method and blocking (Lockhead, 1962). During the past 20 years, except for experiments on "all-or-none" acquisition, the anticipation format was used almost exclusively by many if not all of the more prolific investigators of PA learning. Consequently, the anticipation format came to be regarded as the standard format for PA learning.

The shift from use of the recall to use of the anticipation format was for reasons other than demonstrations of faster acquisition, better retention, and other advantages of the anticipation to the recall format. Indeed, when the present set of experiments was planned, apparently only Battig and Brackett (1961) had undertaken a direct comparison of acquisition under anticipation and recall formats. The stimulus members of their 12-pair list were nonsense figures, the response members were 12 of the two-digit numbers from 12 to 98. Nine trials under anticipation or recall formats followed a first trial under the recall format. The curve for correct responses for the recall format was consistently and markedly above the curve for the anticipation format.

If comparisons of acquisition of paired associates under prompting and confirmation formats are considered pertinent, somewhat more information was available. Under the prompting format, each learning trial involves presentation of the stimulus member followed shortly by appearance of the response member and practice in saying the response member. The interval between presentation of the stimulus member and of the response member is too short for anticipation to occur. Under the confirmation format, each learning trial involves presentation of the stimulus member alone with sufficient time for anticipation to occur and then information about correctness of anticipations in the form of appearance of response members. Under both formats every nth trial is a test trial in which stimulus members alone are presented. Thus, the prompting format is essentially a recall format with several occurrences of each pair before appearance of the stimulus members alone rather than single presentations of all pairs of stimulus and response members alternating with single presentations of stimulus members alone. The confirmation format resembles the anticipation format on the several learning trials and the recall format on the test trial. Confirmation, therefore, combines anticipation and recall formats but is closest, perhaps, to the anticipation format.

In three closely related studies (Cook, 1958; Cook & Kendler, 1956; Cook & Spitzer, 1960), prompting led to better acquisition than confirmation. Sidowski, Kopstein, and Shillestad (1961) also obtained faster learning under two variations of prompting than under two variations of confirmation or under a combination of confirmation and prompting. Therefore, if the prompting and confirmation formats are considered approximations of the recall and anticipation formats, respectively, the superiority of prompting to confirmation provided sufficient corroboration of Battig and Brackett's (1961) results to warrant undertaking additional comparisons of acquisition under recall and anticipation formats.

One reason for undertaking additional comparisons, therefore, was simply to provide more information about relative rates of acquisition under anticipation and recall formats. Another and more important reason was that none of the previous findings were with trigram pairs, adjective pairs, or trigram-adjective pairs, which have been the stimuli of most investigations of PA learning. Assessments of effects of anticipation and recall formats on acquisition of pairs made up of these more conventional stimuli were desirable. Moreover, in none of the preceding studies was difficulty of the PA units or lists varied. Conceivably, recall might prove superior to anticipation at only one level or some levels of difficulty. The two formats, therefore, should be compared with lists and with pairs representing different levels of difficulty. One way of varying difficulty was by combining stimulus members of high or low meaningfulness or similarity with response members of high or low meaningfulness or similarity. In Experiment 7, meaningfulness of stimulus and of response members were varied.

METHOD

Lists. The unmixed lists of six PA units were generated from the two sets of CVCs of high meaningfulness and the two sets of low meaningfulness shown in the upper half of Table A16. Noble (1961) m' values for these CVCs are in parentheses. Table A17 shows the manner in which these sets were combined to obtain lists representing the combinations of low-low, high-low, low-high, and high-high meaningfulness of stimulus and response members. The CVCs for each set had no or only one letter in common and, except for vowels, there were only a few consonants common to sets of high and low meaningfulness. CVCs with common letters were not paired. Thus, similarity was low among stimulus members, among response members, and between stimulus and response members.

New sets of CVCs were used to generate the lists of Experiment 7 and subsequent experiments for two reasons. One was that none of the sets of lists employed in the earlier experiments was satisfactory for generating new lists of the particular numbers of units which were desired. More importantly, the CVCs of the previous experiments had been limited to nonwords. In this and subsequent experiments, the intention was to extend differences re-

TABLE A16

Sets of CVCs of High or Low Meaningfulness, Low Similarity
for Experiments 7, 9, and 11 and of High or Low Similarity,
Intermediate Meaningfulness for Experiments 8 and 10

High		Low	
A	B	C	D
Meaningfulness Varied, Low Similarity			
LOG (4.16)[a]	HIT (4.01)	ZOX (1.07)	ZEH (1.02)
FUR (4.08)	LAW (4.25)	NUQ (1.13)	VUY (1.07)
COW (4.38)	JOB (4.25)	KUH (1.20)	XUK (0.73)
JET (4.01)	RED (4.16)	FOV (1.17)	WIJ (0.85)
SIN (4.03)	BUS (4.23)	GIC (1.39)	MEF (1.43)
DAM (4.00)	PEN (4.12)	YEB (1.17)	QAP (1.23)
Mean (4.11)	(4.17)	(1.19)	(1.06)
Similarity Varied, Intermediate Meaningfulness			
WOD (2.33)	KUD (2.35)	BIM (2.46)	VEX (2.07)
WOB (2.42)	KUP (2.23)	LIR (2.21)	NIS (2.11)
WOT (2.06)	KUB (2.09)	TAQ (2.25)	REJ (2.33)
YOW (2.42)	HUK (2.15)	SAH (2.19)	CAG (2.32)
ZOW (2.26)	MUK (2.47)	GED (1.99)	QAL (2.19)
FOW (2.30)	JUK (2.03)	CEY (2.14)	PIV (2.09)
Mean (2.30)	(2.22)	(2.21)	(2.18)

[a]Noble m' values are in parentheses.

lated to meaningfulness as far as possible by the use of words as the CVCs of high meaningfulness.

The pairs of each list and stimulus members alone for the recall phase under the recall format were in the six different orders of a 6×6 Latin Square. These orders were presented in a random sequence within the restriction of no repetition of one order of the pairs or of stimulus members alone before the other orders had been presented.

TABLE A17

Manner of Combining the Sets of Stimuli of Table A16 to Obtain
Unmixed Lists for Experiments 7 and 11 Representing Combinations
of High or Low Meaningfulness of Stimulus and Response Members
and Unmixed Lists for Experiment 8 Representing Combinations of
High or Low Similarity of Stimulus and Response Members

High-High	Low-High	High-Low	Low-Low
AB (4)[a]	CA (2)	AC (2)	CD (4)
BA (4)	DA (2)	AD (2)	DC (4)
	CB (2)	BC (2)	
	DB (2)	BD (2)	

[a]Number of subjects with each list is enclosed in parentheses.

Apparatus and procedure. The lists were administered to subjects individually by means of a memory drum. Under the anticipation format, stimulus members were presented alone for 2 sec. and then together with response members for 2 sec. Under the recall format, all pairs of stimulus and response members were presented, each for 2 sec., and then all stimulus members were presented alone in a different order, each for 2 sec. Acquisition was to a criterion of one perfect trial or for 36 trials. Two trials followed in which response members alone were presented at a 2-sec. rate for subjects to indicate the stimulus member with which the response member had been paired. Intertrial intervals were about 10 sec.

Subjects. Undergraduates were assigned to counterbalanced cycles to the eight combinations of formats, meaningfulness of stimulus members, and meaningfulness of response members until there were eight subjects in each combination. Assignment to a combination was in order of appearance within the restriction of approximately equal proportions of males and females in each of the combinations.

RESULTS

Acquisition was expressed as trials through criterion with a score of 37 assigned arbitrarily to subjects who had not reached criterion in 36 trials. Recall of stimulus members was expressed as number correct. Twelve was the maximum possible score.

Acquisition. Means and standard deviations of numbers of trials through criterion under anticipation and recall formats for each of the combinations of meaningfulness of stimulus and response members are presented in Table A18. Across all combinations and for three of the combinations of meaningfulness of stimulus and response members, fewer trials were required to reach criterion under the recall than under the anticipation format. In the low-low combination, acquisition was faster under anticipation than under recall.

TABLE A18

Means and Standard Deviations of Trials through Criterion under Anticipation and Recall Formats and of Stimulus Members Correct in Backward Recall for Combinations of Meaningfulness in Experiment 7 and of Similarity in Experiment 8

Stimulus members	Response members	Trials through criterion				Stimulus members correct			
		Anticipation		Recall		Anticipation		Recall	
		Mean	SD	Mean	SD	Mean	SD	Mean	SD
Exp. 7 (Meaningfulness varied, low similarity)									
High	High	11.0	6.8	9.1	4.4	8.5	3.0	8.1	3.7
Low		17.8	7.9	11.0	4.9	3.1	2.4	6.1	2.8
High	Low	24.6	7.7	19.4	9.8	4.8	3.6	6.6	2.7
Low		29.6	4.2	32.5	7.0	2.6	1.8	1.2	1.2
Exp. 8 (Similarity varied, intermediate meaningfulness)									
Low	Low	22.8	8.8	23.2	11.4	4.1	3.9	3.1	2.4
	High	26.5	5.0	26.2	13.4	4.0	2.1	3.2	1.8
High	Low	30.0	6.5	21.4	5.9	4.8	2.5	5.5	3.2
	High	31.4	6.3	34.1	3.8	3.8	0.9	2.1	1.8

TABLE A19

Analyses of Variance on Trials through Criterion and of Analyses of Variance and Covariance on Stimulus Members Correct in Backward Recall in Experiments 7 and 8

| Source | df | Exp. 7 (Meaningfulness varied, low similarity) | | | | | | Exp. 8 (Similarity varied, intermediate meaningfulness) | | | | | |
| | | Trials through criterion | | Stimulus members correct | | | | Trials through criterion | | Stimulus members correct | | | |
		MS	F	MS	F	Adj MS[a]	F	MS	F	MS	F	Adj MS	F
Anticipation or recall (AR)	1	121.00	2.27	9.77	1.12	2.16		31.64		5.06		8.86	1.31
St	1	715.56	13.43**	221.27	25.32**	117.80	15.36**	328.52	5.73*	1.56		12.91	1.91
Response members (R)	1	3277.56	61.52**	112.90	12.92**	4.68		435.76	7.60**	22.56	2.98	4.20	
AR×St	1	10.56		0.01		0.36		37.52		1.56		0.21	
AR×R	1	39.06		4.51		1.40		112.89	1.97	3.06		0.14	
St×R	1	90.26	1.69	0.01		1.70		54.39		22.56	2.98	14.41	
AR×St×R	1	169.00	3.17	43.89	5.02*	21.80	2.84	147.01	2.56	32.25	4.25*	27.65	4.10*
Error	56[b]	53.28		8.74		7.67		57.34		7.58		6.74	

[a] Analysis of covariance adjustment of differences in means of stimulus members correct in backward recall for differences in trials through criterion.

[b] For analysis of covariance, $df = 56 - 1 = 55$.

$*p \leq .05.$

$**p \leq .01.$

The nonsignificant F for formats in the analysis of variance summarized in Table A19 indicates that the smaller number of trials through criterion under recall than under anticipation was not a significant advantage. Moreover, formats entered into no significant interactions with the stimulus variables alone or combined.

Significant direct relationships were obtained for meaningfulness of stimulus members and meaningfulness of response members with the latter the more potent. Under both anticipation and recall formats, acquisition was faster in the order low-low, high-low, low-high, and high-high combinations of meaningfulness.

Backward recall of stimulus members. Under both anticipation and recall formats, means of numbers of stimulus members recalled correctly as responses to response members increased in the order low-low, low-high, high-low, and high-high meaningfulness of stimulus and response members (Table A18). Slightly more stimulus members were recalled correctly following acquisition under the recall than under the anticipation format. In comparisons for each combination, recall was superior for the low-high and high-low combinations, and anticipation was superior for the high-high and low-low combinations.

In the analysis of variance (Table A19), the F for formats was not significant. Significant Fs were obtained for the direct relationships between stimulus members correct and meaningfulness of stimulus and of response members. The significant F for the interaction of formats and the two stimulus variables could be attributed to the inversions in the superiority of recall to anticipation among the four combinations.

Meaningfulness of stimulus members and of response members had both been related directly to rate of acquisition. Consequently, the significant direct relationships between these variables and stimulus members correct might have been due to indirect effects of meaningfulness of stimulus and of response members through differences in acquisition rate rather than, presumably, to effects of meaningfulness of stimulus and of response members during recall of stimulus members. To reduce or eliminate possible effects of differences in acquisition rates, differences among means of stimulus members correct in backward recall were adjusted for differences in trials to criterion. The analysis of covariance involving such adjustments is also summarized in Table A19. Formats remained nonsignificant; the F for meaningfulness of stimulus members remained significant; and the Fs for meaningfulness of response members and for the interaction of formats and the two stimulus variables were no longer significant.

DISCUSSION

Acquisition. With respect to differences in rate of acquisition under recall and under anticipation formats, the results were ambiguous. Across the four combinations of meaningfulness of stimulus and response members, acquisition was faster under recall than under anticipation. But the difference was not significant. The failure to obtain a significant difference might have been due to the inversion of the general superiority of recall to anticipation for the low-low combination. Examination of absolute and relative values of the means for the four combinations under recall and for those under anticipation suggested that more trials were required for the low-low combination under recall than might have been expected. The other three means under recall were each lower than the means for the corresponding combination under anticipation. The difference between the low-low and high-low combinations under anticipation was 5.0. The difference under recall was 13.1. Were the mean for the low-low combination under recall too high because of sampling factors, such as inclusion of a disproportionate number of slow learners, recall would otherwise have been consistently superior to anticipation. Because of this possibility, replication seemed desirable. To anticipate, this was the purpose of Experiment 11.

Meaningfulness of stimulus and response members had typical direct effects on acquisition rate. Also, the order of increasingly rapid acquisition for low-low, high-low, low-high, and high-high combinations under both formats was that expected on the basis of modal findings of greater potency of meaningfulness of response members than of meaningfulness of stimulus members.

Backward recall of stimulus members. The differences between stimulus members correct in backward recall both across all combinations and for the four combinations separately were not sufficient in magnitude or consistency to suggest any superiority of one format to the other.

Occurrence of increasing backward recall in the order low-low, low-high, high-low, and high-high combinations of meaningfulness under both formats agreed with generalizations based on findings of previous studies. In backward recall, response members function as stimulus members and stimulus members function as response members. Thus, the observed order was consistent with the generally greater potency of meaningfulness of response members than of meaningfulness of stimulus members. Meaningfulness of stimulus members, which now functioned as response members, proved significant in both the analysis of variance and the analysis of covariance. Meaningfulness of response members, which now functioned as stimulus members, proved significant in the analysis of variance but not in the analysis of covariance.

SUMMARY

Unmixed lists of six PA units representing combinations of low or high meaningfulness of stimulus and response members were presented under anticipation and under recall formats. The eight subjects in each of the eight combinations acquired the lists to a criterion of one perfect trial or for 36 trials. Acquisition was followed by two trials of presentation of response members alone for backward recall of stimulus members.

Acquisition was faster under recall than under anticipation across all four and for three of the combinations of stimulus attributes. However, neither the F for the over-all difference for formats nor the Fs for interactions involving formats were significant. Direct relationships to acquisition rate were obtained for meaningfulness of stimulus members and of response members with the latter the more potent variable.

Both in an analysis of variance and in an analysis of covariance which adjusted for differences in acquisition rate, a significant direct relationship obtained between number of stimulus members correct and meaningfulness of stimulus members. The direct relationship between stimulus members recalled correctly and meaningfulness of response members was significant in the analysis of variance but not in the analysis of covariance. In neither analysis did the F for formats approach significance.

EXPERIMENT 8

Acquisition of Unmixed Lists Presented under Recall and Anticipation Formats as Functions of Similarity of Stimulus and Response Members

WITH *Nancy A. Mello*

PURPOSE AND DESIGN

In Experiment 8, unmixed lists representing the four combinations of high or low similarity of stimulus and response members were acquired under anticipation and recall formats. Substitution of similarity for meaningfulness was the only essential difference between Experiment 8 and Experiment 7. As previously, the general purpose was to determine whether or not acquisition was generally faster under one format than the other and whether or not direction and extent of the differences varied among combinations of similarity of stimulus and response members.

METHOD

Lists. Shown in the bottom half of Table A16 are the two sets of CVCs of high similarity and the two sets of low similarity used to generate the lists of six PA units of Experiment 8. These sets were also combined in the manner shown in Table A17 to obtain lists representing combinations of high-high, high-low, low-high, and low-low similarity of stimulus and response members.

The CVCs of the sets of high similarity each had a vowel and a consonant in common. The other six consonants were unique to each CVC. The CVCs of the sets of low similarity had no or only one consonant or vowel in common. All were of intermediate Noble (1961) m' values.

Randomization of the orders of these pairs and of the sequence of orders was the same as in Experiment 7.

Apparatus and procedures. Except for the use of different lists, the apparatus and the procedures for acquisition and for backward recall of stimulus members were those of Experiment 7.

Subjects. As in Experiment 7, undergraduates were assigned to each of the eight combinations of formats, similarity of stimulus members, and similarity of response members in counterbalanced cycles. There was a restriction of approximately equal proportions of males and females in each combination.

RESULTS

The measures for acquisition and for backward recall of stimulus members were, respectively, trials through criterion and stimulus members correct. Subjects who did not reach criterion in 36 trials received an arbitrary score of 37.

Acquisition. Means and standard deviations of trials through criterion for each of the eight combinations are shown in the bottom half of Table A18. No consistent superiority of recall to anticipation or the converse is evident. The F for formats was less than unity (Table A19).

Under the anticipation format, acquisition was increasingly more rapid for the high-high, high-low, low-high, low-low combinations; under the recall format, the order was high-high, low-high, low-low, high-low. Disregarding formats, the order was high-high, low-high, high-low, and low-low. The F for similarity of stimulus members was less than the F for similarity of response members to indicate that the latter was the more potent variable. None of the interactions was significant.

Backward recall of stimulus members. Both across all combinations and for three of the four combinations, more stimulus members were correct in backward recall following acquisition under the anticipation format than under the recall format. But the Fs for formats in the analysis of variance and the analysis of covariance did not approach significance.

Under both formats, more stimulus members were correct in response to response members of low than of high similarity. Also under both formats, more stimulus members of high than of low similarity were recalled correctly. But the Fs for similarity of stimulus members and similarity of response members were not significant either in the analysis of variance or in the analysis of covariance. The only significant F in the analysis of variance and also in the analysis of covariance was for the interaction of formats and the two stimulus variables. The apparent basis was a greater difference between the high-high and low-low combinations under the recall format than under the anticipation format.

DISCUSSION

Neither the results for acquisition nor those for backward recall of stimulus members provided marked or consistent evidence of a superiority of recall to anticipation or the converse. Battig and Brackett (1963) also failed to obtain significant differences between acquisition under anticipation and recall formats both across all three combinations of low-low, medium-medium, and high-high similarity among stimulus and among response members and for each combination separately. The additional variables of %ORM and familiarization were combined orthogonally with formats and similarity. Except where %ORM was also a variable, formats and familiarization did not enter into significant interactions.

The interaction of formats and %ORM was significant as were the interactions of similarity, formats and %ORM and of familiarization, formats and %ORM. The first of these interactions was due to superiority of the recall to the anticipation format under 100% ORM and the converse under 50% ORM. The suggested superiority of recall to anticipation under 100% ORM is seemingly inconsistent with the results of Experiment 8 across all combinations of similarity. But the F for the interaction of formats and %ORM obtained by Battig and Brackett was significant only at .05. In view of the inversion in relationships between means which produced this F, it seems doubtful that the difference between 14.12 correct responses under recall and 12.71 correct responses under anticipation was significant. The other two interactions have only tangential significance for the results of Experiment 8, and hence are not described.

Lockhead (1962) presented lists of nine pairs of CVCs of intermediate meaningfulness, low similarity under anticipation, recall (blocking), and random formats. In the random format, pairs of stimuli and stimulus members alone were presented in a random order within the restriction of presentation of all pairs and stimulus members alone before repetition of any one. No knowledge of results or knowledge of results in the form of the experimenter saying "right" or "wrong" immediately after each response was the second variable. Regardless of knowledge of results, differences among the three formats were not significant for trials to criterion, number of correct responses on Trials 1–8, and number of trials required by the first 15 subjects in each group to make three correct responses.

The superiority of the high-low to the low-high combination under the recall format and across formats in Experiment 8 was the basis for the stronger inverse relationship for similarity of response members than for similarity of stimulus members. This outcome was not consistent with typical findings of greater potency of similarity of stimulus members than of response members. The source of the discrepancy is not known.

The results for backward recall of stimulus members did not agree with expectations. Neither similarity of stimulus members nor similarity of response members had significant effects. Moreover, under both formats, the largest numbers of stimulus members recalled correctly were with the high-low combination. More stimulus members correct were expected for both the low-low and low-high combinations.

SUMMARY

The unmixed lists of Experiment 8 represented combinations of low or high similarity of stimulus and response members. Neither acquisition nor backward recall of stimulus members was consistently better under the recall format than under the anticipation format or the converse. The apparent failure to obtain differential effects of format was consistent with findings reported by Battig and Brackett.

The inverse relationship between acquisition rate and similarity of stimulus members was less pronounced than that for similarity of response members. These variables did not influence backward recall of stimulus members.

EXPERIMENT 9

Acquisition of Mixed Lists Presented under Recall and Anticipation Formats as Functions of Meaningfulness of Stimulus and Response Members, Length of List, and Whole or Part-Whole Presentation

WITH *Nancy J. Cobb* AND *Sally L. Perry*

PURPOSE AND DESIGN

In the design of Experiment 9, mixed lists of four or 12 PA units representing combinations of low or high meaningfulness of stimulus and response members were acquired under anticipation and recall formats. Following acquisition of all three of the four-unit lists, they were combined in a 12-unit list. Thus, acquisition by the whole mode of presentation, in which all 12 units were presented from the beginning, could be compared with acquisition by the part-whole mode of presentation, in which subsets of units were first presented separately and then combined.

One purpose of Experiment 9 was to compare acquisition under anticipation and recall formats both across all and for each of the combinations of meaningfulness in mixed lists. Somewhat incidentally, effects of meaningfulness of stimulus and response members on acquisition of unmixed and mixed lists could again be compared. Another purpose was to test the possibility of no or small differences in acquisition rates under anticipation and recall formats with lists of small numbers of units but appreciable differences with lists of relatively larger numbers of units. Still another purpose was to obtain additional information on rate of acquisition under whole and part-whole modes of presentation of lists. Some information about acquisition of PA lists under both modes was available (Orbison, 1944), but it was not extensive.

METHOD

Lists. One of the 12-unit lists of Experiment 9 is shown in Table A20. The stimulus and response members of this list were reversed to obtain the other 12-unit list. The four-unit lists were constituted of pairs in the first row, the second row, and the third row within each of the four combinations of meaningfulness of stimulus and response members. The CVCs of these lists were those of the sets of CVCs used to generate the lists of Experiment 7. Similarity among stimulus members, among response members, and between stimulus and response members was low.

The different random orders of the pairs of the four-unit lists formed a 4×4 Latin Square. Stimulus members alone appeared in the same orders but the orders of pairs and of stimulus members alone in a given trial differed. The pairs and stimulus members alone of the four-unit lists appeared in the same orders in the 12-unit lists. All orders of the pairs and of stimulus members alone were presented before any one was repeated. Otherwise the sequence of orders was random.

Apparatus and procedure. The lists were presented on a memory drum. As in Experiments 7 and 8, under the anticipation format, stimulus members were presented alone for 2 sec. and then with response members for an additional 2 sec. Under the recall format, all pairs were presented for 2 sec. each and then all stimulus members for 2 sec. each. Acquisition of each list was to a criterion of one perfect trial or for 32 trials.

Subjects assigned to four-unit lists learned all three lists in counterbalanced orders. They then learned the 12-unit lists comprised of those same pairs to complete the part-whole mode of presentation. Subjects assigned to 12-unit lists learned with 12 units throughout all trials.

Subjects. Sixteen undergraduates were assigned to the 12-unit lists to be acquired under the anticipation format; 16 more were assigned to the 12-unit lists to be acquired under the recall format. Twenty-four other under-

TABLE A20

Lists of CVCs of High or Low Meaningfulness of Stimulus and Response Members,
Low Similarity for Experiment 9 and of High or Low Similarity of Stimulus and
Response Members, Intermediate Meaningfulness for Experiment 10

		Exp. 9 (Meaningfulness varied, low similarity)		Exp. 10 (Similarity varied, intermediate meaningfulness)	
Stimulus members	Response members	Stimulus members	Response members	Stimulus members	Response members
High	High	JET (4.01)[a]	LAW (4.25)	WOT (2.06)	JUK (2.03)
		SIN (4.03)	JOB (4.25)	FOW (2.30)	KUP (2.23)
		LOG (4.16)	HIT (4.01)	YOW (2.42)	MUK (2.47)
		Mean (4.07)	(4.17)	(2.26)	(2.24)
Low		GIC (1.39)	PEN (4.12)	WOD (2.33)	LIR (2.21)
		ZOX (1.07)	RED (4.16)	WOB (2.42)	SAH (2.19)
		FOV (1.17)	BUS (4.23)	ZOW (2.26)	GED (1.99)
		Mean (1.21)	(4.17)	(2.34)	(2.13)
High	Low	COW (4.38)	VUY (1.07)	REJ (2.33)	KUB (2.09)
		DAM (4.00)	XUK (0.73)	PIV (2.09)	KUD (2.35)
		FUR (4.08)	ZEH (1.02)	QAL (2.19)	HUK (2.15)
		Mean (4.15)	(0.94)	(2.20)	(2.20)
Low		NUQ (1.13)	WIJ (0.85)	VEX (2.07)	TAQ (2.25)
		YEB (1.17)	QAP (1.23)	NIS (2.11)	CEY (2.14)
		KUH (1.20)	MEF (1.43)	CAG (2.32)	BIM (2.46)
		Mean (1.17)	(1.17)	(2.17)	(2.28)

NOTE: With the exceptions of the high-high and low-low combinations for similarity
varied, intermediate meaningfulness, the pairs of the first row of each combination
formed one four-unit list, those of the second row another four-unit list, and those
of the third row the remaining four-unit list.

[a] Glaze M_a values are in parentheses.

graduates acquired the four-unit lists under the anticipation format and 24
more acquired them under the recall format. These 80 subjects were assigned
to the combinations of formats and numbers of units in counterbalanced
cycles. Half of the subjects in each combination of formats and number of
units learned the lists shown in Table A20; half learned the reversed lists.

RESULTS

Acquisition was scored in two ways. One way was the trial on which the
first correct response occurred with the unit of four-unit lists representing
a particular combination of meaningfulness, or the trial on which correct
responses occurred for all three units representing a particular combination
in 12-unit lists. A score of 33 was assigned arbitrarily to all combinations
not acquired in 32 trials. These are trials through criterion for particular

combinations. The other way was trials through the criterion of one perfect trial for entire four-unit or 12-unit lists, disregarding meaningfulness of stimulus and response members.

Trials through criterion for particular combinations. Means and standard deviations of numbers of trials through criterion under each format for subsets of PA units representing different combinations of meaningfulness of stimulus and response members are shown in the upper half of Table A21. The values under "12 (Whole)" are for the 12-unit list. The means for each combination under "Four" were calculated from means for each subject of the numbers of trials through criterion for all three of the four-unit lists. The values under "4,4,4-12 (Part-Whole)" were based on the mean for each subject of the numbers of trials through criterion for all three of the four-unit lists, plus the number of trials through criterion for each combination in the 12-unit lists. The values designated "List" are for trials through criterion for entire lists. They are described later.

Twelve comparisons can be made of acquisition under recall and anticipation formats for combinations of meaningfulness separately. The comparisons for "4,4,4-12 (Part-Whole)," however, are not independent of those for "Four." In all 12 comparisons, the means for trials through criterion under a recall format were lower than those for acquisition under an anticipation format. In all six comparisons among combinations of meaningfulness of stimulus and response members, acquisition was increasingly rapid in the order low-low, high-low, low-high, and high-high.

In the first analysis of variance summarized in Table A22, number of units or length of lists was a variable along with formats, meaningfulness of stimulus members, meaningfulness of response members, and lists with stimulus and response members in the order shown in Table A20 (original) or in the reversed order (reversal). *F*s significant at <.01 indicated that acquisition was faster under recall than under anticipation, with lists of four units than of 12 units, with stimulus members of high meaningfulness than of low meaningfulness, and with response members of high meaningfulness than of low meaningfulness. Across these four variables, lists in original and reversed orders were equivalent.

Formats entered into only two significant interactions. The interaction of formats with meaningfulness of stimulus members and of response members reflected a greater difference between low-low and high-high combinations under anticipation than under recall. The interaction of these three variables and length could also be attributed to differences among differences between low-low and high-high combinations within the four combinations of formats and length.

The interactions of meaningfulness of stimulus members and also of meaningfulness of stimulus members with length, with reversal, and with length and reversal were significant at from .05 to $<.01$. The interaction of meaningfulness of stimulus members and length reflected a more pronounced effect of meaningfulness with 12-unit than with four-unit lists. Differences in effects of meaningfulness with original and reversed orders were sufficient to produce the interaction of meaningfulness of stimulus members and reversal and of meaningfulness of stimulus members, length and reversal. But acquisition was always faster with stimulus members of high than of low meaningfulness.

The interactions of meaningfulness of response members with length, with reversal, and with both variables also reflected differences in the superiority of high meaningfulness to low meaningfulness. The more pronounced effect of meaningfulness of response members with 12-unit than with four-unit lists held both across original and reversed orders and for each order separately.

In the second analysis of variance summarized in Table A22, whole or part-whole modes of presentation replaced length as a variable. Again acquisition was faster under recall than under anticipation, for stimulus members of high than of low meaningfulness, and for response members of high than of low meaningfulness. Differences between means of trials through criterion for the two modes of presentation were not consistent among combinations. The F for the over-all difference between whole and part-whole modes was less than unity. Reversal of orders made no difference.

The one significant interaction involving formats was with the two stimulus variables. Under the anticipation format, meaningfulness of stimulus members was more potent with response members of high than of low meaningfulness; under the recall format, meaningfulness of stimulus members was more potent with response members of low than of high meaningfulness.

Meaningfulness of stimulus members entered into significant interactions with length, with reversal, and with both variables. Effects of meaningfulness were more pronounced with the 12-unit than with the four-unit lists. Effects of meaningfulness differed with original and reversed orders. While direct relationships were obtained between acquisition and meaningfulness of stimulus members with 12-unit lists in original and reversed orders and with the four-unit lists in reversed order, the relationship was inverse with four-unit lists in the original order. This pattern occasioned the significant interaction of meaningfulness of stimulus members, length and reversal.

The interactions of meaningfulness of response members with length and with reversal reflected the patterns of relationships described above for the interactions of meaningfulness of stimulus members with these variables. The interaction of meaningfulness of response members with both variables, however, reflected greater potency of meaningfulness with 12-unit than with four-unit lists in the original order and the converse with those lists in the reversed order.

TABLE A21

Means and Standard Deviations of Trials through Criterion under Anticipation and Recall Formats for Subsets of PA Units Representing Different Combinations of Meaningfulness in Experiment 9 and of Similarity in Experiment 10 for Lists of 12 Units Learned in Whole and Part-Whole Modes of Presentation and for Lists of Four Units

Stimulus members	Response members	12 (Whole)				4,4,4-12 (Part-Whole)				Four			
		Anticipation		Recall		Anticipation		Recall		Anticipation		Recall	
		Mean	SD	Mean	SD	Mean	SD	Mean	SD	Mean	SD	Mean	SD
		Exp. 9 (Meaningfulness varied, intermediate similarity)											
High	High	9.3	3.7	7.0	4.3	12.5	3.7	9.1	3.2	3.0	0.5	1.7	0.7
Low	High	14.7	9.0	9.9	5.9	17.2	8.5	10.9	6.0	4.0	1.4	2.8	1.1
High	Low	19.4	7.4	13.9	8.2	18.8	7.8	13.0	7.8	5.1	1.6	3.5	1.8
Low	Low	23.8	6.6	21.8	7.1	21.0	9.1	17.3	8.6	5.7	1.8	4.7	1.2
	List	25.9	6.3	24.0	7.1	26.2	9.4	20.8	10.0	9.5	3.1	7.1	2.5
		Exp. 10 (Similarity varied, intermediate meaningfulness)											
Low	Low	11.8	5.3	16.8	8.4	16.0	3.9	13.1	7.1	4.0	1.2	3.0	1.1
Low	High	26.7	5.9	22.6	8.4	25.1	8.8	18.4	10.6	5.2	1.7	4.5	1.6
High	Low	24.8	7.5	27.1	6.7	29.2	9.5	23.5	12.0	5.0	1.4	4.6	1.7
High	High	25.6	10.3	26.9	7.4	33.9	8.4	25.9	13.9	5.8	2.0	4.8	2.2
	List	30.6	4.6	30.3	4.7	38.0	8.2	33.2	10.7	11.0	3.3	9.4	3.2

TABLE A22

Analyses of Variance on Trials through Criterion under Anticipation and Recall Formats for Lists of 12 and Four Units Embodying Combinations of Meaningfulness in Experiment 9 and of Similarity in Experiment 10; Interactions Yielding Fs < 2.50 Omitted

| Source | df | Exp. 9 (Meaningfulness varied, intermediate similarity) | | | | Exp. 10 (Similarity varied, intermediate meaningfulness) | | | |
| | | 4 vs. 12 | | 4,4,4–12 vs. 12 | | 4 vs. 12 | | 4,4,4–12 vs. 12 | |
		MS	F	MS	F	MS	F	MS	F
AR	1	393.03	9.79**	1507.89	13.87**	0.15		742.74	3.79
Length or mode (L)	1	9541.19	237.70**	.01		25386.41	441.04**	10.35	
Reversal (Rv)	1	10.02		156.91	1.44	38.52		53.08	
AR×L	1	110.55	2.75	25.04				921.35	4.70*
L×Rv	1			357.21	3.29	208.65	3.63	648.25	3.31
AR×L×Rv	1					187.74	3.26	633.95	3.24
Error	72	40.14		108.73		57.56		195.98	
St	1	561.85	46.29**	1296.05	148.94**	811.82	63.60**	5977.16	161.85**
St×L	1	334.97	27.60**	68.25	7.84**	648.23	50.79**	207.37	5.62*
St×Rv	1	126.76	10.44**	911.25	104.72**	64.49	5.05*	997.57	27.01**
St×AR×Rv	1			33.80	3.88			158.22	4.28*
St×L×Rv	1	62.79	5.17*	56.72	6.52*	70.42	5.52*	117.53	3.18
St×AR×L×Rv	1	41.23	3.40	28.03	3.22				
/St×Ss	72	12.14		8.70		12.76		36.93	
R	1	1937.30	194.86**	3781.25	86.26**	580.58	33.97**	2305.88	48.33**
R×AR	1					88.51	5.18*	290.70	6.09*
R×L	1	1118.25	112.48**	367.50	8.38**	370.08	21.66**		
R×Rv	1	406.49	40.89**	638.45	14.56**	67.50	3.95	517.65	10.85**
R×AR×L	1					114.28	6.69*		
R×L×Rv	1	349.08	35.11**	210.68	48.06**				
/R×Ss	72	9.94		43.84		17.09		47.71	

Source	df	MS	F	MS	F	MS	F	MS	F
St×R	1	36.90	4.68*	145.80	8.06**	416.35	36.15**	771.90	31.25**
St×R×AR	1	24.17	3.06	88.20	4.88*	36.20	3.14	87.16	3.53
St×R×L	1					398.74	34.62**	194.45	7.87**
St×R×Rv	1					96.19	8.35**		
St×R×AR×L	1	35.94	4.56*	68.45	3.78	52.59	4.57*	73.14	2.96
St×R×AR×Rv	1								
St×R×AR×L×Rv	1								
/St×R×Ss	72	7.89		18.09		11.52		24.71	

*$p \leq .05$.

**$p \leq .01$.

Entire lists. In all three comparisons of trials to one perfect trial for entire lists, fewer trials were required under the recall than under the anticipation format (Table A21). Lists of four units were learned faster than lists of 12 units. Under the anticipation format, lists were learned at essentially equal rates with presentation by whole and part-whole modes; under the recall format, there was a slight superiority of the part-whole mode to the whole mode.

In the analyses of variance summarized in Table A23, the *F*s for formats were both significant at .05. The *F* for length was significant but not that for modes of presentation. None of the interactions was significant.

TABLE A23

Analyses of Variance on Trials through Criterion in Experiments 9 and 10 for Entire Lists of 12 and 4,4,4–12 or Four Units under Anticipation and Recall Formats

Source	df	Exp. 9 (Meaningfulness varied, intermediate similarity)				Exp. 10 (Similarity varied, intermediate meaningfulness)			
		4 vs. 12		4,4,4–12 vs. 12		4 vs. 12		4,4,4–12 vs. 12	
		MS	F	MS	F	MS	F	MS	F
AR	1	98.26	4.21*	322.65	4.25*	21.66	1.30	181.90	2.87
L	1	5317.61	227.71**	41.80		7832.91	470.22**	510.43	8.06**
Rv	1	1.79		140.50	1.85	0.74		242.66	3.83
AR×L	1	1.04		57.63		7.07		97.44	1.54
AR×Rv	1	18.05		5.00		2.80		80.06	1.27
L×Rv	1	54.03	2.31	328.42	4.33	17.00	1.02	86.41	1.37
AR×L×Rv	1	3.50		0.05		56.76	3.41	262.64	4.15*
Error	72	23.35		75.84		16.66		63.29	

*p ≤ .05.
**p ≤ .01.

DISCUSSION

The results indicated that acquisition was faster under the recall format than under the anticipation format for all four combinations of meaningfulness of stimulus and of response members within mixed lists of four and of 12 units. Disregarding the meaningfulness variables, the entire four-unit and 12-unit lists were acquired faster under the recall format than under the anticipation format. The superiority of the recall format held in the comparison involving acquisition of all 12 units by whole and part-whole modes of presentation.

The consistency of the superiority of recall to anticipation in Experiment 9 was in contrast to the inconclusive results of Experiment 7 and the failure to find differential effects of formats in Experiment 8. Also, in the discussion of the results of Experiment 8, Battig and Brackett's (1963) results for

100% ORM were interpreted as failing to show a significant superiority of the recall to the anticipation format. And Lockhead (1962) clearly failed to obtain differences between anticipation and recall formats.

The failure to obtain a superiority of recall to anticipation in Experiment 7 was viewed as possibly due to unexpectedly slow acquisition under recall of the list representing the low-low combination. The failure to obtain differences due to format in Experiment 8 and, seemingly, in Battig and Brackett's experiment might be attributed to manipulation of similarity rather than meaningfulness. But why differences due to formats were not obtained with manipulation of similarity and might be obtained with manipulation of meaningfulness is not clear.

Interpretation of the results of Experiment 9 is complicated further by Battig and Brackett's (p. 513) statement that, "In this connection, however, it should be noted that two recently completed studies in this laboratory have shown recall-method performance on low similarity CVC lists to be significantly and consistently superior to the anticipation method (a) over a wide range of conditions of S and R term meaningfulness; (b) under both constant and varied serial orders; and (c) for bidirectional (both S-R and R-S associations) as well as unidirectional learning conditions." These results appear entirely consistent with those of Experiment 9.

With respect to effects of meaningfulness of stimulus and response members, the consistent findings of direct relationships between acquisition rate and meaningfulness of stimulus members and of response members agreed with generalizations based on the results of other investigations. The typical order of increasingly rapid learning with low-low, high-low, low-high, and high-high combinations occurred.

As expected, lists of four units were acquired more rapidly than lists of 12 units. Thus, increasing the number of PA units increased the numbers of trials required to learn each unit of lists disproportionately. But the possible interaction of a more pronounced difference between formats with the 12-unit than with the four-unit lists did not obtain.

Lists were acquired slightly but not significantly faster when presented by the whole than by the part-whole mode. Orbison's (1944) findings suggested that for lists of 12 units, acquisition should be faster by the part-whole than by the whole mode of presentation. Which among the many differences between the lists and procedures of his experiment and those of Experiment 9 might account for this discrepancy is not known.

SUMMARY

Mixed lists of four and 12 units with, respectively, one or three units representing combinations of low or high meaningfulness of stimulus and response members were acquired under anticipation and recall formats of presentation. All three of the four-unit lists whose units were those of the 12-unit list were acquired by subjects assigned to the four-unit lists. These lists were then combined into 12-unit lists so that acquisition by this part-whole mode of presentation could be compared with acquisition by the whole mode of presentation in which subjects were administered lists of 12 units throughout all trials.

The CVCs of high or low meaningfulness used to construct the lists were of low intra-list similarity. The lists were presented by means of a memory drum for acquisition to a criterion of one perfect trial for all pairs of a list or for 32 trials.

Acquisition was expressed as trials through criterion for the one or three units representing each particular combination of meaningfulness and as trials through criterion for entire lists, disregarding meaningfulness. In comparison of trials through criterion for particular combinations, with length of list, formats, and reversal of lists as additional variables, acquisition was faster under the recall than under the anticipation format, with four-unit than with 12-unit lists, with stimulus members of high than of low meaningfulness, and with response members of high than of low meaningfulness. Reversal did not have significant over-all effects. The two significant interactions involving formats were interpreted in terms of differences between and among differences between low-low and high-high combinations of meaningfulness of stimulus and response members. The interactions of both meaningfulness of stimulus members and meaningfulness of response members with length, with reversal, and with length and reversal reflected differences in the potency of meaningfulness of stimulus and of response members at different levels and at different combinations of levels of the other variables.

In the analysis of trials through criterion for particular combinations in which mode of presentation replaced length, the results for the significant effects of formats, meaningfulness of stimulus members, meaningfulness of response members and reversal alone and in combination were essentially those obtained in the analysis with length as a variable. Acquisition by the whole mode was not sufficiently faster than acquisition by the part-whole mode to produce a significant difference.

Entire lists were acquired faster under the recall than under the anticipation format. The superiority of recall to anticipation held at each level of length and of modes of presentation.

The suggested generally faster acquisition under the recall than under the anticipation format was discussed in relation to other inconclusive findings and to other findings of no differences between formats. Also noted was a corroborative report of general superiority of the recall to the anticipation format.

EXPERIMENT 10

Acquisition of Mixed Lists Presented under Recall and Anticipation
Formats as Functions of Similarity of Stimulus and Response Members,
Length of List, and Whole or Part-Whole Presentation

WITH *Nancy J. Cobb* AND *Sally L. Perry*

PURPOSE AND DESIGN

Experiment 10 differed from Experiment 9 only in the use of mixed lists
representing combinations of high or low similarity of stimulus and response
members rather than of meaningfulness. Thus, the variables were similarity
of stimulus and of response members and the variables employed in Experiment 9 of formats, number of units, and presentation by whole or part-whole
modes. The purposes of Experiment 10 were those of Experiment 9.

METHOD

Lists. One of the 12-unit lists of Experiment 9 is shown in Table A20.
This list was reversed to obtain the other 12-unit list. By mistake, one
four-unit list had two high-high pairs and another had two low-low pairs.
Otherwise the three four-unit lists were derived from the first, second, and
third rows within each of the combinations of meaningfulness of stimulus
and response members. Across all three four-unit lists, the results indicated
that the deviation from three four-unit lists in which each combination was
represented was of no discernible consequence.

The CVCs of these lists were those of the sets of CVCs used to generate
the lists of Experiment 8. Both stimulus and response members were of
medium meaningfulness. Randomization of orders of pairs and of stimulus
members alone was in the manner described in Experiment 9.

Apparatus and procedure. The memory drum was that used for Experiment
9 as was the procedure.

Subjects. The 80 subjects were assigned to each of the combinations of
format and numbers of units in the numbers and manner of Experiment 9.
Half learned the lists of Table A20; half learned the reversed lists.

RESULTS

The two ways of scoring acquisition of Experiment 9 were used again.
Thus, results are described in terms of trials through criterion for particular
combinations and for entire lists.

Trials through criterion for particular combinations. Means and standard
deviations of trials through criterion for each format for subsets of pairs

representing each combination in 12-unit lists, in four-unit lists, and in the "4,4,4-12 (Part-Whole)" mode are shown in the bottom half of Table A21. In all four comparisons for the four-unit lists and in all four comparisons for the part-whole mode, means of trials through criterion under the recall format were lower than the corresponding means under the anticipation format. In three of the four comparisons for the 12-unit lists, however, the means for acquisition under anticipation were lower than the corresponding means under recall.

In three of the six comparisons among combinations of similarity of stimulus and response members, means of trials through criterion decreased in the order high-high, high-low, low-high, and low-low. For 12-unit lists under the anticipation format, the positions of the high-high and low-high combinations were reversed; for the 12-unit lists under the recall format, the positions of the high-high and high-low combinations were reversed; and for the four-unit lists under the anticipation format, the positions of the high-low and low-high combinations were reversed.

In the analysis of variance involving lists of four units versus those of 12 units (Table A22), the F for formats was not significant. The four significant interactions in which formats was a variable are considered in connection with results for those other variables.

The highly significant Fs for similarity of stimulus members and similarity of response members were due to more rapid acquisition with low than with high similarity. Similarity of stimulus members was more potent than similarity of response members. Disregarding the other variables, reversal made no difference; it was involved in several significant interactions.

Similarity of stimulus members entered into significant interactions with length, reversal, and length and reversal. The difference between high and low similarity of stimulus members was much larger for lists of 12 units than of four units, and was somewhat larger with the reversed than with the original order. Differences between high and low similarity of stimulus members increased in the order four units and original order, four units and reversed order, 12 units and original order, and 12 units and reversed order to produce the interaction among all three variables.

Similarity of response members interacted with formats, with length, and with formats and length. Similarity of response members had somewhat more pronounced effects under the anticipation than under the recall format and with 12 units than with four units. The third interaction reflected greater differences between effects of similarity of response members with 12-unit and four-unit lists under the anticipation than under the recall format.

The interaction of similarity of stimulus and response members was due to a greater difference between stimulus members of high and low similarity for response members of high than of low similarity. The same relationships held with four-unit lists and 12-unit lists separately and were sufficiently more pronounced with the 12-unit lists to produce an interaction of the two stimulus variables and length. The remaining two significant interactions of all variables but reversal and of all five variables might also be described in terms of differences in the potency of similarity of stimulus members at levels of high and low similarity of response members among combinations of the other variables. Further, more detailed descriptions of these patterns are not warranted here.

The analysis of variance in which mode of presentation replaced length as a variable is summarized in the last two columns of Table A22. The F for whole versus part-whole modes was below unity. The F for formats approached significance at .05, and the F for the interaction of formats and mode was significant at $<.05$. For acquisition by the whole mode of presentation, the rates were the same under both formats. But for acquisition by the part-whole mode, the rate was faster under recall than under anticipation. Formats was involved in two more significant interactions; these are described in connection with effects of the similarity variables.

Significant inverse relationships between acquisition rate held for both similarity of stimulus members and similarity of response members with the former the more potent variable. The interactions of similarity of stimulus members with length and with reversal reflected a larger difference between means for high and low similarity of stimulus members with the four-unit than with the 12-unit lists and with the reversed than with the original order. The pattern of differences among means for similarity of stimulus members and reversal held under both anticipation and recall formats but the difference between these differences was sufficiently larger under recall than under anticipation to produce the significant interaction of similarity of stimulus members, formats, and reversal.

The difference between means for high and low similarity of response members was larger under anticipation than under recall and with the original than the reversed order. These differences underlie the significant interactions of similarity of response members with formats and with reversal.

The interaction of similarity of stimulus and of response members reflected a larger difference between means for stimulus members of high and low similarity with response members of low than of high similarity. Both of these differences were larger with four-unit than with 12-unit lists to produce the interaction of both variables with length.

Entire lists. In the analyses of variance on trials through criterion for entire lists (Table A23), the only significant F in the analysis in which length was a variable was for length. The only significant Fs in the analysis in which mode of presentation was a variable were for mode and the interaction of formats, mode and reversal. Entire lists of four units were acquired faster than lists of 12 units and entire lists of 12 units were acquired faster with presentation by the whole than by the part-whole mode. The triple interaction reflected superiority of recall to anticipation for the combinations of four-unit lists and the original order and for 12-unit lists and the reversed order, and slight superiority of anticipation to recall for the other two combinations.

DISCUSSION

The results of Experiment 10 do nothing to resolve the problem of possible differences in rates of acquisition under anticipation and under recall formats of presentation. Supporting a conclusion of faster acquisition under recall than under anticipation are the comparisons which show a superiority of recall for the four combinations of similarity of stimulus and response members with the four-unit lists and for presentation by the part-whole mode. Also, entire lists of four units and of 12 units, when presented by the part-whole mode, were acquired faster under recall than under anticipation. However, the differences between means for trials through criterion. in these comparisons were sometimes as small as 0.4, and the comparisons for lists of 12 units acquired by the part-whole mode are not independent of those for lists of four units.

Supporting a conclusion of no difference in acquisition rates under the two formats are faster acquisition under anticipation than under recall for three of the four combinations of similarity of stimulus and response members for 12-unit lists presented by the whole mode, and the almost identical means for trials through criterion for those entire lists. That formats was involved in only a few significant interactions suggests that the failure to obtain significant differences across the other variables could not be attributed to opposite effects of anticipation and recall at different levels and combinations of levels of the other variables. Moreover, such opposite effects did not appear in the patterns of significant interactions involving formats.

Considering the results of Experiment 10, those of Experiment 8, and those of Battig and Brackett's (1963) experiment in which similarity of stimulus and response members were varied, the most defensible conclusion is, at most, of slightly more rapid acquisition under the recall than under the anticipation format. But, at least for acquisition, the possible advantage of recall is of little practical significance. Moreover, a conclusion of no differences in effects of formats both across and for specific combinations of levels of other variables is still tenable. Whether variations in meaningfulness constitute an exception to this conclusion is considered in the discussion of the results of Experiment 11.

In three of six comparisons among combinations of similarity of stimulus and response members, acquisition was increasingly rapid for high-high,

high-low, low-high, and low-low combinations. This is the order expected on the basis of findings in the majority of other experiments involving the same combinations of similarity of stimulus and response members. The differences between means of trials through criterion which produced exceptions to this order in the other three comparisons were sufficiently small to be attributable to chance factors. As mentioned in the description of the lists, there was no evidence that the deviation from all four combinations in each of the four-unit lists was responsible for these discrepancies between observed orders and the expected order. In contrast to the results of Experiment 8, similarity of stimulus members was more potent than similarity of response members. Unidentified peculiarities in the lists of Experiment 8, or other factors, may have been responsible for the discrepancy between effects of similarity of stimulus and response members in that experiment and in Experiment 10 along with the majority of other experiments.

In agreement with the results of Experiment 9, subjects required more trials to reach criterion with lists of 12 units than of four units. Also, acquisition proceeded at essentially equal rates for presentation by whole and part-whole modes with no evidence of interactions of modes with stimulus attributes separately or combined.

The over-all effect of reversal was not significant in either Experiment 9 or Experiment 10. In both experiments there were interactions of reversal with meaningfulness of stimulus and response members and with their similarity. These interactions suggested that the particular set of CVCs which served as stimulus members or response members of high or low meaningfulness or similarity influenced the magnitude of effects of the four variables. Closer examination of the sources of these interactions showed the manner in which they were produced by reversal. Those sets of CVCs which functioned as stimulus and response members in the original order functioned as response and stimulus members in the reversed order. Thus, when the effects of meaningfulness or similarity with particular sets of stimulus members were greater with the reversed order than with the original order, the effects of meaningfulness or similarity with those particular sets of response members were greater with the original than with the reversed order.

SUMMARY

Experiment 10 differed from Experiment 9 only in the variation of similarity of stimulus and response members rather than of their meaningfulness. In comparisons of trials through criterion for the different combinations of similarity both for four-unit lists and for 12-unit lists acquired by the part-whole mode of presentation, acquisition was consistently faster under the recall than under the anticipation format. But the opposite effect obtained in three of the four comparisons for 12-unit lists acquired by the whole mode of presentation. The Fs for formats in the analysis involving particular combinations were not significant nor were those in the analyses for entire lists, disregarding combinations. Formats entered into only a few interactions. These were not of a form which would produce significant interactions but nonsignificant effects across other variables of the interactions.

The inverse relationship between acquisition rate and similarity of stimulus members was more pronounced than that relationship for similarity of response members. In three of six comparisons, acquisition rate increased in the order high-high, high-low, low-high, and low-low combinations of similarity. There were inversions in the other three comparisons. Similarity of stimulus members and of response members entered into some significant interactions involving formats, length and reversal. These interactions were described in terms of differences among inverse effects of similarity at different levels or combinations of levels of the other variables.

Four-unit lists were acquired faster than 12-unit lists but acquisition of 12-unit lists was at essentially equal rates whether presented by whole or part-whole modes.

The results were viewed as failing to resolve the problem of possible differences in rates of acquisition under anticipation and under recall formats. Particularly for variations in the similarity of stimulus and response members, available data were interpreted as supporting a conclusion of no or at most slight differential effects of formats.

EXPERIMENT 11

Replication of Experiment 7

WITH *Nancy J. Cobb*

PURPOSE AND DESIGN

Experiment 11 replicated Experiment 7 in all important respects. Replication of Experiment 7 seemed desirable because of the possible superiority of the recall to the anticipation format in that experiment and because of the consistent superiority of recall to anticipation obtained in Experiment 9 and reported by Battig and Brackett (1963) for variations in meaningfulness of stimulus and response members.

In Experiment 7, the over-all difference between acquisition under anticipation and under recall was not significant. But examination of absolute and relative values of the names for the eight combinations of meaningfulness of stimulus members, meaningfulness of response members, and formats suggested that acquisition for the low-low combination under recall might have been atypically slow. It seemed possible, therefore, that the failure to obtain significantly faster acquisition under recall than under anticipation was due to some chance factor such as assignment of a disproportionate number of slow learners to the low-low combination under recall. Experiment 11 checked this possibility.

METHOD

The lists, apparatus, procedure, and details concerning subjects were those of Experiment 7. They are described there.

RESULTS

For convenient comparison, means of trials through criterion obtained in both Experiment 7 and in Experiment 11 are shown in the upper half of Table A24. Means for stimulus members correct in backward recall are shown in the lower half.

TABLE A24

Means of Trials through Criterion and of Stimulus Members Correct
in Backward Recall in Experiments 7 and 11 Separately and
Combined for Each Combination of Meaningfulness
under Anticipation and Recall Formats

Stimulus members	Response members	Anticipation			Recall		
		Exp. 7	Exp. 11	Both	Exp. 7	Exp. 11	Both
		Trials through criterion					
High	High	11.0	8.4	9.7	9.1	12.5	10.8
Low		17.8	16.5	17.1	11.0	12.9	11.9
High	Low	24.6	15.8	20.2	19.4	14.4	16.9
Low		29.6	36.2	32.9	32.5	33.3	32.9
		Stimulus members correct					
High	High	8.5	6.6	7.6	8.1	7.0	7.6
Low		3.1	2.1	2.6	6.1	4.0	5.1
High	Low	4.8	8.2	6.5	6.6	7.8	7.2
Low		2.6	0.5	1.6	1.2	2.2	1.8

Acquisition. In Experiment 11, disregarding combinations of meaningfulness of stimulus and response members, acquisition was slightly faster under the recall format than under the anticipation format. The superiority of recall to anticipation held for all combinations but the high-high which was acquired faster under anticipation. However, neither the F for formats nor the Fs for interactions involving formats were significant (Table A25).

TABLE A25

Analyses of Variance on Trials through Criterion and Analyses of Variance and Covariance for Stimulus Members Correct in Backward Recall for Experiment 11 and for Experiments 7 and 11 Combined; Interactions Yielding Fs $\leq$ 2.50 Omitted

| Source | df | Exp. 11 | | | | | | Exps. 7 and 11 | | | | | |
| | | Trials through criterion | | Stimulus members correct | | | | Trials through criterion | | Stimulus members correct | | | |
		MS	F	MS	F	Adj MS^a	F	MS	F	MS	F	Adj MS^a	F
AR	1	15.01		12.25	1.61	8.95	1.31	110.64	2.12	21.95	2.69	10.25	1.43
St	1	2292.01	44.67**	430.56	56.73**	209.14	30.62**	2784.45	53.24**	634.57	77.67**	315.08	43.82**
R	1	2347.89	47.51**	1.00		30.19	4.42*	5684.45	108.69**	67.57	8.27**	5.81	
Replications (Rp)	1							4.14		3.45		2.46	
AR×St	1	87.90	1.71	14.07	1.85	6.35		18.75		7.50		4.53	
St×R	1	953.27	18.58*	33.07	4.36*	2.91		815.06	15.58**				
St×Rp	1							223.12	4.27*				
R×Rp	1							31.00		46.32	5.67*	36.26	5.04*
AR×St×R	1	37.51		0.55		2.41		182.89	3.50	17.26	2.11	5.05	
St×R×Rp	1							228.46	4.37*				
AR×St×R×Rp	1									27.19	3.33	20.52	2.85
Error	56,112^b	51.31		7.59		6.83		52.30		8.17		7.19	

^{a} Analysis of covariance adjustment of differences in means of stimulus members correct in backward recall for differences in trials to criterion.

^{b} df for Exp. 11 and for Exps. 7 and 11 combined, respectively. For analyses of covariance the df are 56—1=55 and 112—1=111.

*$p \leq$ .05.
**$p \leq$ .01.

Across anticipation and recall formats and under the recall format, acquisition was increasingly more rapid for the low-low, high-low, low-high, and high-high combinations of meaningfulness of stimulus and response members. Under the anticipation format, acquisition was slightly faster for the high-low than for the low-high combination. The Fs for the direct relationships between acquisition rate and meaningfulness of stimulus and of response members were both significant with the latter slightly the more potent. The significant F for the interaction of these two variables reflected a more pronounced effect of meaningfulness of response members for stimulus members of low than of high meaningfulness.

Except for the means for the high-low combination under anticipation, the values for means of trials through criterion obtained for each of the combinations of formats and meaningfulness of stimulus and response members in Experiments 7 and 11 were in reasonable agreement. Accordingly, the means obtained in both experiments were combined as more reliable estimates of effects of formats and stimulus attributes.

Disregarding the stimulus variables, acquisition was faster under the recall than under the anticipation format in both Experiment 7 and Experiment 11. Hence, acquisition was faster under recall for the two experiments combined. In the analysis of variance for both experiments combined, however, the F for formats was still not significant. Although the differences between formats for the four combinations were not consistent in direction or magnitude, formats did not enter into any significant interactions with the stimulus variables. Nor was the interaction of formats and the additional variable of replications significant.

Across both experiments, acquisition was increasingly rapid for the low-low, high-low, low-high, and high-high combinations of meaningfulness of stimulus and response members for each format separately and for the two combined. Meaningfulness of response members was considerably more potent than meaningfulness of stimulus members. The significant interaction of the stimulus variables reflected a larger difference due to meaningfulness of response members for stimulus members of low than of high meaningfulness.

Disregarding the other variables, the F for replications was not significant. Indeed, the general means obtained in the two experiments were almost identical. However, replications was involved in two significant interactions. The effects of meaningfulness of stimulus members were sufficiently greater in Experiment 11 than in Experiment 7 to produce the interaction of replications and meaningfulness of stimulus members. The interaction of replications with meaningfulness of stimulus and of response members reflected only slightly faster acquisition with the low-high than with the high-low combination in Experiment 11 and considerable superiority of the low-high combination in Experiment 7.

Backward recall of stimulus members. In Experiment 11, disregarding the stimulus variables, slightly more stimulus members were recalled correctly following acquisition under recall than under anticipation. Means for stimulus members correct were higher for acquisition under recall than under anticipation for all but the high-low combination for which the mean for stimulus members correct was .04 higher under anticipation. In the analysis of variance, however, the effects of formats were not sufficient to produce a significant over-all F and none of the interactions involving formats was significant. The same outcomes obtained in the analysis of covariance involving adjustments for differences in trials through criterion.

Increasing numbers of stimulus members were recalled correctly for the low-low, low-high, high-high, and high-low combinations of meaningfulness of stimulus and response members. In both the analysis of variance and the analysis of covariance, significantly more stimulus members of high than of low meaningfulness were recalled correctly. In the analysis of variance, the F for meaningfulness of response members was not significant. In the analysis of covariance, the F for meaningfulness of response members was significant due to a higher adjusted mean for low meaningfulness of response members than for high meaningfulness of response members.

The values for means of responses correct in backward recall for the combinations of formats and meaningfulness of stimulus and response members were in reasonable agreement. The exception, again, was the means for the high-low combination under anticipation. Accordingly, means for stimulus members correct in both experiments were combined. For three of the four combinations of meaningfulness of stimulus and response members and across combinations, the combined means for stimulus members correct were higher following acquisition under recall than under anticipation. But again the Fs for formats in the analyses of variance and covariance were not significant. Nor did formats enter into interactions with the stimulus variables in either analysis.

Under both formats, means of stimulus members correct increased in the order low-low, low-high, high-low, and high-high meaningfulness of stimulus and response members. The F for meaningfulness of stimulus members was significant in both the analysis of variance and the analysis of covariance. The F for meaningfulness of response members was significant in the analysis of variance but not in the analysis of covariance. The significant interaction of meaningfulness of stimulus members and replications in both analyses reflected a greater effect of meaningfulness of stimulus members in Experiment 11 than in Experiment 7.

DISCUSSION

Results for acquisition in Experiment 11 and in the preceding four experiments are discussed primarily in terms of the problem of differences in acquisition rates between anticipation and recall formats. In the discussion of results for backward recall of stimulus members in Experiments 7, 8, and 11, effects of formats are also emphasized. Effects of meaningfulness of stimulus and response members in Experiment 11 are, however, considered briefly in relation to findings of other experiments.

Acquisition. Acquisition may be faster under the recall format than under the anticipation format. Formats may have no consistent differential effects. At present, these are the possible conclusions. Little evidence has been reported in favor of the third conclusion of faster acquisition under the anticipation format than under the recall format.

The results of Experiment 9 and those described by Battig and Brackett (1963, p. 513) for variations in meaningfulness of stimulus and response members support the first conclusion. Although acquisition was faster under recall than under anticipation both across all combinations and for three of the four combinations in Experiment 7 and in Experiment 11, the results of these experiments are probably best interpreted as supporting a conclusion of no significant effects of formats. Failure to obtain significant over-all Fs for the experiments separately and for the two combined is one reason for this conclusion. A related reason is the failure for formats to enter into significant interactions and, particularly, into significant interactions reflecting effects of formats in the same direction at different levels or combinations of levels of the other variables.

The results of Experiments 8 and 10 and those reported by Battig and Brackett for variations in similarity are more in accord with a conclusion of no differential effects of formats. Lockhead (1962) did not vary meaningfulness or similarity of stimulus and response members. But his failure to obtain significant differences between anticipation and recall formats cannot be construed as favoring faster acquisition under recall than under anticipation.

In Experiment 11, faster acquisition in the order low-low, high-low, low-high, and high-high meaningfulness of stimulus and response members obtained for acquisition under the recall format and across both formats. The inversion in the ranks of the low-high and high-low combinations under anticipation is based on such small differences in means that chance factors cannot be ruled out as the most likely explanation. The combined results of Experiments 7 and 11 were in the low-low, high-low, low-high, and high-high order for formats separately and combined. Thus, the results of Experiment 7 and of Experiments 7 and 11 combined were consistent with findings in the majority of previous experiments.

Backward recall of stimulus members. In Experiment 11, none of the relationships obtained in backward recall of stimulus members suggested the occurrence of differential effects of formats. Except for the higher means for the high-low than for the high-high combination, the rank orders of stimulus members correct in backward recall were those expected with a reversal in functions of the stimulus members and response members of acquisition. The significant direct relationship between stimulus members correct and meaningfulness of stimulus members was not altered by adjustment of means for differences in acquisition rate. But such adjustment changed the nonsignificant direct relationship for meaningfulness of response members to a significant inverse relationship.

Except for high-low combinations under recall, the values of the means obtained for the same combinations of formats and meaningfulness of stimulus and response members in Experiments 7 and 11 were in reasonable agreement. Combining the results for formats did not produce any evidence of differential effects of formats. Both under anticipation and under recall, however, the means for stimulus members correct increased in the order low-low, low-high, high-low, and high-high. Thus, the more reliable means were in the order consistent with modal prior findings. The direct effect of meaningfulness of stimulus members held in both the analysis of variance and the analysis of covariance; the direct effect of meaningfulness of response members suggested in the analysis of variance vanished in the analysis of covariance.

SUMMARY

In purpose and method, Experiment 11 replicated Experiment 7 in which the variables were anticipation and recall formats of presentation along with meaningfulness of stimulus and response members realized in unmixed lists. In Experiment 7 and for the combined results of Experiments 7 and 11, formats had no significant differential effects on acquisition either across the stimulus variables or for different combinations of meaningfulness of stimulus and response members. Formats also had no differential effects on backward recall of stimulus members.

Across both formats and under the recall format in Experiment 11 and also across formats and for formats separately in the combined results of Experiments 7 and 11, acquisition rates increased in the order low-low, high-low, low-high, and high-high meaningfulness of stimulus and response members. This is the order typically obtained. In Experiment 7, backward recall of stimulus members increased in the order low-low, low-high, high-high, and high-low. But in the combined results of Experiments 7 and 11, backward recall increased in the modal order of previous findings of low-low, low-high, high-low, and high-high.

Results of Experiment 11 were discussed in relation to those of Experiments 7, 8, 9, 10 and other experiments. The pattern of these results was considered as equivocal with respect to the problem of no or differential effects of formats for variations in meaningfulness of stimulus and response members. A conclusion of no differential effects of variations in similarity was suggested.

EXPERIMENT 12

Acquisition of Mixed Lists as Functions of Percentages of Occurrence of Stimulus Members and Response Members, Meaningfulness of Stimulus Members, and Meaningfulness of Response Members

WITH *Bruce N. Gregory*

PURPOSE AND DESIGN

The variables of Experiment 12 were percentages of occurrence of stimulus members (%OSM) and of response members (%ORM), along with meaningfulness of stimulus and response members realized in mixed lists of four PA units. Experiment 12 was conceived as the first experiment in a series designed to extend Experiments 9 and 10 and also Experiment 1 and earlier experiments (Goss, Nodine, Gregory, Taub, & Kennedy, 1962).

The extension of Experiments 9 and 10 was in the introduction of the variables of %OSM and %ORM. The condition of 100% occurrence of both stimulus and response members, here designated 100% OSRM, served as the origin for variations in both %ORM and %OSM. Thus, with levels of 25% ORM and 25% OSM, only three percentages of occurrence of stimulus and response members were needed to realize these two variables. In Experiments 9 and 10, formats and mode of presentation had proved ineffectual. Therefore, these variables were ignored in Experiment 12. Length of lists, which was significant in both Experiments 9 and 10, was excluded temporarily as were similarity of stimulus and of response members, the stimulus attributes varied in Experiment 10.

The extension of Experiment 1 and the earlier experiments was in the introduction of %OSM and in the use of mixed rather than unmixed lists. Combinations involving both meaningfulness and similarity were excluded temporarily.

METHOD

Lists. One of the three four-unit lists of Experiment 9 was selected to provide the combinations of low or high meaningfulness of stimulus and response members. Only one of the three was used because results with this list had been representative of those across all three lists. The pairs of the particular list selected were KUH, MEF (low-low), FUR, ZEH (high-low), FOV, BUS (low-high), and LOG, HIT (high-high). This list was reversed to obtain a second list. The Noble m' values of these CVCs are in parentheses in Table A16.

Units of the lists were presented in four different random orders which constituted a 4×4 Latin Square.

Apparatus and procedure. The lists were presented under an anticipation format to subjects individually by means of a memory drum. Under 100% OSRM, stimulus members appeared alone for 2 sec. and were always accompanied by their response members for an additional 2 sec. Under 25% ORM, stimulus members always appeared alone for 2 sec. On only 25% of their occurrences were they then accompanied by response members during the next 2 sec. Only one of the response members occurred on a given trial; each response member appeared once in each block of four trials.

Under 25% OSM, each stimulus member appeared only once in each block of four trials. When stimulus members occurred alone for 2 sec., they were always accompanied by response members during the next 2 sec. When stimulus members did not occur, response members appeared alone during the last 2 sec. of the 4 sec. allowed for each unit.[8] The particular schedule of occurrences of stimulus members matched that for response members under 25% ORM. On the trial the response member of a pair appeared under 25% ORM, the stimulus member of that pair appeared under 25% OSM.

Acquisition was to a criterion of one perfect trial plus four trials or for 32 trials.

Subjects. Undergraduates were assigned to the six combinations of percentages of occurrence and original or reversed lists in order of their appearance. Five counterbalanced cycles were run to yield 10 subjects for each of the percentage conditions.

RESULTS

One measure of acquisition was the trial of the occurrence of the first correct response for each unit representing one of the combinations of meaningfulness of stimulus and response members. The other measure was trials to criterion for entire lists. The scoring for each unit under 25% OSM involved the problem of the separation of trials on which a particular stimulus member appeared by, on the average, three trials on which the other stimulus members appeared. Following an incorrect response to a presented on Trial $n+1$, the response might have occurred correctly. In-particular stimulus member on Trial n, had that stimulus member been

---

[8]Exposure to response members alone was thus shorter than exposure to stimulus members alone which might have provided some advantage in familiarization of and discrimination among stimulus members under 25% ORM relative to familiarization of and discrimination among response members under 25% OSM. However, duration of response members alone was not increased to 4 sec. in part to approximate the conventional PA procedure as closely as possible. Also, even without response members present, subjects could rehearse the response members seen previously, thus minimizing any possible disadvantage of their shorter duration.

stead, the stimulus member was not presented again until Trial $n+4$, which would add three trials in which, had subjects had the opportunity, they might have responded correctly. Thus, subjects' rate of acquisition could be underestimated by up to three trials.

To assign three trials as the amount of underestimation assumes that, between successive appearances of the stimulus member of a particular unit, no changes occurred which might have influenced probability of a correct response on the second appearance of the stimulus member of that unit. During the intervening three trials, however, subjects might have increased integration-availability of responses, rehearsed the associations, or both which, in turn, could contribute to the probability of a correct response to the stimulus member on Trial $n+4$. Subtracting three trials, therefore, might err in the direction of overestimation of acquisition rate. With no rational basis for selecting a value between zero and three for the correction, the risk of underestimating acquisition rate by not subtracting any correction was chosen.

Under 25% OSM, a minimum of four trials was necessary for presentation of all four stimulus members and, because of the random orders, up to three of the pairs might have been repeated before a particular pair appeared a second time. Therefore, trials to criterion on entire lists was defined as trials to the trials during which subjects were correct on each different pair with no incorrect responses on any intervening repeated pairs.

Means and standard deviations of trials of the first correct response for pairs representing each combination of low or high meaningfulness of stimulus and response members under 100% OSRM, 25% ORM, and 25% OSM along with means and standard deviations of trials to criterion for entire lists are shown in Table A26. For each combination separately and for entire lists, acquisition was most rapid under 100% OSRM and least rapid under 25% OSM. Had three trials been subtracted from each of

TABLE A26

Means and Standard Deviations of Trials on Which the First Correct Response Occurred for Different Combinations of Meaningfulness and of Trials to Criterion for Entire Lists under Different Percentages of Occurrence of Stimulus and Response Members in Experiment 12

Stimulus members	Response members	100% OSRM		25% ORM		25% OSM	
		Mean	SD	Mean	SD	Mean	SD
High	High	4.4	4.1	5.0	3.4	16.6	8.4
Low		5.7	3.5	9.2	6.2	24.7	8.8
High	Low	6.7	3.0	13.6	7.5	14.1	10.6
Low		6.3	4.7	12.4	5.9	23.6	7.8
Entire lists		13.9	6.1	22.3	7.4	31.1	3.8

the means for particular combinations under %OSM, all but the means for the high-low combination would still have been appreciably higher than its corresponding mean under 25% ORM. The F for percentages of occurrence of stimulus and response members obtained in the analysis of variance on trials of the first correct response for each combination was significant at <.01 (Table A27). The F for differences among percentages for entire lists was also significant at <.01.

TABLE A27

Analysis of Variance on Trials of the First Correct Response for Different Combinations of Meaningfulness and on Trials to Criterion for Entire Lists under Different Percentages on Occurrence in Experiment 12

Source	df	Combinations		Entire lists	
		MS	F	MS	F
Percentages (%)	2	2051.11	30.96*	739.81	18.95*
Error	27	66.26		39.03	
MS	1	385.21	10.37*		
%×MS	2	206.86	5.57*		
/MS×Ss	27	37.14			
MR	1	102.68	1.70		
%×MR	2	149.42	2.47		
/MR×Ss	27	60.52			
MS×MR	1	27.08			
%×MS×MR	2	28.98			
/MS×MR×Ss	27	31.80			

*$p \leq .01$.

Under 100% OSRM and 25% ORM, acquisition rate increased in the order high-low, low-low, low-high, and high-high. Under 25% OSM, the order was low-high, low-low, high-high, and high-low. In the analysis of variance, the direct relationship between trials of the first correct response and meaningfulness of stimulus members was significant at .01, but the direct relationship for meaningfulness of response members was not significant. The interaction of the variables was not significant. The significant interaction of percentages and meaningfulness of stimulus members reflected increasing differences in the superiority of high to low meaningfulness of stimulus members under 100% OSRM, 25% ORM and, particularly, 25% OSM.

Acquisition was faster for high than for low meaningfulness of response members under 100% OSRM and 25% ORM and the opposite under 25% OSM. Neither this pattern nor the differences in orders of the combinations between the two former percentages and the latter percentage were sufficient to produce significant interactions of percentages and meaningfulness of response members or of percentages and both stimulus variables.

DISCUSSION

The faster acquisition under 100% OSRM than under 25% ORM was consistent with findings in Experiments 1, 2, and 3 and in earlier experiments (Goss, Nodine, Gregory, Taub, & Kennedy, 1962) with unmixed lists administered both to subjects individually and in groups. %OSM had not been a variable in Experiments 1, 2, and 3 or in the earlier experiments. Thus, the faster acquisition under 100% OSRM and 25% ORM than under 25% OSM has no precedent within these particular series of experiments. However, Mandler (Cofer & Musgrave, 1963, p. 156) has described an experiment by Fletcher and Tulving in which 50% ORM led to faster acquisition than 50% OSM. The former was referred to as stimulus familiarization and the latter as response familiarization. Schulz (Postman & Underwood, 1963, p. 213) is reported as describing experiments involving %ORM and %OSM but which variation produced the faster acquisition was not stated.

As mentioned above, 25% ORM and 25% OSM can be viewed, respectively, as providing opportunity for familiarization of and discrimination among stimulus members and among response members. That the shorter duration of response members alone than of stimulus members alone did not occasion differential opportunity for familiarization and discrimination is assumed. On this assumption, the results of Experiment 12 and those reported for Fletcher and Tulving suggest that familiarization of and discrimination among stimulus members had greater weight than did such changes among response members. Such an interpretation does not seem in accord with the generally greater potency of meaningfulness of response members. Nor is this outcome consistent with the suggestion that any facilitative effects which might be occasioned by familiarization are more likely with familiarization of response members than of stimulus members.

Conceivably some factor or factors other than or in addition to familiarization of and discrimination among stimulus and among response members was involved. Schulz is reported as mentioning rehearsal (Postman & Underwood). Rehearsal of associations between stimuli produced by recognition responses to stimulus members and to response members might have occurred with greater ease and frequency under 25% ORM than under 25% OSM. When the Schulz data are reported in detail, the issue may be resolved. Whatever the basis for the superiority of 25% ORM to 25% OSM in Experiment 12 and in Fletcher and Tulving's experiment, the results of Experiment 12 show that %OSM as well as %ORM is a variable of significance in acquisition of PA lists.

The stimulus variables were of importance in Experiment 12 primarily as means of exploring possible differences in effects of %ORM and %OSM among combinations of meaningfulness of stimulus and response members.

A significant interaction of percentages with meaningfulness of stimulus members was obtained but the interactions of percentages with meaningfulness of response members and with both stimulus variables were not significant. The former interaction was due to a greater difference in rate or acquisition with stimulus members of high or low meaningfulness under 25% OSM than under 100% OSRM or 25% ORM. With rehearsal controlled, Schulz is reported as obtaining a significant interaction of %ORM and pronunciability but not of %OSM and pronunciability. Control of rehearsal may account for the apparent lack of accord between his results and those of Experiment 12.

The slightly faster acquisition with the low-low than with the high-low combination was in contrast to the faster learning with the high-low than with the low-low combination with four-unit lists under the anticipation format in Experiment 9. With only one pair representing each combination, and only 20 and 12 subjects in each cell in Experiments 12 and 9, respectively, these discrepancies may be due to chance factors.

Despite the nonsignificant interaction of percentages, meaningfulness of stimulus members, and meaningfulness of response members, meaningfulness of response members was seemingly more potent than meaningfulness of stimulus members under 100% OSRM and 25% ORM, and meaningfulness of stimulus members more potent than meaningfulness of response members under 25% OSM. The reversal in potency under 25% OSM relative to 100% OSRM and 25% ORM was sufficient to produce the significantly greater potency across percentages of meaningfulness of stimulus members than of meaningfulness of response members.

SUMMARY

Mixed lists of four units with one unit representing each combination of low or high meaningfulness of stimulus and response members were acquired under schedules of 100% occurrence of both stimulus and response members (100% OSRM), 25% ORM, and 25% OSM. The lists were presented by means of a memory drum to subjects individually until they reached a criterion of one perfect trial for the entire lists plus four trials or for 32 trials.

Acquisition of pairs representing each combination and of entire lists was increasingly more rapid under 25% OSM, 25% ORM and 100% OSRM. The significant interaction of percentages and meaningfulness of stimulus members reflected a greater difference between stimulus members of low and high meaningfulness under 25% OSM than under 100% OSRM and 25% ORM. None of the other interactions involving percentages and stimulus variables was significant.

References

Adams, H. E., & Vidulich, R. N. Dogmatism and belief congruence in paired-associate learning. *Psychol. Rep.*, 1962, **10**, 91-94.

Allport, G. W., Vernon, P. E., & Lindzey, G. *A study of values.* Boston: Houghton, Mifflin, 1951.

Anderson, N. S. Associations to various things. Paper read at New York meeting of Psychonomic Society, 1961.

Anisfeld, M. A comment on "The role of grapheme-phoneme correspondence in the perception of words." *Amer. J. Psychol.*, 1964, **77**, 320-321.

Anisfeld, M., & Lambert, W. E. When are pleasant words learned faster than unpleasant words? Department of Social Relations, Harvard University, and Department of Psychology, McGill University, 1964.

Archer, E. J. A re-evaluation of the meaningfulness of all possible CVC trigrams. *Psychol. Monogr.*, 1960, **74**, Whole No. 497.

Archer, E. J. Some comments on Noble's "Measurement of association value (*a*), etc. . . . ." *Psychol. Rep.*, 1961, **9**, 679-680.

Arnoult, M. D. Familiarity and recognition of nonsense shapes. *J. exp. Psychol.*, 1956, **51**, 269-276.

Arnoult, M. D. Stimulus predifferentiation: some generalizations and hypotheses. *Psychol. Bull.*, 1957, **54**, 339-350.

Arnoult, M. D. Prediction of perceptual responses from structural characteristics of the stimulus. *Percept. mot. Skills*, 1960, **11**, 261-268.

Asch, S. E., & Lindner, M. A note on "strength of association." *J. Psychol.*, 1963, **55**, 199-209.

Atkins, R. E. An analysis of the phonetic elements in a basal reading vocabulary. *Elementary Sch. J.*, 1926, **26**, 595-606.

Attneave, F. A method of graded dichotomies for the scaling of judgments. *Psychol. Rev.*, 1949, **56**, 334-340.

Attneave, F. Ability to verbalize similarities among concepts and among visual forms. *Amer. Psychologist*, 1951, **6**, 270 (Abstract.)

Attneave, F. Psychological probability as a function of experienced frequency. *J. exp. Psychol.*, 1953, **46**, 81-86.

Attneave, F. *Applications of information theory to psychology.* New York: Holt, 1959.

Baddelay, A. D. Stimulus-response compatibility in the paired-associate learning of nonsense syllables. *Nature*, 1961a, **191**, 1327-1328.

Baddelay, A. D. Sequential dependencies among letters and the learning of nonsense syllables. Paper presented at the London meeting of the Experimental Psychology Society, 1961b.

Baddelay, A. D., Conrad, R., & Thomson, W. E. Letter structure of the English language. *Nature*, 1960, **186**, 414-416.

Bailey, J. H., & Jeffrey, W. E. Response strength and association value in stimulus prediffer-entiation. *Psychol. Rep.*, 1958, **4**, 715-721.

Barclay, A. The influence of variations in paradigms and associative values on mediated transfer in paired-associates learning. Department of Psychology, St. Louis University. Progress Report on Grant MH 06957-01, 1964.

Battig, W. F. Scaled difficulty of nonsense-syllable pairs consisting of syllables of equal association value. *Psychol. Rep.*, 1959, **5**, 126.

Battig, W. F. Comparison of two methods of scaling nonsense-syllable pairs for ease of learning. *Psychol. Rep.*, 1960, **6**, 363-366.

Battig, W. F. Interrelationships between measures of association and structural character-istics of nonsense shapes. *Percept. mot. Skills*, 1962, **14**, 3-6.

Battig, W. F. Organizational processes in complex learning. Department of Psychology, University of Virginia, Final Progress Report on M-05769-02, 1964.

Battig, W. F., & Brackett, H. R. Comparison of anticipation and recall methods in paired-associate learning. *Psychol. Rep.*, 1961, **9**, 59-65.

Battig, W. F., & Brackett, H. R. Transfer from verbal-discrimination to paired-associate learning: II. Effects of intralist similarity, method, and percentage occurrence of response members. *J. exp. Psychol.*, 1963, **65**, 507-514.

Battig, W. F., & Spera, A. J. Rated association values of numbers from 0-100. *J. verb. Learn. verb. Behav.*, 1962, **1**, 200-202.

Battig, W. F., Brown, S. C., & Nelson, D. Constant vs. varied serial order in paired-associate learning. Department of Psychology, University of Virginia. Report of research under Cooperative Research Program of the U. S. Office of Education and under Grant M-5769 from the National Institute of Mental Health, 1962.

Battig, W. F., Williams, J. M., & Williams, J. G. Transfer from verbal discrimination to paired-associate learning. *J. exp. Psychol.*, 1962, **63**, 258-268.

Beck, R. C., Phillips, W. R., & Bloodsworth, W. D. Associative reaction time as a function of association value of nonsense syllable stimuli. *Psychol. Rep.*, 1962, **10**, 517-518.

Beecroft, R. S. Verbal learning and retention as a function of the number of competing associations. *J. exp. Psychol.*, 1956, **51**, 216-221.

Benedetti, D. T. The stratification of words in cognitive organization. *J. gen. Psychol.*, 1958, **58**, 249-258.

Besch, N. F. Paired-associates learning as a function of anxiety level and shock. *J. Pers.*, 1959, **27**, 116-124.

Besch, N. F. Pre-training effects in paired-associate learning. Paper presented at New York meeting of the Psychonomic Society, 1961.

Besch, N. F., Thompson, V. E., & Wetzel, A. B. Studies in associative interference. *J. exp. Psychol.*, 1962, **63**, 342-352.

Biase, V., & Marshall, G. R. Single response free word association norms to 122 abstract words or phrases. Department of Psychology, Adelphi College and Bell Telephone Laboratories, 1964.

Blanchard, R. J. The effects of response familiarization on paired-associate learning. Un-published Ph.D. dissertation, State University of Iowa, 1962.

Bloomer, R. H. Stimulus properties of words: variables related to spelling difficulty. Un-published Ph.D. dissertation, University of Southern California, 1959.

Bourne, C. P., & Ford, D. F. A study of the statistics of letters in English words. *Information & Control*, 1961, **4**, 48-67.

Bousfield, W. A. The problem of meaning in verbal learning. In C. N. Cofer (Ed.), *Verbal learning and verbal behavior*. New York: McGraw-Hill, 1961.

Bousfield, W. A., & Cowan, T. M. Immediate memory spans for CVC trigrams. *J. gen. Psychol.*, 1964, **70**, 283-293.

Bousfield, W. A., & Samborski, G. The relationship between strength of values and the meaningfulness of value words. *J. Pers.*, 1955, **23**, 375-380.

Bousfield, W. A., Whitmarsh, G. A., & Berkowitz, H. Partial response identities in associative clustering. *J. gen. Psychol.*, 1960, **63**, 233-238.

Bousfield, W. A., Whitmarsh, G. A., & Danick, J. J. Partial response identities in verbal generalization. *Psychol. Rep.*, 1958, **4**, 703-713.

Bousfield, W. A., Cohen, B. H., Whitmarsh, G. A., & Kincaid, W. D. The Connecticut free associational norms. Department of Psychology, University of Connecticut. Tech. Rep. No. 35, Contract Nonr 631(00), 1961.

Bower, G., & Trabasso, T. Concept identification. In R. C. Atkinson (Ed.), *Studies in mathematical psychology*. Stanford: Stanford Univer. Press, 1964.

Bower, H. Factors influencing visual imagery for letter groups. *Amer. J. Psychol.*, 1932, **44**, 775-779.

Brener, R. An experimental investigation of memory span. *J. exp. Psychol.*, 1940, **26**, 467-482.

Brody, N. Anxiety and the variability of word associates. *J. abnorm. soc. Psychol.*, 1964, **68**, 331-334.

Brown, S. C., Battig, W. F., & Pearlstein, R. Effect of successive addition of stimulus elements on paired-associate learning. Department of Psychology, University of Virginia, Research Grants M-05769-02 and HD-00929-03, 1964.

Brown, W. P. *Conceptions of perceptual defense*. Cambridge: Cambridge Univer. Press, 1961.

Buchanan, M. A. *A graded Spanish word book*. Toronto: Univer. Toronto Press, 1927.

Buchwald, A. M. The generality of norms of word association. *Amer. J. Psychol.*, 1957, **70**, 233-237.

Bugelski, B. R. Presentation time, total time, and mediation in paired-associate learning. *J. exp. Psychol.*, 1962, **63**, 409-412.

Bummer, B., & Rosenthal, R. Anxiety level and the retention of neutral and affectively toned verbal material. *J. proj. Tech.*, 1963, **27**, 47-50.

Busemann, A. Lernen und Behalten: Beiträge zur Psychologie des Gedächtnisses. *Z. f angew. Psychol.*, 1911, **5**, 211-275.

Buss, A. *The psychology of aggression*. New York: Wiley, 1961.

Carroll, J. B. Transitional probabilities of English phonemes. Progress Report on Project 52. School of Education, Harvard University, 1952.

Carroll, J. B. The assessment of phoneme cluster frequencies. *Language*, 1958, **34**, 267-278.

Carroll, J. B., & Burke, B. L. Parameters of paired-associate verbal learning: length of list, meaningfulness, rate of presentation, and ability. *J. exp. Psychol.*, in press.

Carroll, J. B., & Sapon, S. M. *The modern language aptitude test*. New York: Psychological Corp., 1958.

Cason, H. Association between the familiar and unfamiliar. *J. exp. Psychol.*, 1933, **16**, 295-305.

Cassen, N., & Kausler, D. H. Supplementary report: effects of stimulus association value and exposure duration on R-S learning. *J. exp. Psychol.*, 1962, **64**, 94.

Castaneda, A., Fahel, L. S., & Odom, R. Associative characteristics of sixty-three adjectives and their relation to verbal paired-associate learning in children. *Child Develpm.*, 1961, **32**, 297-304.

Chang, J. J., & Shepard, R. N. Meaningfulness in classification learning with pronounceable trigrams. *J. verb. Learn. verb. Behav.*, 1964, **3**, 85-90.

Chapman, F. L., & Gilbert, L. C. A study of the influence of familiarity with English words upon the learning of the foreign language equivalents. *J. educ. Psychol.*, 1937, **28**, 621-628.

Cieutat, V. J. Supplementary report: stimulus and response meaningfulness (m') in paired-associate learning by hospitalized mental patients. *J. exp. Psychol.*, 1959, **58**, 490.

Cieutat, V. J. Differential familiarity with stimulus and response in paired-associate learning. *Percept. mot. Skills*, 1960a, **11**, 269-275.

Cieutat, V. J. Group paired-associate learning: recognition vs. recall as a criterion of learning. *Percept. mot. Skills*, 1960b, **11**, 305-308.

Cieutat, V. J. Group paired-associate learning: stimulus vs. response meaningfulness. *Percept. mot. Skills*, 1961, **12**, 327-330.

Cieutat, V. J. Stability of meaningfulness (m) values for verbal material. *Percept. mot. Skills*, 1962, **14**, 398.

Cieutat, V. J. Association indices for 446 randomly selected English monosyllables, bisyllables, and trisyllables. *J. verb. Learn. verb. Behav.*, 1963, **2**, 176-185.

Cieutat, V. J., & Cieutat, L. G. Meaningfulness (m), verbal ability, and social adjustment in paired-associate learning. *Percept. mot. Skills*, 1961, **12**, 171-174.

Cieutat, V. J., Stockwell, F. E., & Noble, C. E. The interaction of ability and amount of practice with stimulus and response meaningfulness (m, m') in paired-associate learning. *J. exp. Psychol.*, 1958, **56**, 193-202.

Clement, D. E. Uncertainty and latency of verbal naming responses as correlates of pattern goodness. *J. verb. Learn. verb. Behav.*, 1964, **3**, 150-157.

Cliff, N. Adverbs as multipliers. *Psychol. Rev.*, 1959, **66**, 27-44.

Cochran, S. W., & Wickens, D. D. Supplementary report: rated association values of numbers from 0–100. *J. verb. Learn. verb. Behav.*, 1963a, **2**, 373-374.

Cochran, S. W., & Wickens, D. D. Prediction of learning by group-rated association values versus individual-rated association values. *J. verb. Learn. verb. Behav.*, 1963b, **2**, 509-512.

Cofer, C. N. Associative commonality and rated similarity of certain words from Haagen's list. *Psychol. Rep.*, 1957, **3**, 603-606.

Cofer, C. N. Comparison of word associations obtained by the methods of discrete single words and continued association. *Psychol. Rep.*, 1958, **4**, 507-510.

Cofer, C. N. A repetition and extension of Glanzer's comparison of content and function words as parts of response triplets in paired associate learning. Paper presented at Niagara Falls, Ontario meeting of the Psychonomic Society, 1964.

Cofer, C. N., & Musgrave, B. S. (Eds.) *Verbal behavior and learning: problems and processes.* New York: McGraw-Hill, 1963.

Cofer, C. N., & Shevitz, R. Word-association as a function of word-frequency. *Amer. J. Psychol.*, 1952, **65**, 75-79.

Cohen, B. H., Bousfield, W. A., & Whitmarsh, G. A. Cultural norms for verbal items in 43 categories. Department of Psychology, University of Connecticut. Tech. Rep. No. 22, Contract Nonr-631(00), 1957.

Cohen, J. C., & Musgrave, B. S. Effect of meaningfulness on cue selection in verbal paired-associate learning. *J. exp. Psychol.*, 1964a, **68**, 284-291.

Cohen, J. C., & Musgrave, B. S. Effects of formal similarity on cue selection in verbal paired-associate learning. Paper presented at the Niagara Falls meeting of the Psychonomic Society, 1964b.

Coleman, E. B. The association hierarchy as an indicator of extraexperimental interference. *J. verb. Learn. verb. Behav.*, 1963, **2**, 417-421.

Coleman, E. B. Generalizing to a language population. *Psychol. Rep.*, 1964, **14**, 219-226.

Conrad, R. Practice, familiarity and reading rate for words and nonsense syllables. *Quart. J. exp. Psychol.*, 1962, **14**, 71-76.

Cook, J. O. Supplementary report: processes underlying learning a single paired-associate item. *J. exp. Psychol.*, 1958, **56**, 455.

Cook, J. O. Response analysis in paired-associate learning experiments. In A. A. Lumsdaine (Ed.), *Student response in programmed learning*. Washington, D. C.: National Academy of Sciences-National Research Council, 1962.

Cook, J. O., & Brown, J. E. Familiarity and novelty of stimulus and response terms in paired-associate learning. *Psychol. Rep.*, 1963, **12**, 535-545.

Cook, J. O., & Kendler, T. S. A theoretical model to explain some paired-associate learning data. In G. Finch & F. Cameron (Eds.), *Symposium on Air Force human engineering, personnel, and training research*. Washington, D. C.: National Academy of Sciences-National Research Council, 1956.

Cook, J. O., & Spitzer, M. E. Supplementary report: prompting versus confirmation in paired-associate learning. *J. exp. Psychol.*, 1960, **59**, 275-276.

Coombs, C. H. An application of a nonmetric model for multidimensional analysis of similarities. *Psychol. Rep.*, 1958, 4, 511-518.

Cooper, C. J. Some relationships between paired-associates learning and foreign-language aptitude. *J. educ. Psychol.*, 1964, **55**, 132-138.

Crawford, J. L., & Vanderplas, J. M. An experiment on the mediation of transfer in paired-associate learning. *J. Psychol.*, 1959, **47**, 87-98.

Crothers, E. J. Paired-associate learning with compound responses. *J. verb. Learn. verb. Behav.*, 1962, **1**, 66-70.

Dallett, K. M. Implicit mediators in paired-associate learning. *J. verb. Learn. verb. Behav.*, 1964, **3**, 209-214.

DeBold, R. C. Effect of forced paired-comparison on paired-associate learning and meaningfulness. *Psychol. Rep.*, 1964, **14**, 871-878.

Deese, J. Free association frequencies to 444 stimulus words. Purple-dittoed report, The Johns Hopkins University, 1959.

Deese, J. On the structure of associative meaning. *Psychol. Rev.*, 1962, **69**, 161-175.

Dewey, G. *Relativ frequency of English speech sounds*. Cambridge: Harvard Univer. Press, 1923.

Dietze, D. The facilitating effect of words on discrimination and generalization. *J. exp. Psychol.*, 1955, **50**, 255-260.

Dietze, D. A. The effects of sequence and similarity of responses on concept formation. Unpublished Ph.D. dissertation, University of Washington, 1959.

DiMascio, A. Learning characteristics of nonsense syllables: a function of letter frequency. *Psychol. Rep.*, 1959, **5**, 585-591.

Dixon, T. R., & Dixon, J. F. The impression value of verbs. *J. verb. Learn. verb. Behav.*, 1964, **3**, 161-165.

Doehring, D. C. Value, frequency, and practice in visual word recognition. *Psychol. Rec.*, 1962, **12**, 209-216.

Dollard, J., & Miller, N. E. *Personality and psychotherapy*. New York: McGraw-Hill, 1950.

Duncan, C. P. Letter response hierarchies within and among subjects. *Psychol. Rep.*, 1960, **6**, 291-297.

Dunlap, K. *List of 43,000 dissyllable words and paralogs*. Washington, D.C.: National Research Council, 1933.

Eaton, H. S. *An English-French-German-Spanish word frequency dictionary*. New York: Dover, 1940.

Elliott, L. L., & Tannenbaum, P. H. Factor-structure of semantic differential responses to visual forms and prediction of factor-scores from structural characteristics of the stimulus-shapes. *Amer. J. Psychol.*, 1963, **76**, 589-597.

Ellis, H. C., & Bessemer, D. W. Associative scaling of random tactual stimuli. *Percept. mot. Skills*, 1962, **14**, 89-90.

Epstein, S., & Levitt, H. The influence of hunger on the learning and recall of food related words. *J. abnorm. soc. Psychol.*, 1962, **64**, 130-135.

Epstein, W. Backward association as a function of meaningfulness. *J. gen. Psychol.*, 1962, **67**, 11-20.

Epstein, W. The effect of stimulus and response meaningfulness when response availability is equated. *J. verb. Learn. verb. Behav.*, 1963, **2**, 242-249.

Epstein, W., & Streib, R. The effect of stimulus meaningfulness and response meaningfulness in the absence of response learning. *J. verb. Learn. verb. Behav.*, 1962, **1**, 105-108.

Epstein, W., Rock, I., & Zuckerman, C. B. Meaning and familiarity in verbal learning. *Psychol. Monogr.*, 1960, **74**, Whole No. 491.

Ervin, S. M., & Landar, H. Navaho word associations. *Amer. J. Psychol.*, 1963, **76**, 49-57.

Estes, W. K. Learning theory and the new "mental chemistry." *Psychol. Rev.*, 1960, **67**, 207-223.

Estes, W. K., Hopkins, B. L., & Crothers, E. J. All-or-none and conservation effects in the learning and retention of paired-associates. *J. exp. Psychol.*, 1960, **60**, 329-339.

Federer, W. T. *Experimental design: theory and application.* New York: Macmillan, 1955.

Feldman, M. J., Lang, P. J., & Levine, B. J. Word association disturbance, learning, and retention. *Psychol. Rep.*, 1959, **5**, 607-608.

Feldman, S. M., & Underwood, B. J. Stimulus recall following paired-associate verbal learning. *J. exp. Psychol.*, 1957, **53**, 11-15.

Flavell, J. H. Abstract thinking and social behavior in schizophrenia. *J. abnorm. soc. Psychol.*, 1956, **52**, 208-211.

Flavell, J. H. Meaning and meaning similarity: I. A theoretical reassessment. *J. gen. Psychol.*, 1961a, **64**, 307-319.

Flavell, J. H. Meaning and meaning similarity: II. The semantic differential and co-occurrence as predictors of judged similarity in meaning. *J. gen. Psychol.*, 1961b, **64**, 321-335.

Flavell, J. H., & Flavell, E. R. One determinant of judged semantic and associative connections between words. *J. exp. Psychol.*, 1959, **58**, 159-165.

Flavell, J. H., & Johnson, B. A. Meaning and meaning similarity: III. Latency and number of similarities as predictors of judged similarity in meaning. *J. gen. Psychol.*, 1961, **64**, 337-348.

Flavell, J. H., & Stedman, D. J. A developmental study of judgments of semantic similarity. *J. genet. Psychol.*, 1961, **98**, 279-293.

Foster, H. W. Stimulus predifferentiation in transfer of training. Unpublished Ph.D. dissertation, University of Michigan, 1953.

Fowler, M. Herdan's statistical parameter and the frequency of English phonemes. In E. Pulgram (Ed.), *Studies presented to Joshua Whatmough on his sixtieth birthday.* The Hague: Mouton, 1957.

Freedman, J. L., & Mednick, S. A. Ease of attainment of concepts as a function of response dominance variance. *J. exp. Psychol.*, 1958, **55**, 463-466.

French, N. R., Carter, C. W., Jr., & Koenig, W., Jr. The words and sounds of telephone conversation. *Bell System tech. J.*, 1930, **9**, 290-324.

Gagné, R. M. The effect of sequence of presentation of similar items on the learning of paired associates. *J. exp. Psychol.*, 1950, **40**, 61-73.

Gannon, D. R., & Noble, C. E. Familiarization (*n*) as a stimulus factor in paired-associate verbal learning. *J. exp. Psychol.*, 1961, **62**, 14-23.

Garner, W. R., & Clement, D. E. Goodness of pattern and pattern uncertainty. *J. verb. Learn. verb. Behav.*, 1963, **2**, 446-452.

Garskof, B. E., & Houston, J. P. Measurement of verbal relatedness: an idiographic approach. *Psychol. Rev.*, 1963, **70**, 277-288.

Garskof, B., Houston, J. P., & Ehrlich, N. J. Inter- and intra-hierarchical verbal relatedness. *J. verb. Learn. verb. Behav.*, 1963, **2**, 229-233.

Gerjuoy, I. R. Discrimination learning as a function of the similarity of the stimulus names. Unpublished Ph.D. dissertation, State University of Iowa, 1953.

Gibson, E. J. A systematic application of the concepts of generalization and differentiation to verbal learning. *Psychol. Rev.*, 1940, **47**, 196-229.

Gibson, E. J. Retroactive inhibition as a function of degree of generalization between tasks. *J. exp. Psychol.*, 1941, **28**, 93-115.

Gibson, E. J. Intra-list generalization as a factor in verbal learning. *J. exp. Psychol.*, 1942, **30**, 185-200.

Gibson, E. J. On the perception of words. *Amer. J. Psychol.*, 1964, **77**, 667-669.

Gibson, E. J., Osser, H., & Pick, A. D. A study of the development of grapheme-phoneme correspondence. *J. verb. Learn. verb. Behav.*, 1963, **2**, 142-146.

Gibson, E. J., Bishop, C. H., Schiff, W., & Smith, J. Comparison of meaningfulness and pronunciability as grouping principles of the perception and retention of verbal material. *J. exp. Psychol.*, 1964, **67**, 173-182.

Gibson, E. J., Pick, A., Osser, H., & Hammond, M. The role of grapheme-phoneme correspondence in the perception of words. *Amer. J. Psychol.*, 1962, **75**, 554-570.

Glanzer, M. Grammatical category: a rote learning and word association analysis. *J. verb. Learn. verb. Behav.*, 1962, **1**, 31-41.

Glaze, J. A. The association value of non-sense syllables. *J. genet. Psychol.*, 1928, **35**, 255-269.

Goldstein, A. G. Spatial orientation as a factor in eliciting associative responses to random shapes. *Percept. mot. Skills*, 1961, **12**, 15-25.

Goss, A. E. A stimulus-response analysis of the interactions of cue-producing and instrumental responses. *Psychol. Rev.*, 1955. **62**, 20-31.

Goss, A. E. Comments on Professor Noble's paper. In C. N. Cofer & B. S. Musgrave (Eds.), *Verbal behavior and learning: problems and processes.* New York: McGraw-Hill, 1963.

Goss, A. E. Verbal mediation. *Psychol. Rec.*, 1964, **14**, 363-382.

Goss, A. E., & Cobb, N. J. Formation, maintenance, generalization and retention of response hierarchies. *J. exp. Psychol.*, in press.

Goss, A. E., & Greenfeld, N. Transfer to a motor task as influenced by conditions and degree of prior discrimination training. *J. exp. Psychol.*, 1958, **55**, 258-269.

Goss, A. E., Nodine, C. F., & Levitt, H. Stimulus characteristics and percentages of occurrence of response members in paired-associates learning under group administration. Paper presented at the New York meeting of the Psychonomic Society, 1961.

Goss, A. E., Nodine, C. F., Gregory, B. N., Taub, H. A., & Kennedy, K. E. Stimulus characteristics and percentage of occurrence of response members in paired-associates learning. *Psychol. Monogr.*, 1962, **76**, Whole No. 531.

Gougenheim, G., Michea, R., Rivenc, P., & Sauvageot, A. *L'Elaboration du Français élémentaire.* Paris: Didier, 1956.

Haagen, C. H., Synonymity, vividness, familiarity and association value ratings of 400 pairs of common adjectives. *J. Psychol.*, 1949, **27**, 453-463.

Hakes, D. T. Familiarization (n) as a stimulus factor in paired-associate verbal learning: a replication. Paper presented at the Chicago meeting of the Midwestern Psychological Association, 1961a.

Hakes, D. T. The role of stimulus and response familiarization in paired-associate learning. Unpublished Ph.D. dissertation, University of Minnesota, 1961b.

Haraguchi, M. Transfer in re-paired lists. Unpublished B.A. thesis, Kyoto University, 1957.

Harleston, B. W. Task difficulty, anxiety level, and ability level as factors affecting performance in a verbal learning situation. *J. Psychol.*, 1963, **55**, 165-168.

Harleston, B. W. & Cunningham, S. M. Task difficulty and anxiety level as factors affecting performance in a verbal learning situation. *J. Psychol.*, 1961, **52**, 77-86.

Haspiel, G. S., & Bloomer, R. H. Maximum auditory perception (MAP) word list. *JSHD*, 1961, **26**, 156-163.

Haun, K. W. Measures of association and verbal learning. *Psychol. Rep.*, 1960, **7**, 451-460.

Havens, L. L., & Foote, W. E. The effect of competition on visual duration threshold and its independence of stimulus frequency. *J. exp. Psychol.*, 1963, **65**, 6-11.

Hawker, J. R. The influence of training procedure and other task variables in paired-associate learning. *J. verb. Learn. verb. Behav.*, 1964, **3**, 70-76.

Hayden, R. E. The relative frequency of phonemes in General-American English. *Word*, 1956, **6**, 217-223.

Henmon, V. A. C. A French word book based on a count of 400,000 running words. *Univer. Wisconsin Bur. Ed. Res. Bull.*, 1924.

Herdan, G. *Language as choice and chance.* Groningen: Noordhoff, 1956.

Higa, M. Interference effects of intralist word relatedness in verbal learning. *J. verb. Learn. verb. Behav.*, 1963, **2**, 170-175.

Hilgard, E. R. Methods and procedures in the study of learning. In S. S. Stevens (Ed.), *Handbook of experimental psychology.* New York: Wiley, 1951.

Hill, F. A., & Wickens, D. D. The effect of stimulus compounding in paired-associate learning. *J. verb. Learn. verb. Behav.*, 1962, **1**, 144-151.

Holzberg, J. D., Bursten, B., & Santiccioli, A. The reporting of aggression as an indication of aggressive tension. *J. abnorm. soc. Psychol.*, 1955, **50**, 12-18.

Horn, E. A basic writing vocabulary. *Univer. Iowa Monogr. in Educ.*, Series 1, No. 4, 1926.

Horowitz, A. E. The effects of variations in linguistic structure on the learning of miniature linguistic systems. Unpublished Ph.D. dissertation, Harvard University, 1955.

Horowitz, L. M. Associative matching and intralist similarity. *Psychol. Rep.*, 1962, **10**, 751-757.

Horowitz, L. M., & Larsen, S. R. Response interference in paired-associate learning. *J. exp. Psychol.*, 1963, **65**, 225-232.

Horowitz, L. M., Lippman, L. G., Norman, S. A., & McConkie, G. W. Compound stimuli in paired-associate learning. *J. exp. Psychol.*, 1964, **67**, 132-141.

Horton, D. The effects of meaningfulness, awareness, and type of design in verbal mediation. *J. verb. Learn. verb. Behav.*, 1964, **3**, 187-194.

Houston, J. P., & Garskof, B. E. Correlation between word association strength and associative overlap. *Psychol. Rep.*, 1963, **13**, 866.

Howe, E. S. Probabilistic adverbial qualifications of adjectives. *J. verb. Learn. verb. Behav.*, 1963, **1**, 225-242.

Howes, D. On the interpretation of word frequency as a variable affecting speed of recognition. *J. exp. Psychol.*, 1954, **48**, 106-112.

Hull, C. L. The meaningfulness of 320 selected nonsense syllables. *Amer. J. Psychol.*, 1933, **45**, 730-734.

Hultzen, L. S., Allen, J. H. D., Jr., & Miron, M. S. *Tables of transitional frequencies of English phonemes.* Urbana: Univer. Illinois Press, 1964.

Hunt, R. G. Meaningfulness and articulation of stimulus and response in paired-associate learning and stimulus recall. *J. exp. Psychol.*, 1959, **57**, 262-267.

l'Institut Pédagogique National. *Le Français fondamental* (1er degré). Paris, 1959a.

l'Institut Pédagogique National. *Le Français fondamental* (2e degré). Paris, 1959b.

Iscoe, I., & Semler, I. J. Paired-associate learning in normal and mentally retarded children as a function of four experimental conditions. *J. comp. physiol. Psychol.*, 1964, **57**, 387-392.

Jacobs, A. Formation of new associations to words selected on the basis of reaction-time-GSR combinations. *J. abnorm. soc. Psychol.*, 1955, **51**, 371-377.

Jantz, E. M., & Underwood, B. J. R-S learning as a function of meaningfulness and degree of S-R learning. *J. exp. Psychol.*, 1958, **56**, 174-179.

Jenkins, J. J. Degree of polarization and scores on the principal factors for concepts in the Semantic Atlas study. *Amer. J. Psychol.*, 1960, **73**, 274-279.

Jenkins, J. J. Mediated associations: paradigms and situations. In C. N. Cofer & B. S. Musgrave (Eds.), *Verbal behavior and learning: problems and processes.* New York: McGraw-Hill, 1963a.

Jenkins, J. J. Stimulus "factionation" in paired-associate learning. *Psychol. Rep.*, 1963b, **13**, 409-410.

Jenkins, J. J. The 1952 word association norms. In L. Postman (Ed.), *Norms of word associations.* New York: Academic Press, in press.

Jenkins, J. J., & Bailey, V. B. Cue selection and mediated transfer in paired-associate learning. *J. exp. Psychol.*, 1964, **67**, 101-102.

Jenkins, J. J., & Russell, W. A. Basic studies on individual and group behavior. Department of Psychology, University of Minnesota, Annual Rech. Rep., Contract N8 onr-66216, 1956.

Jenkins, J. J., & Russell, W. A. Systematic changes in word association norms: 1910-1952. *J. abnorm. soc. Psychol.*, 1960, **60**, 293-304.

Jenkins, J. J., Russell, W. A., & Suci, G. J. An atlas of semantic profiles for 360 words. *Amer. J. Psychol.*, 1958a, **71**, 688-699.

Jenkins, J. J., Russell, W. A., & Suci, G. J. A table of distances for the Semantic Atlas. Department of Psychology, University of Minnesota, Tech. Rep. No. 20, Contract N8 onr-66216, 1958b.

Jenkins, J. J., Russell, W. A., & Suci, G. J. A table of distances for the Semantic Atlas. *Amer. J. Psychol.*, 1959, **72**, 623-625.

Jenkins, P. M., & Cofer, C. N. An exploratory study of discrete free association to compound verbal stimuli. *Psychol. Rep.*, 1957, **3**, 599-602.

Jensen, A. R., & Rohwer, W. D., Jr. Verbal mediation in paired-associate and serial learning. *J. verb. Learn. verb. Behav.*, 1963a, **1**, 346-352.

Jensen, A. R., & Rohwer, W. D. The effect of verbal mediation on the learning and retention of paired-associates by retarded adults. *Amer. J. ment. Defic.*, 1963b, **68**, 80-84.

Johnson, P. E. Associative meaning of concepts in physics. *J. educ. Psychol.*, 1964, **55**, 84-88.

Johnson, R. C. The meaningfulness of eighty English words. *Psychol. Rep.*, 1961, **9**, 431.

Johnson, R. C. Reanalysis of "Meaningfulness and Verbal Learning." *Psychol. Rev.*, 1962, **69**, 233-238.

Johnson, R. C., & Fehmi, L. G. Aural-oral and written word frequency as related to rate of learning stimulus materials. *J. gen. Psychol.*, 1963, **69**, 125-129.

Johnson, R. C., & Zara, R. C. The influence of word meaningfulness on visual duration thresholds at various frequency levels. *J. gen. Psychol.*, 1964, **70**, 235-239.

Johnson, R. C., Frincke, G., & Martin, L. Meaningfulness, frequency, and affective character of words as related to visual duration threshold. *Canad. J. Psychol.*, 1961, **15**, 199-204.

Johnson, R. C., Thomson, C. W., & Frincke, G. Word values, word frequency, and visual duration thresholds. *Psychol. Rev.*, 1960, **67**, 332-342.

Johnson, R. C., Weiss, R. L., & Zelhart, P. F. Similarities and differences between normal and psychotic subjects in responses to verbal stimuli. *J. abnorm. soc. Psychol.*, 1964, **68**, 221-226.

Johnson, R. E. Meaningfulness and retention of a single paired-associate, *Psychol. Rep.*, 1964, **14**, 951-957.

Jung, J. Effects of response meaningfulness (*m*) on transfer of training under two different paradigms. *J. exp. Psychol.*, 1963, **65**, 377-384.

Kanarick, A. F. A study of the occurrence and distribution of substitution errors in paired-associate learning. Unpublished M.S. thesis, North Carolina State, 1963.

Kanungo, R., & Lambert, W. E. Paired-associate learning as a function of stimulus and response satiation. *Brit. J. Psychol.*, 1963, **54**, 135-144.

Kanungo, R. N., Lambert, W. E., & Mauer, S. M. Semantic satiation and paired-associate learning. *J. exp. Psychol.*, 1962, **64**, 600-607.

Karen, R. L. Recognition as a function of meaningfulness and intention to learn. *Amer. J. Psychol.*, 1956, **69**, 650-652.

Karwoski, T. F., & Berthold, F., Jr. Psychological studies in semantics: II. Reliability of free association tests. *J. soc. Psychol.*, 1945, **22**, 87-102.

Karwoski, T. F., & Schachter, J. Psychological studies in semantics: III. Reaction times for similarity and for difference. *J. soc. Psychol.*, 1948, **28**, 103-120.

Kazusa, K. The mechanism of generalization and differentiation in paired-associate learning. *Jap. J. Psychol.*, 1961, **32**, 287-294.

Keading, F. W. *Haufigkeitsworterbuch der deutschen Sprache*. Berlin: E. S. Mittler & Sohn, 1898.

Keller, F. S., & Taubman, R. E. Studies in International Morse Code. 2. Errors made in code reception. *J. appl. Psychol.*, 1943, **27**, 504-509.

Kent, G. H., & Rosanoff, A. J. A study of association in insanity. *Amer. J. Insan.*, 1910, **67**, 317-320.

Keppel, G. Word value and verbal learning. *J. verb. Learn. verb. Behav.*, 1963, **1**, 353-356.

Kimble, G. A., & Dufort, R. H. Meaningfulness and isolation as factors in verbal learning. *J. exp. Psychol.*, 1955, **50**, 361-368.

Kjeldergaard, P. M., & Higa, M. Degree of polarization and the recognition value of words selected from the Semantic Atlas. *Psychol. Rep.*, 1962, **11**, 629-630.

Klemmer, E. T. The perception of all patterns produced by a seven-line matrix. *J. exp. Psychol.*, 1961, **61**, 274-282.

Koen, F. Polarization, *m*, and emotionality in words. *J. verb. Learn. verb. Behav.*, 1962, **1**, 183-187.

Kothurkar, V. K. Effect of stimulus-response meaningfulness on paired-associate learning and retention. *J. exp. Psychol.*, 1963, **65**, 305-308.

Kothurkar, V. K. Effect of meaningful relation on learning and retention of paired-associates. *Amer. J. Psychol.*, 1964, **77**, 116-119.

Kott, M. G. Learning and retention of words of sexual and nonsexual meaning. *J. abnorm. soc. Psychol.*, 1955, **50**, 378-382.

Kristofferson, A. B. Word recognition, meaningfulness, and familiarity. *Percept. mot. Skills*, 1957, **7**, 219-220.

Krueger, W. C. F. The relative difficulty of nonsense syllables. *J. exp. Psychol.*, 1934, **17**, 145-153.

Kuraishi, S. On the reproduction of simple thought-configurations by using the method of paired-associates. *Jap. J. Psychol.*, 1937, **12**, 578-602.

L'Abate, L. Manifest anxiety and the learning of syllables with different associative values. *Amer. J. Psychol.*, 1959, **72**, 107-110.

L'Abate, L. Recognition of paired trigrams as a function of associative value and associative strength. *Science*, 1960, **131**, 984-985.

L'Abate, L. Transfer of learning with differences in associative value and in manifest anxiety. *Amer. J. Psychol.*, 1962, **75**, 251-258.

LaBerge, D. L., & Lawrence, D. H. Two methods for generating matrices of forms of graded similarity. *J. Psychol.*, 1957, **43**, 77-100.

Laffal, J. The learning and retention of words wtih association disturbances. *J. abnorm. soc. Psychol.*, 1952, **47**, 454-462.

Laffal, J. Response faults in word association as a function of response entropy. *J. abnorm. soc. Psychol.*, 1955, **50**, 265-270.

Laffal, J., & Feldman, S. The structure of single word and continuous word association. *J. verb. Learn. verb. Behav.*, 1962, **1**, 54-61.

Laffal, J., & Feldman, S. The structure of free speech. *J. verb. Learn. verb. Behav.*, 1963, **2**, 498-503.

Lambert, W. E., & Jakobovits, L. A. Verbal satiation and changes in the intensity of meaning. *J. exp. Psychol.*, 1960, **60**, 376-383.

Ledgerwood, R. A comparison of methods in determining the affective value of words. *Amer. J. Psychol.*, 1932, **44**, 796-797.

Lepley, W. M. An hypothesis concerning the generation and use of synonyms. *J. exp. Psychol.*, 1950, **40**, 527-530.

Levitt, H. The effects of sound intensity (drive) on paired-associates learning. Unpublished Ph.D. dissertation, University of Massachusetts, 1959.

Levitt, H., & Goss, A. E. Stimulus attributes and drive in paired-associate learning. *J. exp. Psychol.*, 1961, **62**, 243-252.

Leytham, G. W. H. Frequency, recency, associative value and tachistoscopic identification. *Brit. J. Psychol.*, 1957, **48**, 216-218.

Lifton, H., & Goss, A. E. Aural-visual transfer of paired-associates learning. *J. gen. Psychol.*, 1962, **66**, 225-234.

Lindquist, E. F. *Design and analysis of experiments in psychology and education.* New York: Houghton-Mifflin, 1953.

Little, K. B. Connotations of the Rorschach inkblots. *J. Pers.*, 1959, **27**, 397-406.

Lockhead, G. R. Methods of presenting paired-associates. *J. verb. Learn. verb. Behav.*, 1962, **1**, 62-65.

Lorge, I. *The semantic count of the 570 commonest English words.* New York: Columbia University Teachers College, 1949.

Lorge, I., & Thorndike, E. L. *A semantic count of English words.* New York: Columbia University Teachers College, 1938.

Lovaas, O. I. The relationship of induced muscular tension, tension level, and manifest anxiety in learning. *J. exp. Psychol.*, 1960a, **59**, 145-152.

Lovaas, O. I. Supplementary report: the relationship of induced muscular tension to manifest anxiety in learning. *J. exp. Psychol.*, 1960b, **59**, 205-206.

Malamud, D. I. Value of the Maller Controlled Association Test as a screening device. *J. Psychol.*, 1946, **21**, 37-43.

Maller, J. B. *A controlled association test.* New York: Author, 1936.

Mandler, G. Response factors in human learning. *Psychol. Rev.*, 1954. **61**, 235-244.

Mandler, G. Associative frequency and associative prepotency as measures of response to nonsense syllables. *Amer. J. Psychol.*, 1955, **68**, 662-665.

Mandler, G., & Campbell, E. H. Effect of variation in associative frequency of stimulus and response members on paired-associate learning. *J. exp. Psychol.*, 1957, **54**, 269-273.

Mandler, G., & Huttenlocher, J. The relationship between associative frequency, associative ability and paired-associate learning. *Amer. J. Psychol.*, 1956, **69**, 424-428.

Markel, N. N., & Hamp, E. P. Connotative meaning of certain phoneme sequences. *Studies in Linguistics*, 1961, **15**, 47-61.

Marshall, G. R., & Cofer, C. N. Associative indices as measures of word relatedness: a summary and comparison of ten methods. *J. verb. Learn. verb. Behav.*, 1963, **1**, 408-421.

Marshall, M. A., & Runquist, W. N. Facilitation of performance in paired-associate learning by distributed practice. *J. verb. Learn. verb. Behav.*, 1963, **1**, 258-263.

Martin, C. J. The role of repetition in the acquisition of verbal associations. Unpublished Ph.D. dissertation, Wayne State University, 1963.

Martin, E., & Schulz, R. W. Aural paired-associate learning: pronunciability and the interval between stimulus and response. *J. verb. Learn. verb. Behav.*, 1963, 1, 389-391.

Mayzner, M. S., & Tresselt, M. E. The ranking of letter pairs and single letters to match digram and single-letter frequency counts. *J. verb. Learn. verb. Behav.*, 1962, 1, 203-207.

McCullers, J. C. Effects of associative strength, grade level, and interpair interval in verbal paired-associate learning. *Child Develpm.*, 1961, 32, 773-778.

McCullers, J. C. An analysis of some factors underlying intralist associative transfer in paired-associate learning. *J. exp. Psychol.*, 1963, 65, 163-168.

McGuire, W. J. A multi-process model for paired-associate learning. *J. exp. Psychol.*, 1961, 62, 335-347.

McLaughlin, G. H. *Newspaper vocabularies.* Mimeographed Report, Northampton College of Advanced Technology, London, 1962.

Mednick, S., & Halpern, S. Ease of concept attainment as a function of associative rank. *J. exp. Psychol.*, 1962, 64, 628-630.

Merikle, P. M., & Battig, W. F. Transfer of training as a function of experimental paradigm and meaningfulness. *J. verb. Learn. verb. Behav.*, 1963, 2, 485-488.

Miller, G. A. *Language and communication.* New York: McGraw-Hill, 1951.

Miller, G. A., & Nicely, P. E. An analysis of perceptual contusions among some English consonants. *J. acoust. Soc. Amer.*, 1955, 27, 338-352.

Miller, N. E., & Dollard, J. *Social learning and imitation.* New Haven: Yale Univer. Press, 1941.

Mordkoff, A. M. An empirical test of the functional antonymy of semantic differential scales. *J. verb. Learn. verb. Behav.*, 1963, 2, 504-508.

Morgan, B. Q. *A German frequency word book.* New York: Macmillan, 1928.

Morikawa, Y. Studies in paired-associate learning: II. Forward-backward recognition gradient. *Tohoku J. exp. Psychol.*, 1958, 2, 57-62.

Morikawa, Y. Functions of stimulus and response in paired-associate verbal learning. *Psychologia*, 1959a, 2, 41-56.

Morikawa, Y. Studies in paired-associate learning: III. The influence of meaningfulness and familiarity of stimulus and response on learning and recall. *Jap J. Psychol.*, 1959b, 30, 153-167.

Murdock, B. B., Jr. Effects of task difficulty, stimulus similarity, and type of response on stimulus predifferentiation. *J. exp. Psychol.*, 1958, 55, 167-172.

Murdock, B. B., Jr. Response factors in learning and transfer. *Amer. J. Psychol.*, 1960, 73, 355-369.

Musgrave, B. S. The effect of nonsense-syllable compound stimuli on latency in a verbal paired-associate task. *J. exp. Psychol.*, 1962, 63, 499-504.

Musgrave, B. S., & Cohen, J. C. Effects of two-word stimuli on recall and learning in a paired-associate task. *J. exp. Psychol.*, 1964, 68, 161-166.

Musgrave, B. S., Goss, A. E., & Shrader, E. Compound nonsense-syllable stimuli presented without an intervening space. *J. exp. Psychol.*, 1963, 66, 609-611.

Newbigging, P. L. The perceptual redintegration of frequent and infrequent words. *Canad. J. Psychol.*, 1961a, 15, 123-132.

Newbigging, P. L. The perceptual redintegration of words which differ in connotative meaning. *Canad. J. Psychol.*, 1961b, 15, 133-142.

Newbigging, P. L., & Hay, J. M. The practice effect in recognition threshold determinations as a function of word frequency and length. *Canad. J. Psychol.*, 1962, 16, 177-184.

Newman, E. B., & Gerstman, L. J. A new method for analyzing printed English. *J. exp. Psychol.*, 1952, 44, 114-125.

Newman, S. E. A selective mediation model of paired-associate learning. Paper presented at the Chicago meeting of the Psychonomic Society, 1960.

Newman, S. E. Studies of paired-associate learning. Paper presented at the New York meeting of the Psychonomic Society, 1961.

Newman, S. E. Response hierarchies in paired-associate learning. Paper presented at Symposium on "Theory and Method in Verbal Learning" at the Miami Beach meeting of the Southeastern Psychological Association, 1963a.

Newman, S. E. Effects of two techniques for identifying discriminative stimulus-term elements on performance during paired-associate training. Department of Psychology, North Carolina State College, Tech. Rep. No. 7, Contract Nonr 486(08), 1963b.

Newman, S. E. A replication of paired-associate learning as a function of S-R similarity. *J. exp. Psychol.*, 1964, **67**, 592-594.

Newman, S. E., & Buckhout, R. S-R and R-S learning as functions of intralist similarity. *Amer. J. Psychol.*, 1962, **75**, 429-436.

Newman, S. E., & Gray, C. W. S-R vs. R-S recall and R-term vs. S-term recall following paired-associate training. Department of Psychology, North Carolina State College, Tech. Rep. No. 8, Contract Nonr 486(08), 1963.

Newman, S. E., & Taylor, L. R. Context effects in paired-associate learning as a function of element-sharing among stimulus terms. *J. verb. Learn. verb. Behav.*, 1963, **1**, 243-249.

Noble, C. E. An analysis of meaning. *Psychol. Rev.*, 1952, **59**, 421-430.

Noble, C. E. The meaning-familiarity relationship. *Psychol. Rev.*, 1953, **60**, 89-98.

Noble, C. E. The familiarity-frequency relationship. *J. exp. Psychol.*, 1954. **47**, 13-16.

Noble, C. E. The effect of familiarization upon serial verbal learning. *J. exp. Psychol.*, 1955, **49**, 333-338.

Noble, C. E. Emotionality (*e*) and meaningfulness (*m*). *Psychol. Rep.*, 1958a, **4**, 16.

Noble, C. E. Tables of the *e* and *m* scales. *Psychol. Rep.*, 1958b, **4**, 590.

Noble, C. E. Measurements of association value (*a*), rated associations (*a'*), and scaled meaningfulness (*m'*) for the 2100 CVC combinations of the English alphabet. *Psychol. Rep.*, 1961, **8**, 487-521.

Noble, C. E. Reply to comments on the measurement of CVC trigrams. *Psychol. Rep.*, 1962, **10**, 547-550.

Noble, C. E. Meaningfulness and familiarity. In C. N. Cofer & B. S. Musgrave (Eds.), *Verbal behavior and learning: problems and processes.* New York: McGraw-Hill, 1963.

Noble, C. E., & McNeely, D. A. The role of meaningfulness (*m*) in paired-associate learning. *J. exp. Psychol.*, 1957, **53**, 16-23.

Noble, C. E., & Parker, G. V. C. The Montana scale of meaningfulness. *Psychol. Rep.*, 1960, **7**, 325-331.

Noble, C. E., Stockwell, F. E., & Pryer, M. W. Meaningfulness (*m'*) and association value in paired-associate syllable learning. *Psychol. Rep.*, 1957, **3**, 441-452.

Nodine, C. F. Stimulus durations and stimulus characteristics in paired-associates learning. *J. exp. Psychol.*, 1963, **66**, 100-106.

Norcross, K. Effects of discrimination performance of similarity of previously acquired stimulus names. *J. exp. Psychol.*, 1958, **56**, 305-309.

Nunnally, J. C., & Flaugher, R. L. Correlates of semantic habits. *J. Pers.*, 1963, **31**, 192-202.

Nunnally, J. C., Flaugher, R. L., & Hodges, W. F. Measurement of semantic habits. Department of Psychology, Vanderbilt University, 1963.

Orbison, W. D. The relative efficiency of whole and part methods of learning paired-associates as a function of the length of list. Unpublished Ph.D. dissertation, Yale University, 1944.

Osgood, C. E., Suci, G. J., & Tannenbaum, P. H. *The measurement of meaning.* Urbana: Univer. Illinois Press, 1957.

Otten, M. W., & Van de Castle, R. L. A comparison of set "A" of the Holtzman inkblots with the Rorschach by means of the semantic differential. *J. proj. Tech.*, 1963, **27**, 452-460.

Paivio, A. Learning of adjective-noun paired-associates as a function of adjective-noun word order and noun abstractness. *Canad. J. Psychol.*, 1963, **17**, 370-379.

Paivio, A. Abstractness, imagery, and meaningfulness in paired-associate learning. Department of Psychology, University of Western Ontario, 1964.

Palermo, D. S., & Jenkins, J. J. Free association responses to the primary responses of the Palermo-Jenkins word association norms for grade school children. Department of Psychology, Pennsylvania State University, Research Bulletin 37, Research Grants MH-04286 to University of Minnesota and MH-8490 and HD-00961 to The Pennsylvania State University, 1963.

Palermo, D. S., & Jenkins, J. J. Changes in the word associations of fourth and fifth grade children from 1916 to 1961. Department of Psychology, Pennsylvania State University, Research Bulletin 41, Research Grant HD-00961 to The Pennsylvania State University, 1964a.

Palermo, D. S., & Jenkins, J. J. *Word association norms: grade school through college.* Minneapolis: Univer. Minnesota Press, 1964b.

Palermo, D. S., Flamer, G. B., & Jenkins, J. J. Association value of responses in the paired-associate learning of children and adults. *J. verb. Learn. verb. Behav.*, 1964, **3**, 171-175.

Parker, G. V. C., & Noble, C. E. Experimentally produced meaningfulness (*m*) in paired-associate learning. *Amer. J. Psychol.*, 1963, **76**, 579-588.

Peixotto, H. E. The recognitive value of three hundred nonsense syllables. *Amer. J. Psychol.*, 1948, **61**, 352-360.

Peters, H. N. Mediate association. *J. exp. Psychol.*, 1935, **18**, 20-48.

Peterson, M. J. Verbal response strength as a function of cultural frequency, schedule of reinforcement, and number of trials. *J. exp. Psychol.*, 1956, **52**, 371-376.

Peterson, M. J., & Blattner, K. C. Development of a verbal mediator. *J. exp. Psychol.*, 1963, **66**, 72-77.

Phipps, G. T. Meaningfulness (*m*) and overlearning experimentally controlled in paired-associate learning. Unpublished Ph.D. dissertation, Pennsylvania State University, 1959.

Pierce, J. Some sources of artifact in studies of the tachistoscopic perception of words. *J. exp. Psychol.*, 1963, **66**, 363-370.

Pimsleur, P., Sundland, D. M., Bankowski, R. J., & Mosberg, L. Further study of the transfer of verbal materials across sense modalities. *J. educ. Psychol.*, 1964, **55**, 96-102.

Plotkin, L. Stimulus generalization in Morse code learning. *Arch. Psychol.*, 1943, **27**, 504-509.

Pollio, H. R. A simple matrix analysis of associative structure. *J. verb. Learn. verb. Behav.*, 1963, **2**, 166-169.

Pollio, H. R. Some semantic relations among word-associates. *Amer. J. Psychol.*, 1964a, **77**, 249-256.

Pollio, H. R. Composition of associative clusters. *J. exp. Psychol.*, 1964b, **67**, 199-208.

Postman, L. The present status of interference theory. In C. N. Cofer (Ed.), *Verbal learning and verbal behavior.* New York: McGraw-Hill, 1961.

Postman, L. The effects of language habits on the acquisition and retention of verbal associations. *J. exp. Psychol.*, 1962, **64**, 7-19.

Postman, L. Acquisition and retention of consistent associative responses. *J. exp. Psychol.*, 1964, **67**, 183-190.

Postman, L. (Ed.), *Norms of word association.* New York: Academic Press. To be published.

Postman, L., & Conger, B. Verbal habits and the visual recognition of words. *Science*, 1954, **119**, 671-673.

Postman, L., & Phillips, L. W. The effects of variable contexts on the acquisition and retention of paired-associates. *Amer. J. Psychol.*, 1964, **77**, 64-74.

Postman, L., & Underwood, B. J. Second California conference on verbal learning and verbal behavior. *J. verb. Learn. verb. Behav.*, 1963, **2**, 203-215.

Price, L. E. Learning and performance in a verbal paired-associate task with preschool children. *Psychol. Rep.*, 1963, **12**, 847-850.

Reed, H. B. Associative aids: I. Their relation to learning, retention and other associations. *Psychol. Rev.*, 1918a, **25**, 128-155.

Reed, H. B. Associative aids: II. Their relation to practice and the transfer of training. *Psychol. Rev.*, 1918b, **25**, 257-285.

Reese, H. W. Motor paired-associate learning and stimulus pretraining. *Child Develpm.*, 1960, **31**, 505-513.

Restle, F. Conditioning and discrimination: the all-or-none processes in paired-associate learning. Department of Psychology, Indiana University, Tech. Rep. Contract Nonr 908(16), 1962.

Richardson, J. The relationship of stimulus similarity and number of responses. *J. exp. Psychol.*, 1958, **56**, 478-484.

Richardson, J., & Erlebacher, A. Associative connection between paired verbal items. *J. exp. Psychol.*, 1958, **56**, 62-69.

Riegel, K. F. A study of verbal achievements of older persons. *J. Geront.*, 1959, **14**, 453-456.

Riegel, K.F., & Riegel, R. M. Prediction of word-recognition thresholds on the basis of stimulus parameters. *Lang. Speech*, 1961, **4**, 157-170.

Riegel, K. F., & Riegel, R. M. Changes in associative behavior during later years of life: a cross-sectional analysis. *Vita humana*, 1964, **7**, 1-32.

Rock, I., & Heimer, W. Further evidence of one-trial associative learning. *Amer. J. Psychol.*, 1959, **72**, 1-16.

Rocklyn, E. H., Hessert, R. B., & Braun, H. W. Calibrated materials for verbal learning with middle- and old-aged subjects. *Amer. J. Psychol.*, 1957, **70**, 628-630.

Rosen, E. Connotative meanings of Rorschach inkblots, responses, and determinants. *J. Pers.*, 1960, **28**, 413-426.

Rosen, E., & Russell, W. A. Frequency-characteristics of successive word-association. *Amer. J. Psychol.*, 1957, **70**, 120-122.

Rosenzweig, M. R. Word associations of French workmen: comparisons with associations of French students and American workmen and students. *J. verb. Learn. verb. Behav.*, 1964, **3**, 57-69.

Rosenzweig, M. R., & McNeill, D. Uses of the semantic count in experimental studies of verbal behavior. *Amer. J. Psychol.*, 1962, **75**, 492-495.

Rotberg, I. C. An experimental hypothesis of intralist generalization. *Psychol. Rep.*, 1963, **13**, 359-363.

Rotberg, I. C. Verbal paired-associate learning as a function of grouping similar stimuli or responses. *J. exp. Psychol.*, 1964, **67**, 298-299.

Rotberg, I. C., & Woolman, M. Verbal paired-associate learning as a function of grouping similar stimuli or responses. *J. exp. Psychol.*, 1963, **65**, 47-51.

Rothkopf, E. Z. A measure of stimulus similarity and errors in some paired-associate learning tasks. *J. exp. Psychol.*, 1957, **53**, 94-101.

Rothkopf, E. Z. Stimulus similarity and sequence of stimulus presentation in paired-associate learning. *J. exp. Psychol.*, 1958, **56**, 114-122.

Rothkopf, E. Z. Two predictors of stimulus equivalence of paired-associate learning. *Psychol. Rep.*, 1960, **7**, 241-250.

Runquist, W. N., & English, J. M. Response pretraining and forced availability in paired-associate verbal learning. *Psychon. Sci.*, 1964, **1**, 121-122.

Russell, W. A., & Jenkins, J. J. The complete Minnesota norms to 100 words from the Kent-Rosanoff word association test. Department of Psychology, University of Minnesota, USN Tech. Rep. No. 11, Contract N8 onr-66216, 1954.

Saltz, E. Similarity and differentiation in verbal learning. Paper presented at the Chicago meeting of the Psychonomic Society, 1960.

Saltz, E. Response pretraining: differentiation or availability. *J. exp. Psychol.*, 1961, **62**, 583-587.

Saltz, E. Compound stimuli in verbal learning: cognitive and sensory differentiation versus stimulus selection. *J. exp. Psychol.*, 1963, **66**, 1-5.

Saltz, E., & Ager, J. W. Issues in scaling meaningfulness: Noble's revised CVC norms. *Psychol. Rep.*, 1962, **10**, 25-26.

Saltz, E., & Myers, T. I. A method for group presentation of paired-associates learning materials. Paper read at Chicago meeting of Midwestern Psychological Association, 1955.

Saltz, E., Metzen, J. D., & Ernstein, E. Predifferentiation of verbal stimuli in children. *Psychol. Rep.*, 1961, **9**, 127-132.

Schlosberg, H., & Heineman, C. The relationship between two measures of response strength. *J. exp. Psychol.*, 1950, **40**, 235-247.

Schoer, L. Effect of intralist item similarity on paired-associate learning by learners of high and low verbal ability. *J. educ. Psychol.*, 1963, **54**, 249-252.

Schulz, R. W., & Lovelace, E. A. Meaningfulness and the associative phase of paired-associate learning: a methodological consideration. *Psychon. Sci.*, 1964, **1**, 37-38.

Schulz, R. W., & Martin, E. Aural paired-associate learning: stimulus familiarization, response familiarization, and pronunciability. *J. verb. Learn. verb. Behav.*, 1964, **3**, 139-145.

Schulz, R. W., & Runquist, W. N. Learning and retention of paired adjectives as a function of percentage occurrence of response members. *J. exp. Psychol.*, 1960, **59**, 409-413.

Schulz, R. W., & Tucker, I. F. Supplementary report: stimulus familiarization in paired-associate learning. *J. exp. Psychol.*, 1962a, **64**, 549-550.

Schulz, R. W., & Tucker, I. F. Stimulus familiarization and length of the anticipation interval in paired-associate learning. *Psychol. Rec.*, 1962b, **12**, 341-344.

Schulz, R. W., Miller, R. L., & Radtke, R. C. The role of instance contiguity and dominance in concept attainment. *J. verb. Learn. verb. Behav.*, 1963. **1**, 432-435.

Schwartz, F., & Rouse, R. O. The activation and recovery of associations. *Psychol. Issues*, 1961, 3, Monogr. 9.

Seibel, R. *Letter sequences (n-grams): I. Frequencies in samples of text from the (London) Times.* Yorktown Heights, N.Y.: Thomas J. Watson, IBM, 1963.

Semler, I. J., & Iscoe, I. A comparative and developmental study of the learning abilities of Negro and white children under four conditions. *J. educ. Psychol.*, 1963, **54**, 38-44.

Shapiro, S. S. Word-association norms for grade-school-aged children. Unpublished M.S. problem, University of Massachusetts, 1963a.

Shapiro, S. S. Verbal paired-associates learning in grade-school children. Unpublished Ph.D. dissertation, University of Massachusetts, 1963b.

Shapiro, S. S. *Word associations to CVCs by grade-school-aged children.* Amherst: Department of Psychology, University of Massachusetts, 1963c.

Shapiro, S. S. Meaningfulness values for 52 CVCs for grade-school-aged children. *Psychon. Sci.*, 1964, **1**, 127-128.

Sheffield, F. D. The role of meaningfulness of stimulus and response in verbal learning. Unpublished Ph.D. dissertation, Yale University, 1946.

Shepard, J. F., & Fogelsonger, H. M. Studies in association and inhibition. *Psychol. Rev.*, 1913, **20**, 290-311.

Shepard, R. N. Stimulus and response generalization: tests of a model relating generalization to distance in psychological space. *J. exp. Psychol.*, 1958, **55**, 509-523.

Sherman, J. A. Performance in paired-associates learning as a function of achievement imagery, motivational instructions and degree of competition of verbal learning list. Unpublished Ph.D. dissertation, State University of Iowa, 1957.

Sidowski, J. B., Kopstein, F. F., & Shillestad, I. J. Prompting and confirmation variables in verbal learning. *Psychol. Rep.*, 1961, **8**, 401-406.

Simon, S., & Wood, G. Backward learning and the stimulus-familiarization inhibitory effect. *J. exp. Psychol.*, 1964, **67**, 310-315.

Sines, J. O. An approach to the study of the stimulus significance of the Rorschach inkblots. *J. proj. Tech.*, 1960, **24**, 64-70.

Sines, J. O. An indication of specificity of denotative meaning based on the semantic differential. *J. gen. Psychol.*, 1962, **67**, 113-115.

Smith, D. E. P., & Raygor, A. L. Verbal satiation and personality. *J. abnorm. soc. Psychol.*, 1956, **52**, 323-326.

Smith, T. A., Jones, L. V., & Thomas, S. Effects upon verbal learning of stimulus similarity, number of stimuli per response, and concept formation. *J. verb. Learn. verb. Behav.*, 1963, **1**, 470-476.

Solomon, L. N. Semantic approach to the perception of complex sounds. *J. acoust. Soc. Amer.*, 1958, **30**, 421-425.

Solomon, L. N. Search for physical correlates to psychological dimensions of sounds. *J. acoust. Soc. Amer.*, 1959a, **31**, 492-497.

Solomon, L. N. Semantic reactions to systematically varied sounds. *J. acoust. Soc. Amer.*, 1959b, **31**, 986-990.

Spear, N. E., Ekstrand, B. R., & Underwood, B. J. Association by contiguity. *J. exp. Psychol.*, 1964, **67**, 151-161.

Spence, J. T. Contribution of response bias to recognition thresholds. *J. abnorm. soc. Psychol.*, 1963a, **66**, 339-344.

Spence, J. T. Associative interference on paired-associate lists from extraexperimental learning. *J. verb. Learn. verb. Behav.*, 1963b, **2**, 329-338.

Spence, J. T., & Lair, C. V. Associative interference in the verbal learning performance of schizophrenics and normals. *J. abnorm. soc. Psychol.*, 1964, **68**, 204-209.

Spence, K. W. *Behavior theory and conditioning.* New Haven: Yale Univer. Press, 1956.

Spence, K. W., Farber, I. E., & McFann, H. H. The relation of anxiety (drive) level to performance in competitional and non-competitional paired-associates learning. *J. exp. Psychol.*, 1956, **52**, 296-305.

Spence, K. W., Taylor, J., & Ketchel, R. Anxiety (drive) level and degree of competition in paired-associates learning. *J. exp. Psychol.*, 1956, **52**, 306-310.

Staats, A. W., & Staats, C. K. Meaning and *m*: correlated but separate. *Psychol. Rev.*, 1959, **66**, 136-144.

Staats, C. K., Staats, A. W., & Schutz, R. E. The effects of discrimination pretraining on textual behavior. *J. educ. Psychol.*, 1962, **53**, 32-37.

Stoddard, G. D. An experiment in verbal learning. *J. educ. Psychol.*, 1929, **20**, 452-457.

Strassburger, F., & Wertheimer, M. The discrepancy hypothesis of affect and association values of nonsense syllables. *Psychol. Rep.*, 1959, **5**, 528.

Sundland, D. M., & Wickens, D. D. Context factors in paired-associate learning and recall. *J. exp. Psychol.*, 1962, **63**, 302-306.

Sutton, J. T. Verbal learning, palmar skin conductance, and response latency as a function of intralist stimulus similarity and warming up. Unpublished Ph.D. dissertation, Vanderbilt University, 1958.

Tanaka, Y., Oyama, T., & Osgood, C. E. A cross-culture and cross-concept study of the generality of semantic spaces. *J. verb. Learn. verb. Behav.*, 1963, **2**, 392-405.

Taylor, J. A. Meaning, frequency, and visual duration threshold. *J. exp. Psychol.*, 1958, **55**, 329-334.

Taylor, J. D. The meaningfulness of 320 words and paralogs. Unpublished Ph.D. dissertation, Duke University, 1959.

Terman, L. M., & Miles, C. C. *Sex and personality*. New York: McGraw-Hill, 1936.

Terwilliger, R. F. Note on familiarity and verbal learning. *Psychol. Rep.*, 1962, **10**, 409-410.

Terwilliger, R. F. Free association patterns and familiarity as predictors of affect. *J. gen. Psychol.*, 1964, **70**, 3-12.

Thorndike, E. L. Word knowledge in the elementary school. *Teachers College Record.*, 1921, **22**, 334-370.

Thorndike, E. L. *The teacher's word book.* (2nd Ed.) New York: Columbia Univer. Teachers College, 1927.

Thorndike, E. L. *Teacher's word book of 20,000 words.* New York: Columbia Univer. Teachers College, 1931.

Thorndike, E. L., & Lorge, I. *The teacher's word book of 30,000 words.* New York: Columbia Univer. Press, 1944.

Thornton, T. E. Stimulus generalization in schizophrenic, brain-injured and normal subjects. Unpublished Ph.D. dissertation, Northwestern University, 1958.

Tobias, J. V. Relative occurrence of phonemes in American English. *J. acoust. Soc. Amer.*, 1959, **31**, 631.

Torgerson, W. S. *Theory and methods of scaling.* New York: Wiley, 1958.

Trapp, E. H., & Kausler, D. H. A revision of Hull's table of association values for 320 selected nonsense syllables. *Amer. J. Psychol.*, 1959, **72**, 423-428.

Tresselt, M. E., & Mayzner, M. S. The Kent-Rosanoff word association: word association norms as a function of age. *Psychon. Sci.*, 1964, **1**, 65-66.

Trnka, B. *A phonological analysis of present day standard English.* Prague: Charles University, Studies in English, v. 5, 1935.

Tucker, I. F. Articulation vs. nonarticulation of stimulus units during paired associate learning. Unpublished Ph.D. dissertation, State University of Iowa, 1962.

Umemoto, T. Association values of 1016 Japanese nonsense syllables. *Jap. J. Psychol.*, 1951a, **21**, 23-28.

Umemoto, T. The relative weights of stimulus versus response words in rote learning. *Jap. J. Psychol.*, 1951b, **21**, 46-55.

Umemoto, T. Similarity between stimulus and response words in paired associate learning. *Tohoku J. exp. Psychol.*, 1958, **2**, 95-102.

Umemoto, T. Paired-associate learning as a function of similarity: semantic similarity between stimulus- and response-items. *Amer. J. Psychol.*, 1962, **75**, 85-93.

Umemoto, T. Association methods in the analysis of verbal learning and verbal behavior. Kyoto University, *Studies*, No. **9**, 1963.

Umemoto, T., & Hilgard, E. R. Paired associate learning as a function of similarity: common stimulus and response items within the list. *J. exp. Psychol.*, 1961, **62**, 97-104.

Umemoto, T., Morikawa, Y., & Ibuki, M. The non-association values and meaningfulness of 1892 Japanese two-letter syllables and words. *Jap. J. Psychol.*, 1955a, **26**, 148-155.

Umemoto, T., Morikawa, Y., & Ibuki, M. Familiarity and similarity scales of Japanese adjectives. *Kyoto Univer. Res. Studies in Educ.*, 1955b, **1**, 85-116.

Underwood, B. J. Studies of distributed practice: II. Learning and retention of paired-adjective lists with two levels of intralist similarity. *J. exp. Psychol.*, 1951, **42**, 153-161.

Underwood, B. J. Studies of distributed practice: VIII. Learning and retention of paired nonsense syllables as a function of intralist similarity. *J. exp. Psychol.*, 1953a, **45**, 133-142.

Underwood, B. J. Studies of distributed practice: IX. Learning and retention of paired adjectives as a function of intralist similarity. *J. exp. Psychol.*, 1953b, 45, 143-149.

Underwood, B. J. Intralist similarity in verbal learning and retention. *Psychol. Rev.*, 1954, **61**, 160-166.

Underwood, B. J. An evaluation of the Gibson theory of verbal learning. In C. N. Cofer (Ed.), *Verbal learning and verbal behavior*. New York: McGraw-Hill, 1961.

Underwood, B. J., & Keppel, G. Retention as a function of degree of learning and letter-sequence interference. *Psychol. Monogr.*, 1963, **77**, Whole No. 567.

Underwood, B. J., & Postman, L. Extraexperimental sources of interference in forgetting. *Psychol. Rev.*, 1960, **67**, 73-95.

Underwood, B. J., & Richardson, J. Some verbal materials for the study of concept formation. *Psychol. Bull.*, 1956, **53**, 84-95.

Underwood, B. J., & Schulz, R. W. *Meaningfulness and verbal learning*. Philadelphia: Lippincott, 1960a.

Underwood, B. J., & Schulz, R. W. Response dominance and rate of learning paired associates. *J. gen. Psychol.*, 1960b, **62**, 153-158.

Underwood, B. J., & Schulz, R. W. Studies of distributed practice: XXI. Effect of interference from language habits. *J. exp. Psychol.*, 1961, **62**, 571-575.

Underwood, B. J., Ham, M., & Ekstrand, B. Cue selection in paired-associate learning. *J. exp. Psychol.*, 1962, **64**, 405-409.

Underwood, B. J., Runquist, W. N., & Schulz, R. W. Response learning in paired-associate lists as a function of intralist similarity. *J. exp. Psychol.*, 1959, **58**, 70-78.

Vander-Beke, G. E. *French word book*. New York: Macmillan, 1929.

Vanderplas, J. M., & Garvin, E. A. The association value of random shapes. *J. exp. Psychol.*, 1959a, **57**, 147-154.

Vanderplas, J. M., & Garvin, E. A. Complexity, association value, and practice as factors in shape recognition following paired-associates training. *J. exp. Psychol.*, 1959b, **57**, 155-163.

Voelker, C. H. A sound count for the oral curriculum. *The Volta Rev.*, 1936, **25**, 55-56.

von Restorff, H. Über die Wirkurg von Bereichsbildung im Spurenfeld. *Psychol. Forsch.*, 1933, **18**, 299-342.

Walker, E. L., & Tarte, R. D. Memory storage as a function of arousal and time with homogeneous and heterogeneous lists. *J. verb. Learn. verb. Behav.*, 1963, **2**, 113-119.

Wallace, J. Concept dominance, type of feedback, and intensity of feedback as related to concept attainment. *J. educ. Psychol.*, 1964, **55**, 159-166.

Waters, R. H. The law of acquaintance. *J. exp. Psychol.*, 1939, **24**, 180-191.

Weiss, E. Backward association in paired associate learning; a test of stimulus availability theories. Unpublished Ph.D. dissertation, New School for Social Research, 1962.

Weiss, E. Mixed list interference, stimulus meaningfulness and backward association. Paper presented at the New York meeting of the Eastern Psychological Association, 1963.

Weiss, J. H. Further study of the relation between the sound of a word and its meaning. *Amer. J. Psychol.*, 1963, **76**, 624-630.

Weiss, R. L. The role of association value and experimentally produced familiarity in paired associate learning. Unpublished Ph.D. dissertation, University of Buffalo, 1958.

Weiss, W., & Margolius, G. The effect of context stimuli on learning and retention. *J. exp. Psychol.*, 1954, **48**, 318-322.

West, M. *A general service list of English words, with semantic frequencies and a supplementary word-list for the writing of popular science and technology.* New York: Longmans, Green, 1953.

Wicklund, D. A., Palermo, D. S., & Jenkins, J. J. The effects of associative strength and response hierarchy on paired-associate learning. Department of Psychology, Pennsylvania State University, Research Bulletin 38, Research Grants GB-1958 and HD-00961, 1964.

Wiggins, J. S. Two determinants of associative reaction time. *J. exp. Psychol.*, 1957, **54**, 144-147.

Wilcoxon, H. C., Wilson, W. R., & Wise, D. A. Paired-associate learning as a function of percentage of occurrence of response members and other factors. *J. exp. Psychol.*, 1961, **61**, 283-289.

Williams, J. E. Connotations of color names among Negroes and Caucasians. *Percept. mot. Skills*, 1964, **18**, 721-731.

Williams, J. M., & Derks, P. L. Mode of presentation and the acquisition of paired-associates that differ in pronunciability and association value. *J. verb. Learn. verb. Behav.*, 1963, **2**, 453-456.

Williams, J. P. A test of the all-or-none hypothesis for verbal learning. *J. exp. Psychol.*, 1962, **64**, 158-165.

Wilson, K. V. Multidimensional analyses of confusions of English consonants. *Amer. J. Psychol.*, 1963, **76**, 89-95.

Wilson, W. R., & Becknell, J. C. The relation between association value, pronunciability, and affectivity of nonsense syllables. *J. Psychol.*, 1961, **52**, 47-50.

Wimer, C. An analysis of semantic stimulus factors in paired-associate learning. *J. verb. Learn. verb. Behav.*, 1963, **1**, 397-407.

Winer, B. J. *Statistical principles in experimental design.* New York: McGraw-Hill, 1962.

Winzen, K. Die Abhangigkeit per paarweisen Assoziation von der Stellung des besser haftenden Gliedes. *Z. Psychol.*, 1921, **86**, 235-252.

Witmer, L. R. The association value of three-place consonant syllables. *J. genet. Psychol.*, 1935, **47**, 337-360.

Woodrow, H., & Lowell, F. Children's association frequency tables. *Psychol. Monogr.*, 1916, **22**, Whole No. 97.

Woodworth, R. S., & Schlosberg, H. *Experimental psychology.* (Rev. Ed.) New York: Holt, 1954.

Wright, B., & Rainwater, L. The meanings of color. *J. gen. Psychol.*, 1962, **67**, 89-99.

Yelen, D. R., & Schulz, R. W. Verbal satiation. *J. verb. Learn. verb. Behav.*, 1963, **1**, 372-377.

Young, R. K. Paired-associate learning when the same items occur as stimuli and responses. *J. exp. Psychol.*, 1961, **61**, 315-318.

Yule, G. U. *The statistical study of literary vocabulary.* Cambridge: Cambridge Univer. Press, 1944.

Yum, K. S. An experimental test of the law of assimilation. *J. exp. Psychol.*, 1931, **14**, 68-82.

Zax, M., & Benham, F. G. The stimulus value of the Rorschach inkblots as perceived by children. *J. proj. Tech.*, 1961, **25**, 233-237.

Author Index

343

Subject Index